Propaganda and World Public Order

The Legal Regulation of the Ideological Instrument of Coercion

by B. S. Murty

The ideological instrument, or propaganda, has attained formidable influence in this century, with rapid advances in the technology of communication and an increased sophistication in the methods of influencing human attitudes and behavior. Concern over the effects of propaganda on international peace has spurred discussion in various international forums, but attempts to evolve a pattern of regulation by treaty have met with little success.

What distinguishes persuasion from coercion, and permissible from nonpermissible propaganda? Mr. Murty has employed a policy-oriented jurisprudential approach to seek solutions to the tangled problems of propaganda regulation, bringing to bear the allied disciplines of psychology, communication research, and international politics. New policies, he suggests, must aim at promoting freedom of information and maintaining minimum world public order, and he emphasizes the present and potential role of the United Nations in regulating the use of propaganda.

Mr. Murty is head of the department of law at Andhra University in India, and is one of the authors of a manual of international law, now in preparation, sponsored by the Carnegie Endowment for International Peace.

"Undoubtedly the most profound and comprehensive study of this important subject yet available. . . . [He] writes about the linkages between ideological coercion and such complex matters as norms prohibiting aggression, the doctrine of non-intervention, criminal responsibility, [and] free speech with clarity and erudition."—RICHARD A. FALK, *Princeton University.*

"The present work is superior to anything I have read on the subject. It is more comprehensive, being based on a synthesis of disciplines. . . . It is particularly strong in its consideration of factors of policy. . . . The author writes with conviction, but with scholarly reserve and moderation."—J. B. WHITTON.

PROPAGANDA AND WORLD PUBLIC ORDER

Propaganda and World Public Order

THE LEGAL REGULATION OF THE IDEOLOGICAL INSTRUMENT OF COERCION

BY B. S. MURTY

New Haven and London, Yale University Press, 1968

Designed by John O.C. McCrillis,
set in Electra type,
and printed in the United States of America by
The Vail-Ballou Press, Inc., Binghamton, N.Y.
Distributed in Canada by McGill University Press.

Library of Congress catalog card number: 67-24505

Published with assistance from the foundation
established in memory of Amasa Stone Mather
of the Class of 1907, Yale College.

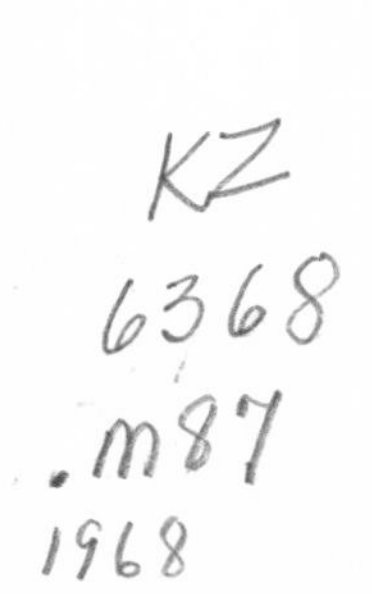

To my teacher

MYRES S. MCDOUGAL

Foreword by Harold D. Lasswell

AMONG the major tasks of decision-makers, advocates, and commentators who specialize in the law of the world community is that of clarifying or applying authoritative prescriptions that harmonize the several instruments of national policy with the goals of minimum or maximum public order. In common parlance the instruments are diplomatic, economic, military, and ideological. It is not far wide of the mark to say that confusion is greatest when controversies relate to ideological policy, or the use of managed communication to influence large audiences. No small part of the difficulty is to be found in a conception of law that fails to locate official decision-makers and claimants in the social process, or to distinguish between the communicative and other dimensions of a collective act. Professor Murty has successfully dealt with these basic matters.

Professor Murty distinguishes the process of claim and decision within the context of the whole social process. Hence it is clear from the beginning that law, defined as authoritative and controlling decision, is a component of the larger process. It is made explicit that a continuous gradation leads from an interaction whose principal feature is communication to an interaction whose significance is something else, such as trading or fighting. The illuminating point is that, to some degree, communication is always present, since communication is understood to occur whenever words, gestures, and their equivalents are employed as mediators between the subjectivities of the initiator and the recipient of messages. It is demonstrated that in certain circumstances the use of communication is coercive. Murty's analysis shows that if a decision-maker is to make reliable inferences about the content of any sequence of communication, including its causes and consequences, the total context must be scrutinized by systematic methods.

Working within this framework it is possible for Professor Murty to demonstrate why piecemeal, noncontextual approaches have so often led to unsatisfactory results: they have been divorced from the guiding principles required to ascertain when ideological strategies facilitate or block results that are compatible with world public order. For example, it has often been suggested that the trend of official decision is to affirm the impermissibility of "war propaganda," and that this negative prescription ought to be embodied in a formal treaty. Murty throws persuasive doubt on the occurrence of the alleged trend and indicates that a formal treaty would inhibit rather than foster the realization of the basic goals of public order.

The author's contextualism enables him to propose criteria that aid in disentangling past claims, decisions, and recommended norms from one another in delimiting the responsibility of official and of private wielders of the ideological instrument; past commentators have been remarkably unenlightening in their discussion of these issues. Another example—one of many—of Professor Murty's success is his outline of a workable conception of one of the most treacherous and highly sloganized doctrines in the entire repertory of international law, namely, "ideological aggression."

The fascinating question is why Professor Murty's predecessors have been relatively unsuccessful in bringing systematic discipline to the field. It is fair, I think, to assert that the chief source of difficulty is intellectual, not from incapacity, of course, but from the over-incorporation of certain latent assumptions and sentiments that are tightly linked with both ordinary and professional language. The remarkable fact about language, when considered as a component of culture, is that it conveys so much more than it says.

The manifest content of every message—the seemingly "plain and natural meaning"—is a small fraction of the designative and evocative significations of the whole, whether on the part of the senders or the receivers. For instance, in many societies ordinary and professional languages often contain statements to the effect that law itself is words. Thus, law is a "rule," or it is a "clause of the constitution" or a "statute." Such lexical conceptions are so patently absurd—since, at most, words are *among* the bases of inference relevant to authoritative expectations—that it is hardly astonishing to find that ordinary discourse declares or implies many other definitions. We are sometimes told that whatever is enforced is law—which is a monstrosity, since the definition includes naked power along with authoritative control.

Professor Murty is able to thread his way confidently among existing connotations because his scientific standpoint is sufficiently comprehensive to put each assertion in its appropriate place, either as an unofficial interaction or as part of a process of official claim or decision. We underline the point that a commentator's position in the flow of communicative and noncommunicative events must be clearly defined before he can *deal with* rather than *succumb to* an unrecognized use of the ideological instrument.

Whatever imperfections of detail there may be in the execution of Professor Murty's formidable undertaking, it is as sure as any prognosis can be that his work will be accepted as the landmark treatise on an elusive topic. The timing is fortunate, since we are gingerly entering the era of satellite-expedited employment of the ideological instrument, and a host of new technological innovations must soon be evaluated in terms of the minimum and maximum goals of world public order.

Acknowledgments

THIS BOOK would not have been possible without the generous help and encouragement I have received from various sources, of varied character, and over a period of years. Of the debt owed Professors Myres S. McDougal and Harold D. Lasswell, the book itself speaks with sufficient eloquence. But for the interest evinced by them, I perhaps would have abandoned the project at a very early stage, and its completion is a product of their inspiration and guidance. I am further indebted to Professor Lasswell for writing the foreword and to Professor McDougal for accepting the dedication of the book.

My study of this subject began in 1954 when I was a graduate student at Yale Law School. My doctoral thesis, *The International Regulation of the Ideological Instrument of Coercion,* was accepted in June 1957 and awarded the Carolinda Waters Prize in the Law School that year. In October 1957 I had to return to my own country, and, due to other preoccupations, revision of the text for publication could not be completed for several years.

At the stage of writing the thesis, Mr. William T. Burke, professor of law at Ohio State University, who was then on the Yale Law School faculty, spent a great deal of time reading the drafts, discussing the issues, and making many helpful suggestions. At that stage I also received assistance from other faculty members: Dr. Gerhard Bebr, Associate Dean Jack Bernard Tate, and Professor Ralph Sharp Brown. After submission and acceptance of the text, Professor Leon Lipson, Professor Quincy Wright, and Mr. Charles Runyon gave generously of their penetrative and constructive criticism, which helped a great deal in the revising process. The kind interest of Dean Eugene V. Rostow was abiding throughout.

I am grateful to all the officers of the Yale University Press who in various ways have contributed to the task of publication. The suggestions made by reviewers for the Press were very helpful, and I am profoundly thankful to Mrs. Ruth D. Kaufman for her highly valuable editorial assistance. However, I assume full responsibility for the shortcomings in the book and for the views expressed therein.

On the material side, I am indebted to the United States Department of State, as it was a Smith-Mundt and Fulbright grant in 1954 that enabled me to go to Yale. The Yale Law School was generous in financing my stay there during the years 1955 to 1957. The Asia Foundation and the Law School financed my trip to the United States and stay at Yale during 1965–66, in connection with a companion study on the diplomatic instrument, and the occasion was utilized to effect some changes in the present text. The Andhra University, where I am now professor of law and head of the Department of Law, was generous in granting leave to spend long periods at Yale and in financial assistance to support my family at home.

Finally, I wish to express my appreciation of the sacrifice made by my wife, children, and aged mother in permitting me to stay abroad for fairly long periods of time in pursuit of this study.

Waltair, India B. S. M.
August 1967

Contents

Abbreviations

A.J.I.L.	*American Journal of International Law*
Brit. Parl. Papers, Cmd.	British Parliamentary Papers, Command
B.Y.B.I.L.	*British Yearbook of International Law*
Dept. of State Bull.	*Department of State Bulletin*
E.S.C.O.R.	Economic and Social Council, Official Records
For. Rel. of U.S.	*Foreign Relations of the United States*
G.A.O.R.	General Assembly, Official Records
Hague Recueil	Academy of International Law (The Hague), *Recueil des Cours*
I.C.J.	International Court of Justice
Int'l and Comp. L.Q.	*International and Comparative Law Quarterly*
Int'l. Conciliation	*International Conciliation*
Int'l. Org.	*International Organization*
Law and Contemp. Problems	*Law and Contemporary Problems*
L.O.N. Doc.	League of Nations Document
L.N.T.S.	League of Nations Treaty Series
Mich. L. Rev.	*Michigan Law Review*
Proc. Am. Soc. Int'l. L.	*Proceedings of the American Society of International Law*
S.C.O.R.	Security Council, Official Records
Trans. Grot. Soc.	*Transactions of the Grotius Society*
U.N.C.I.O.	United Nations Conference on International Organization, Documents
U.N. Doc.	United Nations Document
U.N.T.S.	United Nations Treaty Series
Yale L.J.	*Yale Law Journal*

1

Introduction

The use by an elite of communication with the rank and file to shape the attitudes and behavior of the latter for political purposes, or the use of the ideological instrument as we propose to refer to it in this study, appears to be as old as the history of mankind. The reference here is mostly to what is generally called propaganda.[1] In Kautilya's *Arthasastra,* a treatise on the strategy of worldly possessions, written in India about 300 B.C.,[2] the author states that the king should send his secret agents to silence the disloyal among his subjects. The agents are to be assigned the mission of carrying on disputations, in places where people congregate, on the short-comings of the king, his merits, the benefits flowing from ordered government, and the divine ordainment of kings. The conclusion must always be in favor of the view which upholds loyalty to the ruler. The people must be warned that divine and earthly punishments will visit those who might indulge in acts of treachery toward the king. The author states in another place, "When the conqueror is desirous of seizing an enemy's village, he should infuse enthusiastic spirit among his own men and frighten his enemy's people by giving publicity to his power of omniscience and his close association with gods." [3] He further suggests that the conqueror's spies should "sow the seeds of dissension" among the enemy people. In all likelihood what Kautilya wrote corresponded in considerable measure to the practices obtaining in his time. In the West the use of propaganda in the political arena can be traced to the time of the Greeks and perhaps even earlier.[4] Demosthenes cautioned the Athenians against Macedonian ag-

1. More precise definitions of *propaganda* and *ideological instrument* will be given later.

2. According to one view the work was produced about 600 years later, but the exact date is not very material here.

3. Trans. R. Shamasastry (4th ed. Mysore, Sri Raghuveer Printing Press, 1951), pp. 22–23, 423.

4. For a detailed account of the history of propaganda in the West, John B. Whitton and Arthur Larson, *Propaganda, Towards Disarmament in the War of Words* (New York, Oceana, 1963), Chap. 2; Lindley Fraser, *Propaganda* (London, Oxford University Press, 1957), Chap. 2.

gressions, and Hannibal of Carthage, while marching on Rome, proclaimed that he was coming as a friend of the people and not as a conqueror.

Claims affirming the legitimacy or otherwise of some of the patterns of the practice, which are of interest to students of modern international law, appear from the time of the French Revolution.[5] There were two reasons for their appearance at this time. The first was that the Revolution was followed by a period of crisis and war, of efforts on one hand to spread the Revolution and, on the other, to suppress it by force, open and otherwise. The second was the crystallization in the eighteenth century of the doctrine of nonintervention in the internal affairs of a state as a prescription of international law; [6] without that development, the claim of illegitimacy of forcible exportation of an ideology, or its suppression abroad, would have been unsustainable. The French Revolution was followed by a century of ferment marked by movements toward democracy and nationalism, directed against the monarchical, imperialist, aristocratic, and privileged order that prevailed in Europe. Often the leaders of unsuccessful rebellions against the established order, or overthrown regimes, escaped to neighboring states that offered them asylum and from there carried on the struggle. The media of communication available to them then were human agents and the press. Their propaganda activity occasioned diplomatic exchanges, and the outcome of some of these exchanges was the adoption in the municipal law of some countries of measures to punish certain varieties of propaganda activity.

In the twentieth century, among the events that led to the outbreak of World War I was the Serbian propaganda directed against Austria-Hungary for recovery of Bosnia and Herzegovina.[7] During the war the Allies made full use of propaganda for building up public opinion in favor of their cause and for demoralizing the enemy civilian population and armed forces. The legality of incitement of enemy armed forces to desertion was first questioned but later accepted.[8] After the war the League of Nations was established providing an institutional setup which facilitated the collective, organized effort of nations to maintain international peace. During its existence, the League had to be a witness to intensification of propaganda activity in Europe.

Diplomatic controversy between the government of the U.S.S.R. and the governments of other states frequently arose as a result of Soviet propaganda activity. The splitting up of the two Eastern European empires

5. On the French propaganda of this period, Robert B. Holtman, *Napoleonic Propaganda* (Baton Rouge, Louisiana State University Press, 1950).

6. P. H. Winfield, "The History of Intervention in International Law," 3 *B.Y.B.I.L.* 130, 136 (1922–23); Sir G. Butler and S. Maccoby, *The Development of International Law* (London, Longmans, 1928), pp. 70–71.

7. Whitton and Larson, pp. 2–3.

8. See below, Chap. 8.

after World War I and their reconstitution into states based upon the principle of nationality, leaving in the process national minorities in each of the newly created states, led to the rise of irredentist movements. This factor, and the growth of radio broadcasting as a medium of communication, intensified propaganda activity in the political life of Europe to a point where it was thought to constitute a menace to the peace. The question of regulation of propaganda activity was consequently brought before the League of Nations for discussion. At the time of the Geneva Disarmament Conference in 1932, and subsequently, this question was considered at length. But, apart from the Broadcasting Convention of 1936,[9] which did not prove significant in its practical effects, the discussions produced no new pattern of regulation. The less powerful European states suggested measures that would have occasioned the imposition of certain limitations on the freedom of speech and the press in addition to those already in existence; and the more powerful liberal democracies with traditions of these freedoms readily rejected them. The Axis powers made full use of the ideological instrument in furthering their programs of aggression, and this activity figured in the charges preferred in the postwar trials of the leaders of those powers and in the judgments.

After World War II, the states of a major part of the world—having witnessed, and some experienced, the devastations of the war and the brutal suppression of human rights by the dictators—began to construct the edifice of the United Nations, apparently reposing high hopes in it for a new pattern of life. In the first few years after the founding of the United Nations, proposals were put forward that the Organization should adopt measures to promote freedom of information;[10] and almost simultaneously came proposals for controlling propaganda. The latter originated from the countries of the communist bloc.

The two questions, promotion of freedom of information, and regulation of propaganda, were discussed at the Conference on Freedom of Information, Geneva, 1948, and have engaged the attention of the General Assembly ever since 1946. During these debates, and on other occasions, the liberal democracies sought to influence other states to accept their concept of freedom of information, an important premise of which is that the best remedy for propaganda is free discussion; and the Soviet Union tried to obtain acceptance of an obligation on the part of the democracies to suppress certain types of utterances, especially so-called war propaganda

9. M. O. Hudson, *International Legislation*, 7 (Washington D.C., Carnegie Endowment, 1941), 409.

10. The General Assembly in its Resolution 59(I), 14 December 1946, adopted the proposal of the Philippines delegation to convene an international information conference to devise ways and means by which information could be freely gathered in, transmitted, and published through all the media of public information, press, film, and radio, in all countries, avoiding all discriminatory practices.

and warmongering. The less powerful, underdeveloped, noncommunist states, which could not match the more powerful and what to them seemed to be still imperialistic, liberal democratic states in any propaganda contest, sought to obtain acceptance of certain limited propaganda controls, in the hope that it would equalize their position.[11] After prolonged efforts, the West gave up the attempt to obtain acceptance of the liberal democratic concept of freedom of information, and assumed the negative posture of opposing all moves directed toward imposing limitations on freedom of information in order to control political propaganda.

But other governments have not lessened their exertions on behalf of restrictive regulation. The Soviet Union included provisions for such regulation in its definition of aggression,[12] and raised the question of prohibition of war propaganda in the Eighteen-Nation Committee on Disarmament.[13] More recently, the question was raised before the General Assembly's Special Committee on Principles of International Law concerning Friendly Relations and Cooperation among States.[14] The Draft Convention on Freedom of Information, originally prepared at Geneva in 1948, was taken up for active consideration by the General Assembly in 1959, after an interval of six years, and the Third Committee completed the drafting of four articles in three successive sessions. During these discussions there was a restatement of previous positions, and the draft languished again. On every occasion when propaganda or freedom of information is discussed, positions are based on these three major points of view.

The General Assembly has, however, on December 16, 1966, unanimously adopted the international covenants on human rights and opened them for signature, ratification, and accession. Of these, the Covenant on Civil and Political Rights, in Articles 19 and 20, obligates the parties to recognize, and ensure enjoyment in their respective jurisdictions of, the right to freedom of expression, and to prohibit propaganda for war and certain other types of propaganda. This is a significant departure from the

11. For the attitudes adopted by the various delegations at Geneva and subsequently in the U.N. organs, S. de Palma, "Freedom of the Press—An International Issue," 24 *Dept. of State Bull.* 724 (1949); E. D. Canham, "International Information," 14 *Law and Contemp. Problems,* 584 (1949); C. Binder, "Freedom of Information and the United Nations," 6 *Int'l. Org.* 210 (1952); D. Exley, "International Transmission of News and the Right of Correction," 30 *Journalism Quarterly* 198 (1953).

12. See below, pp. 160–62.

13. See below, pp. 235–37.

14. *Report of the Special Committee on Principles of International Law concerning Friendly Relations and Cooperation among States,* U.N. Doc. A/5746 (16 Nov. 1964), and especially paras. 27 and 28 for the proposals of Czechoslovakia and Yugoslavia; *Report of the 1966 Special Committee on Principles of International Law concerning Friendly Relations and Cooperation among States,* U.N. Doc. A/6230 (27 June 1966), paras. 25, 26, 28, and 29.

previous trend, but one can at best find in the two articles a basis for solution of some of the problems connected with freedom of information and propaganda and not a comprehensive system of regulation.

While the discussions within international organizations to devise a regime to control propaganda have thus been mostly inconclusive, juristic studies made in the past have neither satisfactorily explained the intricacies of the problem nor suggested workable policies or means of regulation. The few studies that were made before World War II dealt solely with the question whether a state was responsible for revolutionary propaganda carried on against foreign governments by its officials and state-subsidized organizations.[15] The approach was for the most part legalistic. Policy questions did not receive appreciable attention.

Since the close of World War II attention has become more focused upon the problem. Examining the question in the light of the Nazi and Fascist use of propaganda before the war, the postwar trials, the long-standing complaint against the Soviet Union of its subversive propaganda against noncommunist states, and the cold war, writers dealt with such questions as whether "war propaganda," "war mongering," or incitement of foreign people to civil war was permissible.[16] The results arrived at are somewhat surprising. For instance, Professor Whitton and Dr. Larson reach the conclusion that there is already a considerable body of customary international law and treaties controlling propaganda, and put forward suggestions for more effective application of the customary prescriptions and treaties by governments and the United Nations. On the other hand, Mr. Martin maintains that there are very few customary prescriptions, and that the difficulties of enforcing them and the existing treaty obligations are practically insurmountable. He reaches the conclusion that, so long as sovereignty is recognized, it is inconceivable that international law will ever control propaganda and the control will remain "in the municipal law of states and the bargaining power of diplomacy." [17]

On a question which is very material to the regulation of propaganda, whether there is a right of free communication across state boundaries so as to legitimize the efforts at penetrating an "iron curtain," there was a

15. The most important of such studies were H. Lauterpacht, "Revolutionary Propaganda by Governments," 13 *Trans. Grot. Soc.* 143 (1928); and "Revolutionary Activities by Private Persons Against Foreign States," 22 *A.J.I.L.* 106 (1928); L. Preuss, "International Responsibility for Hostile Propaganda Against Foreign States," 28 *A.J.I.L.* 649 (1940).

16. Whitton and Larson, *Propaganda;* John B. Whitton, "Propaganda and International Law," 72 *Hague Recueil* 577 (1948); Quincy Wright, "The Crime of War Mongering," 42 *A.J.I.L.* 128 (1948); L. J. Martin, *International Propaganda, Its Legal and Diplomatic Control* (Minneapolis, University of Minnesota Press, 1958).

17. See ibid., Chap 9, p. 207.

somewhat heated discussion at the 44th annual meeting of the American Society of International Law.[18] During the discussion, a number of leading members expressed the view that by virtue of the territorial sovereignty of states it is permissible, in the absence of treaty obligations, for governments to raise an "iron curtain" if they so choose.[19] Professor Fenwick, however, took the view that under modern conditions such an action would constitute a crime against the world community. His argument was that if a powerful country were to do so it would menace the security of other states.

These differences of opinion among scholars by themselves would justify another effort at the study of the subject. But actually there is greater justification. The studies so far made have been concerned mainly with the discovery of the "rules" of international law. The policy issues which arise in the context of the subject are clarified to a certain extent, but are not subjected to such rigorous analysis as the complexity of the subject demands. The question—when a decision-maker is confronted with a set of claims and counterclaims—of what factors should guide him in making a decision as to the "legality" of the activity is not adequately considered. For instance, Whitton and Larson find that international law prohibits warmongering propaganda but does not prohibit propaganda in favor of such use of force as is legitimate under the U.N. Charter. Some questions that arise from this statement include who is to decide whether a particular propaganda activity is of the permitted or prohibited variety, by applying what criteria, under what conditions, with what objectives and what effects, and what overriding policy goals ought to guide the decision-maker. These questions were not fully explored. The possibility of presentation of conflicting claims, one affirming that an activity is nonlegitimate propaganda and the other that it is a legitimate process of communication of factual information, is clearly observed by Mr. Martin. This possibility, the difficulty of defining nonlegitimate propaganda, and the relatively undeveloped machinery of enforcement of law in the contemporary international community have led him to the conclusion that there is little scope for international regulation of propaganda.

Anyone who even scans the existing juristic literature cannot fail to notice that it suffers from a major deficiency. One at once finds that the debates are insufficiently related to the factual contexts in the relations between states pertaining to the use of propaganda. These contexts are by no means simple.[20] Their complexity cannot escape attention the moment

18. "Freedom of Communication Across National Frontiers," 1950 *Proc. of Am. Soc. of Int'l. L.*, pp. 95, 116 et seq.

19. Professors Wright, Hazard, Freeman, and Turlington took this view.

20. Professor C. G. Fenwick pointed out, writing in 1938, that propaganda addressed to foreign countries could be anything from mere extolling of one's own achievements

one begins to look at propaganda not merely as the dissemination of words and word-substitutes (pictures), but as a process which has several significant aspects. Stated in a simplified manner, propaganda is the process by which a communicator seeks to influence an audience, situated in a certain environment, to respond in a particular way, by communicating symbols and words. The communication is an act (or act-sequence), and the response it evokes from the audience is the consequence of the communication. The significant features which go beyond the mere focus on the dissemination factor are: the response produced or expected to be produced; the manner in which it is produced, whether as a result of persuasion or, at the other end of the scale, compulsion of a high degree, or coercion.

Propaganda situations which arise in world politics are complicated by still other factors. Let us for convenience adopt here a currently used classification of the practices employed by the elites in states in their interactions in the world arena. These practices—the instruments of policy—are classified as diplomatic, ideological, economic, and military. An elite rarely pursues its policy by means of any single policy instrument; typically it employs combinations, using this or that with greater intensity than others. A context will generally be one of "more or less" rather than "purely this or that." A study which is designed to be in close touch with the realities of world politics should not be focused on propaganda activities alone, but ought to give due weight to the other policy means which leaders employ along with the ideological. The intentions and capabilities of these leaders, the expectations and responses of the targets, and the perspectives of those who make and apply authoritative prescriptions should receive due attention.

This book is an attempt to study the subject from what is currently known as a value- or policy-oriented approach. This is hardly the place to give a detailed description of the method; [21] its significant features will be-

---

to incitement of foreign audiences to revolt. He showed an awareness of the fact that a situation which might arise in practice for legal regulation would not readily fit into one of a few fixed categories such as "revolutionary propaganda." "The Use of Radio as an Instrument of Foreign Propaganda," 32 *A.J.I.L.* 339 (1938).

21. For a detailed exposition of this method, see Myres S. McDougal, "International Law, Power and Policy," 82 *Hague Recueil* 137 (1953); and the works produced by him and his associates with this jurisprudential approach: McDougal, Harold D. Lasswell, and Ivan A. Vlasic, *Law and Public Order in Space* (New Haven, Yale University Press, 1963); McDougal and Florentino P. Feliciano, *Law and Minimum World Public Order: The Legal Regulation of International Coercion* (New Haven, Yale University Press, 1961); McDougal and William T. Burke, *The Public Order of the Oceans: A Contemporary International Law of the Sea* (New Haven, Yale University Press, 1962); McDougal and associates, *Studies in World Public Order* (New Haven, Yale University Press, 1960).

come clear as we proceed. Briefly stated, our main concern is with decisions [22] and decision-makers; with factual contexts and policy alternatives. Our aim is to bring policy clarification to the task of judges, officials, and legal advisors, who apply or expound international law. The judges and officials are themselves participants in the vast, worldwide, interdependent social process. As officials they participate in the authoritatively recognized organizations engaged in the decision processes within individual states and the world arena.

When we speak of decisions ("precedents" or treaties) we do not refer to the mere language in which they are couched. Decisions are to be studied in their total factual contexts. Hence one should ask: what happened when propaganda was used in the past persuasively or coercively, and under what conditions. Further, as legal decisions are events which invariably affect the values of the contending claimants and the community, scholarly inquiry should not stop at a mere analysis of past decisions and the variables that affected them; it should extend to an appraisal of the effects of the decisions on the value processes prevailing at the time. And if the study is to be a useful guide in the future it must clarify how decision-makers will have to respond to maximize preferred values.

The key questions we intend to address in this study are: when the ideological instrument was coercively used in the past, what were the goals sought by those using it, and under what conditions; what were the assertions made in the name of the obligations of the members of the world community in reference to such use; what influenced the course of events and the regulation of the use; what are the present day situations, or situations of the foreseeable future, arising out of the use of the instrument; and assuming we propose to maximize all preferred values, what doctrines and methods seem best suited for the purpose?

In addition to other possible omissions and commissions the author expects the reader to point out that many questions of current interest, or those relating to situations that may arise in the future, pertaining to the legality of the various types of propaganda activity are not categorically answered. Let it be repeated, the purpose of this study is to clarify the task of decision-makers. The attempt here is not to deduce a few supposedly authoritative rules and to advance an opinion as to whether a particular course of conduct is repugnant to those rules or not, but to throw light on these questions: who is likely to decide issues of the specified type; what

22. We use the expression "decision" in a sense wider than a "judicial decision," to include any exercise of power which is "the culminating point of a situation in which the participants entertain certain 'expectations' and 'demands.'" See Lasswell, "The World Revolution of our Time: A Framework for Basic Policy Research," in Harold D. Lasswell and Daniel Lerner, eds., *World Revolutionary Elites* (Cambridge, Mass., M.I.T. Press, 1965), pp. 29, 45–46.

are the facts which the decision-makers have to regard as relevant; what authoritative legal prescriptions are available for them to invoke; and what goals should they bear in mind in making their decisions? Indeed none can foresee all the relevant details of events which may come up for decision in the future. Hence in many cases one can only indicate the categories of pertinent facts and the alternatives of policy. This is what has been attempted here.

The central problem of legal control in the world arena is the prevention or at least the regulation of coercion. Our primary task under the mode of analysis outlined above is to acquaint ourselves with the world political situations which arise as a result of the use of the instruments of policy. We, therefore, examine the interactions among elites and focus attention upon the policy instruments employed, with special reference to the consequences to the world community of any process that involves coercion. As our interest is directed to the coercive use of the ideological instrument we must describe its method and consequences of use in greater detail than others.

Communication is no doubt a vehicle of persuasion, but can it be coercive? Doubt may exist, and hence it is not out of place to lay a basis, making use of the available scientific knowledge, for our characterization of the instrument as susceptible to coercive use. Part of our problem is to supply a set of criteria by means of which it becomes possible to differentiate, at least broadly, a coercive from a persuasive use of the ideological instrument. In the next chapter we shall essay this task. From the foundations laid in Chapter 2, we shall proceed in Chapter 3 to analyze the process of use of the instrument, to identify the recurring problems of legal policy that arise as the instrument is employed by the elites in the world arena in pursuit of transnational values, or producing transnational effects.

In Chapter 4 we shall postulate our preferred policies. These are intended to further the development of controls which counteract or prevent the continued occurrence of adverse effects upon the world community. The discussions that have taken place in the League and the United Nations have disclosed that the question of regulation of propaganda brings into conflict two major policy considerations, namely, the protection and promotion of freedom of information, and the maintenance of peace and security. The goals envisaged in this study will be more comprehensive. They include promotion of human rights in the world community, subjection of transnational coercion to ordered procedures, and affirmative use of persuasion.

In Chapters 5 to 12 we shall examine the trend of legal decisions regarding the various claims and counterclaims put forward in relation to the process of use, appraising the trend in the light of our preferred policies and suggesting the policies that seem to be best adapted to attain the goals.

More specifically, we shall observe the trend of decisions relating to the claims concerning participation in the process of use of the instrument, the objectives of the strategists, situations in which the instrument is employed, the base or instrumental values possessed by the strategists, the strategies employed by them, the outcome and effects of the process, and the process of decision. In Chapter 13 we shall make a final appraisal and put forward suggestions regarding the policies to be adopted by the decision-makers.

2

The Ideological Instrument of Coercion

THE FOUR INSTRUMENTS OF POLICY

In the contemporary world community, which is divided into territorially delimited political communities called states, it is common experience that social processes take place within each state and across state boundaries.

A "social process" may be understood as a continuing flow of influence between people. It is a process by which men interact with each other to obtain satisfaction of their value demands. The whole range of the interactions which take place in the social process may be summed up under the formula that men acting individually or in combination seek to maximize their values by using resources and institutions.[1] A value, stated descriptively, is a desired event; and an institution signifies the practice by which a value is pursued. A detailed itemization of all values may perhaps run into a figure of thousands, depending upon the nation or even the individual involved. For purposes of comparison let us use the following brief list of categories: *power, wealth, well-being, skill, enlightenment, respect, rectitude,* and *affection.*[2]

The expression *power* is understood to mean not merely naked force but participation in the making of policy choices attended by sanctions. *Wealth* is control over goods and services; *well-being* is the health and safety of the organism; *respect* is the value of honor and access to other values without discrimination; *enlightenment* is the knowledge of contemporary and historical facts; *skill* is proficiency in any art or craft; *affection* is the enjoyment of highly congenial interpersonal relations; and *rectitude* is

1. For a detailed analysis of social process, see Harold D. Lasswell and Abraham Kaplan, *Power and Society* (New Haven, Yale University Press, 1950), p. 69; McDougal, "International Law, Power and Policy," p. 165.

2. The definition of value given here, categorization of values, and definitions of the categories are adopted from Lasswell and Kaplan and the writings of Lasswell and McDougal.

moral value, such as virtue and righteousness. Each of these values may be pursued as an end in itself (that is, as a *scope* value) as well as a means to an end (as a *base* value).

In any sizable community, and without saying in a state, it is matter of common experience that the sharing of values among individuals will not be equal. Those who possess a greater share of values may be referred to as the *elite*.

The management of practices by which values are shaped and shared to maximize one's own value position may be referred to as strategy, taking the expression in its comprehensive sense. Strategies may be distinguished from one another according to the practice employed, and also in terms of the objectives immediately sought and the distinctive means adopted to attain them. In a general way the practice of diplomacy may be said to consist of negotiation between leaders; the ideological practice, of manipulation of words and symbols for the purpose of influencing group attitudes and behavior; and the economic and military practices, of giving or withholding goods and services and using violence, respectively. The immediate objective sought in diplomacy is agreement advantageous to the strategists; in ideological strategy the aim is the formation in the audience of attitudes favorable to the strategists; in economic strategy the objective is to improve one's position in regard to resources and production; and in military strategy, to secure one's position in contests of violence.[3] The distinctive means employed in the first is negotiation; in the second, the communication of words and symbols; in the third, goods and services; and in the fourth, instruments of violence.

"Policy" may be understood as "a projected program of goal values and practices." [4] It is any projected course of action in which other persons are also involved. For the elite in any community the diplomatic, ideological, economic, and military practices serve as instruments of policy, both internally and externally. The choices regarding the combination of instruments to be used, and the sequence and relative intensity of their use, are made so as to attain the goal of the policy with minimum cost.[5]

The policy instruments can indeed be used for purposes ranging from persuasion to coercion. About the coercive character of the military instrument there cannot be any doubt. The diplomatic instrument is mainly persuasive, but sometimes it may be used for coercive purposes, as when recognition is withheld in order to extract some concessions. Economic aid

3. See Harold D. Lasswell, *The Analysis of Political Behavior, An Empirical Approach* (London, Oxford University Press, 1948), p. 125.

4. Lasswell and Kaplan, p. 71.

5. Harold D. Lasswell, "The Strategy of Soviet Propaganda," in *Psychological Warfare,* Foreign Policy Headline Series, No. 86 (New York, Foreign Policy Association. 1951), p. 57.

may be given as a means of persuasion, and withdrawn for purposes of coercion. The ideological instrument will be examined in detail presently.

THE IDEOLOGICAL INSTRUMENT

Symbol Manipulation an Instrument of Politics

Language is indeed an instrument of politics, national as well as international. As a matter of fact, not language alone, but pictures, movies, and indeed any visual or aural representation which conveys meaning, can be pressed into service in the political arena. We shall use the expression "symbol" to denote anything which communicates a meaning. It may include an *act* as well, if the act carries important symbolic significance.[6]

At no time in history was man fed more intensely by symbols than he is at present. The rich repast starts with breakfast and continues till sleep overtakes him at night. Newspapers, magazines, radio, television, movies, books of all types, continuously serve him with delicious dishes prepared by expert chefs. To these heavy servings we have to add the occasional snacks supplied by platform speakers, soap-box orators, professional agitators, and gossiping neighbors.

Can we in a strain similar to that of Shakespeare's Sir John Falstaff, say, "What are words? Air," and banish this incessant bombardment with symbols from serious discussion? No serious-minded scholar, in the political, legal, or any other discipline, would suggest it. Political communications possess a few characteristics which very soon capture our attention. Certain words are constantly repeated. Politicians rarely engage in public talk without using them. Some symbols are old ones, though others have entered the scene only recently. The entry of some of these new arrivals was accompanied by the thunders of revolution, while others did not have that pomp and ceremony. The words refer to nations, parties, leaders, causes, hopes, expectations, and possess rich diversity of emotional appeal. In this crowding multitude of symbols one may readily discern at present a few oft-repeated ones, such as "communism," "dictatorship," "democracy," "people's democracy," "free world," "workers," "socialists," "proletariat," "capitalists," "imperialists," "colonialism," "anticolonialism," "neocolonialism," "warmongers," "peace," "revisionists," and so on.

To explain why symbols are frequently used one has to refer to the larger context in which they occur, that is, all political discourse. The language in which political debate is generally carried on has certain distinctive features. For one thing it abounds in frequent references to legal doctrines, political doctrines, and political folklore. It does not take long to explain

6. See Harold D. Lasswell, "Propaganda," in *Encyclopaedia of Social Sciences*, 12 (New York, Macmillan, 1934), 521, 522; Ernst B. Haas and Allen S. Whiting, *Dynamics of International Relations* (New York, McGraw-Hill 1956), p. 186.

this phenomenon. The doctrines and lore obtaining within any community, by and large, articulate the "fundamental assumptions" [7] prevailing among its members about political affairs—assumptions which are believed rather unquestioningly. Communication will naturally be facilitated if discourse is carried on by using symbols which voice these assumptions. We may use the expression *political myth* to refer to the assumptions.

Actually, the importance of myth is more than that of a convenient referent for purposes of effective communication in political debate. It is supposed to legitimize all action in the political arena.[8] Officials and non-officials, political leaders and their followers, judges and litigants, all invoke myth to show justification for their actions, claims, or policies. Myth is indeed central to all action in the political arena.

It is not intended to maintain that a single integrated system of beliefs is essential for the subsistence and functioning of a political community. As a matter of fact, at least in fairly large states, the myth consists of heterogenous and somewhat mutually contradicting parts. Groups aspiring for power may give to the myth interpretations which differ from those espoused by the established authority.[9] Or those groups may challenge parts or the whole of the doctrines professed by the established elite. Political myth, as we understand it, comprises the whole body of political doctrines and beliefs prevailing within a body politic—the established one as well as the heterodoxy. For the sake of convenience, the established myth may be called "ideology" and the heterodoxical portion "counter-ideology." [10]

Nor is it intended to assert here that all political actions are strictly circumscribed by the myth. It is nearer to truth to assert that for true believers, i.e. for those whose predispositions are most deeply affected, it constitutes a code of political behavior. For others who are not deeply affected, it supplies at least an anchoring point to legitimize their conduct or programs. Myth is indeed at once a "conscience-keeper" of its believers and the handmaid of its manipulators.

By virtue of this dual character, myth assumes a highly significant role in the drama of the political arena; and for students of political science it is a fascinating topic of study. The arena of politics is rarely static. Frequently

7. A. V. Dicey, *Lectures on the Relation Between Law and Public Opinion in England during the Nineteenth Century* (London, Macmillan, 1914), p. 20; also see Harold D. Lasswell, Nathan Leites, and Associates, *The Language of Politics* (New York, George Stewart, 1949), p. 9; Harold D. Lasswell, Daniel Lerner and Ithiel de Sola Pool, *The Comparative Study of Symbols: An Introduction* (Stanford, Stanford University Press, 1952), pp. 1–2, and the authors' citations from Plato and the Arab historian and philosopher Ibn Khaldun.

8. See Talcott Parsons, *The Social System* (Glencoe, Ill., Free Press, 1951), p. 349

9. For an elaborate discussion of these diversities, see ibid., p. 355.

10. This terminology is adopted from Lasswell et. al., *The Language of Politics*, p. 3.

the "haves" of power are overthrown by the "have-nots," or are forced to accept a sharing arrangement. Established patterns of recruitment of the elite may be set at naught, and upstarts may force their way to control points in the arena by unconventional and sometimes high-handed methods. When changes such as these take place it is difficult, hazardous, and expensive to seek, by the force of bayonets alone, the acceptance of the new regime by the rank and file and the elite of lower levels. It will be much easier if they can be made to believe that the change is for their own good. Language becomes in such periods of change an important weapon in the hands of strategists.

History supplies abundant evidence that political upheavals are accompanied by striking changes in the language of the political forum. The French Revolution popularized the symbols "liberty," "equality," and "fraternity." The Bolshevik Revolution in Russia marked not only the advent of a sociopolitical system radically different from the traditional ones, but also a set of expressions and doctrines unheard of before from the political elite of that country. Not long ago the world witnessed the rise and fall of the Nazis and the Fascists, and with them the emergence and disappearance of racist and chauvinistic theories, and symbols such as "*lebensraum*" and "The Asian Co-Prosperity Sphere." If an inhabitant of another planet, who had visited ours before World War II, renewed his visit today he would be astounded by the transformations which have taken place in the politician's language, let alone other changes.

There can be little doubt that the above transformations in language were effected by none other than those political strategists who were instrumental in bringing about the changes in the regimes. But it may be pertinent to ask whether the new symbols were consequential. Did they have any effect on the audiences involved? Or one may expand the question: is the ideological strategy, in general, consequential in any situation? In answering questions like these without the aid of any scientific data one is liable either to exaggerate or to minimize the effects of the changes. If the answers are to be reasonably accurate they have to be based upon scientific foundations.

A preliminary step in the direction of obtaining the necessary scientific tools seems to be to devise some method by which the overwhelming collection of political symbols used by the propagandists can be reduced into a few systematic categories. Such categories will facilitate comparison of the various communications. Further, if the basic factors which influence human behavior are known and the communication categories and other operations of the ideological strategy can be related to those factors, there will be a reasonable basis to estimate how consequential a communication is likely to be.

When we speak of the basic factors that influence human behavior we may have in mind a variety of planes of reference. Because of the enormous amount of scholarly research that has gone lately into the fields of history, anthropology, and other social sciences, we are at present more sensitive to the influences of national, racial, and cultural factors on the responses of individuals and groups, officials and nonofficials, statesmen and diplomats, during crisis and intercrisis periods. Important as these various group affiliations may be in shaping human behavior, there is one factor fundamental to study in this area, and that is the character of man himself. The behavior and responses of groups are, in the ultimate analysis, the behavior of the individuals composing them. The several contributions made by social scientists, giving us valuable insights into the behavior of people in society are, by and large, generalizations based upon the data gathered from the observation of individuals. For the purpose at hand, too, it seems appropriate to take the individual as the basic key to understanding the dynamics of human behavior.

A qualification has to be added, however, to what is stated below in regard to the factors influencing behavior. Man is so complex a being that, in spite of all the centuries of effort to study him, he still remains mysterious. There is much to learn about the manner in which human thought processes operate and what ultimately determines the response. Psychology has indeed made considerable strides, but the unsurveyed and even unseen fields are still enormous; and the explorations so far made have not yielded data that are beyond challenge. Therefore, much of what is going to be mentioned is necessarily tentative and based upon fairly undisputed scientific knowledge. It remains, however, open to correction in the light of future developments in the scientific field.

The Analysis of Political Communications

Political communications may be said to consist, for our present purposes, of symbols, slogans, and doctrinal and other statements. A slogan may be described as a group of words which serves the same function as a symbol.[11]

Political symbols (as well as slogans and doctrinal statements) may be classified into those of demand, of expectation, and of identification, according to the meaning they convey. A demand symbol commits its user to a preference or a determination; examples are "equality," "freedom," "revolution," and the like. A symbol of expectation conveys merely an assumption of fact, historical or prospective. A symbol of identification sets the boundaries of the self of its user; e.g. "we workers," "we Americans," "we Arabs," and so on. It may also set the limits of the person or group that is being referred to, and as a necessary consequence indicate those who

11. This definition and the following classifications of symbols etc. are adopted from ibid., p. 13.

remain outside the "self." The demand, expectation, and identification symbols may further be classified into those which appeal mainly to reason and those which appeal to emotions.

The Basic Factors that Influence Human Behavior

At one end of the scale, the response of the organism when subjected to external stimuli may be no more than the functioning of bodily reflexes, with little involvement of psychic processes. Since this study is focused mainly on the responses to verbal communications, the responses produced by the mere functioning of the reflexes are not of much interest. We are concerned with those responses produced as a result of the psyche receiving a verbal message and setting in motion the processes which lead to the response.

The Theory of Conditioned Reflexes

As we turn our attention to such responses, we are drawn rather automatically to the theory of conditioned reflexes propounded by the famous Russian scientist Pavlov, a theory that has inspired several recent works on propaganda and brainwashing techniques.[12] Briefly stated, the theory propounds that if certain irrelevant signals accompany stimuli which evoke responses that satisfy the drives of biological instincts of the organism, after a time the organism becomes conditioned to produce the same responses to the irrelevant signal alone. A dog salivates, Pavlov demonstrated by experiments, on the mere ringing of a bell if, for some time in the past, the ringing has accompanied the giving of food to the dog.[13] He called the response of salivation which becomes thus established a conditioned reflex, as distinguished from the natural reflex of salivation at the sight of food.

The cues which this theory is supposed to supply the propaganda strategists are fairly clear. The inference is that human beings may respond in a desired manner if they are conditioned by verbal or other symbols used in propaganda. To accomplish such conditioning the symbols employed should be sufficiently exciting.[14] If the conditioning is to remain intact the symbols must be repeated continually.[15] By means of highly intensive propaganda it is possible to produce a condition of mass hypnosis.[16] The

12. Among such works may be mentioned Sergei Chakhotin, *The Rape of the Masses* (London, Routledge & Kegan Paul, 1940); William W. Sargant, *Battle for the Mind* (Garden City, N.Y., Doubleday, 1957); J. A. M. Meerloo, *Rape of the Mind* (Cleveland, The World Publishing Co., 1956).

13. I. P. Pavlov, *Conditioned Reflexes, An Investigation of the Physiological Activity of the Cerebral Cortex* (trans. and ed. G. V. Anrep, London, Humphrey Milford, 1927).

14. See ibid., p. 31.

15. Ibid., p. 28.

16. Ibid., lectures 15 and 16.

audiences brought under such hypnosis lose their faculty of discretion and become transformed into passive spectators of events or can easily be influenced by suggestion.

Pavlov's conditioning theory, however, is much in dispute among psychologists for several reasons. In the first place, it is highly doubtful whether certain reflexes, pupillary contractions for instance, are amenable to conditioning.[17] It is likely that a theory which postulates that human behavior is the result of conditioning alone is an oversimplification of the highly complex processes that underlie it. Further, the experiments of Pavlov do not conclusively support the theory; they can be explained on other theoretical assumptions also. One should also note in this connection that Pavlov himself cautioned against an unquestioning extension of theories based on the behavior of dogs to human beings endowed with highly superior psychic mechanisms.[18]

Behavioral, Freudian, and "Gestalt" Psychologists

Leaving aside the theory of conditioned reflexes, we may pass on to the valuable insight supplied by the behavioral scientists, Freudian psychologists, and the gestalt psychologists, regarding human behavior. According to the Freudian theory, and the *hedonistic* theory of behavior which is accepted among a wide section of behavioral scientists, human beings strive to maximize pleasure over pain. The Freudian theory is that the libidinal impulses in man seek gratification and the attendant pleasure through an institution of the personality which is referred to as the *id*. Another institution, the *ego*, too, strives to maximize pleasure over pain at a higher level. As an unrestrained play of impulses is very likely to bring in return, in ordinary day-to-day life, deprivations of various types, the ego institution exercises restraint on the id, with the result that certain pleasures are now given up in order to have a surplus of pleasure in the long run. The *superego*, the third element in the personality, also functions in a comparable manner. Man living in society has to conform to the behavioral patterns demanded of him by the society. Gradually he comes to adopt and internalize the demands made in this connection by parents and parent surrogates, and thereby the superego is formed. The superego controls the ego and the id with a view to protecting the subject from deviant behavior and the attendant societal sanctions.

From the behavioral scientists' point of view, behavior is the organism's response to the stimuli operating upon it rather than an outcome of the functioning of inner psychic institutions. Those who support the hedonis-

17. See Ernest R. Hilgard, *Theories of Learning* (New York, Appleton, 1956), p. 432.

18. Pavlov, p. 395.

tic theory among the behavioral scientists,[19] however, more or less reach the same result as the Freudians. They maintain that the organism selects rewarding responses and avoids painful ones. The rewards may be either the primary ones, such as the gratification of the hunger drive, or secondary ones, such as receiving praise or reducing fear or anxiety.[20] They come near the Freudians in this regard. However, the credit goes to the Freudians for theoretically postulating how the psyche builds up various internal mechanisms to protect the personality from tormenting fears, anxieties, and frustrations likely to be experienced in ordinary life. We shall refer to these mechanisms a little later.

The gestalt psychologists and, among the behavioral psychologists, Tolman, have made a distinctive contribution to the study of behavior by sharply departing from the approach of the behavioral scientists. While the latter explained all learning processes in terms of stimulus and response, gestalt psychologists and Tolman proposed that what the organism learns is not the response, but the signs which guide it to the response.[21] According to this thesis, all behavior is goal-seeking. The path chosen is that which brings the organism to the goal with economy of effort. When confronted with any problem situation, the organism makes use of its cognitive powers to survey the environment, the various paths that lead to the solution, and the tools the environment supplies to reach it, and then makes a choice out of the available alternatives. The choice may be insightful or the result of trial and error, or partly insightful and partly the result of trial and error. The trial need not necessarily take place in the physical world; it may be purely mental. What the organism perceives or expects to perceive will quite naturally influence the choice. Sometimes the organism may take a sign to represent a total situation of which the sign was formerly a part, and respond in a manner appropriate to the total situation.

Some of the behavioral scientists adopt an *associationistic* theory as distinguished from the hedonistic, postulating that if a response occurs in association with certain stimuli, it is likely to repeat itself if the same stimuli are present.[22] Pavlov's dog salivates on the mere ringing of the bell

19. This theory is subscribed to in diverse forms by many modern psychologists.

20. See Neal E. Miller and J. D. Dollard, *Social Learning and Imitation* (New Haven, Yale University Press, 1941), pp. 29–30; for an exposition of C. H. Hull's position in this regard, see Hilgard, *Theories of Learning*, p. 129; O. H. Mowrer, in his *Learning Theory and Personality Dynamics, Selected Papers* (New York, George Ronald, 1950), develops the two-factor theory of learning according to which secondary drives such as fear call forth their own response which he calls "conditioning" (p. 244).

21. For a brief exposition of Tolman's theory and gestalt theories, see Hilgard, *Theories of Learning*, Chaps. 6 and 7.

22. Ibid., p. 53.

because that response followed the stimulus on earlier occasions. The theory indeed throws light on the habit-forming trait of an organism. It is even recognized among other psychologists that some habits persist even in situations which are not adaptive, and accustomed behavior follows even in novel situations which call for new patterns of response.[23] Freudian psychologists, too, affirm that habit-formation is one of the fundamental human traits.[24]

Now a word about two of the mechanisms the ego builds to protect the personality from the painful effects of frustrations and anxieties, and to which reference has been made earlier. The first is *identification*. This mechanism operates in diverse ways. A frustrated person may project and identify himself with another who is successful, and thus seek at least symbolic gratification.[25] A girl, unsuccessful in love affairs, may identify herself with her prettier sister, and seek symbolic gratification through her success. Sometimes the object chosen for identification may be the aggressor himself who is responsible for the frustration, or the cause of the anxiety. A girl afraid of ghosts in the night may start acting like a ghost herself to overcome the fear.[26] A child threatened with punishment by parents for certain conduct may identify himself with the parents and impose on himself the parental injunctions. Another mechanism is *displacement* on to others of hatred against the object which is causing frustration or anxiety. The behavioral trait of displacing aggression which the subject cannot overcome on to irrelevant objects has been experimentally demonstrated by Neal Miller.[27] And history furnishes many instances of creation of scapegoats—a phenomenon of attributing responsibility for an evil to an irrelevant object, and channeling all hatred to it.[28]

Language and Behavior

The importance of language, political communications in particular, in shaping the activities of people may be intelligently observed in the light of

23. Ibid., p. 466.

24. See e.g. Franz Alexander, *Our Age of Unreason, A Study of the Irrational Forces in Social Life* (Philadelphia, Lippincott, 1951), p. 129; Sigmund Freud himself spoke of "repetition-compulsion" in his *Beyond the Pleasure Principle* (trans. J. Strachey, New York, Liveright, 1950), pp. 19–25.

25. See Anna Freud, *The Ego and the Mechanisms of Defense* (trans. C. Baines, New York, International Universities Press, 1946), p. 40.

26. Ibid., p. 118, reports an actual case like this.

27. See J. N. Dollard, Neal E. Miller et al., *Frustration and Aggression* (New Haven, Yale University Press, 1939), p. 41; Hilgard and others, *Psychoanalysis as Science* (Stanford, Stanford University Press, 1952), pp. 10–11; also H. J. Eysenck, *The Psychology of Politics* (London, Routledge and Kegan Paul, 1954), p. 215; Bernard Berelson and G. A. Steiner, *Human Behavior: An Inventory of Scientific Findings* (New York, Harcourt, Brace, 1964), p. 267.

28. See Alexander, p. 221 et. seq.

what has been stated. For one thing, the knowledge a man derives by direct observation is very small when compared to what is received indirectly. A great majority of contemporary events which shape his expectations are brought to the focus of his attention through the medium of language. Also, most of the cultural heritage which gives him ready-made solutions to problems encountered in day to day life, and the insight which helps him in problem-solving and stimulates the thought processes which lead to solutions are transmitted through the medium of language. Impending dangers coming from the environment are communicated to him, and fears are consequently aroused, mostly through the medium of language—as are the expedients to overcome dangers, fears, and anxieties.

Actually, the influence of language is more subtle than that. For our present purposes, we may understand language as a system of signs which carry the same significance to a collection of interpreters of the signs with relative constancy.[29] In behavioral terms, language signs are not mere signals which evoke the related responses but are symbols which represent situations and call forth behavior appropriate to those situations.[30] And it is not this "representational" or "descriptive" function alone that the language signs perform. They have also an "expressive" or "emotive" function.[31] Each sign performs the two functions in varying degrees.[32] The representational or descriptive significance which the signs carry at any time is, however, only relatively constant. As a matter of fact, the response that the signs evoke in terms of the cognitive mental processes (such as thinking, believing, supposing) they stimulate are dependent upon the environment in which the receivers are situated, their previous experience, and the habitual use to which the sign has been put among them.[33] The emotive significance that the signs convey also depends upon the same factors, viz., environment, experience, and habit. The responses to language signs, therefore, are variable within a certain wide range.

In any society, the significance the language signs convey is of vital concern. We have already alluded to the role of the myth. Further, the existence of a society presupposes the subsistence of interpersonal relations of a stable character. The patterns of these relations are prescribed by those

29. For a definition of language from the behaviorist's point of view, see Charles Morris, *Signs, Language and Behavior* (New York, Prentice-Hall, 1946), pp. 35–36.

30. For an explanation of "sign" and "symbol," see ibid., pp. 23–27.

31. Rudolf Carnap, *Philosophy and Logical Syntax* (London, Routledge and Kegan Paul, 1935), p. 27, terms the functions of language "representative" and "expressive"; that is to say, words represent a state of affairs and also express the feelings, mood, or disposition of the person who utters them. Charles L. Stevenson, *Ethics and Language* (New Haven, Yale University Press, 1944), pp. 59–62, uses the expressions "descriptive" and "emotive" to describe the same two functions.

32. Stevenson, pp. 76–78.

33. Ibid., pp. 70–71.

controlling the society, and the prescription is done, at least in part, through the medium of language. The appraisal of events in terms of conformance or deviance from the prescriptions, and disapprovals, are conveyed partly through the medium of language. An individual member soon comes to internalize these signs, as he does all social norms. His response to events, consequently, will depend in part upon the significance of these signs. If interpersonal relations between the members should be harmonious, the prevailing sign system should be conducive to that end. Hence societal control is exercised on the sign system.[34]

When language signs are followed over a long period of time by a particular pattern of responses, the subjects become habituated to react in that way. Emotional attachments of the signs continue with persistence; [35] and cognitive responses, too, tend to become habitual.

The Influence of Political Communications

We may recollect the threefold classification of the political symbols and words adopted earlier. The circulation of the symbols of demand may lead the audience to adopt the demands as their own. The demand may be of self on self, or of self on others. The audience may be induced to demand from others such things as more wages, more rational adjustment of the existing state of affairs, or more sacrifices in the name of God or country. Or a member of the audience may be induced to demand that he himself forego some of his basic wants, yield to reason, follow leaders, sacrifice himself for the sake of his country, and so on. The tenacity with which a demand may be pressed forward, and the choice of alternatives to obtain satisfaction of the demand, will necessarily depend upon the expectations of the audience about past, present, and future events. Expectation symbols will be useful to shape the expectations of the audience.

Symbols of identification serve diverse purposes. They facilitate projection by individuals of self into larger groups such as nations, races, political parties, and religious groups, and obtain at least symbolic gratification of many things which the persons cannot otherwise obtain.[36] Because of this general tendency to project, it has been possible to build up among people group consciousness and group solidarity, and to unify them into nations, tribes, etc.

The insecurities that an individual in a community faces may be due not to inevitable natural events but to the policies pursued by the ruling elite. The frustrations resulting from the policies can certainly be more easily

34. Morris, pp. 207, 208.

35. Ibid., p. 40, states, "Once a word has become ingrained into our habits of emotional expression, it retains its place with no little persistence."

36. J. H. Masserman, "The Dynamic Psychology of War-Time Communications and Morale," 5 *Diseases of the Nervous System* 101 (1944).

suffered if the sufferer identifies himself with the elite. And further, the elite's position is likely to be far more secure if the hatred springing from the frustrations can be displaced on to some irrelevant objects. Symbols of identification may be used to promote, on one hand, identification with the elite; and on the other to spotlight an irrelevant group which is assigned the scapegoat function.

Symbols of expectation may rouse anxieties and fears among the audience, or reduce fears caused by the environment. Identification symbols may serve to overcome fears and anxieties, and in turn strengthen identifications. Thus, in times of real or artificially created insecurity, belief in the infallibility of the leaders, and identification with them, will give relief from anxieties and also strengthen identification with the leaders.

Group Pressures and Individual Behavior

Man being invariably a member of some social group, in fact many groups, the influence that the group exerts on him has to be studied in a comprehensive inquiry into his behavior. Recent studies have brought to light the fact that an individual participates in a fairly large society—let us say a state—not directly, but through various smaller primary groups, such as his family, his club, his professional association, his local community, with which he identifies himself in various ways.[37] These primary groups exercise a high degree of influence on his opinions, attitudes, and behavior. Indeed his opinions and attitudes are not strictly his individual affair, but are inextricably connected with the norms of the groups to which he belongs. Extraneous influences opposed to the group norms have less effect on him than those that accord with the norms. Attempts to change his opinions or attitudes in such a way that they are incompatible with the norms of his group are likely to be vigorously resisted.[38] Furthermore, if subjected to the pressure of the group, he is likely to conform his opinion and judgment to theirs.[39]

The influence of the group on the individual is seen in a more dramatic

37. See Elihu Katz and P. F. Lazarsfeld, *The Part Played by People in the Flow of Mass Communications* (Glencoe, Ill., Free Press, 1955), p. 25; Wilbur L. Schramm, ed., *The Process and Effects of Mass Communication* (Urbana, University of Illinois Press, 1954), p. 20 et seq.

38. Katz and Lazarsfeld, pp. 65, 81.

39. See the experimental study of S. E. Asch, "Some Forms of Interpersonal Influence: Effect of Group Pressure upon the Modification and Distortion of Judgments," Guy Swanson et al., eds., *Readings in Social Psychology* (New York, Holt, 1952). The result is summarized thus: ". . . by means of a simple technique we produced a radical divergence between a majority and a minority, and observed the ways in which individuals coped with the resulting difficulty. Despite the stress of the given conditions, a substantial portion of individuals retained their independence throughout. At the same time a substantial minority yielded, modifying their judgments in accordance with the majority" (p. 10).

form in the context of the behavior of a crowd which is excited and engaged in the pursuit of some specific and aggressive objective.[40] In a crowd of that character there will generally be a minimum degree of conscious identification, tradition, or other elements which go to make it a society. Yet sheer stimulation from other members of the crowd drives many to uncritical actions—actions which they would not indulge in under ordinary conditions.[41] The crowd sets the norm for the moment which the members follow rather like automatons.

The influence of a group on the behavior of its members is readily seen in another context. It is well known that intense fear or anxiety has a disorganizing effect on individuals.[42] It creates panic, to which they may react by extreme passivity or inaction, or a flight-reflex which goads them into highly uncritical actions. However, when organized into a group, individuals are less vulnerable to the panic-creating elements. During the last stages of World War II, in spite of the heavy odds against them, the German armies displayed a surprising degree of morale. This phenomenon has been attributed to the influence which the primary groups in the German army had exercised over individual soldiers.[43] So long as these primary groups satisfied the physical and psychological wants of the soldier his morale did not slacken. It cracked when the primary groups began to disintegrate. By way of contrast, one may note the effect produced in 1938 by Orson Welles' broadcast, "Invasion from Mars." It drove many Americans listening to the radio in their homes to panicky flights. The fact that the listeners were not in an organized and prepared condition to meet this novel danger may provide a partial explanation of the panic.[44]

40. Crowds, it is said, may be classified into four types: *casual* crowd, such as the one that gathers to see a chance spectacle; *conventionalized* crowd, one that gathers and witnesses an event following a conventionalized pattern of behavior (e.g. a crowd watching a tennis match); *acting* crowd, a crowd pursuing an objective aggressively; and *dancing* crowd, a crowd participating in an action in a conventional way. See H. Blumer, "The Crowd, The Public and the Mass," in Schramm, *The Process and Effects of Mass Communication,* p. 363. The reference here is to a crowd of the third type. Lasswell, "The Impact of Crowd Psychology upon International Law," 1 *Philippine International Law Journal* 293, 295 (1962), speaks of crowd response as "a collective situation in which stress towards action is intense, and in which critical, independent and reflective processes are thrust aside by the imperatives of drive and determination."

41. See Blumer, p. 366; Miller and Dollard, Chaps. 14 and 15.

42. See J. A. M. Meerloo, *Patterns of Panic* (New York, International Universities Press, 1950), pp. 27–30.

43. See in this connection the valuable study of E. A. Shils and M. Janowitz, "Cohesion and Disintegration in the *Wehrmacht* in World War II," in Daniel Katz et al., eds., *Public Opinion and Propaganda* (New York, Dryden Press, 1954), p. 553, and particularly the conclusion at p. 582.

44. See H. Cantril, "The Invasion from Mars," in Swanson et al., *Readings in Social Psychology,* p. 198. The author gives some other explanations also for the panicky behavior.

Let us sum up what has been said so far in relation to what influences the behavior of individuals. Behavior is conditioned by factors that may be broken into two broad classes. In the first are the following: perceptions of the situation; demands, the fulfillment of which is pleasurable; persisting habits; insight and the internal trial and error processes; the tendency to attribute to signs various meanings; group norms which the subject internalizes and no longer regards as injunctions imposed from outside; and the mechanisms which the ego has built internally to protect the personality from painful fears, anxieties, and frustrations. Leaving aside the actual perceptions, we may refer to all these diverse factors under the head of predispositional factors. Second, there are the pressures that the groups to which the subject belongs exert on him. The perceptions of the situation and the group surroundings may be referred to as environmental factors.

The Operations of Ideological Strategy

Here we shall observe only the general aspects of the operations and reserve the details for the next chapter. The main objective of ideological strategists is to develop among the audience perspectives and attitudes which accord with the strategists' policies. The expression "perspective" denotes a pattern of demands, expectations, and identifications, and "attitude" means a tendency to act in a manner which externalizes a perspective.[45] A person may have a pro-communist perspective but not necessarily a pro-communist attitude.

The primary function of the strategists is, of course, to select symbols and words suitable for developing the desired perspectives and attitudes and to disseminate them. We have referred to the role of myth in societies, and myth is indeed a collection of symbols that articulate the important part of the perspectives of the members of the society. But symbols selected for one purpose do not necessarily serve for all time. They require redefinition from time to time as the flow of events alters the prevailing expectations of the audience. Events may rouse new anxieties, and a change in the symbolic environment may be helpful in reducing those anxieties and thereby avoiding possible disturbances in the community. Furthermore, with the lapse of time the symbols may cease to be realistic in reference to the environment, and their psychological appeal may consequently be lost. Redefinition of symbols from time to time is thus a compelling task for the strategists.

However, strategists may find it inexpedient in a given situation to adopt radical redefinitions of the prevailing symbols, redefinitions that are likely to encourage demands for corresponding changes in the prevailing system of order. An elite will quite naturally oppose alterations in the symbolic structure when it apprehends that the changes would encourage demands

45. Lasswell and Kaplan, p. 25.

for sacrifices, on its part, of power and other values. If redefinition is not desired, or if the object is to avoid radical changes in the expectations of the audience or anxieties likely to have a disturbing effect in the community, the strategists may resort to the alternative of keeping from the people knowledge of changes in the environment. This can be accomplished by manipulating the process of enlightenment.

The enlightenment process in any community—that is, the process by which the members of the community come to know about contemporary and historical facts—consists of three aspects: intelligence, correlation, and dissemination.[46] Members of the elite survey the environment, gather intelligence of all developments in the environment, and bring it to certain centers and subcenters where it is interpreted in the light of the problems confronting the community. At the present time, intelligence is brought to the foreign offices of governments, editorial offices of newspapers and journals, and to a certain extent to educational institutions. Correlation is performed in these centers, and the facts gathered and interpreted are disseminated from some centers and subcenters.

The strategists may control the correlation process or the dissemination process. They may interpret, or permit interpretation of, events only in a manner which accords with their overall strategy. When it is deemed desirable, information may be withheld from circulation. When this suppression is done officially, we refer to it as censorship.

We have already noted the influence of the norms of a group on its members. If the strategists want to minimize the impact on a people of any particular type of information coming from outside, it is expedient for them to promote the formation of such groups and group norms as would absorb and blunt the communication impact. It is equally expedient to prevent the formation or functioning of groups that are likely to be receptive to the outside communications. Controlled communication is useful to manage the formation and functioning of desired groups, and when favorable groups are established and controlled, communication becomes an easy process. It is not difficult in this light to understand why expansionist totalitarian elites impose severe restrictions on freedom of association within their countries, and at the same time build up transnational political parties and nurture dissident groups in foreign states.

Actually, the control of groups yields a richer harvest to the strategists than may be thought from what has been just stated. It has been found in recent studies on mass communication that the influence of communications on individuals within the audience is more indirect than direct.[47] Contrary to general belief, influence operates through intermediaries within the audience groups. Each group generally possesses its "opinion

46. See Lasswell, "Attention Structure and Social Structure."

47. Katz and Lazarsfeld, Chap 2; and Schramm, p. 20.

leaders," that is, those who receive the message in the first instance and pass it on to others in an effective way. They serve as points of relay from which the message communicated through the mass media may be further transmitted. After all, it has to be borne in mind that person-to-person communication still remains the most effective medium of communication of ideas, for it provides an intrinsic feedback mechanism;[48] that is, the effect produced on the listener may be studied at once and further messages can be suitably patterned. Individual members of groups not only serve as effective relay stations to transmit the messages communicated by the mass media, but perform another useful function. They may consolidate or reinforce the results obtained by the media. If the strategists can control intragroup communications they can definitely obtain increased returns for their operations, can accentuate the effects from their own communications, and the messages disseminated by opposing strategists may be rendered relatively innocuous.

Disintegration of groups is equally significant in the management of the strategy, if the prevailing norms of groups are uncongenial to the opinions and attitudes intended to be formed. Furthermore, disintegration of a group renders its individual members more vulnerable to fear-arousing communications and panic.

If the strategists want their audiences to accept what is communicated to them most uncritically, it is expedient to create a crowd atmosphere. Large audiences can be subjected to fire-breathing harangues, and if so desired, awesome symbols, martial music, and marching may be employed. The environment, the mutual stimulation that the members of the crowd obtain from each other, and the mass hypnosis which very intense stimuli may on occasion create, increase the impact of the communication and facilitate unquestioning acceptance of the message. The effects thereby obtained may be preserved by subsequent reinforcement by other means such as the mass media of communication, agitators, and so on. Hitler and Mussolini made utmost use of these methods.

The chief aspects of the ideological strategy are, to sum up: the selection and dissemination of symbols, controlling the process of enlightenment, building up or disintegrating groups, controlling the formation and functioning of groups, and creating a "crowd" environment when it is so desired.

PERSUASION OR COERCION?

Now we come to the question which is central to this chapter: is the ideological instrument persuasive or coercive? Hard words break no bones, so runs an old adage. Words may indeed enter our brains but do not break the skulls. We can by no means compare the hurling of words with that of

48. Schramm, ibid.

stones, bullets, or grenades. However, it has to be noted that it is not the use of violence itself that is generally referred to as coercion. Coercion is a process, or an end result, and violence is one of the means used to accomplish it.

Coercion may be defined as "moral or physical compulsion by which a person is forced to do or to refrain from doing some act apart from his own voluntary action." [49] Moral coercion may be said to have been exercised when a person is subjected to a high degree of constraint in the choice of alternatives in shaping his conduct.[50] A persuasive process may be defined as one which leaves for the person whose opinions, attitudes, or behavior are sought to be influenced a number of alternatives with expectations of high gains and low cost. A coercive process is one in which few such alternatives are left, and the available ones are attended with expectations of high cost and low gains.[51]

The question then comes down to this: is it possible to subject persons to a high degree of constraint directed toward adoption of a particular course of conduct by exposing them to the use of the ideological instrument? If it is, how does the coercive use of the instrument differ from its persuasive use? It may not be possible to draw the line that separates the two patterns of use with mathematical precision,[52] but it is possible at least to supply useful criteria to distinguish the two for purposes of choice of legal policy.

We are concerned here with persuasion as a process by which persons are influenced to accept a desired opinion, adopt a desired attitude, or act in a desired manner.[53] Using words as means, a person's opinions, attitude, or behavior may be altered by bringing relevant facts to his notice, and also by suggesting how these facts may be correlated and adapted to the solu-

49. *Encyclopaedia Britannica* (Chicago, 1951), 5, 953; the heading "coercion" is dropped in recent editions. H. M. Kallen, "Coercion," *Encyclopaedia of Social Science* (New York, 1930), 3, 617–19.

50. On nonviolent coercion, see C. M. Case, *Non-Violent Coercion* (London, Century Co., 1923), p. 402.

51. See McDougal and associates, *Studies in World Public Order*, p. 29 n.

52. It is indeed difficult to say precisely when a process of communication designed to influence those addressed ceases to be persuasive and becomes coercive. See F. E. Lumely, *Means of Social Control* (New York, 1925), p. 13.

53. On may refer here to the definition of "persuasive communication" given by C. I. Hovland, I. L. Janis, and H. M. Kelly, *Communication and Persuasion* (New Haven, Yale University Press, 1953), p. 10. The authors mention the characteristics of a persuasive communication to be these: It contains a recommendation of an opinion; it produces on the part of the person communicated with the response of thinking about the recommended opinion and his previous opinion on the subject; and it produces the response of accepting the recommended opinion because of its intrinsic logical appeal, or the promises or rewards or threats of punishment conveyed by it.

Opinion in a group may be termed a "demand or expectation controvertible in the group" (Lasswell and Kaplan, p. 38).

tion of the problems confronting him. In other words, by changing expectations about facts, and about the paths that lead to the solution of problems, it is possible to influence a person's opinions, attitudes, or behavior. But the means employed need not be limited to the presentation of facts and reasoning based on facts. They may include appeals to diverse emotions. A speaker may persuade his listeners by using words which have emotive content, by his rhetorical cadence, by employing various figures of speech which make communication effective, by his appealing tones, his gestures, his deportment and so on.[54]

There is nothing ethically wrong in appealing to emotions in order to influence opinions or actions. It is not reason alone that governs human actions, nor does it supply answers to all problems. It may be that in some situations men do not have the time required to reason out all the pertinent aspects of the problems they are confronted with before they act. Emotion often accounts, at least in part, for our choice of any course of conduct. Furthermore, when we seek to influence others by means of words we cannot keep the method "purely" rational. The inherent character of language makes it impossible to use "pure" reason in any human context.[55] Since all words may possess "emotive" as well as "descriptive" significance, even the most logical argument may be expected to contain a modicum of emotional appeal.

If persuasion by words has been cleared of any ethical stigma that might be attached to it because it can involve play on the emotions, it seems also necessary to state that no undue sanctity need be attributed to it. Surely we do not permit a person to persuade another to commit murder or any other crime. If certain acts are condemned by virtue of their injurious character to the community, persuasion to commit those acts may equally be regarded as reprehensible.

Doubtless within a wide range the ideological instrument may be used in a purely persuasive manner. Its wielders may apprise the audiences of facts and interpretations that help them to find solutions to political problems, and may touch various chords of emotion while remaining strictly within the limits of persuasion.

To determine when the use of the ideological instrument becomes coercive, let us look at a few hypothetical situations. We shall first confine attention to the operations undertaken by the elite in the territory which is under its exclusive control, and in reference to each of the situations, raise the following questions: Is the audience's choice of alternatives severely restricted as a result of the use of the instrument? Is the possibility of the audience responding to the flow of political events in a manner different from the one desired by the strategists severely reduced?

Let us suppose that the strategists have roused emotions such as fear,

54. Stevenson, *Ethics and Language*, p. 139.
55. Ibid., pp. 141–42.

hate, and anger to such an extent that they have created an excited "crowd." It is then possible to say that the audience's choice of alternatives has become restricted to a high degree, and the possibility of their acting in a manner different from what the strategists desire is considerably reduced.

We may assume that the strategists have started manipulating the enlightenment process so that the facts which now come to the attention of the audience are not realistic, but only those that they choose to supply. The strategists make it appear that all the alternatives except those that they suggest entail high costs and low gains, while it is not in fact so. The processes of cognition of the environment which normally go on in the psyche—in Freudian terminology, the ego functions—before a course of conduct is selected are now shackled. And if the strategists have introduced a regime of terror, and presented the audience with the alternatives of either suffering severe penalties or of accepting and internalizing the pseudo reasons which the strategists supply and acting as directed, the results are likely to be those described by Professor Lasswell: [56]

> Cut off from the means by which statements can be tested in reality, cut off from the quickening support of institutions of genuine inquiry, independent minds are cast adrift from their moorings. They are no longer in a position to exercise the kind of criticisms which they themselves most respect; for, by nature, independent minds respect information and inquiry. The impoverished pabulum available to the ego first weakens the ego and typically ends in transforming the conscience. The ego is constrained to admit that given the miserable sources of current intelligence, the individual has little more than his suspicions to contribute to the consideration of public policy. And the coercive menaces of the ruling regime provide strong incentives against speaking up and demanding wider access to intelligence sources.

Let us again suppose that the strategists have operated over a long period of time and popularized among the people of their state language symbols which are "pathic" signs; [57] that is, signs which distort reality and evoke highly inexpedient responses to situations. It is no doubt true that many political symbols do not accurately and realistically represent situations, and language signs rarely perform the work of photographic reproduction. However, if the people who use the signs have freedom to inquire whether

56. "Propaganda and Mass Insecurity," in A. H. Stanton and E. Perry, eds., *Personality and Political Crisis* (Glencoe, Ill., Free Press, 1951), pp. 15, 21. See also E. Kriss and Hans Speier, *German Radio Propaganda, Report on Home Broadcasts During the War* (London, Oxford University Press, 1944), p. 3.

57. The expression "pathic sign" is taken from Morris, *Signs, Language and Behavior,* p. 199.

the signs faithfully represent reality, and to redefine them if they are not healthy, it is possible to minimize the mischief of inaccurate representation inherent in language symbols. But if the strategists have interdicted all such inquiries and redefinitions, as is done by totalitarian elites, a stage will again come when the audiences will have to act more as the strategists desire than of their own choice.

Let us assume that the strategists have imposed a strict regime over the formation and functioning of all groups within the state and established a tight control on all intragroup communications by introducing secret agents. The response evoked from the audience can hardly be designated as free choice.

It may be seen that by adopting any of these methods it is possible for the strategists in large degree to constrain the audience to respond in the desired manner. It may be difficult to say when the rousing of emotions reaches the stage of creating a "crowd" situation. It may be difficult to say what degree of suppression of factual information severely cuts down the free choice of alternatives of the audience. Indeed for reasons of the safety of state it may be quite necessary for the strategists to withhold some facts from circulation. It may be difficult to say when the popularization of "pathic" symbols and interdiction of inquiry into their "healthy" character reaches a stage when the audience has to behave only according to the strategists' desire. It may be difficult to say what degree of control over the organization and functioning of groups and on intragroup communications subjects the audience to severe constraint. It may be difficult to say how stringent the regime imposed by the strategists should be in order that the audience may be strongly compelled to accept and internalize the suggested pseudo reasons. However, as the strategists adopt these methods with increasing rigor, either individually or in combination, a stage is likely to be reached when the audience will have no real choice left. It will have to respond to events more under the influence of the use of the instrument than out of its own choice of alternatives. The possibility of acting in a manner different from what the strategists desire is likely to be reduced to a phantom.

We would admit readily that the line-drawing between persuasion and coercion has been done here in a manner that would hardly satisfy those who might insist upon precise criteria which can be mechanically applied to dispose of cases that arise in practice. We cannot supply precise instruments by which the degree of coercion can be assessed. Unfortunately life situations are so complex that such criteria and instruments can very rarely be ever obtained. We have a continuous process by which strategists seek to shape the opinions, attitudes, and behavior of groups, by managing the flow of mass communication. At one end of the process there is persuasion, and at the other end there is constraint of a high degree, or coercion. Between these two extremes, there is an infinite variety of situations depending upon the combinations of methods the strategists use, and the rigor which they bring to bear in the operations. In this factual continuum it may be difficult to mark precisely when the process becomes coercive and to measure the degree of coercion. However, for the purpose of formulating legal policy in the contexts relevant to this study, the important thing is not whether we can demarcate the boundary in advance and estimate the degree of coercion. It suffices that the indices we have supplied will help the decision-makers to form realistic expectations of the outcome of the operations, and to make rational policy choices.

The diverse operations of the ideological strategy referred to above may very conveniently be undertaken by strategists within their own state. They cannot obviously carry on some of the operations in foreign states to the same extent as within their own. But if they possess means of communication and personnel to use them effectively, they may be able to swamp all versions of facts, including those of the elite of the target state, in the flood of their own version. They may rouse fears and anxieties. If necessary, they may, by exerting diplomatic and economic pressure or displaying force, create an environment in which the threats they hold out seem realistic. They may build up dissident groups which facilitate easy communication of what they desire to convey, apart from being serviceable as subversives. It is also possible for them to popularize among the groups "pathic" symbols, and to disintegrate the groups loyal to the target state.

The Coercive Effects of the Strategy on the Elite of the Target State

The strategists' communications are very likely to reach the elite in a foreign state, too, who may be persuaded or coerced, as the case might be, to adopt the policies desired. We are not interested here in this type of outcome of the strategy, but only with the possible outcome which the strategy of a foreign unfriendly elite will have on the target elite if the groups within the target state begin to respond favorably to the strategy.

People being one of the bases of power, if the people of a state respond favorably to the use of the ideological strategy of a foreign unfriendly elite, it will constitute a threat to the power of the home elite. The possibility of loss of power is likely to constrain it in a high degree to make policy choices it would not otherwise make. For instance, let us assume that the officials of state A have presented a diplomatic démarche to the officials of state B demanding certain concessions, and simultaneously they are able to call forth demonstrations from groups within B favoring the granting of those concessions. The officials of B will definitely have less freedom of choice in responding to the demand than if there were no such demonstrations. Or, suppose that A and B are at war, and the officials of B are faced with having to choose either to continue fighting or to surrender. If the people of their state are averse to prolonging the war, and if there is widespread incidence of sabotage of the war effort, defection in the army, and so on, all due to the propaganda of A, the officials of B will definitely be constrained in a high degree in making their policy choice.

Or let us assume that the strategists of A have, devoting effort over a long period of time, nurtured subversive groups within B which may be called to action whenever the strategists choose. The officials of A have presented a demand for concessions and threatened to use force if the demand is not acceded to. The officials of B, with knowledge of the insecurity at home, cannot definitely take a firm stand against the demand. Let us again assume that the strategists of A are offering great inducements in return for B's accepting the policies suggested by the former. More concretely, let us say, the members of a coalition, having gained a victory in a battle, call upon state B, which is remaining neutral in the war, to join their alliance and share the spoils of war. The people of B respond to the appeal with great enthusiasm. It may be difficult to say in this case that the people of B are subjected to coercion. It is no doubt conceivable that persons' freedom of choice of alternatives may be reduced to a high degree by holding out promises of rewards for choosing one alternative. Whether we can say definitely that coercion has or has not been exercised, it is possible to say with assurance that the officials of B are under great constraint in choosing their policy.[58]

Theoretically speaking, the elite of a state will begin to feel the coercive effects the moment the people under its control begin to respond favorably to the operations of the strategy of the unfriendly elite. However, so long as the elite feels that it can undo the effects by presenting its own version of facts and arguments, it is not likely to feel the coercive effects in a palpable form. And when the elite realizes that the effects cannot be so overcome, it starts protesting, and may then also adopt measures designed for the protection of its own position. These can include, on one hand, countermeasures of coercion against the strategists' state and, on the other, curtailment of civil liberties within its own state. For operational purposes, it seems convenient to regard this moment—that is, when the target elite feels it cannot counteract the effects of the strategy by argument—as the starting point of coercive use of the instrument against the elite.

The ideological instrument delineated above includes a wide range of operations. It may be described as the whole process of management of mass communications to influence the attitudes and behavior of peoples.

58. We may regard constraint to mean limitation of choice of alternatives, coercion as constraint of a high degree. See Lasswell and Kaplan, p. 97. It may be noted that in these examples we are not appraising lawfulness.

And propaganda is the manipulation of symbols and words to influence behavior and attitudes.[59] But when we refer to propaganda, the assumption is that the dissemination of symbols is made in a context where argument can be met by argument, and allegations of facts can be disputed and falsehoods exposed.[60] Ideological strategy, it has been seen, can be so operated that the strategists come to monopolize the forum and restrict severely free discussion and debate.

59. Lasswell, "Propaganda," pp. 521–22; Lasswell and D. Blumenstock, *World Revolutionary Propaganda* (New York, Knopf, 1939), p. 9.

60. Lasswell remarks, "Propaganda is advocacy, a form of persuasion; it implies a modicum of doubt, some contemplation of alternatives, some exercise of critical judgment, some clash of opinion." See his "Propaganda and Mass Insecurity," p. 20.

3

The Problem Situations

We may now proceed to the task of identifying the important, recurring problems of legal regulation that present themselves as the ideological instrument is used in the world arena. In order to do this satisfactorily it is necessary to analyze the process of communication in which the instrument is employed, the different types of claims made to authoritative decision regarding the permissibility of the various uses of the instrument, and the more important features of the comprehensive world process of authoritative decision as they bear upon these controversies.

THE PROCESS OF USE OF THE INSTRUMENT

The process of use of the instrument by the elites in the contemporary world arena may be described in a fairly comprehensive way in terms of: the participants in the process of communication, the audiences sought to be influenced, the objectives sought by the strategists, the situations in which the instrument is employed, the relative capabilities of those operating the strategy and against whom it is directed, the various strategies employed, the prevailing conditions, and the outcome and effects of use of the instrument.

Because this study is mainly a legal one, the analysis and description of the process given here are designed, as far as possible, to be such as can be related to legal prescriptions and their application. Our task is to spotlight the features of the process that are relevant to the making and applying of general community policies.

In order to make our description relatively simple, we shall assume that the elite group as a whole in a state operates an integrated ideological strategy. In point of fact, however, this is very near the truth only in a totalitarian state. In democracies, it is possible for each group among the elite to operate a strategy that differs in varying degrees from the strategies of other groups. The strategies of all groups, however, tend to be shaped to achieve certain basic goals; and in times of crisis a high degree of integration might result by virtue of the voluntary cooperation of all the groups.

Participants

The operations of the ideological strategy of an elite may be regarded, just as international propaganda is referred to in nonlegal literature, as the activity of a state, or in terms of a transnational political movement, like communism, controlled by the elite. Description of participants in these terms is, however, of limited use in discussing the application of some of the well established legal prescriptions such as those relating to state responsibility; nor is it adequate for the purpose of estimating the probable effects of the activity, or for discussing rationally the issues of legal policy.

Participants may be identified as officials of states and non-officials. Such identification is useful when determining the responsibility of a state for such use of the instrument as constitutes an international delinquency. In that context it is also necessary to split the first category into executive, diplomatic, legislative, and judicial officials. If the elite of a state happens to gain control of an international organization, it may succeed in employing the personnel and resources of the organization in the operations of its own strategy.[1] Officials of such an organization may, for the present purpose, be treated as non-officials.

We may now look at the contemporary scene to note to what extent persons belonging to each of the above categories participate in the operations of ideological strategies of the elites.

Executive, Diplomatic, Legislative, and Judicial Officials

Participation by the executive officials in the selection and dissemination of symbols and facts is now quite common, and is on an extensive scale. The governments of many states have information, publicity, or propaganda departments, which are well organized, staffed, and generously financed, functioning at home as well as abroad.[2] Governments now exer-

1. Normally this is not possible, and it may not be good policy for the state that gains influence to compromise the international character of the organization. Nor would the personnel of the organization be ready always to compromise their position as international civil servants. Only in those situations when the organization, at the instance of the influential state, decides to apply coercive measures against a state are the personnel of the organization likely to take part and the resources of the organization permitted to be used. It may however be noted that in the past there were occasions when representatives of member states complained that U.N. officials in their individual capacity delivered speeches critical of their states. E.g. see G.A.O.R., 6th Sess., Fifth Comm. (1952), p. 296.

2. During World War I, the British government established a Ministry of Information and the well-known Lord Northcliffe's Committee at the Crew House to organize wartime propaganda, but these were abolished soon after the war. The Ministry of Information was revived during World War II and continues to be in existence. As a matter of fact, in Britain now a number of ministries, government departments, and two public corporations—the B.B.C. and the British Council—are entrusted with

cise varying degrees of control over the processes of education and public information, and in totalitarian states such control is comprehensive and strict.[3] And there are among leaders of governments and government officials mass orators who keep fairly busy and some of whom can address to crowds highly emotional and lengthy speeches.[4]

At present diplomatic officials have a useful role to play in the operations of the ideological strategy. At the legations, they gather intelligence about local conditions and transmit it to their government for the purpose, among others, of using it in preparing propaganda material. They also function as important agents for dissemination of propaganda to foreign audiences.[5]

---

propaganda and information activities. For details, see Martin, *International Propaganda,* pp. 34–46. The U.S. had no governmental agency entrusted with such work before World War II. But since then a vast governmental organization has been built and at present the United States Information Agency, established in 1953, holds an important place in the U.S. bureaucracy. The U.S.I.A. now manages information agencies all over the world and the "Voice of America" radio programs. For details see ibid., pp. 22–30; *The U.S. Ideological Effort: Government Agencies and Programs,* Study Prepared by the Legislative Reference Service (Washington, U.S. Govt. Printing Office, 1964), pp. 6–25; S. K. Padover, *Psychological Warfare,* Foreign Policy Headline Series, No. 86 (New York, Foreign Policy Association, 1951); J. P. Warburg, *The Unwritten Treaty* (New York, Harcourt, Brace, 1946); W. E. Daugherty and M. Janowitz, *A Psychological Warfare Case Book* (Baltimore, Johns Hopkins University Press, 1958), pp. 120–45. In the Soviet Union, the radio and a section of the press are under government ownership. For detailed information see A. Inkeles, *Public Opinion in Soviet Russia* (Cambridge, Harvard University Press, 1951), p. 226 et seq. The Soviet Foreign Office in Moscow and the International Book Publishing Corporation, a branch of the Soviet Ministry of Foreign Trade, are notable governmental agencies established for managing Soviet ideological strategy. Regarding the People's Republic of China, see Houn, *To Change a Nation* (Glencoe, Ill., Free Press, 1961).

3. For an idea as to the dimensions such control can reach see Houn.

4. One may call to mind in this connection leaders like Fidel Castro of Cuba.

5. Till the close of the last century, it was considered a breach of etiquette for statesmen to appeal to the people on an issue of international policy. See H. G. Nicolson, *Diplomacy* (2d ed. London, Oxford University Press, 1950), p. 168. Our contemporary situation is far from that position. See, in this connection, Chester Bowles' statement in his *Ambassador's Report* (New York, Harper, 1954), p. 16: "The fact that the Point Four people plus the USIS staff actually outnumbered the regular Embassy employees, emphasizes the changed nature of modern diplomacy. An Ambassador's job is no longer a relatively simple one of carrying out the policy of his government on a high level in the country to which he is assigned. As I see it, his job is to also reach the people and give them some understanding of the objectives and policies of the United States." Mrs. Clare Booth Luce, former U.S. Ambassador to Italy, "American Diplomacy at Work," *32 Dept. of State Bull.* 616 (1955), observes, "An ambassador these days becomes in the widest sense the representative of his people to the people—as well as the Government—of the country in which he works." Diplomats no longer remain in the sanctum of secrecy, but come out into the open, cultivate relations with the press, make public addresses explaining the policies of their respective governments.

These officials, accorded immunities and privileges in the state in which they function, and also commanding considerable prestige, are at considerable advantage in playing a role in ideological operations. However, intensive activity on their part, especially when it happens to give offense to the government to which they are accredited, involves risks: the host government can order the activity stopped, demand the recall of the offending officials, or order their expulsion.[6] Hence, diplomatic officials, unless they are tactless or are deliberately desirous of offending the receiving government, are likely to subject themselves to considerable restraint in carrying on propaganda activity.

Legislators engage in extensive speechmaking; often, when they speak within the legislature, their aim is more to influence the people outside than their fellow legislators. The people addressed need not be the people of their state only, they may include foreign audiences as well.

The extent of the legislators' freedom to participate in operations independent of the strategy of executive officials of that state depends upon the relationship that exists between the two groups in that state. If the legislators are virtually selected by the executive, it is inconceivable that they would have any noticeable degree of freedom to make statements that conflict with the policies of the executive. On the other hand, if put in office by a free election, their freedom to make statements unpalatable to the executive is not likely to be subject to formal restriction. However, several factors, such as political party affiliations and party discipline, may have indirect influence in restraining them from dissenting sharply from the executive. In a state in which more than one political party is allowed to function, the members of the party not in power will have a greater degree of freedom to criticize the policies of the executive than in a totalitarian state. However, sentiments of patriotism may influence the members of the opposition to refrain from statements that severely conflict with the basic objectives of the executive. In a communist state, a single party controls the government as well as all the processes by which the legislators are selected. It is very likely, then, that in such a state the legislators' participation tends to be in close conformity with the executive's policies.

6. See in this connection G. H. Hackworth, *Digest of International Law* (8 vols. Washington, D.C., U.S. Govt. Printing Office, 1940–), 4, sec. 393 (hereafter cited as Hackworth, *Digest*, 4). In 1959, the government of India, annoyed at the propaganda activity of the Chinese Embassy in relation to the Sino-Indian boundary dispute, asked all foreign missions not to circulate articles and writings critical of the government. At the same time the government stated that there was no objection to reproduction in the embassy bulletins of official statements of foreign governments. See *The Hindu*, Sept, 28, 1959. The Indian government's endeavor to restrain the Chinese Embassy's propaganda culminated in a refusal to renew the visa of the Chinese press attaché, who was suspected of sending slanted reports to Peking about Indian policy and public opinion on the border dispute. See 6 *Foreign Affairs Record* 187 (Ministry of External Affairs, External Publicity Division, Government of India, 1960).

It is only very rarely that judicial officials take up the role of participants. A judge may occasionally assume, however, the role of a propagandist while making his judicial pronouncements, with varying degrees of expectation that what he says will be published in the press and will be widely read. He may also, now and then, make public speeches to influence opinion. But, by and large, judges are not likely to take an appreciable part in intensive operations.

Non-Officials

Private persons and organizations of varied character now form highly significant participants in the ideological strategies of the elites of states. Most of the operations of ideological strategy of liberal democratic countries are managed by non-officials. It is beyond doubt that their participation may produce sometimes very significant results.[7]

Furthermore, for diverse reasons, the private press in many countries tends to exaggerate and emotionalize facts, or distort and suppress them, and the facts relating to international events are no exception. Commercialism on the part of the owners of the press is one reason. But the major reason is the pattern of our contemporary social organization. The rise of nationalism has pushed to the background local symbols and brought to prominence national symbols. The growth of democracy has increased the importance of the common man and his attitudes and opinions. The spread of literacy has given him, however, only a modicum of education. The partly educated reader requires crude stimuli to arouse him, and hence national symbols are intensely manipulated to develop in him love of his nation and hatred of the opposing nation.[8]

Limitations of the Official vs. Nonofficial Categorization

Description of participants in terms of officials and non-officials, even with the subcategories mentioned, suffers under modern conditions from some shortcomings. In reference to participants in totalitarian as well as nontotalitarian states it conceals some highly significant facts.

In totalitarian states a single political party controls both the government and all the media of public information. In the Soviet Union, for

7. Kent Cooper, a well-known journalist, writes about the influence the private press in the United States exerted in the last century on decisions of Congress to enter wars: "The probable and improbable propaganda that got into newspaper stories on Spain's inhuman methods in trying to suppress Cuba's struggle for independence, and the propaganda cries incited by the sinking of the battleship *Maine* in Havana harbor, led Congress to declare war on Spain." See his *The Right to Know* (New York, Farrar, Straus and Cudahy, 1956), p. 10. He concludes his narration thus: "The propaganda that pushed the American people into all its own nineteenth-century wars, therefore, was generated at home entirely by the people and their newspapers—not by their government" (p. 102).

8. See Harold D. Lasswell, *World Politics and Personal Insecurity* (New York, McGraw-Hill, 1935), p. 205.

example, though some sections of the press are owned by the government, some by the Communist party, and some by trade unions and local organizations, the party controls them all.[9] The means employed are varied.[10] First, the persons who operate all the sections of the press are selected and trained by the party. Second, the party issues directives from time to time to those who operate the press agencies in regard to the policies that should be adopted. Third, the party supervises the performance of all these sections of the press with the help of the party machinery. Criticism of leaders and government officials is permitted to appear in the press only if it does not touch the top leaders of the party.[11] The radio broadcasting

9. See Inkeles, p. 151. To get a general idea of the pattern of press ownership in the Soviet Union, it may be noted that *Izvestia* is owned by the government, being the organ of the Praesidium of the Supreme Council, *Pravda* is owned by the Communist party, *Komsomolskaia Pravda* by the Youth Organization, *Literatournais Gazeta* by the Union of Soviet Writers, and *Trud* by the syndicates of the labor organizations. All printing is done by print shops operated by the state or a cooperative association of printers where censoring is done. See also Houn, for information about the People's Republic of China.

10. For the manner in which control is exercised by the party on all sections of the press, see Inkeles, pp. 150 et seq. *The Press in Authoritarian Countries* (International Press Institute Survey No. 5, Zurich, 1959), pp. 28–43, notes that control is exercised in respect of printing, publication, and even distribution, by systematic planning. The Department of Agitation and Propaganda of the Central Committee of the Party (AGITPROP) at Moscow exercises this control. The governmental organization *Glavit* (Chief Administration for Literary Affairs and Publishing) is entrusted with the function of censoring publications. But this organization's importance has gradually diminished, and in the post-Stalin era the editors have come to be assigned greater responsibility, limiting *Glavit's* responsibility to censorship of publications exported from foreign countries. In the post-Stalin "liberalization" period, the editorial staffs of newspapers and journals have obtained considerable freedom to present news in a more interesting and readable form, and to express divergent views. But control has by no means diminished. In other communist countries the same techniques of control are employed but with minor variations. In Poland and Yugoslavia a certain degree of freedom is enjoyed by the press, but party control is nevertheless present; see ibid., Part II. Houn says that China still permits a small section of the press to operate under private ownership, but control by means of the party machinery is quite strict.

11. See Inkeles, p. 215. It may be noted that the Soviet doctrine of *Samokritika* permits self-criticism, but within certain bounds. It is employed more to discipline the rank and file of the party and factory leaders, and to control the bureaucracy. Soviet newspapers allot a great deal of space to "Letters to the Editor"; see Mark Arkadyev, "Soviet Newspapers," in U. G. Whitaker, Jr., ed., *Propaganda and International Relations* (San Francisco, Chandler, 1962), pp. 99, 103. See also *The Press in Authoritarian Countries,* pp. 39–41; P. Kecskemeti, "Totalitarian Communication as a Means of Control—A Note on Sociology of Propaganda," 14 *Public Opinion Quarterly* 224, 229 (1950). The criticism is never allowed to touch the top leaders of the party and the major policies of the party. In 1956, for instance, the editorial staff of *Veprossy Istori,* a historical review, was dismissed because it went much further on the history of "destalinization" than the party leaders were prepared to approve. See *The Press in Authoritarian Countries,* p. 42.

stations are government owned but the party controls their operation. The motion picture concerns are owned by joint stock companies and cooperatives but over them, too, party control is systematically organized and exercised.[12]

In Nazi Germany the party press was under the control of the Nazi party chiefs who simultaneously held high positions in the government. For instance, Dietrich was the head of the party press as well as the press section of the Ministry of Propaganda. A good section of the press was allowed to remain under private ownership, but by various means the Nazis were able to reduce the possibility of opposition to their policies from that section of the press.[13] By exerting economic pressure and by governmental fiat they were able to wipe out the press owned by their political opponents. By insisting that only a member of the Press Chamber constituted by the Ministry of Propaganda could enter or remain in the journalists' profession, and by giving power to the President of the Chamber to expel any one, all the journalists were held under the strict control of government and the party. Radio was under government ownership, and other media of mass communication were kept under the control of the respective chambers constituted by the Ministry of Propaganda. By these methods the Nazis were able to maintain strict control over all the media of public information, official as well as nonofficial.

In liberal democracies, governments do not generally possess formal power which can be directly applied to compel the press and other information agencies to follow any particular ideological policy. But on broad policy matters, by and large, there will be a certain degree of conformance on the part of the private press with the governmental line. Kingsley Martin, a leading journalist of the United Kingdom, writes: "A hint of change in the direction of policy may come from the Foreign Office to the press, and from the press the public gradually learns of the malice of one country and the friendship of another."[14] E. H. Carr writes that, before World War II, although the British government denied responsibility for publications in the private press, whenever foreign governments protested them the British government successfully persuaded the operators of the press to exercise restraint.[15] Persuasions such as these do generally have effect. In times of crisis, persuasion aimed at self-restraint in promotion of the national interest will have much greater effect. The effectiveness of the sys-

12. See Inkeles, pp. 225 ff., 311 ff.

13. See D. Sington and A. Weidenfeld, *The Goebbels Experiment* (New Haven, Yale University Press, 1943), pp. 76, 104–19.

14. Kingsley Martin, *The Press the Public Wants* (London, Hogarth Press, 1947), p. 82.

15. *Propaganda in International Politics*, Pamphlets on World Affairs Series, No. 16 (Oxford, Clarendon Press, 1939), p. 21.

tem of voluntary censorship in the United States during World War II amply demonstrates this point.[16]

It may be noted further that strict control over the press and other means of public information is not a feature exclusively confined to communist states. There are other authoritarian states in which similar control is exercised by governments by means of censorship, directives, intervention in the matter of selection of editorial staff, and economic and other sanctions which can be used for applying indirect pressure.[17] By such means the governments are able to enforce conformance to the approved governmental line, restrain deviation, or render opposition to government almost impossible. Even in democratic countries, constitutional law, press laws, penal laws, and laws relating to security afford means to compel the press to adopt any desired ideological policy.[18] Furthermore, controls are exercised in many countries over imports of newsprint and printing machinery and their distribution, and these controls are abused in some to compel the press to adhere to a particular policy.[19] However, it has to be noted that these and other various indirect means are actually employed to restrict the freedom of the press only by governments which are either authoritarian or weak, unstable, and arbitrary in their choice of methods to safeguard their position.[20] But quite significant effects can be obtained by using the means; in regard to Egypt, a survey by the International Press Institute observed:

> In actual fact, there no longer exists in the Egyptian press a single newspaper which could really constitute a menace to the new regime, and one can go so far as to say that all the press has become an in-

16. See in this connection T. F. Koop, *The Weapon of Silence* (Chicago, University of Chicago Press, 1946), p. 44.

17. See *The Press in Authoritarian Countries*, p. 199, and Part II generally.

18. See *Government Pressures on the Press*, The International Press Institute Survey No. 4 (Zurich, 1955), pp. 9–55. A more detailed survey covering press, movies, and radio, is F. Terrou and L. Solal, *Legislation for Press, Film and Radio, A Comparative Study of the Main Types of Regulations Governing the Information Media* (Paris, UNESCO, 1951).

19. These are mentioned among the indirect means of control in the *Memorandum of the U.N. Secretary General on Measures to Facilitate International Transmission of Information, Notes on Censorship, to the U.N. Conference on Freedom of Information*, U.N. Doc. E/Conf.6/14 (1948). A more elaborate account of the indirect means of pressure on the press is *Government Pressures on the Press*, pp. 61–114. Among these are listed subsidies, bribes, newsprint distribution, official advertising, trade union pressures, discriminatory practices, direct and indirect political pressures.

20. This emerges from *Government Pressures on the Press*, and also *The Press in Authoritarian Countries*, Part II. The noncommunist countries that come out badly in these surveys from the point of view of freedom of information are Spain, Portugal, Turkey, Egypt, some Latin American and Central American states, and Formosa. The surveys, of course, did not cover all the countries in the world.

strument of propaganda for the regime. In this respect, Egypt's newspapers have the mission of supporting and supplementing the intensive propaganda campaigns of Radio Cairo in Arab countries.[21]

It is also possible that governments, overtly or covertly, encourage or give support to private organizations to carry on propaganda. The Nazi government of Germany used the *Fichte* League, an organization founded in 1914 with pan-German ideology, to disseminate Nazi propaganda in Austria, Hungary, South Africa, Argentina and Mexico.[22] The Communist parties in various countries are widely known to receive assistance and inspiration from Moscow, and some from Peking, to carry on communist propaganda. The "Free Europe Committee," a private, incorporated body formed under the New York State laws, which disseminates propaganda to Eastern European countries, commands the sympathies and support of the United States government.[23]

21. *The Press in Authoritarian Countries*, p. 183.

22. Sington and Weidenfeld, pp. 85–87.

23. The Free Europe Committee was started as a nonofficial incorporated committee in New York in 1949 to deal with the problems of refugees from Eastern European countries. It has since developed three instrumentalities: Free Europe Press, Free Europe Exile Relations, and Radio Free Europe. Radio Free Europe transmits broadcasts to Eastern European countries and Free Europe Press transmits printed leaflets to those countries, one of the means of transmission adopted in the past being plastic balloons. With the help of the U.S. government, Radio Free Europe has been able to obtain facilities for installing high powered radio transmission stations in West Germany and Portugal. Radio Free Europe possessed in 1956 a radio network consisting of the Voice of Free Poland, Free Czechoslovakia, Free Hungary, Free Romania, Free Bulgaria, the output of which was over 3,000 transmission hours per week, and more than 2,000 persons were working in its operations in several places in Western Europe and in New York. It had in 1956 29 transmitters, very efficient and modern, some as powerful as 100 kilowatts. In 1950 the Crusade for Freedom was launched, to collect money to finance the activities of Free Europe Press and Radio Free Europe. The campaign enjoyed the support of the United States government and was allowed to publish appeals for contributions on U.S. mail postmarks. One may refer in this connection to President Eisenhower's message to Radio Free Europe in 1953 (32 *Dept. of State Bull.* 295 [1953]), to understand the nature of the encouragement received from the United States government. Robert T. Holt, who wrote on Radio Free Europe says "However private the organization may be, it [RFE] must . . . be assessed as an instrument of American foreign policy" (*Radio Free Europe*, Minneapolis, University of Minnesota Press, 1957), p. 200. The same author remarks, "Radio Free Europe provides an example par excellence of use of propaganda against an adversary in the cold war." Ibid., p. 4.

There is also a private association, the American Committee for Liberation of refugees from the U.S.S.R. It owns Radio Liberty, which broadcasts to the U.S.S.R., located near Munich and functioning since 1953. In 1956, its total broadcasting hours per day were 228 hours. For a brief account of this organization, see *Sparks into the USSR* (Press and Publications Division, American Committee for Liberation, New York, undated), generally, and p. 4; see also N. Gordon, J. Falk, and W. Hodapp, *The Idea Invaders* (New York, Hastings House, 1963), p. 177.

Thus it will be seen that the classification into officials and non-officials corresponds to reality only to the extent that the former hold an official status, and the latter do not, in the state under reference. The classification does not reveal the extent to which the former class does, in a given context, by direct or indirect, formal or informal, means, control or encourage the activities of the latter and vice versa; nor does it indicate the extent to which both classes, designedly or otherwise, act in collaboration with each other. Further, as will appear below, the classification is of limited usefulness in estimating the effectiveness of the activity, for it cannot be maintained as a general rule that propaganda by officials is more effective than by non-officials or vice versa.

Audience

The audience groups which strategists might endeavor to influence may be divided into two classes: internal and external. The latter class may further be divided into groups within friendly and uncommitted states, and those in opposing states.

When the instrument is employed to influence the audience in a foreign state, the groups the propaganda is aimed at may be selected ones,[24] or the general mass of people. Communist propaganda is at present transmitted through two channels, one used to address the general mass of people, and the other the cadres of Communist parties.[25]

From the point of view of forming an expectation about the likely impact on the audience of a given set of symbols and words, one may distinguish the audience as one which is favorably disposed to the propaganda or not so disposed; or one likely to be influenced or unlikely to be influenced. In order to distinguish thus one has to take note of a variety of factors relating to the audience—national, racial, cultural, historical, religious, etc. Indeed, the probability of being influenced may be higher or lower, depending upon such factors.

It is indeed quite difficult under modern conditions to say one thing to

24. Thus before World War II, the Nazis devoted greater attention to German national groups in foreign countries than to others. See H. C. Wolfe, *Human Dynamite, The Story of European Minorities,* Foreign Policy Headline Series No. 20 (New York, Foreign Policy Association, 1939), pp. 73–92. Also R. E. Murphy and others, *National Socialism* (Washington, D.C., U.S. Dept. of State, 1943), p. 97. The Egyptian broadcasts to neighboring countries are addressed especially to Arab groups and Moslems; see the *New York Times,* March 1, 1956, and February 16, 1957, for the Ethiopian protests over Cairo's broadcasts to Moslem minorities in Ethiopia. All irredentist propaganda, indeed, is addressed to limited groups.

25. See G. A. Almond, *The Appeals of Communism* (Princeton, Princeton University Press, 1954), pp. 79–80; for a detailed account of communist propaganda, see F. B. Evans, ed., *Worldwide Communist Propaganda Activities* (New York, Macmillan, 1955); F. C. Barghoorn, *Soviet Foreign Propaganda* (Princeton, Princeton University Press, 1964).

one audience and another to others. But when the media of mass communication of limited range are employed, when suitable languages are used and means adopted, it is quite possible to do so. A totalitarian government, for instance, which strictly prohibits the flow of information from its territory to outside, may say one thing to its internal audience, while its agents and radio broadcasting stations transmitting in a foreign tongue may disseminate quite different things to outside groups.[26]

Objectives

The objectives generally pursued by the strategists may be described and classified in various ways. In a very abstract way, the objective may be spoken of in terms of the value or values which the elite operating the strategy seeks to maximize for itself as against other elites. In such a description may be included the broad objectives pursued by all elites in the world arena, in order to protect or extend their own position in reference to all values, and to weaken or destroy the value positions and the bases of values of the opposing elites or potential opponents.[27]

In a more concrete manner the objective may be described in terms of the specific response sought from the audience, and thereby from the opposing elite. The object may be to have the audience *abstain* from adopting a certain attitude or behaving in a certain manner, give up a certain attitude (*withdrawal*), or develop an attitude of *cooperation* with the elite operating the strategy; [28] and hence to see that an external elite, due to the pressure of public opinion and attitudes prevailing generally and within the home state in particular, refrains from adopting a particular policy (abstention), withdraws from a position it has taken, or extends cooperation to the strategists operating the strategy. Or the objective may be *reconstruction* of the decision-making process in a foreign state.[29] The

26. If the strategists build up exclusive groups, communication to them can be quite esoteric and radically at variance with the communication to the general mass of people.

27. McDougal and Feliciano, *Law and Minimum World Public Order*, p. 14, suggest this as the most general way of description.

28. The objectives may be characterized as *abstention, withdrawal,* and *cooperation.* All objectives in general may be descriptively categorized as *abstention, withdrawal, cooperation, modification,* and *reconstruction,* as suggested by Lasswell in "Political Factors in the Formulation of National Strategy," 6 *Naval War College Rev.* 19, 34, 35 (1954). In times of war, the objective sought in influencing the people of the enemy state is that the latter abstain from lending support to the war effort in their state, or refrain from putting up resistance to invading forces.

29. *Reconstruction* may be used to describe the objective of the strategy that the Soviet Union successfully pursued in Eastern Europe after World War II, and the Nazis in Austria before the war. The Russian strategists applied economic pressure, maneuvered communists into official positions to control the security police and radio broadcasting, and into positions of control over youth and women's organizations, trade unions, and peasant parties. They held in the background the threat to use military

objective may also be described in terms of whether it is long-term or short-term. Thus the objective may be the short-term one of eliciting a specific response such as abstention from a particular attitude or behavior, or withdrawal from a particular attitude or it may be the fairly long-term objective of *modification*. The objective may also be a continuing one such as *conservation* of the prevailing attitudes among the audience.

While descriptions and categorizations on lines such as these are useful for some purposes, their utility from the point of view of clarification, determination, or appraisal of legal policy in reference to situations involving mutual application of elaborate, intense transnational coercive processes seems to be limited. For these purposes the following aspects of the objectives appear to be relevant and merit notice.[30]

Consequentiality

Three questions may be raised in reference to any objective sought by strategists: how many participants in the world arena are likely to be adversely affected in the pursuit of the objective; what values are sought in the pursuit; and what is the range of the demand in respect of each of the values? The value demand may be presented to one state, a number of them, or to practically the whole world. The objective may be some gain in power or some economic advantage; it may be some influence over the government of a foreign state, or, at the extreme, a world empire. Speaking more concretely, the objective may be to create a good image of oneself among the audience, to persuade a foreign government to yield a small concession, to replace that government by another which is fully amenable to the influence of the elite operating the strategy, or to conquer other states and absorb them by means of overt or covert violence.

Inclusiveness or Exclusiveness

In pursuing the objective, the strategists may be prepared to admit others, in varying degrees, to the enjoyment of the values demanded, or

force if necessary, and were thereby able to substitute communist regimes in the place of the existing governments. For a full account of this process of transformation, see H. Seton-Watson, *From Lenin to Malenkov* (New York, Praeger, 1953), p. 254. In 1948 in Czechoslovakia an institutional system was overturned to install a communist regime. See in this connection P. Selznick, *The Organizational Weapon* (New York, McGraw-Hill, 1952), p. 264. In communist strategy and tactics, propaganda is not merely a means of persuasion but a weapon to build up powerfully organized groups which can be manipulated to undermine or destroy by covert violence the institutional system of the intended victim state. See also S. T. Possony, *A Century of Conflict* (Chicago, Regnery, 1953), p. 111.

30. Characterization on these lines is suggested by McDougal and Feliciano, pp. 15–20.

not willing to admit others at all.[31] The objective may thus have degrees of inclusiveness or exclusiveness; it may be such as would further the interests of a group, a political party, a nation or race, or entire humanity. Although strategists rarely profess the exclusiveness of their objective, in a concrete situation it may not be difficult for a decision-maker to find the true character of the objective.

Extension or Conservation

The objective of the strategists may be to acquire new values or to defend what they already have.[32] The preservation of the general pattern of value shaping and sharing within their state forms one of the constant endeavors of the elite of any state. The objective of the ideological strategy may be limited to that. Or it may extend to obtaining satisfaction of value demands presented to other states. In this context, too, it must be noted that strategists always claim that their objective is a purely defensive one, and the validity of all such claims has to be determined in accordance with the standards implicit in the world community prescriptions, by those who are given the competence to make such determination.

Relation of the Objective to the Public Order of the World Community

The objective may or may not be in conformity with world community prescriptions and the decisions of authoritative decision-makers,[33] whose intervention is invoked in consequence of the activity directed toward the pursuit of the objective. Whether the objective accords with the prescriptions and authoritative decisions is an important aspect to be noted.

31. The Nazis were prepared to admit only the Germans to the enjoyment of the fruits of their conquests. Communist propaganda promises to the proletariat of all the world the enjoyment of values in the future world communist state.

32. During the past decade and a half the Soviet Union has charged that Western propaganda has been designed to foment an aggressive war against the Soviet Union, whereas the West maintained that it was a defensive effort designed to prevent communist expansion. However, the "rollback" of communist power was also professed as an objective on many occasions.

Further, a participant may profess his objective to be not expansion, but recovery of what he once had but lost due to the improper or illegal deprivation caused by others. One may observe the current Communist Chinese claim that their aspiration of unification of the motherland must be realized (R.I.I.A., *Survey of International Affairs, 1959–1960*, p. 206), and the claim of Arab nations that the situation existing before the establishment of Israel must be restored. In such a situation whether the objective is expansion or conservation largely depends upon the time reference adopted by the decision-maker.

33. The most important of such authorities at present are the Security Council and the General Assembly acting under the "Uniting for Peace" Resolution.

SITUATION

What about the situation in which the instrument is employed? In the first place, the *geographical* situations of the strategists making coercive use of the instrument and the elite against whom it is directed require notice. The latter's expectation of attack on its values obviously is likely to be higher and more immediate if the strategists operate from a neighboring territory rather than from a distant land. But the importance of the geographical factor is inversely proportional to the range of reach of the strategists by means of other instruments, and when the reach is great the importance of distance may be negligible.

The *temporal duration* of the activity has to be noted next. A single intemperate utterance indeed creates on the part of those affected an expectation which is quite different from a sustained activity over a period of time.

The degree to which the situation has become *institutionalized* also is important. If a practice has come to be established as normal, an activity which conforms to this practice creates an expectation different from the one produced by a new pattern of activity. Presently, the press in general around the world displays a bias in favor of national policies and leaders, and leaders of friendly countries and their policies, and against the policies of the opposing states and their leaders.[34] There is also the phenomenon of peoples all over the world looking at all foreigners as fitting into a few stereotypes[35] possessing typical characteristics, and so long as the phenomenon persists it is bound to color communication. Propaganda disseminated in a situation may contain mostly symbols already in circulation or a new set of symbols of a revolutionary type. Radio broadcasting to reach foreign audiences is now practiced by almost all states, and these broadcasts generally contain explanations of the policies pursued by one's own state and criticisms of the policies of the opposing states.

Lastly, the level of *crisis* in general, and of the situation in which the audience is placed in particular, should be noticed. The reference is to conditions which cause high expectations of violence; its outbreak may appear to be imminent, or it may have already broken out. It will be seen below that this level is one of the factors that affect the outcome of the use of the instrument.

34. For the manner in which the climate of international relations affects publications in the press, see Lasswell, "The Climate of International Action," H. C. Kelman, ed., *International Behavior* (New York, Holt, 1965), pp. 339, 350.

35. See W. Buchanan and H. Cantril, *How Nations See Each Other, A Study in Public Opinion* (Urbana, University of Illinois Press, 1953).

Relative Capabilities

The capabilities of the strategists in employing the instruments of coercion to cause destruction or deprivation of values shape the expectations of the outcome of the application of coercion—the expectations of the elite which is the target of coercion and of the authorized decision-makers.[36] The alliances the strategists have built up, the diplomatic leverages they command in the world arena, the influence they have in international organizations, the control they possess over the wealth processes affecting the targets of coercion and others, the military resources available to them and their allies, the media of mass communication and personnel trained in the techniques of the ideological instrument at their disposal, are all relevant. It is to be noted that all the base values at the disposal of strategists, not merely *power* and *wealth,* are significant in this context. In connection with the use of the ideological instrument the *respect* value, for instance—the prestige commanded by those who speak, or their reputation for speaking truth [37]—is an important factor. Equally significant are the capabilities of the target elite, its base values and vulnerabilities to coercive processes.

Strategies

Inasmuch as in any context the strategists employ a combination of instruments, a factual analysis should bring out a picture of the whole strategy and not merely of the use of the ideological instrument.[38] Intensive propaganda may synchronize with threats or actual use of force, military demonstrations, assassination of top leaders, or extensive destruction of property by sabotage. On the other hand, propaganda may be resorted to to bring about an economic boycott. In a third situation, it may be used by the strategists to demonstrate to the home audience that, while their own government is prepared for a diplomatic settlement, the opposing government does not desire such a settlement. Or it may be used to im-

36. The relevance of the relative capabilities will be apparent from the statements of the U.S. and Cuban representatives in the Security Council on a Cuban complaint in March 1962; see S.C.O.R., 17th year, 993rd Mtg., 15 March 1962, paras. 96–98, and 994th Mtg., 16 March 1962. The U.S. representative charged Cuba with propaganda and subversive activity and the Cuban representative pleaded that the baseless character of the charges was apparent from the relative capabilities of Cuba on the one hand and of the United States and Latin American countries on the other.

37. For the relevance of credibility, see below, p. 64.

38. In many cases the allegations of propaganda appear along with allegations regarding the use of other instruments of policy. See, for example, the charges of the United Kingdom against the Yemeni Republic, S.C.O.R., 19th year, 1109th Mtg., 7 April 1964, paras. 4–15; also the U.S. allegations mentioned in note 36.

press upon the opposing government that the state of public opinion at home does not permit yielding further concessions. The expectations of the outcome of the activity in these varied situations are obviously not the same. And these expectations cannot be estimated with reasonable precision unless reference is made to the other instruments used and the intensity of the use; nor would it be possible to determine community policy in a rational way without such reference.

After due attention is given to these other instruments, the techniques and tactics employed in the ideological strategy require observation, for the expectations of the outcome of the strategy necessarily bear a significant relation to these techniques and tactics. The main operations [39] may, for analytic purposes, be divided into two major parts: (1) selection of symbols and words, and (2) management of the process of communication.

Selection of Symbols and Words

Broadly speaking, symbols and words are communicated by the strategists to serve any of the following purposes: (1) to shape or change the demands, expectations, and identifications of the audience, or to maintain the existing ones; (2) to control the frame of attention of the audience; (3) to create stress toward action on the part of the audience; and (4) to channel any existing insecurities or to give specific direction to expected behavior. The symbols used comprise one of the factors that shape expectations regarding the likely response of the audience. They may also reveal the objectives of the strategists.

It is outside the scope of this study to describe in elaborate detail how strategists select their materials to communicate to their audience, and how they present them. For such descriptions one may look into the large body of literature written on propaganda, especially on propaganda during wars.[40] It will suffice here to note the general and broad patterns of propagandistic disseminations.

Disseminations intended to influence the expectations of the audience are generally given the following form: With reference to any human value, the audience is informed that it is situated in an advantageous or disadvantageous position, and if the course of behavior suggested in the communication is followed, the advantages can be retained, disadvantages overcome, or improvement in position attained. For example, in reference to the value of power, the propaganda of an elite generally conveys the idea that the opposing elite has denied or will deny the audience access to power, and that the home elite favors policies which give wide access to

39. The attempt here is not to give an elaborate description of the techniques generally employed, but only to state the important aspects of the techniques in an analytic form.

40. The literature is cited in this study, passim.

power. It is common to paint oneself as a lover of democracy and freedom, and the opponent as an autocrat.

Events as they happen affect the expectations of the audience, and the strategists conducting ideological operations suitably interpret the events, distort facts, give a slant to them, suppress them, or invent new ones. Communications designed to shape the demands of the audience are so prepared as to strengthen or weaken existing demands or popularize new ones. Suggestions may be added that the policies put forward by the strategists lead to satisfaction of the demands, and those of the opposing elite do not.

The strategists also circulate symbols of identification which help to fortify or weaken the existing identifications or to create new ones. The communists started with such symbols as "workers," "proletariat," seeking to substitute them for preexisting nationalistic symbols. Nationalistic, cultural, racial, or religious symbols may be manipulated to influence any section of the population in a foreign country to identify itself as a minority and clamor for special rights of protection. Irredentist movements are generally sustained by intensive manipulation of nationalistic symbols.

Communications which affect the expectations, demands, and identifications of the audience will cause the elite against which the strategy is directed to anticipate creation of a bias against the elite among the audience, popularized demands that affect the elite's value position, and the fostering of identifications that menace the cohesion or safety of the elite's state, and to fear either an immediate response from the audience or a gradual change in its predisposition.

A person's knowledge is obviously limited to what comes to his attention. By controlling the frame of attention it is possible to maximize or minimize the impact of the flow of infrmation on the audience.[41] When facts unfavorable to the strategists are likely to come to the knowledge of the audience its attention may be diverted to favorable ones.

The attention frame of a person expands in an environment in which he is threatened with deprivations, except when the resulting anxiety inhibits the learning process. Hence strategists might try to control the attention frame of the audience by exaggerating to a certain extent, or understating, the expected deprivations or promises of rewards. If the strategists desire that the audience should not get a realistic perspective of the flow of events, they may reduce the attention frame of the audience by intensifying anxieties. Terror propaganda may sometimes be used with this objective. Communications of this kind obviously affect expectations about the impact and outcome of propaganda.

Strategists may create among the audience a stress toward action by appealing to the id and the superego aspects of personality. Highly emotion-

41. See in this connection Lasswell, "Attentional Structure and Social Structure."

alized and sentimentalized communications may be used for this purpose.

A stress toward action, of such type as jeopardizes social cohesion, may possibly be produced by fear-arousing communications which play upon human flight-reflexes and possibly produce panicky actions.[42] If communications of this type are disseminated, we may expect a response in the form of an overt act.

When the conditions in a state increase the level of insecurity among its people, and the elite expects incidents which might deprive it of power and other values, it may attempt to displace hatreds among the people toward some internal or external groups. The same technique may be adopted in using the instrument to influence external audiences. It is common for propagandists to hold out a particular individual or group in the opposing state as the source of all the evils of that state.

Communications designed to achieve some of the above purposes may be converted into compressed verbal signs or slogans, to facilitate easy communication and intensive appeal to emotions and sentiments.

Management of the Process of Communication

The communication process is maintained by *disseminating symbols from some centers* by means of *some media of communication.*

CENTERS OF COMMUNICATION

Symbols and words selected by the strategists are disseminated from selected centers. These centers may be divided into three classes: centers within the strategists' own state, those within a foreign state, and international forums. The expectation of the outcome of the communication depends partly upon the importance attached by the audience to the center in terms of the credibility to be attributed to what is disseminated from it.

Centers within the strategists' state may be divided into two groups, official centers and nonofficial centers. They may be divided in a twofold way from a different point of view—into centers primarily devoted to dissemination of information to the public, and those primarily devoted to other objectives. Under the first category are the press, the radio broadcasting stations, etc. In the latter category fall such forums as legislatures, courts,

42. On the subject of fear, panic, and "freezing" with fright, see Meerloo, *Patterns of Panic*, pp. 27–30. It may be noted that if the strategists desire that the audience should act as they suggest, only communications inducing minimal fear and accompanied by assurances that the impending danger can be avoided by following the suggested course of behavior are useful. On the other hand, communications arousing intense fear make the audience only more receptive to counter-propaganda which gives relief from the tension caused by the fear. See in this regard I. L. Janis and S. Feshback, "Effects of Fear-Arousing Communications," 48 *Journal of Abnormal and Social Psychology* 78 (1953). It seems that extreme "terror" propaganda can produce only rather momentary effects of fright, panic, and inhibition of the learning process.

and clubs. In some, such as the courts, propagandistic communications are likely to occur only rarely, while in others, such as legislatures, keen debate may be expected as a general rule.

It needs no special mention that the expectation as to the range of audience that might be reached when anything is disseminated from these centers varies considerably. In some cases, the dissemination may be expected to reach even external audiences.

Centers within foreign states may also be divided into two categories, official and nonofficial. Under the first category come all information centers managed by diplomatic legations. Private agencies may, either for commercial or political purposes or for promoting cultural values, organize centers of dissemination. Such centers may be made use of by the strategists. The foreign centers may also be divided into centers fed by overt channels of communication, and centers fed by covert channels of communication. Under the latter group come whatever segments of the press in the foreign state that are secretly subsidized by the strategists.[43] The covert channels of communication may also be transnational political parties, or even cultural organizations.[44] Communications, if addressed by covert channels, may create an expectation of subversive design on the part of the strategists.

The forum of international organizations may be used to disseminate propaganda material. At the present time the United Nations, and in particular the General Assembly, serves as a very useful center of dissemination.[45]

MEDIA OF COMMUNICATION

The medium employed indicates the speed and reach of the communication and the expectations likely to be formed about its impact on the

43. Thus during the Russo-Japanese War, the Russian Ambassador in France, Isvolsky, paid large sums of money to French journalists to create public opinion in favor of Russia. See R. B. Mowat, *Diplomacy and Peace* (London, Williams and Norgate, 1935), p. 236. During the Second World War, the Nazis subsidized a number of press organizations in Latin America; see C. G. Fenwick, "Intervention by Way of Propaganda," 35 *A.J.I.L.* 626 (1941). And it is not difficult to discover similar instances in the present day.

44. For instance, the Fichte League in 1937 functioned as a secret channel for the Nazis to distribute pamphlets in Hungary which were anti-Jewish and anti-communist. In Austria, before the *Anschluss,* when the government banned all German official publications, the Fichte League posed as a cultural organization but distributed pro-Nazi propaganda material.

45. See H. G. Nicolson, *The Evolution of Diplomatic Method* (London, Constable & Co., 1954), p. 91; L. B. Pearson, *Democracy in World Politics* (Princeton, Princeton University Press, 1955), pp. 68–69; see also *Report on Hearing on U.S. Participation in the I.L.O.* (Subcommittee on International Organization and Movements, Committee on Foreign Affairs, 88th Congress, 1st Sess., 1963), p. 8, for the concern expressed over the use of the I.L.O. forum by the communist delegations for disseminating anti-U.S. propaganda.

audience. The following are the most common media of communication employed by the strategists:

Human Beings. In the previous chapter mention was made of the efficiency of human beings as a medium of transmission of propaganda. Travelers, traders, students, scholars, agents of political parties, people working in secret intelligence services, public information agencies of governments, all serve the function of channels of dissemination and/or intelligence. The extent to which each of these classes of persons functions, and their efficacy, indeed vary. Mention was also made of the advantages that strategists may derive by organizing or disintegrating groups, and by controlling intragroup communication processes. It may be noted here that the elite which vigorously employs the ideological strategy generally takes to organization of strictly disciplined groups in its own state and in the opposing states. It also builds transnational political parties and tries to infiltrate men into other groups, either to disintegrate or gain control over them.[46]

Mails. In addition to written and printed materials transmitted through the mails, postal markings and stamps may be used to disseminate propaganda symbols.[47] As a means of transnational communication the potentiality of mails is limited, for the territorial authority may censor, refuse to transmit, or confiscate the mails if anything is found in or on them prejudicial to its interests.

Censorship of mail serves another purpose also, and that is to learn some secret information which the opponent is supressing. Especially during war, censoring of mail may yield considerable useful information regarding the enemy.[48]

Printed Materials. These constitute a very important medium of communication. When used as a means of transnational communication, the effectiveness of the medium can be minimized by the government of the territory to which the materials are despatched by adopting measures such as seizure at the customs posts.[49] If the opposing elite tightens the frontier

46. See generally Sington and Weidenfeld.

47. For instances, see *New York Times,* March 27, 1957; the Crusade For Freedom postmarks were placed on the mails transmitted from the U.S.A. to Hungary and stopped by the Hungarian government. For controversy between the governments of India and Pakistan over similar use of the postal markings by Pakistan, see 6 *Foreign Affairs Record* 86 (Ministry of External Affairs, Government of India, External Publicity Division, 1960). See also in this connection the editorial in the *New York Times,* April 19, 1962, on communist propaganda through the mails.

48. See Koop, p. 5 et seq.

49. In September 1963, Soviet officials searched 92 Chinese passengers, army officers proceeding to the U.S.S.R. for training, at the railway station at Zabaikalski; when they refused to surrender some newspapers and printed materials alleged to be anti-Soviet, they were not permitted to proceed further and were sent back. See *New York Times,* Sept. 14, 1963.

controls, printed materials may be transmitted by air-dropping, shooting leaflet-shells, and dropping by means of plastic balloons.[50]

Telecommunications. Under this head may be included telegraph, telephone, and wireless communications transmitted either in Morse code, or by teleprinter, or in the form of multidirectional radio communications.[51] Although these channels provide very rapid means of transmission of intelligence to processing centers and the processed materials to centers of dissemination, the extent to which strategists could use them in ideological strategy is limited by one factor: the government of the territory in which the transmission or reception points are located may exercise a high degree of control, weeding out anything likely to prejudice the government's interests.

Radio Broadcasting. This is by far the most effective means of mass communication available now to reach instantaneously audiences practically all over the world, and is believed to be the most efficacious means of transnational communication. The government that does not make use of this medium is exceptional. The Soviet Union initiated its use for transnational propaganda and all the leading states have since the 1930s copied its example.[52]

The government of the state to which transmission is made may, however, attempt to prevent its people from listening to the broadcasts by prohibiting listening to foreign broadcasts, jamming the radio waves, and denying to the people radio sets capable of receiving foreign broadcasts. Limiting reception to transmission by wire is another device. It was reported in 1951 that in the Soviet Union 18 per cent of the receiving sets were capable of direct reception and the rest were useful only for reception by wire.[53] In addition, the Soviet Union's jamming operations were at one

50. For a description of the operations of leaflet drops by plastic balloons, see *New York Times*, Feb. 11, 1956; balloons were used as early as 1871 (Whitton and Larson, p. 24).

51. For a description of the various means by which telecommunications are currently used to transmit news, see F. Williams, *Transmitting World News, A Study of Telecommunications and the Press* (Paris, UNESCO, 1953).

52. The Voice of America, in 1956, broadcast in 43 languages to Europe, Latin America, the Near East, South Asia, Africa, and the Far East; see Martin, p. 28. The B.B.C., by 1946, was broadcasting on 31 transmitters, in 46 languages, for 616 hours weekly; ibid. p. 38. In regard to the U.S.S.R., see ibid. p. 47; Whitton and Larson, p. 50; regarding Communist China, see Houn, pp. 156–58.

53. Inkeles, p. 238; also see H. N. Graves, Jr., *War on the Short-Wave*, Foreign Policy Headline Series No. 30 (New York, Foreign Policy Association, 1941), p. 52. The author says that the Nazis introduced a receiving set called the "People's Set" which was incapable of receiving foreign transmissions. In 1938, only about one third of the sets in Germany were capable of receiving foreign transmissions. After the war broke out, listening to foreign broadcasts was banned. See also Sington and Weidenfeld, p. 145. In Japan, from 1933, possession of short-wave sets was banned and penalties

time employed on a colossal scale.[54] However, restrictive measures such as these to prevent listening to foreign broadcasts may rouse the curiosity of the audience and induce them to adopt a good number of devious methods to circumvent the measures.

Television may for all practical purposes be included in the category of radio broadcasting. It supplies additionally the advantage of combining visual image with aural communication.[55] The advent of the communication satellites has tremendously increased the reach of television broadcasting.

Movies. Movies are a very effective medium of mass communication. But they can be used in an opposing state only within the limits permitted by its government.

It is not possible to say categorically that one medium of communication is more effective than another. Each has its merits and shortcomings. There is little doubt, however, that the most effective means of influencing the audience are communication by mass media followed by face to face contact by human agents.[56]

Tactics

Within the limited scope of this study a detailed description of all the possible tactics of ideological strategy can hardly be attempted; we will in-

---

were provided for listening to foreign broadcasts. In occupied territories, as for example in Burma, the receiving sets of the people were remodeled. See Peter de Mendelssohn, *Japan's Political Warfare* (London, Allen and Unwin, 1944), p. 33; Communist China uses extensively wire-transmission (Houn, pp. 162–66).

54. For details of the transmitters used for jamming when the cold war was intensifying, see 21 *Dept. of State Bull.* 312 (1949); also the speech of the U.S. representative before the U.N. General Assembly (G.A.O.R., Fifth Sess., 3rd Committee, 1950, p. 279). However, in recent years there has been a progressive decrease in jamming operations. President Kennedy reported at a press conference on October 10, 1963, that for many months the Voice of America broadcasts had not been jammed by the Soviet Union. See *The Hindu,* Oct. 11, 1963.

55. It is said that at present, apart from the United States, 82 nations have television broadcasting. There are about 56 million receiving sets and 995 broadcasting stations outside the United States. In the United States there are over 500 TV broadcasting stations. See Gordon, Falk, and Hodapp, pp. 137–38.

56. For detailed information see J. T. Klapper, "The Comparative Effects of the Various Media," W. Schramm, ed., *The Process and Effects of Mass Communication,* pp. 104–05, and the editorial note, p. 91 et seq. Four factors, it is said, are relevant in this context: (1) *time-space* (i.e. whether the communicator has control over the material to be communicated and when to introduce it); (2) *participation* (by the audience in the communication process); (3) *speed;* and (4) *permanence.* Printed material has the advantage of fairly good time-space control and of permanence, but is not useful if the audience cannot read, and is slower than radio broadcasting. In favor of radio broadcasting are factors 2 and 3, but not 1 and 4. Human agents have in their favor factors 1 and 2.

dicate only the general trends. The tactics employed in a given context will indicate the likely outcome of the activity.

The success of the use of the ideological instrument in influencing audiences and evoking from them the desired response is a function of the environmental conditions in which the audiences are placed and their predispositions; hence the operations must be attuned to these environmental and predispositional factors. By using the instrument over a fairly long time the strategists might succeed in modifying the predispositions of the audience addressed, but they could hardly change the environmental conditions. The strategists must at all times operate subject to the limitations which the environmental and predispositional factors impose.

Taking these factors as given, the strategists have to set their objectives,[57] and select participants and techniques suitable to the objectives.[58] In selecting, the principle of economy of effort,[59] which is observed in all operations of successful strategy, will be adhered to as far as possible. Participants and techniques likely to produce maximum effect but to occasion no unacceptable complications or adverse effects will generally be selected.

The selection of words and symbols is generally correlated to the objective sought. If the objective, for example, is that the opponent should relinquish the advantage he enjoys by withholding certain information from publication, circulation of false information which is highly disadvantageous to him may compel him to disclose it.

The operations of the strategy are always so shaped that the strategy of the opponents is counteracted, and an advantage is gained over them. In this process, quite naturally, strategists endeavor to keep their channels of communication as efficient as possible, and to block to the extent they can the channels available to the opponents, while preventing the opponents from blocking their channels of communication. And on the other hand, they might censor all messages to and from their territory and restrict freedom of communication within their boundaries.

Conditions

In order comprehensively to describe the conditions under which the instrument may be employed in the foreseeable future, one should give an

57. By way of illustration, it may be noted that the Soviet ideological strategists originally had the objective of world revolution, but later a more limited one of consolidation of power at home and building up pro-communist groups in foreign states.

58. Proper timing of the operations is an essential part of the tactics. An operation initiated when conditions are unfavorable is not likely to be successful. Ill-timed propaganda operations are known to produce boomerang effects. The Japanese psychological warfare operations during World War II were least successful because they were, it is said, badly timed and ineptly executed. See Mendelssohn, p. 11.

59. For a statement of this principle with reference to military strategy, see B. H. Liddell Hart, *Strategy* (New York, Praeger, 1954), p. 339.

account of all facts relating to the power capabilities of all the participants in the contemporary world arena, their demands, the trends of their policies to obtain satisfaction of these demands, and the expectations of themselves and of others regarding their capabilities with reference to all the instruments of policy. For the present purpose it may suffice to state the main alignments of powers in the arena, the facts that indicate the extent to which we may expect intense use of the ideological instrument, and those facts from which reasonable, broad expectations may be formed about the effects of the use.

It is now commonplace to say that the power structure in the global arena has assumed a highly bipolarized pattern, with the two giants and their allies and satellites ranged on either side. There are strains in both blocs; the Sino-Soviet rift in the Communist bloc and the French–United States differences in the Western bloc have reached such a stage that they seriously undermine the cohesion of the respective blocs. From this may result cooperative agreements across the line dividing the blocs and some lessening of East-West tensions. Intrabloc conflicts may occasion intensive use of the propaganda instrument, as is being witnessed now in the context of the Sino-Soviet rift: intensified use of the radio by both sides against each other, vigorous efforts by the Chinese to smuggle into the U.S.S.R. printed materials highly critical of the Russian Communist party's ideology, and equally strong measures by the Soviet Union to stop transmission and circulation.[60] Unattached to the two power blocs are the so-called "neutrals," but these nonaligned states, which are not militarily very strong and are not prepared to form a close association, do not make the arena a tripolarized one, nor are they likely to in the foreseeable future.

The communist elite's faith in the ultimate global triumph of communism is as firm as ever, and the various national Communist parties have not given up their transnational posture or their goal of global triumph. The expansionist character of communism is as live a factor now as at any time, and the danger seems to be greatest from the Chinese quarter at the present time.[61]

The use of the military instrument having become too expensive, risky, and dangerous beyond description in this nuclear age, all the elites with expansionist tendencies—not exclusively the communists—have come to rely more on nonmilitary instruments of policy, keeping the military in-

60. See *New York Times*, Sept. 14, 1963.

61. It would be more accurate perhaps to say that at present the Soviet Union, with tremendous military power but in a mood to consolidate the gains obtained in various fields, constitutes a lesser danger than Communist China, which is militarily far less powerful but ideologically more militant. The latter's capability to trouble others by the use of the ideological instrument seems to be on a level corresponding to its capability in respect of the military instrument.

strument as far as possible in the background. Propaganda and covert violence have become significant instruments of strategy.[62] The intensity of use of the ideological instrument, however, for tactical reasons is likely to be kept low in certain geographical areas, such as some developing nations. The communist elites are likely to use it against the West for conservation and for expansion purposes. In response to this, the Western elites will probably continue to use the instrument to maintain anticommunist sentiment at a very high level in their own countries and, to the extent possible, to endeavor to foster the same sentiment in communist and noncommunist countries. But neither of the two major blocs is ordinarily likely to use the instrument against a nonaligned state in such a manner as to drive it into the opposite camp.

Apart from the major East-West conflict, there will inevitably be some anticolonial conflicts, conflicts between major and small powers, and between smaller powers over outstanding differences, conflicts which will also occasion the use of the ideological instrument.

The audiences at whom large-scale use of the ideological instrument will be directed in years to come are varied. At one extreme are those who are likely to be least influenced by external propaganda, and at the other those likely to be most affected. For the present purpose, they may be divided into three broad groups. First are those belonging to the advanced Western countries, where the highly industrialized pattern of social organization is ordinarily assumed to breed tensions that can be easily exploited by propagandists.[63] Yet these peoples enjoy the benefits of a very high standard of living, highly developed social services, and free educational and information processes, and therefore are most resistant to the influence of the ideological strategy of opposing external elites. Second, there are the people living in communist countries, under less favorable conditions of life, a regime of strictly controlled processes of education, public information, and organization. They are thus to some extent insulated against the

62. For a systematic treatment of the use of subversion as an instrument of national policy, see Paul W. Blackstock, *The Strategy of Subversion* (Chicago, Quadrangle Books, 1964).

63. About the character of the social organization of modern industrial societies which produces within them tendencies to violence and destruction, Karl Mannheim writes: "Behind the huge organization of modern society and the comparatively smooth working of the industrial system lies the lurking possibility of violence. It is difficult to determine just when and where, in the sphere of foreign policy or of the inner struggle for mastery, bloody violence will take the place of peaceful compromise. The still unharnessed irrationality is always present in the actual working of modern society, and from time to time, mobilizes impulses of the masses. The same persons who, in their working life in the sphere of industrial organization are extensively organized, can at any moment turn into 'machine-wreckers' and ruthless warriors." See his *Man and Society in the Age of Reconstruction* (London, Routledge and Kegan Paul, 1948), p. 64.

effects of anticommunist propaganda, but there is apparently an expectation on the part of the communist elite that a break in these defenses might affect the cohesion of their communities. Finally, there are the peoples of other countries, many of whom live in poverty, hoping that rapid industrialization will bring about a radical transformation in their conditions of living, and they are at the threshold of the disintegration of established social orders which industrialization ordinarily brings about. These audiences present favorable conditions for the operations of the ideological strategy. But in their case, nationalist sentiment supplies a counterweight to centrifugal forces.[64]

Outcome

An outcome of communication is indeed enlightenment. Even the worst propaganda may convey some information, and depending upon the ability of the audience to critically examine and analyze it, fairly realistic information. The technique of content analysis [65] is currently applied to the propaganda of the opposing elite to obtain intelligence, reliable to a certain degree, about the policies and the expected moves of the elite.

In regard to the response of the audience, writers on propaganda and psychological warfare have differed in regard to the effectiveness of mass communication. At one extreme are writers who have denied to psychological warfare any effectiveness, and expressed the view that its results have been exaggerated by some persons involved in psychological warfare operations during World War II and who were perhaps under the influence of self-suggestion.[66] On the other hand, there are writers who have attributed to modern propaganda techniques, especially those practiced in totalitarian states, the power to destroy all free thinking on the part of the audience and all free action, in fact, the human spirit itself.[67] Others have taken positions intermediate between these two extremes. General MacArthur and General Eisenhower are reported to have valued the psychological warfare operations during World War II very highly. Daniel Lerner says that little is known in any scientific sense about the actual effectiveness of

64. See Blackstock, p. 157; he states that during World War II, in spite of widespread disaffection at home, there was loyalty of a high level among the Russian fighting forces.

65. On the use of content-analysis as a means of predicting the acts of an elite, see B. Berelson, *Content Analysis in Communication Research* (Glencoe, Ill., Free Press, 1952), and pp. 365–66.

66. See in this connection the remarks of Konrad Kellen cited in Daniel Lerner, *Sykewar: Psychological Warfare Against Germany, D-Day to VE-Day* (New York, George W. Stewart, 1951), p. 313; also Renzo Sereno in his "Psychological Warfare, Intelligence and Insight," Stanton and Perry, eds., *Personality and Political Crisis*, p. 121.

67. For typical opinions see generally Chakhotin; Meerloo, *Rape of the Mind.*

propaganda in general, and psychological warfare in particular,[68] and another expert in the field agrees that it is difficult to predict the effects of propaganda. It may be possible to predict to some extent the long-term effects, but it is not at all easy to predict the short-term ones.[69] Still another authority, gauging the effectiveness of the psychological warfare operations of the Allies during World War II, concluded that it is difficult to say what effect the strategic operations had, but the tactical propaganda on the battlefield was really effective.[70]

Such divergence of opinion on the effect of mass communication is not at all surprising. Human behavior being a function of two sets of factors, environmental and predispositional, each set comprising highly complex variables, it is indeed difficult to predict on a reasonably scientific basis what effect the stimulus supplied by mass communication will produce in a given situation. Nor is it possible to establish a scientifically demonstrable causal relationship between a stimulus and a course of behavior or a change in attitude or opinion.

Ideological strategy, however, comprises not merely communication of selected material by means of mass media but also the management of the environmental and predispositional factors appropriate to the accomplishment of the objective. On the basis of the operations of the strategists, and the extent to which they possess the ability to control the relevant variables and actually exercise the control, it seems possible to predict to a certain extent the major trends in the response of the audience.

Internal Audience

In respect of the internal audience the strategists occupy the most advantageous position. The more authoritarian their state, the greater is the advantage they possess. Strictly controlling all educational, information, communication, and social processes, the strategists will be able to build up desired predispositions; and if they cannot construct the environment wholly to their design, at least they can minimize its adverse impact and maximize its favorable impact by creating false images of the environment in the minds of the audience.[71] It is true that even under intense pressure of propaganda a section of the audience will retain its independent thought,[72] and there will always be a segment which defies attempts at mass

68. See Lerner, *Sykewar*, pp. 285–86.

69. See Schramm, *The Process and Effects of Mass Communication*, pp. 23–26.

70. See W. Carroll, *Persuade or Perish* (Boston, Houghton Mifflin, 1948), pp. 363–64.

71. In the totalitarian states internal propaganda is vigorously directed to the objective of controlling the image of reality, though the result obtained is partly a function of reality and partly the work of the image-makers. See Kecskemeti, "Totalitarian Communication," p. 226.

72. See Asch, "Some Forms of Interpersonal Influence."

hypnosis and suggestion or can retain cool thinking in times of emotional upsurge.[73] But even they can be either won over after some time by placing them in a closed forum in which only the information supplied by the strategists is available, or silenced under the threat of deprivation if deviant behavior or dissenting attitudes continue. And those won over can be assigned a militant role in support of the regime.

The world witnessed before and during World War II what the Nazis accomplished in Germany by intensive use of the ideological instrument, silencing all opposition to their programs of aggression and harnessing all the human and material resources of Germany to build up a terrific engine of violence and destruction.[74] A body of eminent Japanese scientists testified after World War II to the fact that the ideological strategy pursued by the Japanese government during the years before the war rendered the enlightened in Japan impotent to create a public opinion opposed to the Japanese programs of aggression.[75] The pressure of internal public opinion, as a factor to restrain aggression and violation of international law and canons of humanity, can be reduced to insignificance, if not completely eliminated.

Even where the strategists do not or are not able to assume nearly exclusive control to shape the predispositions of the audience and their knowledge of the environment, the use of the ideological instrument is likely to give to those wielding it increased support from the people of their state. With it their power in the world arena will increase. With such power they might be able to resist any external elite applying coercion to obtain satisfaction of its demands, or to make use of the power for aggressive purposes against other states.

However, it may be noted that in some situations, even when the audience has adopted the desired attitudes, the elite might lose, in varying degrees, its freedom to shape policies, sometimes far in excess of its anticipations. In other words, the elite might suffer power deprivation. Although it has shaped the perspectives of the audience in a certain way, it may find itself unable to modify the perspective further at its choice, and may have

73. Aldous Huxley, *Brave New World Revisited* (New York, Harper, 1958), p. 116. He says that about one fifth of an audience can be easily hypnotized, one fifth cannot be at all, and the rest less easily than the first fifth.

74. Reference may be made in this connection to L. Frazer, *Germany Between the Two Wars: A Study of Propaganda and War-Guilt* (New York, Oxford Book Co., 1945). In the words of the International Military Tribunal, Nuremberg, "Independent judgment, based on freedom of thought, was rendered quite impossible." See *The International Military Tribunal, Nuremberg, Trial of Major War Criminals* (Nuremberg, 1947), 1, 182.

75. For the text of the opinion, see Hadley Cantril, ed., *Tensions That Cause Wars* (Urbana, University of Illinois Press, 1950), p. 300.

to adopt policies more compatible with the perspectives created than are warranted by the realities of the situation, or lose its position of power. The outcome of British and French propaganda during World War I, generating hatred toward Germany, was the imposition at Versailles of extremely unfavorable terms of peace settlement on Germany, although such a step was then known to be unwise.[76] A regime which uses the ideological instrument internally, creating among the audience demands on the values of other states, may well fear that the propaganda might recoil on them and force them to initiate aggression in pursuit of the demands.[77]

External Audiences

While operating to influence external audiences, especially those in the opposing states, the strategists have to take many things as they are and cannot alter them. By and large they can choose only *to whom* to communicate, *what material,* and by *what available media of communication,* but they must operate upon the existing predispositional and environmental factors. If they endeavor to alter the predispositions, or manipulate the process by which facts about the environment come to the knowledge of the audience, they have to do so in competition with the rival strategists. And the less exclusively the strategists can operate, the more difficult it becomes to predict how successful they will be.

Another point also must be noted here. The strategists may have succeeded in changing the attitudes of an external audience to a certain extent, but the change does not become perceptible until it manifests itself in overt acts. And the audience may, because of fear of deprivations that their regime might impose, refrain from overt acts that manifest the attitudes. The response sought may be long delayed, if not fully internalized by the audience.[78] In such a case it is difficult to say whether the operations have been successful or not.

It may be that only a small section of the external audience sought to be influenced is actually won over by the strategists. But this section may sometimes be used for such diverse purposes as organizing groups opposed to the regime, espionage, sabotage, or demonstrations expressing opposition to the policies pursued by the opposing state. In other words, a partial success of the strategy may be helpful in attaining limited objectives of the strategists.

Here we may note some significant factors which are known to influence the outcome of propaganda, in reference to all audiences, internal as well

76. See Kingsley Martin, *Propaganda's Harvest* (London, Routledge and Kegan Paul, 1941), p. 23.

77. Lasswell, "The Impact of Crowd Psychology," p. 295.

78. See Hans Speier, "Elite v. Mass," 4 *World Politics* 308 (1952).

as external. On the basis of the presence of these factors, their magnitude, and other techniques and tactics adopted, it may be possible to estimate the outcome of the propaganda operations.

The nature of the communicator is one important factor. If he commands a reputation for credibility or trustworthiness, he is likely to be given serious attention by the audience.[79] The eminence of the communicator and the prestige he commands are likely to contribute to the effectiveness of the communication.[80] For this reason, the fact that the communicator is an official may make considerable difference. If the audience believes that he possesses great power and that they cannot but accept what he says, the communication will have greater effect than otherwise.[81] Common racial, cultural, or economic ties between the disseminators and the audience are influential factors, for generally audiences are receptive to communications from such people.[82]

The extent to which the message accords with the predispositions of the audience is another factor. If the message accords with the predispositions, the latter are reinforced; [83] if it conflicts with the predispositions it may be expected to have very little effect on them.[84] However, in two situations it may tend to weaken the predispositions. If the predispositions are undergoing modifications due to changes in the environment, propaganda accelerates the weakening.[85] So, if the audience belongs to a lower social

79. One of the reasons why British propaganda addressed to the United States during World War II was said to be more effective than the German propaganda was that the British used speakers who enjoyed or succeeded in building up a reputation for speaking truth. See D. Katz, "Britain Speaks," in H. L. Childs and J. B. Whitton, eds., *Propaganda by Short-Wave* (Princeton, Princeton University Press, 1942), p. 11. And as a matter of good tactics, the British permitted their speakers even to criticize the government, and this enhanced their reputation for speaking the truth. Also see Schramm, *Mass Communication*, p. 212.

80. W. Schramm, "The Effects of Mass Communication: A Review," 26 *Journalism Quarterly* 397 (1949); but H. B. Lewis, "An Experiment on the Operation of Prestige Suggestion," Swanson et al., p. 28, says that when the matter to be judged is clear and unambiguous, prestige suggestion would not affect the judgment, and that the central and focal beliefs of a person will remain unaffected by such suggestion.

81. Kecskemeti mentions this as a factor contributing to the success of internal propaganda of totalitarian governments. See also Meerloo, *Rape of the Mind*, p. 47.

82. Lasswell, "Propaganda," *Encyclopedia of Social Sciences*, 12, 521.

83. Lasswell and Kaplan, *Power and Society*, p. 113. "Propaganda in accord with predispositions strengthens them, propaganda counter to predispositions weakens them only if supported by other factors." The process of strengthening or weakening is likely to be slow and not easily perceptible. See also Schramm, *Mass Communication*, p. 397, who says that the effect tends to be reinforcement rather than change.

84. In war, the well-indoctrinated soldier is not likely to be easily affected by propaganda for this reason. See Carroll, p. 157.

85. Lasswell and Kaplan, p. 113; also Kris and Speier, *German Radio Propaganda*, p. 48, speak of propaganda as "accelerator of accomplishments and eliminator of dissent."

stratum, communications that conflict with the mores of its community may weaken its perspectives much faster than will be true among persons belonging to higher social orders.[86]

The environmental conditions, insofar as they produce insecurities among the audience, are pertinent factors. If the level of insecurity is low, the propaganda disseminated might have no more than cathartic effect, dissipating the insecurity. On the other hand, if the level is high, propaganda might lead the audience to discover more rapidly contradictions in the environment, and to resort to means other than the normal ones—such as violence or breach of the law—to obtain the removal of the contradictions.[87] Propaganda is known to be more effective in times of crisis.

We noted in the previous chapter the influence of the group on behavior. When the audience is socially well organized, the insecurities arising due to environmental changes are at least partially overcome by influences such as identification, approved patterns of behavior in the group, and the guidance supplied by the group leaders. On the other hand, in times of disintegration of the social organization, group influences become progressively more feeble and, what is more, the disintegration increases the level of insecurity. At such times propaganda will have greater impact than in normal times. For this reason tactical psychological warfare operations are likely to yield favorable results when the enemy suffers defeats and his forces become disorganized.[88]

The content of the message communicated is indeed important. In particular, if it shows a way of overcoming the anxieties or insecurities created by the environment, it is likely to be given attention and favorable reception. If it merely rouses anxieties, but suggests no way of overcoming them, it is likely to be given less attention. Furthermore, by skillfully managing the anxieties so roused and projecting the hatreds present on to the strategists, the rival strategists will be able to produce effects quite opposite from those intended.[89] Emotionalized and sentimentalized symbols may produce cathartic effects, or precipitate overt acts suggested in the message, depending upon the prevailing insecurities.

The outcome of sustained use of the instrument will vary, depending upon the matter communicated and the audience's factual knowledge about the environment. If the strategists are able to create an image of the

86. Hovland, Janis, and Kelly, *Communication and Persuasion*, p. 153. This explains the success of communist propaganda addressed to peoples in the lower social orders especially in the underdeveloped world.

87. Lasswell, *World Politics and Personal Insecurity*, p. 114; also Lasswell and Kaplan, p. 114; Harold D. Lasswell, *Propaganda Technique in the World War* (New York, Knopf, 1927), p. 190; also his "Propaganda."

88. In this connection, see the study of Shils and Janowitz, "Cohesion and Disintegration in the *Wehrmacht*."

89. See Janis and Feshbach; and Hovland, Janis, and Kelly, p. 63.

environment which supports the propaganda themes, the outcome is likely to be a desired strengthening of the predispositions of the audience. If the factual knowledge of the audience does not support the propaganda themes, repeated dissemination of the same propaganda material is likely to have little effect and the previous predispositions favorable to the strategists are likely to weaken or disappear. In Pavlovian terminology, in the absence of reinforcement, repetition of the conditioning stimulus will wither away the conditioned response.[90]

The importance of control over the communications system, which includes the channels of intelligence and overt and covert channels of dissemination, needs no mention. An elite which possesses a preponderant advantage over another in respect of such control is likely to be more successful in the operation of ideological strategy and in obtaining coercive effects on the audience.[91]

Successful use of the instrument to influence the external audience in an opposing state implies a relative gain in power to the strategists. The opposing elite, suffering a loss in power, might more easily yield to the demands of the strategists than otherwise. If the strategists are able to reconstruct the decision-making process in the opposing state by means other than the use of violence they will have accomplished a very significant objective with far less expense than otherwise. Military success may be attained more economically if the use of the military instrument is preceded and/or accompanied by successful use of the ideological instrument to dampen or destroy the will to fight of the people of the victim state.

The Target Elite

The use of the instrument, in the first place, shapes the structure of expectations of the target elite regarding the future policies of the elite operating the strategy. In addition, the external target elite is likely to suffer deprivations of power or of respect. The techniques of ideological strategy include criticism of the policies of the opposing external elite, modification of the expectation of the audience about the respect to which the external elite is entitled, and projection of any existing hatreds onto them. In consequence of such techniques, the elite or its individual members might suffer loss of some of the respect in which they were previously held among

90. Berelson and Steiner, *Human Behavior*, p. 137.

91. Schramm, *Mass Communication*, p. 65, says that the most favorable condition for changing opinions and attitudes is monopoly of propaganda control; see also P. E. Lazarsfeld and R. K. Merton, "Mass-Communication, Popular Taste, and Organized Social Action," in Swanson et al., pp. 75, 82. In this connection it may also be noted that according to Pavlov's theory, conditioning to a stimulus can be more easily effected where there are not other disturbing stimuli. For the implications of this theory in regard to estimating the effects of mass communication, see Meerloo, *Rape of the Mind*, pp. 43–54; also Lasswell, "Propaganda and Mass Insecurity."

the audience. And respect being a base of power, loss of respect might occasion loss of power. The strategists might, instead of attacking individuals and their policies, attack the respect in which the institutions of the target state are held. If the audience loses respect for the institutions, loss of power to the opposing external elite could follow. Finally, whether the strategists so intend or not, the use of the ideological instrument might provoke some among the audience to resort to assassination and acts of terrorism. One may recall the Sarajevo incident of 1914 when Prince Ferdinand was murdered by Serbian irredentists, and the assassination of King Alexander of Yugoslavia and M. Barthou of France in 1934, at Marseilles.

Effects of the Use of the Ideological Instrument of Coercion on Community Values

Jeopardy to Peace and Security in the World Community

Intensive use of the ideological instrument by elites in the world arena creates recurring problems relating to the maintenance of peace and security in the world community. The chain of action and reaction which the coercive use of the ideological instrument by an elite—either exclusively or in combination with the coercive use of other nonviolent instruments of policy—might produce is likely to give rise to a threat to the peace at some stage, or might cause an outbreak of violence.

One could produce abundant evidence to show that governments and statesmen have long since regarded propaganda as a disturbing factor to peaceful relations between states. Evidence can be produced from the time of the French Revolution. The discussions that have taken place in the League of Nations and the United Nations on propaganda, and attempts made to draft international conventions to regulate its use, bear eloquent testimony to the fact of such recognition. For the present purpose we may note merely the statements made by two statesmen some years ago in two different contexts. In August 1958, after the United States landed marines in Lebanon, then troubled by civil war, President Eisenhower said before the U.N. General Assembly:

> I believe that this Assembly should reaffirm its enunciated policy and should consider means of monitoring the radio broadcasts directed across national frontiers in the troubled Near East area. It should then examine complaints from these nations which consider their national security jeopardized by external propaganda.[92]

And in 1951, as the East-West cold war was rising in intensity, with the threat of nuclear holocaust hanging over mankind like a Damocles' sword, Prime Minister Nehru stated:

92. See G.A.O.R., 3rd Emer. Special Sess. (1958), pp. 7–8.

> We live in a perilous age. It will be good if all the statesmen of the world controlling the destinies of millions of people keep quiet for a few months. Better still, if the press of the world keeps quiet for a few months. This will advance the cause of peace.[93]

Nehru's words might have been uttered rather in helplessness in the midst of surging cold war, but they indicate the expectations that form in the minds of government leaders as they are confronted with intensive exchanges of propaganda between states.

There is indeed need for regulation of the use of and response to propaganda as a coercive instrument of policy by the elites in the world arena. There is also a need to guard against outbreaks of violence between states in consequence of intensive uses of the instrument.

Interference with Community Value Processes and Destruction of Values

Intensive use of the ideological instrument, adopting all or a number of the techniques mentioned above, interferes with the value processes in the community to the detriment of its population. If the basic premise of democracy is rule by the consent of the governed, this premise is given short shrift by the manipulators of ideology. The consent obtained from the audience subjected to intensive propaganda is by no means a consent based upon a choice made with full awareness of the environmental facts and under conditions of minimum disturbing stimuli which can prevent rational selection of alternatives with due regard to costs and gains.[94] If we accept widest participation in the shaping and sharing of power as a basic principle of democracy, this principle is violated to the advantage of the elite operating the strategy. It has been noted that the strategy involves interference with the enlightenment process, and this results in concentration of enlightenment in the hands of a few. Incitements offered by the strategists can also cause damage to the well-being and wealth values of individuals and groups.[95] We need not invite attention to the possible impact of this interference and destruction of values on other value processes in the community.

THE PROCESS OF CLAIM

We may describe the process of claim by observing the claimants, their objectives, and the typical claims that are presented in relation to the process of communication.

93. *New York Times,* May 30, 1951.

94. Huxley, *Brave New World Revisited,* p. 130.

95. During World War II, the Allied airmen forced to land were sometimes immediately killed by the civilian population. See *I.M.T., Nuremberg, Judgment, Trial of*

Claimants

Traditionally only the governments of states can invoke authority to obtain a cessation of impermissible use of coercion. Non-officials can only exert their influence with governments to make them present claims. At present officials of international organizations, if so authorized by the respective constituent treaties, may invoke such authority; under Article 99 of the U.N. Charter, for instance, the Secretary-General may bring to the attention of the Security Council any matter constituting a threat to the peace.

Objective

The most general objective of the claimants is to secure the prescription and application of community policy to regulate communication alleged to be destructive of common interests. The general objective will, however, manifest itself in the form of specific claims in relation to the process of communication, which may be set out thus: [96]

Specific Claims

Participation

Claim that the identity of the manifest communicator is (is not) relevant to general community policies in the regulation of transnational coercion.

a. Officials of states
b. Non-officials
c. The political party and agencies of public information in a totalitarian state
d. Persons in the service of international organizations

Audience

Claim that the identity of the audience is (is not) relevant.

a. Internal audience
b. Audience in the opposing state
c. Audience in third states

Objectives

1. Claim that the objective of persuasion is permissible.
2. Claim that the objective of deliberate coercion is impermissible.
   a. Major coercion
   b. Minor coercion
3. Claim that even if the immediate objective is coercion, the ulterior objective which is approved by the community renders coercion permissible.

Major War Criminals, 1, 229. Carroll, p. 229, notes that incitements to lynch the airmen were published by the Germans in Hungarian newspapers. See also the "Essen Lynching Case," 1 *Law Rep., U.N. War Crimes Cases* 88 (1945).

96. These claims are referred to in greater detail in the chapters dealing with trends.

a. Securing conformance to the world public order
b. Promotion of self-determination
c. Promotion of the interests of minorities
d. Promotion of human rights

Situation

The characteristics of the situation are (are not) material.

a. Geographical
b. Temporal-duration
c. Institutionalized
d. Crisis:
   i. Before the outbreak of violence
   ii. After violence has broken out

Relative Capabilities

Claim that the relative capabilities of the strategists and the targets of coercion are (are not) material.

Strategies

1. Claim that the use of other instruments of strategy and the varying degrees of intensity in their use, along with the ideological instrument, are (are not) relevant.

2. Claim that the particular techniques and tactics of the ideological strategy employed are (are not) relevant.

a. Content of communication
b. Centers of dissemination
c. Channels of communication

Outcome

Claim that the outcome of the particular use of the instrument, whether or not it increases enlightenment, does (does not) impose deprivation, or create an expectation of deprivation, of the values of the target external elite:

a. Power
b. Respect
c. Well-being

Effects

Claim that the use of the instrument should (need not) be restrained:

a. For maintaining minimum public order.
   i. War propaganda
   ii. Propaganda of hatred
   iii. False and distorted statements
   iv. Offensive statements
b. For minimizing interference with the community value processes (particularly of power, enlightenment, and well-being); in other words, for promoting optimum public order.

Process of Decision

1. Inclusive decision:

a. Claim that the general community does (does not) have competence to decide the lawful or unlawful character of the use of the instrument.

b. Claims relating to the sanctioning measures to be adopted, having regard to the goals of
   i. Prevention
   ii. Deterrence
   iii. Restoration
   iv. Rehabilitation
   v. Reconstruction

2. Exclusive decision:
   a. Claim that a particular state does (does not) have competence to determine whether the communication is lawful or unlawful.
   b. Claim that a particular state does (does not) have competence to determine the appropriate sanctioning measures.

THE PROCESS OF DECISION

The process of decision in relation to the various types of claims specified above may be described similarly in terms of the participants in the process, their objectives, arenas of competence, bases of power, the strategies adopted, the outcome of the decision, and the conditioning factors which affect the decision process.

Decision Makers

The most important decision makers at present are the officials of states, and in previous centuries they were the decision makers. Non-officials can participate in the decision process only indirectly by exerting influence on the officials. International officials may participate in decisions occasionally, as for instance when the United Nations is engaged in a peace-enforcing or peace-keeping operation. In addition to national judicial tribunals which come within the category of state officials, international tribunals such as the International Military Tribunal at Nuremberg or an arbitral tribunal set up by the parties to a dispute also participate in the decision process.

Objectives

The most general objective of the decision makers may be described as identifying the common interests of the participants in the world social process, and affording such interests protection in a manner consistent with the basic goals of world community policy such as maintenance of peace and security, observance of certain humanitarian standards, etc. Inasmuch as the state is presently the most significant group participating in the world social process, it is usually the common interests of states that are sought to be protected.

After the common interests are identified and the policy of protection is formulated and communicated, the next objective sought is to supply the appropriate sanctioning process. For instance, in the past when it was considered that the common interest demanded that libels on heads of states should be prohibited, states began to initiate prosecutions to punish the libelers. The objectives sought in the sanctioning process, relevant to our context, are the following: [97]

Prevention: The goal of prevention may be defined as reducing the probabilities of resort to impermissible coercion. The goal is sought mostly as part of pre-crisis policy, by impressing upon the participants in the social process the advantages to be derived from conformance to prescriptions and the costs likely to be incurred in the event of a breach. Maintaining cordiality in the tone and language of diplomatic communication at this stage is part of a policy of prevention.

Deterrence: The line that separates prevention from deterrence is very thin, reflecting only the degree of imminence of deprivation by unauthorized coercion. The objective is to dissuade the potential violators of the prescription by impressing upon them the consequences of the violation. Warnings issued as to what would be done in the event of the commission of an act, or repetition of it, serve the purpose of deterrence. A threat of counter propaganda, directed to an external elite which seems likely to use propaganda, may serve the purpose of deterrence.

Restoration: This objective refers to a situation when a violation of the prescription has occurred, and it is sought to stop the violation and restore the conditions of interaction obtaining before the violation. Counter propaganda may be employed to induce the elite that has first started using it in an impermissable manner to stop such use.

Rehabilitation: The objective of rehabilitation consists of repairing the destruction of values caused as a result of violation. The objective may be sought in instances of destruction of deferential values (such as respect) as well as material values. When a libel is published on the head of a foreign state, the tendering of an apology by the government concerned to the foreign head of state rehabilitates his injured dignity and respect.

Reconstruction: The objective of reconstruction is transformation of the decision-making process in order to make sure that violations do not recur. The goal of prevention is sought with respect to all, whereas the goal of reconstruction is pursued in reference to a participant who has already resorted to impermissible coercion. It is hoped that a recurrence of coercion will be avoided by transforming the decision-making process. Reconstruction is both a strategic goal of interacting participants and a sanctioning goal of decision makers. After World War II, the objective of recon-

97. For more elaborate discussion of sanctioning objectives, see McDougal, Lasswell, and Vlasic, *Public Order in Space*, p. 416; McDougal and Feliciano, *Law and Minimum World Public Order*, p. 317; Richard Arens and Lasswell, *In Defense of Public Order* (New York, Columbia University Press, 1961), p. 101.

struction was sought in the vanquished countries, and with that end in view steps were taken to wipe out Nazi and Fascist ideologies. In the countries that came under the occupation of the Western powers, liberal democratic doctrines were popularized and institutions built up. In the areas occupied by the Soviet Union, communist governments were established and the communist ideology came to be the established ideology.

Arenas of Decision

The arenas of decision include the entire general structure of authority in the contemporary world community. There are arenas internal and external to the state, and in the external arena both organized and unorganized parts. The organized segment consists of the vast network of international organizations, which facilitate inclusive decisions, that is, those taken on behalf of the community to protect what are regarded as common interests. Traditionally, officials of states have been participating in the unorganized external arena, where decisions taken may be exclusive decisions, that is, taken on one's own behalf by way of self-protection or self-help; or they may be inclusive decisions.[98] Within the states the arena of decision is organized, and the legislature, executive, and judiciary may act to implement policy in regard to communications regarded as impermissible. Such decisions may again be inclusive or exclusive. An illustration of an exclusive decision is the prohibition of revolutionary propaganda directed against the established government within the state; that of an inclusive decision is the law that proscribes incitement to assassination.

Bases of Power

The bases of power of international organizations and their officials may be said to include, first, the formal authority vested in them which gives rise to an expectation that their decisions will be respected and complied with to a high degree. Second, the organizations can offer the values at their disposal as inducements for compliance, and threats of, or actual, withholding of access to these values as a penalty for noncompliance. Third, member states may place at the disposal of the organizations resources and skilled personnel for implementing community policy. The bases of power of the officials of a state are the control the state possesses over resources, people, and institutional arrangements.

98. What may be regarded as inclusive decisions are the policies adopted by the Allies in Germany and Japan after World War II to suppress the propagation of Nazi and militarist doctrines and to develop democratic ideas. A decision to adopt these policies was reached in the Potsdam Agreement. In pursuit of the policies steps were taken affecting public information by mass media such as the press and radio, instruction in schools, and practices of religion. See E. Plischke, "Denazification Law and Procedure," 41 *A.J.I.L.* 807, 819–23 (1947); *Occupation of Japan: Policy and Progress* (U.S. Dept. of State, Far Eastern Series, Pub. No. 2671), p. 33 and also passim.

Strategies

The strategies adopted by the decision makers to reach and implement decisions may be classified in the same manner as the instruments of interaction, that is to say, as *diplomatic, ideological, economic,* and *military.* Policy may be prescribed and applied as a result of consent between the claimant and the counter-claimant. For example, when an utterance is made in a state by one of its officials or a non-official, the officials of the affected state may invoke the doctrine of state responsibility, alleging that the utterance is an impermissible one, and demand from the first state suitable redress. The officials of the state so charged with the responsibility may accept the charge and render redress. In some instances a treaty may be entered into undertaking to carry out the policy agreed upon. If the claimant and counter-claimant are unable to reach an agreement, there may be a resort to the ideological instrument, appealing to the people of the supposedly delinquent state over the head of its rulers. Public opinion has always been considered one of the sanctions of international law.[99] Further, the use of the instrument may be justified as legitimate retaliation, retortion, or nonviolent reprisal. The economic instrument may be employed by holding out a threat to withdraw or actually withdrawing the economic advantages which are being enjoyed by the state charged with delinquency. And lastly, the military instrument may be used where such use is authorized by community prescriptions.

In addition to the four strategies mentioned above, we may mention a fifth, the *correctional strategy.* This sanctioning practice may be directed against individuals or members of groups declared as criminally responsible for impermissible use of the instrument.

The Outcome of the Decision

The outcome may be any one of the phases of prescription and enforcement of policy. Traditionally these phases are categorized as legislative, executive, judicial, and administrative. A sharper classification is: prescribing policy, bringing intelligence to influence prescription of policy, recommending policy, invoking authority, application of policy, appraisal of the effects of application, and termination of policy.

Conditioning Factors

Here we propose to state the factors which have affected so far, and are likely to affect in the foreseeable future, the process of decision in regard to the use of the ideological instrument. This lays a base for the clarification of policy to be presented in the following chapter. The conditioning factors are as follows: (1) The centralized institutions and procedures of au-

99. See below, p. 174 ff.

thority in the global arena are presently so weak and imperfectly developed that an expectation that they will help effectively in identifying and protecting common interests, and providing security from violence and other impermissible forms of coercion is low. (2) In the world arena the expectation of violence is very high, as well as a belief in the effectiveness of nonviolent forms of coercion. The role of the economic instrument in the two world wars and of the ideological instrument in the Nazi and Fascist strategies of aggression are vividly remembered. The transformation of Eastern Europe to a communist pattern without manifest use of violence strongly affects expectations in the West regarding the potentiality of covert transnational coercive processes. (3) There is great inequality among states in terms of power in the diplomatic, ideological, economic, and military contexts. The disparity in the capability of states in regard to the use of the ideological instrument, based upon possession of skilled personnel and resources and the prevailing conditions of internal social organization and stability, is comparable to the disparity in military capability. (4) There are prevailing alignments of powers in the arena, which were formed mainly in search of security. (5) There are diversities in the social systems obtaining in the various states in the arena and in the corresponding ideologies.

These factors affect decision-making in more than one way. Security from outside coercion constitutes the major preoccupation of states, and in their quest for security they are prone to give primary importance to individual, special interests having a bearing upon security, and only secondary importance to common interests. This is clearly perceptible in connection with decision-making relating to the ideological instrument as well. In this connection Professor Lasswell observes,[100]

> In all that pertains to collective psychological problems we shall see that a wavering balance is held between exclusivity and inclusivity. But on the whole it is clear that initiatives on behalf of inclusivity appear to be making little headway in the crucial area of minimum public order. Think of the abortive proposals to widen the scope of international control of any part of the national press (including all mass media) or the contents of history textbooks used in all the schools.

The concern for security affects decision-making in another direction also. The weaker states are prepared sometimes to buy security at the cost of sacrificing a degree of freedom of information and to a certain extent human rights, whereas the stronger powers are ready to risk a little insecurity from violence in order to maintain freedom of information and uphold human rights. Those with low capability to use the ideological instrument and withstand its use by external elites favor restrictive regulation of

100. "The Impact of Crowd Psychology Upon International Law," p. 298.

propaganda, while the stronger insist that the true remedy at all events is a free forum. The weaker use their territorial power to introduce tight restrictions on the circulation of counter ideological symbols, while the stronger favor a liberal regime. An alignment with other powers affects to some extent expectations about security and in consequence the decision-making. By virtue of the diversity of social systems and supporting ideologies, what appears to be a healthy process of public information and education in one state appears to be harmful propaganda, indoctrination, and brainwashing in another, and the elite of each tends to express concern about the opposing elite's activity, sometimes to the point of exaggeration. This reinforces the demand for restrictive regulation of propaganda, as evidenced in the contemporary calls for prohibition of "war propaganda," "subversive propaganda," "ideological aggression," etc., and the trend toward restrictive regulation at the cost of freedom of information.

4

Clarification of Policy

In clarifying the policies to be adopted in relation to the use of the ideological instrument, and the claims and counter-claims presented regarding its use, we shall take up, to the extent that our predispositions permit, the position of a disinterested observer who subscribes to the faith declared in the preamble of the U.N. Charter "in fundamental human rights, in the dignity and worth of the human person." The most fundamental policy we recommend is the upholding of human dignity,[1] or, to express it in a slightly different way, according widest access to the shaping and sharing of all human values.

Communication is a means of enlightenment, and a policy of according widest access to the shaping and sharing of enlightenment demands that the communication process should not be subjected to any restrictions, other than those aimed at sustaining the process in its most optimal form. We recommend a policy of promoting freedom of information, a freedom which finds definition in Article 19 of the Universal Declaration of Human Rights.[2]

However, insofar as the communication process is manipulated to produce coercive effects on the audience groups and opposing elites, and to occasion jeopardy to other human values, the process of communication has to be regulated. A policy of the widest sharing of power and respect

1. There is sufficient justification to introduce the expression "human dignity" into the present discussion for it is now more than an emotionally charged symbol that can be pressed into service for propaganda purposes. Enlightened juristic opinion has come to express the concept of the rule of law in terms of upholding human dignity. The function of the legislature in a society governed by the rule of law, it is said, is the creating and maintaining of conditions "which will uphold the dignity of man as an individual." See "The Delhi Congress of International Commissions of Jurists," 1 *Journal of the Indian Institute of Law* 207 (1959); in particular, the remarks of Lord Denning reported on p. 209.

2. The article runs thus: "Everyone has the right to freedom of opinion and expression; this right includes freedom to hold opinions without interference and to seek, receive and impart information and ideas through any media and regardless of frontiers."

demands that consent and not imposition, persuasion and not coercion, should be the basis of social interaction. Consistently with this policy, all use of coercion should be regulated so as to minimize its incidence. Policy also requires that the use of the instrument should be regulated to minimize the destruction of other human values.

It has been noted before that in an environment in which free inquiry is not permitted coercive effects on the audience will be greater than where it is permitted.[3] And hence, the more general policy of minimization of coercion also calls for promotion of freedom of information.[4]

In regulating the communication process for policy purposes, decision-makers will necessarily be faced in each case with the question whether to permit communication to promote enlightenment, or to impose restrictions to attain the other policy goals. In dealing with such questions, with a view to applying effectively both the policies, we suggest the observance of the two following principles: (1) a communication should be condemned as impermissible only where there is reasonable expectation that any possible undesirable outcome or effect of it is imminent and cannot be prevented by free information or education. (2) The sanctioning measures adopted must be as far as possible compatible with the overall policy of freedom of information.[5] However, it is clear that the application of these principles will leave in practice a number of cases in which decisions will have to be reached by a process of ad hoc balancing of the two major policy considerations outlined above.

The concept of freedom of information we have in mind in formulating the above policy goals is one which fully preserves the freedom of the individual "to seek, receive and impart information and ideas" as specified in Article 19 of the Universal Declaration of Human Rights. The traditional liberal democratic doctrine, which this formula articulates in a large part, faces challenge presently from two quarters. The first is the view adopted in totalitarian and authoritarian countries which assigns an activist social role to the press. The social function of freedom of expression is conceived in the liberal democratic theory as one which, apart from facilitating free dissemination of information, enables the members of the society who desire or oppose a change in the existing state of affairs to present their respective views, so that a group which fails to influence events according to its desires will at least have the satisfaction of having presented its views before the society. Such satisfaction reduces considerably the frustrations resulting from a failure to influence events as desired, and the free airing of

3. See above, pp. 30–31, 61–62.

4. For a detailed statement of the function served by freedom of expression in democratic communities, see Thomas I. Emerson, "Toward a General Theory of the First Amendment," 72 *Yale L.J.* 877, 878–86 (1963).

5. These principles are taken with some modifications from ibid., p. 917.

the views is likely to reduce the tensions in the community by virtue of the catharsis it may produce.[6]

In Soviet theory, the role of public criticism as a means of influencing the power elite is not denied, but the media of public information, particularly the press, are expected not only to inform and mold public opinion but also to promote the progress of the Soviet society.[7] Under such a doctrine those who control the agencies can easily find justification rigorously to exclude from communication all views considered opposed to such progress and to propagate with vigor ideas regarded likely to further the evolution of the society. In authoritarian states the press is also assigned the function of promoting certain ends of the state.[8] Centralization of power, a high degree of control over the media of public information in the form of state ownership, authoritarian control or control by a single political party, and the assignment of an activist role will reduce freedom of expression to freedom to express only what the power elite approves. These conditions also tend to create a monopoly over enlightenment in favor of the elite, and provide greater opportunities for coercive use of the instrument. No one can deny the social responsibilities of the press and other agencies of public information, but one should guard against drastic limitation of freedom in the name of these responsibilities.

The second challenge proceeds from the technological advancement which has converted the media of public information into big industrial concerns requiring large capital outlay. In the absence of state ownership, it is said, the media will be under the control of the wealthy classes. Kingsley Martin compared the freedom of a private citizen to start a newspaper with "the right of a worker in a Sheffield factory to start a steelworks in competition with a steel combine." [9] According to the Soviet view, this position must be rectified by placing at the disposal of the people and their organizations material resources necessary for publication.[10] The Soviet contention indeed highlights the necessity of securing wide access to the media of information, in pursuit of the policy of promotion of freedom of

6. On the social function of freedom of expression in democratic socities, see Emerson, pp. 884–85.

7. See Arkadyev, "Soviet Newspapers," p. 103; also *The Press in Authoritarian Countries*, p. 26; Inkeles, p. 22.

8. See Hilding Eek, *Freedom of Information as a Project of International Legislation* (Uppsala, Lundequistska Bokhandeln, 1953), p. 15.

9. *The Press the Public Wants*, p. 140.

10. According to M. Lomakin, the Soviet representative on the Sub-Commission on Freedom of Information, Commission on Human Rights, a convention on freedom of information should specify as one of its objectives: "To recognize that full freedom of press and information can be secured only under conditions of placing at the disposal of broad masses of the people and of their organizations material means necessary for the publication of organs of the press and for the functioning of other means of information." U.N. Doc. E/CN.4/Sub.1/SR 54 (1948), p. 10.

information.[11] And the present day liberal democratic doctrine is not opposed to the idea of policing the economy to prevent the formation and functioning of private monopolies detrimental to the community. State ownership of the media of information, with fullest autonomy given to the publishing agencies,[12] might effectively promote freedom of information, provided only that there is wide sharing of power in the community and a corresponding sharing of control over the agencies. We wish to emphasize here, without engaging in a doctrinal discussion, that in evolving and applying policy one should not lose sight of the essence of freedom of information, which is the individual's "freedom to seek, receive, and impart information and ideas."

The policies formulated here might be understood as suggesting that in the process of regulating the ideological instrument even the right to propagate "truth" must be restricted. As a matter of fact, as will be observed below, on some occasions in the past those who disseminated propaganda claimed justification for their activity on the ground that they were doing nothing but communicating "truth." In answer to those who stoutly oppose any restriction on the right to propagate truth, it might be stated, taking a cue from an important school of modern philosophers, that truth is not something "real," and it is either an a priori statement connected with other similar statements, or a narration of historical or contemporary facts, or a prediction based upon past experience, and in all these cases there is room for contradiction.[13] Hence there is no such absolute value as "truth" which needs be given protection under all circumstances. However, this study does not intend to take such a stand. According to the present view, world community regulation should leave the process of communication substantially unaffected. When necessary, the extent and form of communication may be regulated to the degree warranted by the importance of the value to be protected. And there should not be any objection to a regulation of that nature, for in municipal law such restriction is accepted as necessary for attainment of certain values. For example, it may be pointed out that scientific or artistic presentation of facts relating to sex is permitted, whereas obscene presentation is not

11. As a matter of fact, as will be noted below, the United Nations and UNESCO have been engaged at least during the past decade in efforts directed to expansion of the media of communication, especially in underdeveloped countries. See below, Chap. 11.

12. This appears to be what is aimed at in Yugoslavia. See the *Report on Developments in the Field of Freedom of Information since 1954* (by Hilding Eek, Special Consultant to the U.N. Secretary-General) to the Economic and Social Council (E.S.C.O.R., 31st Sess., Annexes, Agenda item 10, Part II, 1961, hereafter cited as *Eek's Report*), para. 28.

13. See A. J. Ayer, *Language, Truth, and Logic* (London, Victor Gollancz, 1947), Chap. 5.

tolerated on the ground that it is "truth." Further, in the present day, publication of a set of facts having transnational significance cannot be absolutely interdicted, for disclosure of those facts before a body like the United Nations or a national legislature cannot be prevented. These disclosures and the replies given thereto receive publication in the press and by other media of mass communication. And thus what is intended to be conveyed to the public will receive sufficient publication. In this light it appears that the basic policies suggested here are not open to objection on the ground that they imply restriction on the right to propagate truth.

The manner in which the basic policies specified above may be applied in relation to the various specific claims may now be briefly indicated.[14]

CLAIMS RELATING TO PARTICIPATION

The status of the manifest participant is relevant in several, though not all, contexts. The outcome of participation by an official of a state is normally an expectation that the activity represents the policy of the state vis-à-vis the target elite, while the outcome of participation by a non-official is not ordinarily such an expectation. But there are other factors, such as the official having indulged in what is manifestly an unauthorized act, or the non-official having acted under governmental instigation or authorization, which may produce expectations of a different character. Further, the expectations of the outcome of the activity in the form of an attack launched from the territory of the state in question may arise from official or nonofficial activity, though the expectation in the latter case might be limited to an attack by irregular forces only. The effectiveness of the communication in influencing the attitudes and behavior of the audience addressed does not, it has been noted, depend wholly upon the status of the manifest participant. Inasmuch as the expectation will affect the countermeasures likely to be adopted by the target elite, policy must vary with the expectations produced in each case, and not merely with the status of the manifest participant though the status should form one of the factors influencing the choice. In the case of international civil servants, policy must be based upon the expected effect of the activity on the efficient functioning of the organization in which he is employed.

AUDIENCE

The relevancy of the audience addressed also stems from the variation in the expectations produced as different audience groups are addressed. If the audience is internal, the normal expectation will be that the instrument is being used as a means of internal sociopolitical control; but if the audience is in the opposing state, it is more likely that use will culminate in attacks on the value position of the target elite. But there are situations

14. See above, pp. 69–71.

when internal use can give rise to an expectation that it will culminate in such an attack, and external use may not create such an expectation. When selected groups in an opposing state are addressed, the likely assumption is that the groups will be used as instruments of covert violence. If the audience in a third state is addressed, the expectation may be that use of the ideological instrument is intended to develop friendly attitudes toward the strategists' state or directly hostile attitudes toward the opposing state. For obvious reasons, policy must vary with the expectations produced, and these expectations will depend only in part upon the character of the audience group addressed.

OBJECTIVES

From the basic policies set out, it follows that the use of the instrument for persuasion or negligible coercion should be permissible. Freedom of information implies an opportunity for mutual exchange of views and persuasion among the members of the community. Use for persuasive purposes is not only a harmless process but an indispensable means of bringing about desirable changes in the world arena by peaceful procedures. For clarifying our recommendations about use for coercive purposes, it is necessary first to take a brief look at the policies underlying traditional and contemporary international law in regard to internal and transnational use of coercive processes.

Basic Prescriptions of Traditional International Law and their Underlying Policies

The principle of sovereignty, one of the cardinal principles of traditional international law, gave the elite of each state a high degree of control over the territory and people of the state and freedom from external control. It gave the people of each state freedom to choose the form of government of their liking.[15] A state could give, in particular, extensive or very limited freedom of information to its subjects, and could permit or impose restrictions upon dissemination of ideologies opposed to those professed by the ruling elite. Outside intervention in the internal affairs of a state was prohibited.

These prescriptions implied that the elite was free to use the ideological

15. See W. E. Hall, *A Treatise on International Law* (8th ed. by A. Pearce Higgins, Oxford, Clarendon Press, 1924) (hereafter cited as Hall), p. 50. He says that a "state may place itself under any form of government it wishes, and may frame its social institutions upon any model." Also see L. Oppenheim, *International Law—A Treatise*; Vol. 1, *Peace* (8th ed. by H. Lauterpacht, London, Longmans, 1955) (hereafter cited as Oppenheim-Lauterpacht, 1), p. 287. He says, "In consequence of its internal independence, a state can adopt any constitution it likes, arrange its administration in any way it thinks fit, enact such laws as it pleases." See also C. G. Fenwick, *International Law* (3d ed. New York, Appleton, 1948), p. 249.

instrument internally to produce any degree of coercive effects. There was, it is no doubt true, a doctrine of humanitarian intervention in traditional international law which articulated a claim put forward on some occasions by states, on behalf of the whole community, of a general interest in what transpired within the borders of all states. This general interest was claimed in order to insure that tyranny, oppression, and internecine strife did not reach such levels in a state as would shock the conscience of mankind.[16] But it is doubtful whether this doctrine provided adequate justification for intervention when the ideological instrument was being used very coercively within a state, especially when such use had no perceptible external effects.

In regard to the regulation of transnational coercion, traditional international law was far from satisfactory. States were at liberty to bring into existence a state of war at will.[17] Waging war was regarded as a sovereign prerogative.[18] Apart from allowing the liberty to initiate war at will, the law permitted states to resort to "measures short of war" as a means of obtaining redress for alleged wrongful acts committed by others. These measures were nothing but acts of war themselves, and all that the party against whom they were applied had to do to expose their true character was to say that war had commenced. To speak of legal restraints on the transnational coercive use of the ideological instrument under that law was to indulge in self-delusion.

In contrast to this unfettered freedom to use violence, traditional international law prohibited intervention in the internal affairs of a foreign state. Writers have indeed tried to give the doctrine of intervention a restricted meaning, limiting it to "dictatorial intervention,"[19] or interference which has "an imperative form," or which is either "forcible or backed by the threat of force."[20] But in practice statesmen did not keep its meaning so restricted. They invoked the doctrine even in cases involving minor forms of pressure or coercion.[21] If liberally construed, it seems that this doctrine proscribed the use of the ideological instrument coercively across state boundaries. However, traditional international law had the doctrine of permissible intervention as well, which supplied many justifi-

16. For a statement of "humanitarian intervention" see Hall, pp. 312–13; also Oppenheim-Lauterpacht, 1, 312; Fenwick, p. 242. About the doubtful validity of the doctrine as it is generally stated, see J. L. Brierly, *The Law of Nations* (5th ed. Oxford, Clarendon Press, 1955), p. 310.

17. Hall, p. 80.

18. J. T. Shotwell, *War as an Instrument of National Policy* (London, Constable, 1929), p. 14.

19. Oppenheim-Lauterpacht, 1, 305.

20. Brierly, p. 308.

21. See H. W. Briggs, *The Law of Nations, Cases, Documents and Notes* (2d ed. London, Stevens, 1953), p. 960. See Chap. 6 below.

able grounds for intervention, and inferentially, for transnational coercive use of the ideological instrument.

Incidental to territorial sovereignty, each state was required under traditional international law to prevent the use of its territory as a base for launching hostile activities against foreign states.[22] In particular, the state was to exercise due diligence to see that no private person fitted out expeditions from its territory to overthrow the established regime in a foreign state. However, it is at least very doubtful whether there was a duty to restrict freedom of information within its boundaries, and to take measures to prevent the flow of ideas across its boundaries, in order to safeguard the stability and security of foreign governments against the subversive influences that such ideas might have.[23]

The right of self-defense of states is a long established one. It permitted states to employ forcible means against others to stave off anticipated attack. The right was subject to two well-recognized limitations: (1) there must exist a real necessity for its exercise; and (2) the measures taken in self-defense must be proportional, within the limits dictated by necessity.[24] This principle of the proportionality of the measures taken in self-defense to the necessity was an important aspect of the right.

The principles of necessity and proportionality of the coercive measures taken against foreign states were also applicable under traditional international law to reprisals. According to the law, reprisals must not be "out of all proportion to the act which has motivated them." [25] They must be preceded by a request to the state alleged to have committed the wrongful act to redress the wrong, and failure on the part of that state to do so.[26]

When there was a state of belligerency, however, between two states, the principle of proportionality, other than in the sense of economy of military necessity, had no application. Traditional international prescriptions governing warfare were formulated by reference to two basic principles: (1) Each belligerent must be permitted to do what is militarily necessary for him. (2) He is prohibited from transgressing certain humani-

22. See Fenwick, *International Law*, p. 301.

23. See below, Chap. 5.

24. These limitations are taken as well-established since the *Caroline* Incident; J. B. Moore, *Digest of International Law*, 2 (Washington, D.C., U.S. Gov't. Printing Office, 1906), 409 (hereafter cited as Moore, *Digest*, 2), and have been reiterated in *I.M.T. Nuremberg, Trial of Major War Criminals (Judgment)*, 1, 207.

25. This was stated in the *Naulilaa* arbitration by the tribunal; see Briggs, pp. 951–53.

26. Ibid. Retortions, too, according to Julius Stone, in view of Art. 2(3) of the U.N. Charter, must not now be "excessive when judged by the conduct against which retaliation is made." See his *Legal Controls of International Conflict* (New York, Rinehart, 1954), p. 289; see also A. E. Hindmarsh, "Self-Help in Time of Peace," 26 *A.J.I.L.*, 315 (1932).

tarian considerations and causing needless destruction of human values.[27]

The policy of traditional international law toward shaping and sharing of human values in states, and toward intrastate and transnational coercive processes, may be stated thus in light of the above: It was left to the elite of each state to determine the pattern of shaping and sharing of values within that state; the pattern might be the most progressive one from the point of view of promoting human dignity, or the most unenlightened. The elite was given freedom to use coercive processes internally in whatever degree of intensity, but within the limits of human tolerance of oppression of fellow human beings. In the absence of a centralized machinery to enforce peace between nations, peace was sought amongst them on the basis of mutual abstention from coercion against each other. But, because of the lack of enforcement machinery, each state was given freedom to use coercive process against another or others to prevent, repress, or obtain redress for wrongful acts, under rubrics such as retortions, reprisals, permissible interventions, and self-defense. In applying coercion under these rubrics, however, observance of restraint was insisted upon, and the limiting of the action within the bounds of proportionality constituted an important restraint. And, again for want of machinery to enforce peace between nations, resort to a state of belligerency and mutual application of the most intensive coercion was tolerated. But even during such situations it was insisted that some restraint be observed so as to save certain basic human values and avoid needless destruction of others.

Policy Prescriptions of the U.N. Charter

The Charter of the United Nations, to which almost all the states in the world are now parties, articulates policies which mark a significant advance from the traditional policies noted above. The main purposes of the organization are set out in Article 1 of the Charter; two may be noted here: (1) to maintain international peace and security by means of effective collective measures designed to prevent or remove threats to peace, and to suppress breaches of peace or acts of aggression, and to bring about peaceful adjustment of disputes; and (2) to achieve international cooperation in promoting and encouraging respect for human rights and fundamental freedoms for all.

With a view to achieving the first objective, the Charter has obligated the members of the organization to "settle their international disputes by

27. See L. Oppenheim, *International Law—A Treatise*, Vol. 2, *War and Neutrality* (7th ed. London, 1952), 227 (hereafter cited as Oppenheim-Lauterpacht, 2); he mentions chivalry also as one of the underlying policies of the laws of war, apart from military necessity and humanity; see also McDougal and Feliciano, *Law and Minimum World Public Order*, p. 72.

peaceful means in such manner that international peace and security, and justice, are not endangered" (Art. 2[3]), and proscribed "the threat or use of force against the territorial integrity and political independence of any state, or in any other manner inconsistent with the purposes of the United Nations" by members in their international relations (Art. 2[4]). Article 2(6) has provided that the organization shall ensure that non-members act in accordance with these principles for the maintenance of international peace and security. The Charter has further provided a centralized machinery to deal with cases of threats to the maintenance of peace, threats to the peace, breaches of the peace, and acts of aggression. The Security Council is given power to deal with disputes or situations ranging from those endangering "the maintenance of international peace and security" (Art. 34), to those amounting to "threat to the peace, breach of the peace, or act of aggression" (Art. 39), and to apply measures varying from those of persuasion contemplated in Chapter 6 to measures of coercion provided for under Articles 41 and 42.[28] The General Assembly is given very extensive powers, under Articles 10, 11, and 14, to discuss questions relating to the maintenance of international peace and security and to make recommendations. Under the "Uniting for Peace Resolution" the Assembly has asserted its competence to discuss any situation involving "breaches of peace or acts of aggression" if the Security Council is unable to deal with it because of want of unanimity among the permanent members of the Council, and to make recommendations.

The Charter has not, however, proscribed all uses of force or processes of coercion in international relations. States are bound, if called upon, to participate in the preventive or enforcement measures decided upon by the Security Council. Article 51 of the Charter has left untouched "the inherent right of self-defense if an armed attack occurs against a Member of the United Nations until the Security Council has taken measures necessary to maintain international peace and security." Though it is not above controversy, it can plausibly be maintained that this article has not restricted in any way the traditional right of self-defense.[29] Furthermore,

28. See Waclaw Komarnicki, "Definition De L'Aggresseur," 75 *Hague Recueil* 21 (1949).

29. See McDougal and Feliciano, pp. 232 et seq.; L. M. Goodrich and E. Hambro, *Charter of the United Nations, Commentary and Documents* (2d ed. Boston, World Peace Foundation, 1949), pp. 104–07. C. H. M. Waldock, "The Regulation of the Use of Force by Individual States in International Law," 81 *Hague Recueil* 455, 495 (1952); and for the view that Art. 51 has cut down the traditional right of self-defense, see J.L. Kunz, "Individual and Collective Self-Defense in Article 51 of the Charter of the United Nations," 41 *A.J.I.L.* 872 (1950); Julius Stone, *Legal Controls of International Conflict*, p. 244; N. Bentwitch and A. Martin, A *Commentary on the Charter of the United Nations* (London, Macmillan, 1950), p. 107; W. E. Beckett, *The North*

subject to Article 2(3) and 2(4), in situations not endangering international peace and security and justice, it is open to a member of the United Nations to use coercive procedures "short of war" falling under such traditional rubrics as retortions and reprisals.[30]

The Charter posits not merely the policy of maintaining peace and security but also other parallel and complementary policies articulated in clauses (2) and (3) of Article 1 which run thus:

> (2) To develop friendly relations among nations based upon respect for the principle of equal rights and self-determination of peoples, and to take other appropriate measures to strengthen universal peace;
>
> (3) To achieve international cooperation in solving international problems of an economic, social, cultural, or humanitarian character, and in promoting and encouraging respect for human rights and for fundamental freedoms for all without distinction as to race, sex, language, or religion;

The parallel policies indicated by these clauses are meant to create conditions under which the goal of maintaining peace and security can be effectively realized. In deciding about the legitimacy of any type of coercion, especially the ideological, which is far less destructive than the military instrument, all these policy goals must be regarded as equally relevant and important.[31]

In line with the provisions of the Charter, our position is that all coercion which imminently threatens to deprive a state of its "territorial integrity or political independence" should be regarded as impermissible, unless it is employed in the exercise of legitimate self-defense, individual or collective, or in an authorized enforcement action. Coercions of lesser intensity may be justifiable as self-defense or legitimate measures "short of war," if in accordance with the Charter and traditional international law.

Atlantic Treaty, the Brussels Treaty and the Charter of the United Nations (London, Stevens, 1950), p. 13; A. Martin, *Collective Security, A Progress Report* (Paris, UNESCO, 1952), p. 169.

30. See Stone, *Legal Controls*, p. 287.

31. Professor Quincy Wright takes the view that the Charter gives the dignity of man a place secondary to that of maintenance of peace between nations. See his "International Law and Civil Strife," 1959 *Proc. Am. Soc. of Int'l Law*, p. 145. For contrary opinions see the remarks of Myres S. McDougal during the discussions on Quincy Wright's paper, ibid., p. 166. It seems to the present writer that, even in the atomic age, an absolute priority of maintaining peace over upholding human dignity will not be accepted by mankind. The history of the struggle for human rights, during which detriments to well-being have been most willingly suffered by people, does not encourage a belief that mankind will at any time prefer survival in indignity to extinction.

If coercion is applied with the objective of promoting such policies as self-determination, protection of minorities, and human rights, approved by the Charter, it becomes necessary to balance the policy of maintaining peace and security against the relevant complementary policy approved by the Charter and to allocate a short-term priority to one of the policies.

SITUATION

The geographical, temporal-duration, and institutionalized characteristics are relevant in a consideration of policy for the very simple reason that they affect expectations regarding the outcome of the propaganda activity.

In times of crisis intensive use of the ideological instrument must necessarily be expected, and if violence has not already broken out the outcome of its use will probably be either a catharsis of the tension or precipitation of violence; a policy choice must be preceded in such situations by a reference to the outcome expected in the particular context. This necessitates a reference to all the relevant variables involved in the context.

If violence has broken out, the policy guides to be followed are necessarily those adopted traditionally in relation to the state of belligerency. In such situations, to adopt in relation to the ideological instrument a policy stricter than the one adopted with respect to the military instrument is neither practical nor necessary.

RELATIVE CAPABILITIES

The relative capabilities of those operating the strategy and the elite target of coercion are necessarily relevant inasmuch as they affect the expectations of the outcome of the strategy. A big power's expectations of the outcome of a small power's propaganda, or the harm expected from the policies which seem likely to be adopted by the latter in view of the propaganda, will be quite different from a small power's expectations about the outcome of a big power's propaganda, or the harm from the policies which seem likely to be pursued by the big power.

STRATEGIES

Since the expectation of the outcome of strategy in a given context is dependent upon the use of the instruments of policy by the strategists in the particular context, and their combination and intensity, policy choices must necessarily be preceded by taking into account the various policy instruments being operated and the intensity of the use of each.

The techniques and tactics of ideological strategy employed by the strategists are also relevant to the choice of policy because they would help to form expectations about the response of the audience—whether the response will be limited to a change of opinions previously held, or whether overt acts will materialize causing destruction of community values. The techniques and tactics would also indicate which group will suffer deprivation, whether the opposing elite or a group assigned a scapegoat role. Where the expectation, for instance, is that there will be merely a change of opinion, the sanctioning measures can be limited to a program of information and education. On the other hand, if overt acts causing destruction of community values seem imminent, regulatory measures of a coercive character will become necessary. In between these two extreme positions there may be a variety of situations which require policy choices that seem most appropriate to the situation.

OUTCOME

In the context of the outcome affecting the values of the external elite, two policy considerations come into conflict, thus rendering policy choices exceedingly difficult. The policy of promoting enlightenment suggests that the use of the instrument should be subjected to minimum restrictive regulation. But the tendency of those adhering to the policy of maintaining peace and security in the community will be to suggest that the use of the instrument be regulated so as to avoid deprivation of values to the external elite. The reason generally stated is that the elite expecting deprivations will respond by countermeasures of violence, or measures which lead to outbreak of violence. It should be noted that rational policy choices cannot be made by confining attention exclusively to either the policy of promoting enlightenment or maintaining peace and security. If exclusive attention is given to the claims of the external elite, a stage might come when the policy of promotion of enlightenment will have to languish. An elite which claims that the process of enlightenment should be stopped in order that it may maintain itself in power does not merit community protection. The respect value of an elite cannot be protected at the cost of enlightenment which the community obtains from criticisms of the conduct of those in power, and from discussion of issues relating to public affairs. So it appears that where the two policy goals—promoting enlightenment and avoiding deprivation of the values of an external elite—cannot be pursued simultaneously, policy decisions will have to be reached by balancing the two goals.

EFFECTS

The policy we suggest in regard to the claims relating to effects is regulation of the use of the instrument, but in accordance with the two general principles stated at the outset.

The goals of policy envisaged here, to state them at a lower level of abstraction, are not only the maintenance of peace and security in the world community, or a minimum public order, but also securing optimal production and distribution of all the categories of human values, or an optimum public order. One may postulate the goal of "peace," understood more or less as absence of violence, and suggest that each state should restrain propaganda within its jurisdiction so as to avoid the incidence of violence.[32] This may result in tyrannical or authoritarian regimes demanding suppression of propaganda to insure their safety, to the detriment of enlightenment value. But the view taken here of "peace" is one expressed in terms of a comprehensive public order of human dignity and not merely a minimum public order. The experience of mankind tells us that it is difficult to maintain a minimum public order unless efforts directed toward that end are matched by those which satisfy, adequately if only partially, the demands presented by the members of the community from time to time for wider access to all values.

PROCESS OF DECISION

Our preference is for inclusive decision and as far as possible in the organized arena. Whether the use of the instrument is internal or external, if the interests of the community as a whole are affected, we favor according competence to inclusive decision. The claim to exclusive "domestic jurisdiction," in our view, should not bar community measures designed to promote a comprehensive world public order.

It is not implied thereby that we advocate free use of coercion, in the name of the community, to bring about changes in the value shaping and sharing processes within states, in order to insure optimal production and distribution of values. On the other hand, we recommend that in applying community sanctions the following two principles should be rigorously observed.[33] First, as far as possible, the sanctioning measures should be of a persuasive character and not coercive. As a countermeasure to the use of the ideological instrument—in the place of condemnation of the particular use as impermissible and application of coercive sanctions—a process of information and education that contains practically no appeal to the element of irrationality in human personality may be undertaken. Second, when coercive sanctions are to be applied, there should be strict regard to the principle of economy in the coercion involved, and wherever possible the sanction should be in the nature of an indulgence rather than a deprivation; that is to say, access to some values may be offered as an inducement to stop coercive use. In applying coercive sanctions, further, no more coercion than is strictly necessary in the particular context to protect the minimum public order and promote comprehensive public order should be employed. It should be remembered that condemnation of particular uses

32. For such an approach, see M. R. Garcia-Mora, *International Responsibility for Hostile Acts of Private Persons Against Foreign States* (The Hague, Nijhoff, 1962), p. 11.

33. McDougal, Lasswell, and Vlasic, *Law and Public Order in Space*, p. 409.

as impermissible is not an end in itself but one of the means for regulating unauthorized use of coercion to attain the preferred policy objective of a comprehensive public order.

We recommend that the sanctioning measures be shaped according to the objective sought. The first objective is necessarily *prevention,* and diplomatic, ideological, and economic strategies may be employed to forestall coercive use either internally or externally. The next objective is *deterrence,* and the above strategies may be employed to hold out the possibility of deprivations in case coercive use is resorted to. However, where the expectation is that deterrence will provoke rather than prevent resort to coercion, and will thereby increase the net use of coercion, it may not always be good policy to seek that objective. If coercion actually occurs, measures to stop such use, that is, to attain the objective of *restoration,* have to be brought into operation. Here community measures must bear a close relation to the degree of coercion that is brought into play in violation of community prescriptions. They may start with such procedures as good offices, mediation, conciliation, and adjudication; they may proceed to the use of coercion when nothing else will bring about a cessation of the unauthorized coercion. The policy necessarily implies the use of violence in very extreme and rare cases where it happens to be the only way to protect the "territorial integrity or political independence" of the target of coercion. After the objective of restoration is achieved, *rehabilitation* may be sought by undertaking a program of information to the audience involved, and by encouraging the maintenance of cordiality in the diplomatic exchanges between the parties and voluntary application of remedial measures such as apologizing for the use of abusive language.

In pursuit of the goal of *reconstruction,* one may use the diplomatic instrument to foster among the elite of the delinquent state a disposition not to resort to coercive processes, the ideological strategy to inform and educate the public about the irrational and harmful character of the symbols previously circulated, the economic instrument to reduce the tensions previously arising from economic causes and which occasioned the resort to coercion; and, if there has been an impermissible resort to military force, for a time the military instrument may be used to prevent the resurgence of militarist tendencies. If other conditions favor, the strategy of corrective measures directed against individuals may be employed.

In the contemporary world community, in which full community protection is not assured to individual states against deprivations imposed by others, the right to exclusive decision toward self-protection cannot be denied. In order to protect its internal public order, the state has necessarily to be recognized as having competence to decide whether a particular communication is lawful or unlawful. But from the world community perspective, we suggest that the right to exclusive decision should not include competence to override world community policies; it should be exercised in reasonable conformance to those policies. And in applying sanctioning measures, the state should be required to adhere to the principles of necessity and proportionality of the measures to the expected outcome, the principles which have traditionally governed responsive coercion in self-defense, and measures of coercion "short of war."

5

Trends of Decision: Claims Relating to Participation

CLAIMS RELATING TO OFFICIALS OF STATES AND NON-OFFICIALS

Under traditional international law, the doctrine of state responsibility makes a sharp differentiation between participation by officials of the state and non-officials. According to traditional doctrine, a state is responsible for all acts done by its agents.[1] Acts of officials of states done in the course of discharge of their official duties obviously give rise to state responsibility.[2] Writers are almost unanimously of the view that, by virtue of the doctrine prohibiting intervention in the internal affairs of a foreign state, the responsibility of a state will be engaged if its officials carry on revolutionary propaganda against another state.[3] A recent writer, however, has expressed doubt concerning this position.[4] Beyond the issue of responsibility, he has questioned the existence of any prescription which prohibits the officials of a state from spreading propaganda in a neighboring state hostile to that government.[5] This raises the question whether any, and if so what

1. Oppenheim-Lauterpacht, 1, 337; Hall, p. 268; Clyde Eagleton, *The Responsibility of States in International Law* (New York, New York University Press, 1928), Chap. 3; E. M. Borchard, *The Diplomatic Protection of Citizens Abroad* (New York, Banks Law Pub. Co., 1919), p. 180

2. Oppenheim-Lauterpacht, 1, 341; Hall, p. 268; as a matter of fact, in respect of unauthorized acts also there is responsibility; see Eagleton, p. 57; Borchard, pp. 185–86; Oppenheim-Lauterpacht, 1, 337, 365, says that there is vicarious responsibility in respect of such acts, similar to but more extensive than the responsibility in the case of acts of private persons not authorized by the state.

3. H. Lauterpacht, "Revolutionary Propaganda by Governments"; Whitton, "Propaganda and International Law," p. 569; V. Van Dyke, "The Responsibility of States for International Propaganda," 34 *A.J.I.L.* 58 (1940); L. Preuss, "International Responsibility for Hostile Propaganda Against Foreign States."

4. Stone, *Legal Controls of International Conflict*, p. 319.

5. See also in this connection Martin, *International Propaganda*, p. 203.

type of, propaganda is prohibited against a foreign state, a question that cannot be answered without reference to the several variables to be discussed during the course of our study. However, if the propaganda activity of the officials of a state constitutes a violation of the traditional prescription against intervention, there cannot be any doubt that, according to traditional law, such propaganda will at once engage the responsibility of that state.

Traditional prescriptions do not attribute responsibility to a state for violations of international law committed by non-officials—even its own citizens—outside its territory.[6] Even in respect of violations committed within its territory, the responsibility of a state will be engaged only if the violations have been the result of a failure on the part of the officials of the state to exercise due diligence to prevent their commission.[7] Responsibility may be attributed, however, in respect of violations committed in spite of the exercise of due diligence if the officials of the state fail to procure satisfaction for the wrong by punishing the wrongdoer or compelling him to pay compensation.[8] Traditional doctrines require that no state should permit within its territory commission of acts injurious to a foreign state.[9] In regard to propaganda activities of private individuals carried on within its territory, however, the policy prescribed by decision-makers during the nineteenth century was that the officials of that state need not adopt any measures of restraint.[10] There were recognized exceptions to this policy; if the utterances happened to be libels or incitements to assassination, the officials must adopt repressive and corrective measures.[11] But, by and large, a state was not held responsible for the propaganda activity of private individuals within its territory.

The status of the official whose utterance has given rise to state responsibility is also relevant to the manner in which the responsibility may be discharged. If the official happens to be of lower rank, traditional law permits discharge of responsibility by a disavowal of his utterance and by taking disciplinary measures against him.[12]

6. See Eagleton, p. 78.

7. Oppenheim-Lauterpacht, 1, 365; Hall, p. 268; Eagleton, p. 88; Borchard, p. 213.

8. Hall, p. 269; Oppenheim-Lauterpacht, 1, 365; Borchard, p. 213.

9. Oppenheim-Lauterpacht, 1, 291; Hall, pp. 64–65.

10. See Oppenheim-Lauterpacht, 1, 292; Lauterpacht, "Revolutionary Activities by Private Persons against Foreign States"; and the works cited in note 3 above.

11. Lauterpacht, "Revolutionary Activities by Private Persons against Foreign States."

12. For instances of lower officials making utterances hostile to a foreign government and the government of their state making amends, see E. C. Stowell, "The General Smedley D. Butler Incident," 25 *A.J.I.L.* 321 (1939); also R.I.I.A., *Survey of International Affairs*, 1949–50, pp. 383–84, describing the incident of an official of the Philippines government charging U.S. officials and politicians with corruption. The President of the Philippines apologized and disciplinary action was taken against the official.

In this connection we should note the doctrine of "local remedies," which is an important part of the whole doctrine of state responsibility. When a state is charged with responsibility by another, it is not necessary that the first state should afford redress by some action directly taken by the foreign office. If it were so required, foreign offices would have been flooded with endless correspondence over delinquencies attributed to states.[13] Further, there would not have been any means of testing the claims presented by fair judicial procedures. Hence the responsibility of the state may be discharged by appointing appropriate officials and prescribing procedures by which those officials should afford redress.

The doctrine of "local remedies" is not, however, an absolute one. Although the government of a state may insist that a foreign government or the citizens of a foreign state should first resort to local legal machinery for redress before making a complaint to the offending government directly, the latter need not under certain conditions resort to local remedies: where the machinery does not measure up to the standards set by international law, where under the prevailing conditions it is impossible to obtain a reasonable remedy from the machinery,[14] or where justice has been denied by that machinery.[15] In cases of flagrant violation of law or serious affronts to the dignity of a state, it cannot be expected that the aggrieved government will resort to local remedies for redress.[16]

If the offender is a legislator or a member of the judiciary, the government of the affected state cannot invoke the state responsibility doctrine as freely as in the case of officials of the executive. The basis for attributing responsibility to a state for the acts of its officials being authorization, factual or presumed, to do the particular act on behalf of the state,[17] it becomes necessary before charging a state with responsibility for the acts of its legislators or judges to examine the authorization they possess to do the act in question. Legislators are generally authorized only to participate in the formulation and expression collectively of the legislative will on behalf of their state. Judges are entrusted only with the administration of justice. All acts of legislators and judges which fall outside the scope of their official functions have obviously to be regarded as their private acts. In respect of such acts the responsibility of their state is on principle the same as in the case of acts of private persons.[18]

13. See Eagleton, p. 102.
14. See Eagleton, p. 103; Borchard, pp. 821–25.
15. For the concept of "denial of justice," see Fenwick, *International Law*, p. 276; Eagleton, p. 110.
16. See Eagleton, p. 82; Borchard, p. 823.
17. Oppenheim-Lauterpacht, *1*, 337, 358; Eagleton, p. 45.
18. Oppenheim-Lauterpacht, *1*, 359, says that the responsibility for acts of judicial officials done in their private life does not differ from the responsibility for such acts by private persons.

Even in respect of statements made by legislators and judges while discharging their official functions—that is to say, while participating in the deliberations of the legislature, or making judicial pronouncements—the nature of the redress the respondent state will be able to offer will be different from what is offered when the delinquent is a member of the executive. As the executive generally does not possess direct disciplinary control over these officials, the officials of the respondent state could only disavow the utterance and provide access to the complaining government to seek such remedies as are afforded under the law of the state.[19] The disavowal will indicate that the statement does not represent the policy of the government of that state. Whether the complaining government will accept the response as satisfactory will depend partly upon the latter's opinion as to whether the system of regulation provided for in the respondent state measures up to internationally accepted standards. The position is similar when the person in question happens to be the official of a municipal corporation.[20]

If the utterance comes from a diplomatic official accredited to the state against which the charge is directed, the officials of the aggrieved state have a different set of procedures to follow. They may demand the recall of the diplomatic official or dismiss him.[21] Considerations of reciprocity, however, may have a restraining influence on resort to such procedures.

If the activity in question is that of private persons or organizations, the response of the officials presented with a demand for redress might be to comply with the demand to the satisfaction of the officials of the complaining state, or to disavow the activity and direct the complaining government to pursue such remedies as are provided under the legal system of the respondent state.[22] Whether the complaining government would accept this

19. Thus in reply to the Spanish protest in 1920 about the allegedly offensive statements made by members of the House of Representatives, the U.S. reply was that the Constitution did not permit any measures to be taken by the executive or the judiciary, and only the particular House could deal with the matter. See Hackworth, *Digest*, 2, 144. In 1935, in reply to the German protest over the remarks of a New York magistrate, the U.S. government replied that it had no control over him. See 12 *U.S. Press Releases* 196 (1935).

20. See the incident over the speech of Mayor LaGuardia of New York, Hackworth, *Digest*, 2, 145.

21. See Moore, *Digest*, 4, sec. 640; Hackworth, *Digest*, 4, 472–73. In 1952, when the Soviet Union protested and demanded the recall of U.S. Ambassador Kennan, for remarks made in Berlin comparing conditions in Russia with those in Nazi Germany, the United States, while recalling him, justified Mr. Kennan's statement as a factual description of the situation in the U.S.S.R. See 27 *Dept. of State Bull.* 557 (1952).

22. Many examples of such disavowal can be cited. For instance, see the letter of Lord Hawkesbury, British Foreign Secretary, to M. Otto, French Minister, July 28, 1802, in relation to the French complaint over an article published by one Peltier, 45 *Annual Register* 660 (1803). Other examples will be found below.

response as satisfactory discharge of responsibility depends upon whether it considered the extent of control exercised over private persons in the particular context to measure up to "civilized standards" or not.

POLICY BASES OF THE PRESCRIPTIONS

The prescriptions relating to state responsibility for propaganda arrived at in the nineteenth century deserve more than superficial examination, in order that we may be able to make rational recommendations in relation to contemporary claims.

It may be stated that the nineteenth century was a century of revolutions against monarchical regimes, and quite often the leaders of unsuccessful revolutions or the leaders of overthrown regimes retired to other states for asylum and continued their political struggle from there. Revolutions always find sympathizers and opponents in other countries, and the last century was no exception. Monarchists who fled from the French Revolution and leaders of later revolutionary movements against European monarchies found asylum and supporters in England. Political refugees always found asylum in the United States, and further—the citizens of the United States being persons of different national origins—many revolutionary movements abroad found sympathetic response among sections of the American public. Speeches, writings, and other activities of political refugees and their sympathizers designed to foment trouble in their home countries brought forth protests from the governments of those countries, demanding suppression of such utterances and activities.

The officials of states to whom these claims were presented had to take into account, as against these, claims presented by the members of their respective bodies politic. The nineteenth century was also a century of the rise of democracy. There had been increasing demand for freedom of speech, freedom of the press, abolition of censorship, and adherence to the rule of law. In England, where the movement for democracy started earlier than elsewhere, censorship was abolished as early as 1695, and Fox's Libel Act, 1792, mitigated the rigors of the preexisting common law relating to libels and made the question of guilt of any accused for publishing a libel a matter to be determined by the verdict of a jury, not by the judges of the King's Courts.[23] In the United States the First Amendment passed in 1791 sought to wipe away the much hated common law of sedition.[24] Such being the trend, the governments of the United States and Britain had to give due regard to the claims of their respective peoples not to limit freedom of expression in order to satisfy the demands of foreign rulers.

23. See G. J. Patterson, *Free Speech and a Free Press* (Boston, Little, Brown, 1939), pp. 52, 75.

24. See Z. Chafee, Jr., *Free Speech in the United States* (Cambridge, Harvard University Press, 1948), p. 22.

In the nineteenth-century environment the quantum of harm that rulers of states were likely to suffer as a result of speeches and publications made in other states was not considerable, as the means of transnational communication available were such that the governments of states possessed effective control over them and could arrest the inflow of prejudicial communications at the borders if they so desired. It was during the second half of the nineteenth century that telegraphy developed.[25] And since 1855 governments have asserted and exercised the right to control telegraphic communications and to stop their transmission if they were prejudicial to the security of their states.[26] Governments indeed always possessed legal power to prohibit the importation of harmful printed materials into their territories,[27] and to control movement of persons across their boundaries.

These means of arresting transnational communications might not have been such as to give rulers watertight protection against the flow of ideas reaching their peoples from outside. But states were always conceived as units in the larger community of mankind,[28] and as a normal incident of the life of that community, communication of ideas must have been expected to go on across state boundaries in some degree or other. The rulers of no state could have gone to the absurd length of demanding that other governments should adopt measures to halt the ordinary processes of human communication across its boundaries in order that its power position should remain unaffected. On the contrary, statesmen and writers of the nineteenth century denied the existence of any such obligation on their part.

25. See G. A. Codding, Jr., *The International Telecommunications Union* (Leiden, E. J. Brill, 1952), pp. 7–9.

26. The Berlin Convention on Telegraphy, 1855, entered into by France, Belgium, and Prussia, provided that each government had a right to police and control all traffic. Officials in charge of telegraph stations in the contracting states were given the power to stop or to refuse to accept any telegram which was considered to be contrary to good morals or public security. The right to suspend the service was also recognized. See ibid., p. 18. Similar provisions are contained in the present International Telecommunications Convention, 1952, in Arts. 31 and 32.

27. In 1802, for instance, the British Foreign Secretary informed the French government that, if the latter was dissatisfied with the laws of Britain concerning the press, it could prohibit the importation of foreign newspapers into France and also the sale of such papers. See the letter of Lord Hawkesbury to Mr. Merry, Aug. 28, 1802, 45 *Annual Register* 664 (1803).

28. For instance, Vittoria in *De Indis,* sec. iii (J. B. Scott, *The Spanish Origins of International Law, Francis De Vittoria and His Law of Nations,* Washington, D.C., Carnegie Endowment, 1934, Appendix A., xxxvi), refers to human society as a whole as a "natural society and fellowship." Grotius in his *Freedom of the Seas* (Washington, D.C., Carnegie Endowment, 1916), makes reference to "the social structure of the whole human race" (p. 3), and the "universal state" of human beings (p. 2). Vattel, *The Law of Nations,* 3 (Washington, D.C., Carnegie Endowment, 1916), 5, refers to the "universal society of the human race."

For instance, in 1849, Mr. Bancroft, the Ambassador of the United States to Great Britain, wrote to the British Foreign Secretary, Viscount Palmerston, in connection with British complaints about the activities of sympathizers of Irish revolutionists in the United States, thus: [29]

> In the progress of the human race, nations profit by the experience of one another. Events in the history of America have perhaps contributed to beneficial changes in the conditions of Ireland and they may do so hereafter; but it will never be by rebellions organized at public meetings at three thousand miles distance from the scene of action.

Count Mamiani, Italian jurist and one of the leading writers of the nineteenth century on international law, declared: [30]

> In a judicial point of view all those actions of a State, which are internal, are free; and all those actions are absolutely internal, from which no other immediate effect proceeds outside than by the efficacy of their example, and by the inevitable communication of opinions and sentiments.

Let us look at the statement of Sir Henry Maine which runs in similar strain: [31] "To foreign states, the political or social doctrines which may be exemplified in it [a state], or which may spread from it, are legally immaterial." Thus, communication or diffusion of ideas from the territory of a state to other states, by force of example, or by inevitable communication of opinions and sentiments or, we may add, any process of communication incidental to community life, was not to be regarded as a ground of complaint requiring the officials of the former to adopt preventive measures. The policy of the Holy Alliance Powers during the early part of the nineteenth century, of intervention in the affairs of other states with a view to preventing the spread of revolutionary contagion, was stoutly opposed by the British government, and nonintervention became the accepted policy prescription applicable to such cases.[32]

In addition to environmental conditions, one has to take into account the general attitude adopted by the governments of the United States and Great Britain toward movements for democracy abroad, in order to appreciate properly the policy adopted by them in relation to the above men-

29. Mr. Bancroft to Viscount Palmerston, November 10, 1848, H. R. Exec. Doc. No. 19, 30th Cong., 2d Sess. (1849), p. 4.

30. Count Mamiani, *The Right of Nations* (1859), xx, cited in Sir E. Creasy, *First Platform of International Law* (London, 1876), p. 295.

31. Sir Henry Maine, *International Law* (London, John Murray, 1888), p. 61.

32. See Creasy, pp. 293–95; also John Westlake, *Collected Papers* (L. Oppenheim, ed., Cambridge, Cambridge University Press, 1914), pp. 125–26.

tioned claims. Most often the British government evinced sympathy for democratic movements in European countries, and the government of the United States, too, had similar feelings for such movements abroad. The revolutionary experience of these two countries was indeed responsible for this attitude. When they were called upon to prescribe policy with reference to the above claims, their decisions tended toward promoting freedom of expression within their states, for without such freedom democracy would not thrive. They also tended to give protection to political refugees and subject them to minimum restrictions. At the same time they were prepared to adopt measures designed to protect the elites of foreign states to a certain extent, with a view to maintaining peaceful relations with those countries. To what extent they were prepared to accord that protection will become apparent from the following.

In 1802, the Napoleonic French government demanded that the British government should adopt measures to prevent the appearance in the British press of publications which were seditious to the former; and that they should ask the French refugees, who were, it was alleged, fomenting insurrection in France, to quit British territory.[33] The response of the British government was that they would not restrict the freedom of the press within their country to satisfy the French demand; nor would they ask the refugees to quit unless there was clear proof that the refugees took advantage of their situation in England to incite insurrection in France by such acts as distributing seditious pamphlets in the French coastal areas.[34] In 1851–52, France, Prussia, Austria, Russia, and The Two Sicilies complained to England about the presence of political refugees from those countries in England, who were issuing inflammatory proclamations inciting the people in their home countries to rebellion.[35] The British Foreign Secretary, Earl Granville, while maintaining the right to grant political asylum, assured that his government would adopt measures to prevent the refugees from committing hostile acts against states which were at peace with England.[36] In 1853, when the question of political refugees was raised in the British Parliament, the Foreign Secretary, Viscount Palmerston, declared that the refugees were bound, out of regard for international law as well as the law of England, to abstain from entering into any intrigues, or from pursuing any course intended for the purpose of disturbing the internal tranquility of a foreign country. In the same year the ques-

33. See the letter of M. Otto, Minister of France, to the British Foreign Secretary, Lord Hawkesbury, Aug. 17, 1802, 45 *Annual Register* 661 (1803).

34. See the reply of Lord Hawkesbury, Aug. 28, 1802, ibid., p. 664.

35. See *British and Foreign State Papers, 1852–53*, pp. 408–19, 424–25.

36. See letter from Earl Granville to Her Majesty's Ministers at Vienna and St. Petersburg and Her Majesty's Chargé d'Affaires at Paris and Frankfurt, Jan. 13, 1852, ibid., p. 421. The reply was accepted by the governments concerned with satisfaction. See ibid., pp. 414–38 passim.

tion of political refugees was debated in the House of Lords,[37] and the proceedings deserve detailed examination because of the interesting light they throw on the question.

During the debate a general consensus was expressed that the common law, as it stood then, was adequate to fulfill the international obligations of Britain toward other countries. Lord Lyndhurst, with whose statements of law the other Lords, including the Lord Chancellor, expressed complete agreement, stated the common law position thus:

> If a number of British subjects were to combine and conspire together to excite revolt among the inhabitants of a friendly state . . . and these persons in pursuance of that conspiracy were to issue manifestoes and proclamations for the purpose of carrying that object into effect; and above all, if they were to subscribe money for the purpose of purchase of arms to give effect to that enterprise. . . . such persons would be guilty of misdemeanor.[38]

He further declared: "endeavoring to excite revolt among the subjects of a neighboring state is an offense against the law of nations." [39] But Lord Lyndhurst himself and other speakers were careful to point out the difficulties involved in proving a charge of conspiracy before a court of law. It was pointed out, for instance, that a conviction could not be based on the mere showing that some pamphlets were distributed in a foreign country and the contents of those pamphlets purported to indicate that they were issued from England by a person present there.[40] What evidence would suffice to establish the conspiracy was a matter to be determined by the courts themselves.

The policy prescribed by the British government may be summed up thus: there was no obligation to restrict the freedom of expression in England so as to prevent the publication of anything which a foreign govern-

37. See *Parl. Deb.* (Hansard, 3d ser.), *124* (1853), cols. 805, and 1046 et seq. for the debate on the question.

38. Ibid., col. 1046; however, doubt has been expressed about the accuracy of the proposition of law stated by Lord Lyndhurst. See H. Lauterpacht, "Revolutionary Activities of Private Persons Against Foreign States," n. 73; letter of Mr. Fish, Secretary of State of the United States to Admiral Polo de Bernabe, Ambassador of Spain to the United States, dated April 8, 1874, *For. Rel. of U.S. 1875, 2* (1876), 1178, 1192. Mr. Fish stated, "In view of events which have taken place since that speech was delivered, the undersigned might, were it necessary, feel disposed to doubt whether Lord Lyndhurst correctly interpreted English law, as understood by its administrators." But W. Forsyth, *Cases and Opinions on Constitutional Law* (London, 1869), p. 236, cites the statement of Lyndhurst as authoritative.

39. His authority was "no writer on the law of nations cited otherwise."

40. Apart from Lord Lyndhurst, Lord Brougham also spoke about the difficulties involved in proving the charge of conspiracy; see *Parl. Deb.* (3d ser.), *124*, col. 1051 et seq., for the speech of Lord Brougham.

ment might consider to be offensive, but there was an obligation to prevent the use of its territory as a base of preparation for acts of war against other states,[41] or for planning, preparing, and executing violent revolts against established governments in those states.[42] There was no obligation to interfere with the activities of private individuals unless there was a clear indication that such activities were designed to provoke armed rebellion in a foreign country. In 1802 it was tacitly conceded that the use of the territory as a base for preparation, issuance, and distribution of pamphlets, etc., in a foreign country to provoke insurrection there would give rise to an obligation to adopt measures of repression. During the debate in the Lords in 1853, such activity was termed criminal if committed by a combination of persons. But utterances made in England, whose connection with any plan to provoke armed rebellion abroad was not clearly established, even though intrinsically the utterances were capable of producing disaffection against the established government in a foreign country, need not be penalized.

Further, the British government undertook to take only *punitive* measures against persons who might engage in activities designed for violent overthrow of a foreign government, if such activities should come to light and be proved to the satisfaction of courts. But there was no mention as to what extent they would adopt *preventive* measures to stop all efforts directed from their territory to influence the people of another state by publications, etc., with a view to promoting violent revolution in that state. It would have required stupendous efforts on the part of any government to see that nobody sneaked out of its territory with a bundle of pamphlets to be distributed in a foreign country, and the duty of due diligence would have not called for the exercise of such surveillance.

The policy adopted by the United States was similar, differing only in the standard by which the obligations were determined. It was to the neutrality laws of the United States that the decision-makers made reference. This circumstance is quite explicable. It is a matter of common knowledge that the United States gave a new turn to the law regulating the relations between neutral states and belligerents by virtue of the policy adopted in 1792 in connection with the European war. The United States then assumed duties as a neutral state which were more onerous than those required by the prescriptions existing at that time.[43] To implement the policy Congress enacted legislation in 1794, and subsequently from time to time.[44] The neutrality legislation prohibited the setting on foot, providing,

41. This was admitted in 1852–53; see citation in note 36.

42. This was implicit in Lord Hawkesbury's letter to Mr. Merry, cited in note 27, the statements made during the parliamentary debate, and the statement of Viscount Palmerston, cited in note 37.

43. See Hall, p. 707.

44. For the text of the laws as they stand now, see 18 *U.S.C.A.* sec. 960 (1948).

preparing the means for, furnishing money for, or taking part in any military or naval expedition or enterprise, from the territory of the United States against any state at peace with her. The obligations due to foreign states in preventing injurious acts by private individuals were assimilated by the Department of State to the position laid down by the neutrality statutes. Even the governments of other states generally invoked the neutrality statutes as the yardstick of international obligations of the United States.[45]

The policy adopted by the Department of State, in substance, was that the United States would always enforce its neutrality statutes with due diligence,[46] and would take measures to prevent the "natural consummation" of any revolutionary activities directed against a foreign state, either in actual interference by force or attempt to interfere by force in the affairs of that state.[47] But the Department of State consistently refused to restrict freedom of expression of opinions and sentiments in the United States, however hostile they might be to foreign governments.[48]

The European countries adopted a policy which may appear to be more stringent than the policy of Britain and the United States. The penal laws adopted at an early date in most European states provided for the punishment of activities of private persons detrimental to foreign governments. Thus in 1823, Switzerland adopted a decree by which the cantons were di-

45. For instance, see the letter of the Mexican Ambassador to the United States to the Secretary of State, Jan. 19, 1911, *For. Rel. of U.S., 1911*, p. 397; Mr. Valera Ambassador of Spain to U.S. to the Secretary of State, July 21, 1885, *For. Rel. of U.S., 1885*, p. 776.

46. See Mr. Bayard, Secretary of State, to Mr. Valera, July 31, 1885, *For. Rel. of U.S., 1885*, p. 776; Mr. Knox to Mr. Barra, June 7, 1911, *For. Rel. of U.S., 1911*, p. 393.

47. See the opinion of the Attorney-General of the U.S. given in relation to the complaints of the British government concerning the activities of the sympathizers with the Irish revolutionaries: "The organization, in one country or state, of combinations to aid or abet rebellion in another, or in any other way to act on its political institutions, is undoubtedly a violation of nationality and comity, and an act of wrongful interference in the affairs of other people." The Attorney-General mentions that there were no laws in the United States to punish such conspiracies, and further states, "We do not punish such proceedings until the spirit of interference which induces them reaches its natural consummation, that of attempts to interfere in the affairs of foreign countries by force." *Opinions of the Att. Gen. of the U.S.*, 8 (1856), 216.

48. See Mr. Seward to Mr. Burnley, March 20, 1865, *For. Rel. of U.S., 1866–67*, Part II, p. 103; Mr. Seward to Mr. Adams, March 10, 1886, *For. Rel. of U.S., 1866–67*, Part I, p. 193; F. Wharton, *Digest of International Law*, 1 (2d ed. Washington, D.C., U.S. Gov't Printing Office, 1887), 265–66, for the stand taken by Mr. Frelinghuysen, Secretary of State, in connection with British complaints concerning the activities of Irish revolutionists; and the references cited in note 46. Mr. Knox told the Mexican Ambassador in 1911 that the carrying on "of mere propaganda either by writing or speaking does not constitute an offense against the law of nations," nor under the law of the United States; Mr. Knox to Mr. Barra, June 7, 1911, cited in note 46.

rected to expel political refugees who might follow a course of conduct dangerous to the government of any friendly state, or its peace and internal tranquility.[49] The French and Italian penal laws provided for the punishment of acts of private individuals which might expose their respective states to war or reprisals.[50] The laws of Spain and Norway provided for the punishment of acts endangering the external peace of their respective countries and acts which amounted to violation of the law of nations.[51] The German and Austrian criminal codes provided for the punishment of treasonable acts against foreign governments on a reciprocal basis.[52] The causes which led to the adoption of such legislation were the pressure exerted by the Holy Alliance Powers in the earlier part of the nineteenth century,[53] the anxiety of the governments of weaker states to avoid external troubles, and the policy of autocratic governments of suppressing any form of revolutionary activity against any foreign government on a basis of reciprocity and mutual insurance of their respective internal power positions.[54]

The following facts, however, deserve notice. First, the laws of the European states did not specifically prohibit propaganda activity directed against foreign governments but were couched so broadly that even expressions of opinion offensive to foreign governments could be caught within their purview. They were flexible but compared well in that respect with the elastic common law doctrine of conspiracy. Additionally, in those countries where democracy succeeded, governments were averse to penalizing private individuals for utterances directed against foreign states.[55]

49. See E. Reale, "Droit D'Asile," 63 *Hague Recueil* 472, 549 (1938); Van Dyke, p. 66.

50. Lauterpacht, "Revolutionary Activities of Private Persons Against Foreign States," pp. 118–19; Arts. 84 and 85 of the French Criminal Code, as they stood before amendment in 1939, provided that if a person should by his hostile acts against a foreign state expose the state to a declaration of war or reprisals, he would be liable to be banished. After amendment in 1939, Art. 83 provides that whoever in time of war or peace should injure the external safety of the state would be liable to be punished.

51. In Spain and Norway, acts endangering the external peace or acts amounting to a violation of the law of nations are punishable; see Terrou and Solal, *Press, Film and Radio*, p. 297.

52. Art. 102 of German Penal Code. This provision was repealed by the Allied Control Council Law No. 11, Jan. 30, 1946. The relevant provision in the Austrian law is Art. 66 of the Austrian Penal Code.

53. See Reale, p. 548.

54. See Lauterpacht, "Revolutionary Activities of Private Persons Against Foreign States," p. 112; Harvard Research on "Jurisdiction with Respect to Crime," 29 *A.J.I.L.* Supp. 443, 552 (1935).

55. Lauterpacht, ibid., p. 118, says that in France the provisions in the Penal Code referred to above in note 50 remained practically a dead letter. There was only one prosecution under them and no convictions at all. In Switzerland, the relevant penal provisions have not been invoked since 1888. Ibid., p. 124.

We are now in a position to appreciate better the policy prescribed by nineteenth-century decision-makers, which is generally summed up in the formula that a state is not responsible for the propaganda activities of private persons. It did not imply that private persons were entitled to libel foreign rulers with impunity.[56] When the utterances formed part of a strategy of transnational coercion, traditional prescriptions required the state at least to prevent the culmination of the activity in the form of an attack of violence on the foreign state. It may be noted that the means by which private persons within any state might attempt to attack the power position of the elite in another are the ideological, economic, or military instrument, or any combination of them. We may confine our attention here to the ideological and military instruments as it was with them that the incidents we have discussed were connected. If an elite expected a military attack by private persons in another state, it would necessarily adopt measures of self-defense, which under the traditional doctrines could extend up to preventive military attack. With a view to avoiding the outbreak of violence, traditional law prescribed that the officials of every state should exercise due diligence to prevent the launching of any military attack against other states from its territory.

In a given situation, the activity of private persons within a state might consist of the use of the ideological instrument only; but such use might in fact be preparation for using the military instrument against the elite in another state. That is to say, the private persons might be using the instrument to win over the people in the former and/or the latter state to cooperate actively in the use of violence. That their activity was designed to promote a violent attack might become manifest at a very late stage in the process or at an early stage. The expectation created by their activity at any particular time might, therefore, vary from anticipation of a violent attack against the target elite, to an expectation of no violence at all. But mere expression of opinions and sentiments by private persons within a state, at any time, might not necessarily create an expectation that its proximate outcome would be the initiation of an armed attack from the territory of that state. The nineteenth-century decision-makers, who were desirous of

56. In the letter of Lord Hawkesbury, cited in note 34, it was stated that, while the English law did not permit previous censorship of publications in the press, there was a judiciary in England, independent of the executive, invested with authority to take cognizance "of publications defamatory of those in whose hands the administration of foreign governments is placed," pointing out thereby that if the French government so wished it could institute proceedings against the libelers, including criminal proceedings. Lauterpacht, in "Revolutionary Activities of Private Persons Against Foreign States," pp. 114–15, states that in the course of time the courts refused to recognize statements reviling foreign sovereigns as seditious libels (that is, those affecting the security of one's own state). But, it should be noted that they have always been recognized as libels (affecting reputation).

promoting the enlightenment value as well as regulating transnational coercion, prescribed that—while it was necessary for the officials of a state to prevent the use of its territory as a base for attack of violence against another—it was not necessary to restrict the expression of opinions and sentiments within the first state.

The expectation created by the use of the ideological instrument in a given case might be that it would influence the masses of people in another state to attempt to overthrow the established government by violence. But in the nineteenth century, considering the means of communication available and the extent of control enjoyed by governments over them, that expectation was not likely to be very high. There was certainly little expectation that utterances made within one state would influence the people in another to a substantially higher degree than would ideas that reached them in the normal process of world community life. The expectation should not have been such as would have called for an abridgment of freedom of expression in the first state. Nor would it have called for punishing persons as criminals, contrary to all considerations of human dignity, for merely expressing their feelings and sentiments about peoples and rulers of other countries.[57]

The internal conditions of a state might be such that an exposure of its people to the flow of ideas from outside as an incident of world community life could cause the overthrow of the elite in power. In such situations the expression of opinions and sentiments in another state might indirectly encourage the people in the former to rebel.[58] But world community policy never prescribed that governments should mutually assist each other to maintain power in their respective states against the will of their respective peoples.[59] From this angle, too, the nineteenth-century prescription derived its policy justification.

Let us go back to the situations where the activity of private persons in a state created an expectation that its outcome would be violence against an external elite. And let us look at a situation when the expectation created was of a certain degree, not very high. In such a situation, the elite threatened would necessarily invoke the prescription that no state should allow its territory to be used as a base for acts of violence against another and

57. Mr. Bayard, Secretary of State of the U.S., stated in the letter cited in note 46, "The sympathies of masses of men may be mistakenly bestowed upon unworthy objects, but error of this character is not in itself a crime amenable to the punitive arm of justice."

58. That utterances made in one country might indirectly encourage the people in another to revolt was impliedly admitted by President Cleveland in his fourth annual message (in 1896): "Many Cubans reside in this country, and indirectly promote the insurrection through the press, by public meetings." See J. D. Richardson, *Messages and Papers of the Presidents, 14* (1897), 6146, 6148.

59. See Westlake, *Collected Papers,* p. 124.

demand that the officials of the former state should adopt repressive and corrective measures. To meet such situations, the governments, especially of the European states, armed themselves with laws which could be applied with considerable elasticity in a manner that suited their perspectives. In particular, it was possible for them to vary their decisions suitably to the expectations of the external danger to which the state might be exposed if they did not adopt repressive and corrective measures, their attitude toward the external elite, and their desire to leave the freedom of expression untouched.

In certain circumstances, the activity of private persons might convey the impression to an external elite that the activity had the backing of the officials of the state in which it was being carried on. According to the traditional doctrines, the responsibility of a state would arise if the activity were authorized by the government of the state. In many instances in the past, when the officials of states affected by the propaganda activity of private persons complained, the officials of the state to whom the complaint was made were quick to dissociate themselves from such activity.[60]

An important feature of the pattern of regulation which has come down from the nineteenth century, it will be noticed, is its flexibility. The regulation could be varied according to the status of the participant in the state to which he belonged or within the territory of which he engaged in the activity, and the expectation created thereby regarding the policy likely to be pursued by the government of that state or the outcome of the activity. Participation by officials will most likely create an expectation that the activity accords with the total policy of the government of that state, and the expectation will vary according to the position of the participant in the official hierarchy. It was prescribed that the state was responsible for participation by its officials, and a flexible procedure was provided for discharging that responsibility, which could be varied with the status of the official in question. On the other hand, participation by private persons may not necessarily create an expectation that the activity either represents the policy of the government of the state to which they belong, or within the territory of which they engage in such activity; and therefore, it was prescribed that a state was not responsible for the activity of its private citizens and aliens resident within its territory. If the activity is instigated or encouraged by the officials of the state, and therefore reflects the policy of the government of that state, the state is responsible. Activity of private persons may not have been so instigated or encouraged, but may create an expectation that its outcome will be coercion against another state. The pattern of regulation provided for the responsibility of the state within whose territory the activity was being carried on, and for a variation of the

60. See, for instance, the letter of Mr. Hawkesbury to Mr. Merry cited in note 34; the letter of Earl Grenville cited in note 36; Wharton, *Digest*, 1, 265–66.

responsibility according to the degree of coercion expected as the outcome of the activity.

Recent Trends

From about 1930, claims have been put forward that, as the use of violence as a means of aggression has been proscribed by the League Covenant, the Kellogg Pact, and the United Nations Charter, propaganda by which public opinion is aroused in favor of the use of violence against a state, or which provokes the outbreak of violence, should be deemed impermissible, and that states should assume responsibility to restrain such propaganda. These claims were advanced before World War II mainly by the states which were among the "consumers" of security,[61] and in the post-World War II years by the governments of communist states which had to cope with the propaganda addressed to their peoples. States with high internal tensions have also been among those putting forward such claims.[62] With a view to gaining acceptance of these claims, governments have suggested the adoption of treaty prescriptions, defining the duty of governments to proscribe within their respective jurisdictions certain types of propaganda, irrespective of who the participant might be. What types of propaganda were to be proscribed, whether the prescriptions proposed and the legal formulas suggested merited acceptance, and other allied issues will be discussed at a later stage. Here we will be concerned with the proposals only insofar as they sought to prohibit even private persons from engaging in certain types of propaganda activity and to create state responsibility to secure the enforcement of the prohibition.

The claim that states should restrain the propaganda activities of private persons is based on another ground as well. As it is possible with the aid of modern means of mass communication to produce increased effects on audiences, the traditional community prescriptions should be modified to

61. The expression is used by A. Zimmern in *The League of Nations and the Rule of Law 1918–1935* (2d ed. London, Macmillan, 1939), p. 332. During the pre-World War II years they included France, Belgium, and Central and Eastern European countries. It is interesting to note that the government of Poland was chief among the sponsors of international treaties for regulation of propaganda.

62. For instance, it was the Indian delegation that took a leading role in the U.N. Conference on the Freedom of Information, Geneva, 1948, to sponsor an amendment, generally referred to as the "Indian Amendment," to the draft Convention on Freedom of Information adopted by the conference, which permitted the states to adopt measures to prevent "systematic diffusion of deliberately false or distorted reports which undermine friendly relations between peoples or states." The fact that India was then facing the Hindu-Moslem troubles internally, which constantly threatened also to embroil her with Pakistan, accounts for the enthusiasm of the Indian delegation in this respect. One may also note that some of the South American countries that are constantly afflicted with internecine troubles have been among the proponents of international treaty regulation of propaganda.

prevent the use of the media in such a manner as produces harmful results, in particular, bad relations between states. Nearly thirty years ago, Dr. Raestad, as the President of the Intergovernmental Conference for the Adoption of the Convention Concerning the Use of Broadcasting in the Cause of Peace gave expression to the claim thus:

> Political broadcasting has enormous potentialities as a means of fomenting international discord. Broadcasts have no material substance, and therefore cannot be stopped at frontiers; they can be directed towards any point in space; the political effects may be extensive and immediate; but they are not easy to foresee or control or canalize at need. The underlying ideas of the draft convention are somewhat similar to those that induce Governments to renounce the use of certain means of destruction, which, though indubitably effective, cannot be limited in their action to the real objective.[63]

In 1954, at the Tenth Inter-American Conference at Caracas, the representatives of many American states urged that, as radio broadcasts could attain their objective across state boundaries as effectively as if they were disseminated within the target state, it was necessary that states be obligated to prevent transmission from their territories of broadcasts inciting the people of other states to resort to force against their governments.[64]

The objection to the claims for restraining the propaganda activities of private persons has come from the liberal democracies, and in particular from the United States. The stand taken by the United States has been that, in an attempt to avoid possible harmful effects of propaganda activities of private persons, freedom of expression should not be destroyed. Conforming to this principle the United States has consistently refused to accept any obligation or treaty proposal which was likely to affect the freedom.[65]

63. Cited in J. D. Tomlinson, *The International Control of Radio Communications* (Ann Arbor, Mich., Edwards Bros., 1945), p. 229.

64. The Conference adopted a Protocol to the Convention on Duties and Rights of States in the Event of Civil Strife, Havana, 1928, for the text of which see 48 *A.J.I.L.* Supp. 127 (1954). Also see C. G. Fenwick, "Proposed Control over the Radio as an Inter-American Duty in Cases of Civil Strife," 48 *A.J.I.L.* 289 (1954).

65. Thus, at the Inter-American Conference for the Maintenance of Peace, Buenos Aires, 1936, the U.S. abstained from voting on a resolution which recommended to the North and Central American States that a convention similar to the South American Regional Agreement on Radio Communications, Buenos Aires, 1935, should be entered into by them. At the U.N. Conference on the Freedom of Information, the United States stood as the chief opponent of the "Indian Amendment." At the Inter-American Conference, Caracas, 1954, the United States opposed signing an additional protocol to the Convention on the Duties and Rights of the States in the Event of Civil Strife, Havana, 1928, which sought to obligate the signatories to prevent the dissemination of certain types of broadcasts from their territories. See Fenwick, ibid.

The stand taken by the United States at the Caracas Conference in 1954 deserves closer examination. It was stated that the policy underlying the proposal was a desirable one for the American governments to adopt, but it was not desirable to give effect to the policy by means of a treaty prescription.

> An attempt to fix this general policy, however, into specific international treaty obligations and thus translate it from the area of policy into the regime of law would, in the view of the government of the United States, be fraught with dangers to the freedom of speech, sacred in this Hemisphere and to the democratic countries everywhere.[66]

The opposition of the United States was thus more against a modification of the nineteenth-century prescription by a treaty than to the policy itself.

The claim that states should assume responsibility for restraining the propaganda activity of non-officials has received recognition only in two multilateral conventions so far. One of them is the Broadcasting Convention of 1936 referred to above. The convention prescribed that the governments of contracting states should prevent the transmission of certain types of broadcasts from their territories, such as incitements to war, false and distorted statements which embitter relations between states, and incitements to acts incompatible with the internal security of other states. The provisions of the convention are vague and the convention remained practically a dead letter.[67] The other convention is the South American Regional Agreement on Radio Communications (Revised), Rio de Janeiro, 1937.[68] It obligated the contracting states to ensure that no broadcasts of news and comments which might disturb the good relations between the contracting states, offend the national sentiments of their peoples, or of ideas which might threaten the sovereignty and integrity of those states, were transmitted from their respective territories.

Bilateral treaties which obligated the parties to restrain the propaganda activities of private persons have been rare.[69] On the other hand, the

66. Ibid.

67. See the remarks of Tomlinson, p. 233; T. Grandin, *The Political Use of the Radio*, Geneva Studies, *10*, No. 3 (1939), 93.

68. See Hudson, *International Legislation*, 7, 47.

69. One can mention as a direct example of such a treaty the Indo-Pakistan Agreement of 1948. The text of the Agreement can be found in Economic and Social Council, Commission on Human Rights, Sub-Commission on Freedom of Information and the Press, Memorandum of Secretary-General (U.N. Doc. E/CN.H/Sub.1/105) (1950). A few others—as, for example, between Egypt and Yemen, 1945 (*U.N.T.S.*, *10*, 1947, 118), between Greece and Turkey, 1938 (*L.N.T.S.*, *190*, 1938, 27)—phrase the obligations to restrain certain types of activities of private persons so broadly that they can be interpreted to include propaganda activity.

Thirteenth General Assembly of the League of Nations opposed the introduction of any international regulation which might encourage governments of states to impose restrictions on the freedom of the press.[70] At the United Nations Conference on the Freedom of Information, Geneva, 1948, a large number of the delegations opposed the introduction of any form of international regulation which involved governmental control of propaganda. Furthermore, Article 2(j) of the draft Convention on the Freedom of Information, proposed by the Indian delegation, which permitted (not obligated) the parties to restrict freedom of information with a view to preventing "the systematic diffusion of deliberately false or distorted reports which undermine friendly relations between peoples of States," turned out to be the most controversial of the provisions of the draft.[71]

The professed objectives sought by those who suggested the treaties were avoidance of the outbreak of violence and better means of regulation of relations between states in the contemporary environment of highly developed means of mass communication. If the methods suggested to regulate the activity of non-officials had been such as would have afforded the states security against violence, without imperiling the enlightenment value, there would perhaps have been better response from the governments. The treaties proposed, however, did not go beyond seeking to obligate states to prohibit certain types of utterances, which, in general, have a tendency to produce pro-war public opinion, hatred against other states, or hatred among a people against its own elite. Such treaty prescriptions would not have added substantially to the arrangements for security which were already in existence. During the days of the League, they did not promise to overcome to any considerable degree the shortcomings of the collective security system of the League. If accepted now they are not likely to strengthen the United Nations security system.

If the legal policy objective is the regulation of transnational coercive processes, and toward that end the regulation of the activity of private persons consisting of the use of the ideological instrument, any legal formulas suggested under the proposed treaties should have been such as would have permitted the decision-makers to examine the activity in its total context, and shape the policy suitably to attain the policy objectives. That is, they should have been such as would have permitted the decision-makers to take cognizance of the objectives the participants might be seeking in any given situation, the audiences addressed by them, the techniques and tac-

70. See the Report of Sir Cecil Chelwood, Rapporteur of the 6th Committee of the League General Assembly, 13th Sess. (*L.O.N.* Pub. IX. Disarmament, 1935. IX.4, 2, 392), adopted by the Assembly on October 11, 1932.

71. As for the opposition of the United States, see the *Report of the Delegation of the United States to the Secretary of State,* Dept. of State Pub. 3150 (1948).

tics employed, and the expectations created about the outcome and effects of the activity. Most of the proposals put forward were, on the other hand, such that if adopted they would have limited the range of facts which the decision-makers could have taken into account in shaping policy to the utterances and their general tendency alone. We have noted that the traditional prescriptions provided for an elastic pattern of regulation which permitted officials of states to take into account a wide range of facts attending the activity of private persons and to prescribe a policy to fit the expectations of the state from which the activity emanated and the outcome of the activity. The suggested treaty prescriptions threatened to destroy that flexibility.

The vague character of the suggested treaty obligations, no doubt, promised to leave largely untouched the liberty of the governments of states to shape policies, and thus offered encouragement to accept them. This explains why so many states became parties to the Broadcasting Convention of 1936.[72] But vague treaty obligations presented also the threat that they might be used by stronger states to put pressure on weaker ones to suppress even legitimate expressions of opinion within the latter's jurisdictions. Also a state might use the treaty obligations to charge its opponent with treaty violations and thus make gains in ideological strategy.

In the absence of a treaty, the tendency on the part of governments has been to deny responsibility for the propaganda activity of private persons. Thus, in 1934, when Austria complained of anti-Austrian propaganda coming from Germany, Hitler, who had aggressive designs against Austria, replied that the propaganda was being carried on by political refugees and that such activity should not occasion complaint by anybody.[73] In 1951, Czechoslovakia protested to the United States about broadcasts made from the "Radio Free Europe" stations in the United States occupied zone of West Germany.[74] The Czech government alleged that the broadcasts contained incitements against their government and directions to commit espionage and crime. The United States denied that the broadcasts contained any incitement to crime or espionage, and further maintained that

72. As many as 23 states became parties to it by 1941. See Hudson, *International Legislation,* 7, 409. The U.N. General Assembly by Resolution 841 (IX) of 17 December 1954 decided to request the parties to the convention to signify whether they wished to transfer to the United Nations the functions performed by the League of Nations. Of the 25 states parties to the Convention in 1960, 15 agreed to the transfer. Those that had not signified their consent included Australia, France, New Zealand, and the United Kingdom. Neither the U.S.S.R. nor the United States is a party to the Convention. See *Eek's Report,* para. 22.

73. See R.I.I.A., *Documents on International Relations, 1934,* p. 324.

74. See 25 *Dept. of State Bull.* 12 (1951), for the Czech protest and the reply of the United States.

the organization was a private one, and that international law did not require the imposition of censorship on broadcasts transmitted from any country. The Czech government contended that international law required that states should restrain individuals living within their territories from endangering the safety of other states, and that the Convention Concerning the Use of Broadcasting in the Cause of Peace, Geneva, 1936, prescribed the general duty of the governments of states to prevent transmission from their respective territories of broadcasts which were harmful to foreign states. The reply of the United States to these contentions was that the Czech government overlooked the principle of freedom of information. The United States took the same stand when other communist governments of Eastern Europe raised similar complaints in respect of the activities of refugee organizations operating in West Germany.[75] In the 1920s the Soviet Union had denied responsibility for the publications of its Communist party and of the Third International.[76]

But in these instances, it should be noted, attention was not clearly focused on the various elements of the coercive process involved, its expected outcome and effects, and on the issue whether there was justification for the use of the process.

Garcia-Mora, after a review of several international conventions, maintained that "It may be said to be a principle emerging from the international conventions here reviewed that a state's tolerance of private revolutionary activities and hostile propaganda against foreign nations is not only illegal under modern international law but it is also a disservice to the cause of international peace and security." [77] On a first look at the conventions [78] this conclusion may seem justifiable, but a closer examination might indicate what has escaped attention. It may be noted that a subversive movement organized by private persons in a state and directed against another will pass through several stages before it attains success, beginning with the recruitment of the middle rank leaders at one end and ending with the use or threat of violence.[79] At some intermediate stage in this

75. See the protest of Hungary over leaflet drops by means of plastic balloons released from West Germany, and the reply of the United States, 32 *Dept. of State Bull.* 14 (1935); also the protest of the Soviet officer in charge of E. Germany, Gen. Chuikov, to the United States, the United Kingdom, and France, over the activities of organizations formed in West Germany by refugees, which, it was alleged, were subversive of the East German government and consisted of spreading terrorizing propaganda and propaganda inciting sabotage, and the reply of the United States, 27 *Dept. of State Bull.* 861–63 (1952).

76. See notes 84 and 88 below.

77. See his "International Responsibility for Hostile Acts of Private Persons," p. 108.

78. These conventions are referred to in notes 88 to 90, 92 to 94, and 97.

79. See Blackstock, *The Strategy of Subversion*, pp. 25–80.

process propaganda appears and may grow in intensity. Traditional prescriptions required the state to exercise due diligence to prevent a violent attack on the foreign state, which would call for active steps from the time when an attack is expected to be reasonably imminent. If it is suggested that the steps be taken at an earlier stage, then that stage should be described more fully. But to state in one breath that there should be responsibility for revolutionary activities as well as hostile propaganda is not a meaningful policy recommendation. We may assume neither that the author intended that freedom of speech or association should be interfered with at a stage when very little harm could be expected to the other state, nor that the treaties cited contemplated it.

Whitton and Larson, after an extensive study, reached the conclusion that the state is responsible for the activities of private persons if they assume the form of a hostile expedition against a foreign state, incitement to assassination, and defamation of diplomats. Further, the authors consider that the better view is that a state is under a duty to see that its territory is not used as a base for transmission by radio of war-mongering, subversive, and defamatory propaganda.[80] An examination of the authors' conclusions takes one to an inquiry into what constitutes impermissible war-mongering propaganda, etc.[81] It is, however, submitted that, according to the doctrines of state responsibility, if a particular activity is prohibited by community prescriptions, the state becomes responsible for exercising due diligence to prevent its commission within its territory by private persons, and to take appropriate remedial measures in case the prescriptions are violated in spite of the exercise of such diligence.

It may be observed in passing that the major trend in the process of decision-making has so far been to distinguish the participants as officials and non-officials, and not on the basis of their efficacy as communicators capable of influencing the audience. The element of efficacy has received notice only implicitly, insofar as an official is in general more likely to be credited with authenticity regarding information concerning the state and its policies than a non-official.

CLAIMS RELATING TO THE POLITICAL PARTY AND AGENCIES OF PUBLIC INFORMATION IN A TOTALITARIAN STATE

The question here is how should the traditional prescription that a state is responsible for the activities of its officials and authorized agents be applied with reference to activities of such a party as the Communist party, running a party-controlled press, and transnational political activities from

80. See their *Propaganda*, Chap. 7.
81. See below, Chaps. 10 and 11.

state territory? In the past, liberal democratic states, especially Britain, claimed that the U.S.S.R. should assume responsibility for the pronouncements and propaganda activity of the Communist Party in that country.[82] But the latter claimed that the party should be treated in the same manner as political parties in the liberal democratic states are treated traditionally, that is, as a private organization.[83] The Soviet government went even further and disclaimed responsibility for publications appearing in the government-owned press,[84] while traditionally the governments of states have accepted responsibility for publications in the official press.[85] The activities of the Third International, while it was in existence, occasioned protests from states affected by its propaganda,[86] but the U.S.S.R. claimed

82. See the British Foreign Office note of Feb. 23, 1927, to the Soviet government, *A Selection of Papers Dealing with the Relations between His Majesty's Government and the Soviet Government*, 1921–27 (Cmd. No. 2895, 1927). The British government claimed that the chief organ of the Communist party, the Politburo, being in the position of the de facto government of the U.S.S.R., the U.S.S.R. must assume responsibility for its pronouncements and propaganda.

83. See the reply of M. Litvinov, Feb. 26, 1927, ibid. In 1922, when the Allied powers meeting at Cannes decided to call an economic conference, and in a memorandum sent to the Russian government mentioned that one of the conditions required for the promotion of international trade was that states should refrain from engaging in propaganda subversive of the established political system of others, the Soviet government replied that, if the condition implied that the activities of political parties and organizations in Soviet Russia should be surpressed, such a demand would not be accepted. See *Brit. Parl. Papers* (Cmd. No. 1657, 1922).

84. The British note of protest cited in note 82 made reference to *Izvestiya*, a government-owned paper. In his reply, cited in note 83, Litvinov denied responsibility for publications made in that paper. His contention was that not merely the decisions of the government but all information which would be of interest to the public was published in that paper, and therefore the Soviet government could not assume responsibility.

85. Thus, in 1802, when the French Ambassador to Britain questioned how the British government, which in 1792 considered it necessary to go to war over the writings that had appeared in the *Moniteur*, could tolerate the publication of seditious writings against the French government in the British press, the reply of Lord Hawkesbury, the British Foreign Secretary, was: "The paragraphs in English newspapers, the publications . . . have not appeared under any authority of the British government, and are disavowed and disapproved by them; but the paragraph in the *Moniteur* has appeared in a paper avowedly official, for which the government is, therefore, considered responsible, as His Majesty's government is responsible for the contents of the London Gazette." See Lord Hawkesbury to M. Otto, August 28, 1802, 45 *Annual Register* 661 (1803); in 1858, the French government expressed regret for the publication in the *Moniteur* of statements stigmatizing England as a den of conspirators, after an unsuccessful attempt on the life of Emperor Napoleon III. See 100 *Annual Register, History*, 32 (1858).

86. See the note of the British Foreign Office, Sept. 7, 1921, *Brit. Parl. Papers* (Cmd. 2995, 1927); note of Oct. 24, 1924, ibid.; note of Nov. 2, 1921, ibid.; letter of Mr. Austen Chamberlain, Foreign Secretary, to Mr. Peters, Jan. 6, 1925, ibid. About the protest of the United States, see C. C. Hyde, "Concerning a Russian Pledge," 29 *A.J.I.L.* 656 (1935).

for it the status of a political refugee organization enjoying asylum in that country.[87]

It has been noted before that at the present time, the governments of many states, not communist, possess the means of exercising and do exercise varying degrees of direct or indirect control over the mass media of communication within their respective countries. The traditional doctrine that a state is not responsible for utterances of private persons, and therefore, for publications in the private press, was based on the assumption that, such a press being independent of the government in power, its publications should not give rise to an expectation that they were representative of the policy of the government. In the contemporary situation, the question arises whether the application of the traditional prescription which exempts the government of a state from responsibility for publications by the mass media not under government ownership should be modified so as to attribute responsibility for disseminations by the government-controlled media of mass communication, and if so, what degree of governmental control should exist before responsibility could be attributed. We may first glance at the bilateral treaties which the U.S.S.R. entered into with other countries from 1921 onward, for in some of these treaties the U.S.S.R. undertook an extended degree of responsibility for communist propaganda, thereby enlarging the category of impermissible participants in pro-Soviet propaganda. These treaties may be divided into three broad groups. In the first the official representatives and members of the delegations of the contracting parties were obligated to refrain from conducting, supporting, or encouraging political propaganda directed against institutions of either contracting party.[88] In the second group fall those treaties which obligated either party to prevent within its jurisdiction the formation or functioning of any organization, official or non-official, which had as its objective the overthrow of the political order of the other contracting party by violent means.[89]

87. See the note of the Soviet government dated Sept. 21, 1921, *Brit. Parl. Papers* (Cmd. 2995, 1927).

88. See the Russo-German Treaty, Rapallo, 1922, Supplementary Agreement, 1922, 20 *A.J.I.L.* Supp. 116 (1926); Provisional Arrangement of Commerce between Norway and Russia, 1921, *Martens*, 3d ser., *16* (1928), 249; Provisional Agreement between Denmark and Russia, 1923, *Martens*, 3d ser., *14* (1926), 411. In this category, we may also place the Provisional Treaty of Friendship and Commerce between Russia and Czechoslovakia, *Martens*, 3d ser., *18* (1928), 641.

89. In this category come the following treaties: Protocol Concerning the Reestablishment of the Diplomatic Relations between Bulgaria and U.S.S.R., 1934, *Martens*, 3d ser., 30 (1935), 49; Agreement between the U.S.S.R. and Rumania, Concerning the Mutual Guarantee of the Sovereignty of the Two States, exchange of notes, 1934, *Martens*, 3d ser., *36* (1938), 480; Treaty of Peace between Poland, Russia and Ukraine,

The third group falls midway between the above two groups. It makes participation by organizations receiving support from the government, especially economic, impermissible. Under the Anglo-Soviet Trade Agreement, 1921, each party undertook not to conduct any "official propaganda" encouraging hostile action against the interests of the other party, and the expression "official propaganda" was interpreted to include giving "assistance or encouragement" to any propaganda conducted outside the borders of either state.[90] In the undertaking signed by the U.S.S.R. in 1923, on demand by Britain, the former specifically undertook not to give any financial support to propaganda activities designed to spread discontent in the British Empire.[91] The treaty entered into with Japan in 1925 prescribed that, besides the government or its servants, all organizations receiving any financial assistance from either government should refrain from activities, overt or covert, liable in whatever way to endanger order and security in any part of the territory of the other contracting party.[92] The Roosevelt-Litvinov Agreement, 1933, obligated the U.S.S.R. and the United States to refrain, and to restrain all persons in governmental service, all governmental organizations, and all organizations under governmental control including those which were receiving financial assistance from government, from carrying on propaganda of the type specified in the agreement.[93] Under the Franco-Soviet Nonaggression Pact of 1935, each party undertook to abstain from any action which might help or favor any agitation or propaganda of intervention directed against the territorial integrity of the other contracting party, or to change by force the political or social regime of the other.[94]

The above treaties were the outcome of demands made by states against the U.S.S.R. that the latter should undertake specific treaty obligations to refrain, and to restrain all its agents, from carrying on propaganda directed against their internal order. The governments of these states were apprehensive that the establishment of normal relations with the Soviet Union would enable the latter to use its diplomatic missions to disseminate com-

---

Riga, 1921; Agreement between the Republic of China and the U.S.S.R., Peiping, 1925, 19 *A.J.I.L.* Supp. 53 (1925).

90. Trade agreement between His Britannic Majesty's Government and the Government of the Russian Federal Soviet Republic, 1921, *Brit. Parl. Papers* (Cmd. No. 1207, 1921), 16 *A.J.I.L.* Supp. 141 (1922).

91. For the text, see the British Foreign Office Memorandum to Mr. Krassin, Russian Chargé d'Affaires, May 29, 1923, *Brit. Parl. Papers* (Cmd. No. 2895, 1927).

92. See the Convention Embodying the Basic Rules of Relations between Japan and the U.S.S.R., 19 *A.J.I.L.* Supp. 78 (1925).

93. See exchange of letters between President Roosevelt and Maxim Litvinov, 1933, 28 *A.J.I.L.* Supp. 2 (1934).

94. See *Martens*, 3d ser., 29 (1934), 28.

munist propaganda within their countries, and therefore put forward the demand with a view to minimizing the possibility of spreading such propaganda.[95] The extent to which these treaties proved to be effective in accomplishing this objective is another story.[96]

It will be observed that the treaties of the first of the above three categories proceeded no further than reaffirming the traditional position which made a state responsible for the propaganda of its officials. The treaties of the second group obligated the states to proscribe propaganda of the types specified in the treaties, whether the participants happened to be officials or non-officials. It may be noted that some of the noncommunist states also entered into similar bilateral treaties with a view to excluding certain types of propaganda of a noncommunist character.[97] These treaties relate to something which goes beyond the range of the use of the ideological instrument, though its use might come within their scope. Treaties of the third category are of special interest to us. They prescribe that activities of organizations which receive governmental assistance, particularly financial, are the responsibility of the contracting parties. A significant fact about these treaties is that the U.S.S.R. accepted the obligations under them, though they were (although reciprocal in form) such as would in practice operate only against the Soviet Union. However, financial assistance by itself cannot be taken as the chief criterion for the determination of responsibility, for the reason which we shall presently observe. Let us look at the different bases suggested by scholars for the determination of the responsibility of a state in reference to the propaganda activity of organizations which are not official but have official connections.

95. See, for instance, Secretary Colby's note to the Soviet government of August 10, 1920, refusing to grant recognition, cited in E. C. Stowell, *Intervention in International Law* (Washington, D.C., J. Byrne, 1921), p. 380.

96. The long controversy between the U.S.S.R. and the United Kingdom, from 1921 to 1927, culminating in the severance of diplomatic relations in 1927, indicates how little the agreement entered into by those two countries helped to stop the use of diplomatic missions, etc., as centers for dissemination of propaganda. See *Brit. Parl. Papers* (Cmd. 2895 of 1927), for an account of the controversy.

97. See Preliminary Agreement as to the Resumption of Relations between Germany and Latvia, Berlin, 1920, *L.N.T.S.*, 2 (1920–21), 97; Treaty between the United Kingdom, Iraq, and Turkey regarding the Settlement of the Frontier between Turkey and Iraq, Angora, 1926, *L.N.T.S.*, 64 (1927), 387; Agreement Revising the Convention of Dec. 18, 1923, relating to the Organization and Statute of the Tangier Zone, Paris, 1928, between the United Kingdom, France, Spain, and Italy, *L.N.T.S.*, 87 (1929), 251; Treaty of Neutrality and Non-aggression between Persia and Turkey, 1932, *Martens*, 3d ser., 30 (1935), 668; Additional Treaty to the Treaty of Friendship, Neutrality, Conciliation and Arbitration of 1930, between Greece and Turkey, 1938, *Martens*, 3d ser., 36 (1938), 682; Agreement between Italy and Yugoslavia for Consolidating the Relations of Friendship, Belgrade, 1937, *Martens*, 3d ser., 34 (1938), 330; The Indo-Pakistan Agreement, 1948, cited in note 69, above.

Financial Aid Test

According to Sir Hersch Lauterpacht, the government of a state includes not only its officials but its institutions and resources. Hence the responsibility of a state must extend to acts of "bodies maintained, controlled or subsidized by the state." [98] According to this test the activities of the Third International were attributable to the Soviet Union. He is, however, opposed to holding a state responsible for the activities of a political party in that state, even though it is a single-party state.[99] To hold a multiparty state responsible for the activities of the party in power would be, according to him, "to play havoc with the established rules of state responsibility," and on the principle of parity of legal obligations a single-party state, too, should not be held responsible for the activity of the party.

Lauterpacht's test gains strength from two sources. It is supported by the policy adopted by the British government in relation to the Third International during the years of its existence. The British charged the Soviet Union with responsibility for two reasons: the organization was receiving financial assistance from the Soviet government, and the same persons were holding leading positions in the Third International and the Soviet government.[100] Secondly, in some of the bilateral treaties entered into between the Soviet Union and other countries noted above the test was adopted.

However, on close examination it will be found that financial aid by itself cannot serve as a satisfactory test either on principle or policy, though it may form one of the criteria adopted in this context. In modern political theory it is recognized that one of the important functions of the state is the promotion of the welfare of its citizens. Indeed a majority of persons in a state will receive the benefit of the resources of the government in some form or other. The financial aid test will lead one logically to an acceptance of the position that the state is responsible for the actions of practically all its citizens. Lauterpacht's suggestion is not limited to saying that a state must be responsible for the activities which it finances, but is much wider than that. During the discussion in the Grotius Society in 1927, in reply to a question whether the British government could be held responsible if a professor of London University should attack the constitution of a foreign country, Lauterpacht's answer was in the affirmative.[101] Elsewhere he wrote,

98. See "Revolutionary Propaganda by Governments," p. 159.

99. See his "Boycott in International Relations," 14 *B.Y.B.I.L.* 125, 133–34 (1933).

100. See the British Foreign Office note of Sept. 7, 1921, reproduced in *Brit. Parl. Papers* (Cmd. 2929, 1927).

101. See Lauterpacht, "Revolutionary Propaganda by Governments," p. 164.

> the activites of such bodies [bodies receiving financial aid from the State] do not directly engage the responsibility of the State but the foreign State is entitled to expect that the government will make continued financial support dependent upon the cessation of activities which if conducted by the government as such would create international responsibility on the part of that State.[102]

As educational institutions in many states now receive financial assistance from government, a logical application of the principle will severely limit all academic freedom.

Further, Lauterpacht's exoneration of totalitarian states from responsibility for the activities of the political parties in those states has met with criticism from Friedmann. He questions why a single party state should escape responsibility for the activities of a political party which is integrally associated with its government and controls it. To place the political party of a single-party state in the category of private persons, he asserts, is to "play havoc with elementary rules of international relations." [103]

The Control Test

The suggestion that the fact of control exercised by the government over an agency or organization should be made the criterion has been made by Lauterpacht, and elaborated by Lawrence Preuss. Friedmann also favors this approach.[104] According to this view the measure of responsibility of a state should be the degree of control exercised by the government over private citizens and organizations in that state. Preuss maintains that the state ought to be responsible for the propaganda of an organization which is under the "direct or indirect control" of the government.

These writers, however, do not clearly specify what degree of control should be exercised by the government, in respect of what activities of the organization or agency, and to produce what effects, in order that responsibility may be attributed. While governments at present exercise varying degrees of control over the agencies of public information in varied forms, in some cases it may not be for the purpose of controlling the subject matter of publication but to control only the use of resources, such as newsprint. In the United States, to take one example, the Federal Communications Commission exercises control of the allotment of radio frequencies to broadcasting, and requires the maintenance of certain standards in the pro-

102. See "Boycott in International Relations," p. 133.

103. See W. Friedmann, "The Growth of State Control over the Individual and Its Effects upon the Rules of International State Responsibility," 19 *B.Y.B.I.L.* 118 (1938).

104. Lauterpacht, "Revolutionary Propaganda by Governments," p. 159; L. Preuss, "International Responsibility for Hostile Propaganda Against Foreign States"; Friedmann, "Some Impacts of Social Organization on International Law," 50 *A.J.I.L.* 475, 497 (1956).

grams. In view of the control exercised by the Commission, the question may be asked whether the United States should be responsible for what is broadcast. Friedmann seems to be of the opinion that it should.[105] When the Commission has no more power to control the subject matter of what is transmitted from radio stations than the United States government has to control the publications of the press, it does not stand to reason that there should be responsibility for radio broadcasts but not for the press.

Whitton and Larson seem to be in agreement with Friedmann, provided that what is transmitted falls within one of the categories of propaganda specified by them to be the prohibited ones.[106] This view may not be objected to if we accept their opinions as to what kinds of propaganda are prohibited. But the reasons given require examination. They say that a private broadcaster in the United States must obtain a license which stipulates that the station must be used in public interest whereas the publication of a newspaper can be started without a license. It may be noted that even in the United States freedom of the press is not absolute and may be subjected to reasonable restrictions if public interest demands it. Further, if the requirement of a license is a definitive factor regarding responsibility, many nonauthoritarian states should assume responsibility for publications in their nonofficial press, because it is required in those countries that a license be obtained before commencing publication of a newspaper.[107] It cannot be assumed that the authors intend to imply that requirement of a license places a private broadcaster in the United States in the same position as an official agency. If the authors merely mean that radio broadcasting must be subjected to different standards from those applied to the press, that is a question which may be examined separately.[108]

In order that the control test may be stated in a meaningful form it is necessary to specify what degree of control should be exercised, with reference to what aspects of the functioning of the agency of the public information or other organization, and producing what effects.

Close Association Test

Before discussing the third suggested test, we may note what Preuss suggested as the second aspect of the control test. He said that if a party or an organization "through its actual control over the government constitutes the effective authority within the state" then its activities should be attributed to the state.[109]

Friedmann considers that a state should be responsible for the activities

105. Friedmann, ibid., p. 498.
106. *Propaganda*, p. 160.
107. See Terrou and Solal, pp. 74–75.
108. See below, pp. 212–13.
109. Preuss, "International Responsibility for Hostile Propaganda," p. 668.

of organizations which are sufficiently closely associated with government as to justify their identification with the government. The fact of interdependence between the government and the political party in a totalitarian state, he says, should be sufficient basis for the attribution of responsibility for its activities to the state.[110]

But even here perhaps one has to specify more clearly the criteria for attributing such responsibility: the degree of interdependence or association which must exist and the effects produced by virtue of such association.

The question is under what conditions one can attribute the utterances of persons or organizations other than the government to the state itself. The government of a state may be taken as the body of persons who exercise formal authority and effective control within the state. If the government exercises such an amount of formal or effective control over a person that, whenever that person speaks, he may be reasonably expected to speak only what has been expressly or impliedly authorized, then there is a basis for attributing his utterances to the government and the state. Or if a group of persons possesses such an amount of effective control over the government that, whenever they speak, it may be reasonably assumed to be the voice of the latter, there is again a basis for attributing responsibility. In such a case the formal authority of those occupying the position of government is illusory.

According to this formula the London University professor in Lauterpacht's example need not be subjected to any restraint for he is not compelled by the British government to give expression only to the latter's policies. Nor is the United States government responsible for whatever a broadcasting company in the United States transmits by radio. A liberal democratic state is not responsible for the propaganda activity of a political party within it even though that party happens to be in power for the time being. For in a liberal democracy the party in power cannot be expected to have its way as it pleases, but will have to seek some line of policy balancing its forces against those in opposition.

On the other hand, in a totalitarian state there can be nothing which prevents the single political party from shaping governmental policies in the way the party chooses. And in a country like Communist China, because of the control exercised by the party over the agencies of public information, they cannot be expected to speak what is not expressly or impliedly authorized by the government.[111] If a totalitarian state in practice

110. Friedmann, "Some Impacts of Social Organization," p. 497; "The Growth of State Control," p. 144.

111. Even a communist state, according to our formulation, is not chargeable with publications in the press, etc. if in respect of them the citizens are allowed a high degree of freedom of expression. For example, what is stated in the "letters to the editor" is not attributable to the government.

gives a high degree of freedom to the agencies, this fact may be taken note of in attributing responsibility.

The formulas suggested above may be objected to on the ground that they in effect set up different standards of responsibility for the totalitarian and democratic states. This objection assumes that states should be regarded as ultimate entities, and what obtains behind the façades of the states should not be the concern of decision-makers in the world community. There is no reason for such an assumption. At least it may be pointed out that when the press in a totalitarian state is found to be using intensively the ideological instrument, creating an expectation on the part of the government of a liberal democratic state that the elite of the former will be adopting policies which will cause deprivations to the latter, the latter cannot remain idle spectators. It is relatively far more difficult for the government of a totalitarian state to form expectations about the policies of the government of a liberal democracy from what is published in the press of that country. Hence there exists every basis to apply differential standards of state responsibility.

The formulas suggested here do not tend to limit freedom of expression in the world community to an extent greater than is required to promote the twofold policy of promotion of human rights and maintenance of peace and security.

CLAIMS RELATING TO PERSONNEL IN THE SERVICE OF INTERNATIONAL ORGANIZATIONS

Here we contemplate two possible types of participation by the personnel of international organizations, and the use of the resources and symbols of the organizations in the ideological operations of an elite: (1) the elite of a state gains influence over the organization and thereby is able to influence such participation and use, without any decision by the organization itself reached in accordance with its prescribed procedures; (2) such participation and use follow a decision of the organization.

Attention will be confined here to intergovernmental organizations. For, when nonofficial organizations are involved the same principles will apply as in the case of participation by private persons. We may also omit from this discussion the regional governmental organizations and other governmental organizations having limited membership. For, among the members inter se the concerned organization will rarely be used as a means of coercion. And if so used the prescriptions that will come into operation are, generally speaking, the same as apply in the case of participation by officials of states, except insofar as they have been modified by the treaty prescriptions governing the organization. If a non-member happens to be the object of coercive use of the instrument, the legal position will be the same as in the case of participation by officials of a state. We may, therefore, limit our discussion here to the United Nations and its Specialized Agencies; in fact, to the United Nations only, for whatever applies to the United Nations applies substantially to its affiliates.

The Department of Public Information of the United Nations Secretariat has at its disposal considerable communication equipment. But the General Assembly expressly prohibited its use for "propaganda." Its purpose was declared to be "to promote to the greatest possible extent . . . an informed understanding of the work and purposes of the Organization." It is to depend to a considerable extent on the assistance of the governmental and nongovernmental information agencies in its publicity work.[112] That is to say, it is to function only as an agency supplementing the work of the latter, and not as a primary organization in competition with them.

The personnel of the Organization indeed enjoy certain jurisdictional immunities and privileges in the countries they serve, but the conditions of their service make it impermissible for them to participate in the coercive use of the ideological instrument against any member at the instance of the elite of another state. The jurisdictional immunities and privileges are created under Article 105(2) of the Charter, and the Convention on the Privileges and Immunities of the United Nations.[113] They are granted, in particular, immunity from "legal process in respect of words spoken or written . . . in their official capacity" within the jurisdictions of states which are parties to the Convention.[114] But the immunity was conferred for the benefit of the Organization and not of the individuals, and the Secretary-General is given the power to waive it if he considers that its exercise will impede the course of justice.[115] On the other hand, Article 100

112. See the Report of the Sub-Committee appointed by the General Assembly during its Sixth Session to review the principles underlying the work of the Department, which was adopted by Assembly Resolution 595 (VI), 4 February 1952, report reproduced in *Yearbook of the United Nations*, 1951, p. 135. Indeed, from its inception the purpose of the Department was restricted in this respect; see the Recommendations of the Technical Advisory Committee on Information Concerning the Policies and Functions and Organization of the Department of Public Information, adopted by the Preparatory Commission and approved by the General Assembly on Feb. 13, 1946, *Yearbook of the U.N.* 1946–47, p. 84. See also the discussion in the Fifth Committee of the General Assembly on Recommendations, G.A.O.R. (First Sess., Fifth Comm., 1946), p. 34.

113. For an analysis of the provisions of this Convention in general, see J. L. Kunz, "Privileges and Immunities of International Organizations," 41 *A.J.I.L.* 828 (1947).

114. See sec. 18(a) of the Convention. In the United States, which has not yet ratified the Convention, the position is governed by the International Organizations Immunities Act, 1945.

115. See sec. 20. In the United States, in *Ranollo's Case*, 76 N.Y.S. 2d (1946), 31, it was held that immunity should be available only when necessary to assure proper deliberations in the Organization. It was further held that, in the absence of specific instructions in this regard from the State Department, whether immunity was necessary in the particular case to facilitate those deliberations would form an issue of fact determinable by the court before which immunity was invoked.

of the Charter prohibits the officials of the United Nations from seeking or receiving instructions from any government or authority external to the Organization, and from participating in any activity which might reflect on their position as international officials responsible only to the Organization.

The purport of Article 100 was spelled out in detail in the Staff Regulations,[116] the Report of the Secretary-General on Personnel Policy, submitted to the General Assembly during its Eighth Session,[117] and in the Reports of the International Civil Service Advisory Board.[118] The standards of conduct prescribed by these rules and documents, and particularly the integrity, independence, and impartiality in behavior required of international civil servants,[119] reduce the extent of permissible participation in the coercive use of the ideological instrument against any member state to nothing, except when authorized by the Organization.

The responsibility for the enforcement of the rules and regulations lies with the Secretary-General, and he in turn is responsible to the General Assembly and to other organs of the Organization in connection with matters dealt with by them. It follows that if the Organization is using enforcement measures against a state, these rules lose their relevance so far as that state is concerned. However, in practice the Secretariat has been reluctant in the past to participate in any intensive propaganda activities even in such a situation. At one stage of the enforcement action in Korea the Secretariat adopted the view that the United Nations Organization had to abstain officially from psychological warfare operations.[120]

Persons appointed to discharge any specific mission of the United Nations are granted similar immunities and privileges, which continue even after they cease to be employed on the mission. The objective is to enable

116. See U.N. Doc. ST/SGB/Staff Rules/1, 16 March 1962. See in particular Reg. 1.1 and Reg. 1.4.

117. U.N. Doc. A/2533 (1953). The Secretary-General proposed in that report an amendment to Reg. 1.7 of the Staff Regulations to add the following, "Unless otherwise authorized in accordance with Staff Rules issued by the Secretary-General, staff members shall not engage in any political activities outside the scope of their official duties, other than voting." The proposal was accepted by the General Assembly. See M. Cohen, "The United Nations Secretariat—Some Constitutional and Administrative Developments," 49 *A.J.I.L.* 295 (1955).

118. See U.N. Docs. Coord./Civil Service; in particular, No. 5 of the series (1954). The Board stated, "It is also the duty of the staff members to avoid any action which would impair good relations with governments, or destroy confidence in the secretariat—such as public criticism of, or any kind of interference with policies or affairs of governments. For international civil servants, either individually or collectively, to engage in any active criticism of a government or in any activity which undermines or discredits its authority, is incompatible with their status." The Board recommended the prohibition of activities such as preparing speeches for or supplying arguments to representatives of members on any controversial issues.

119. See Reg. 1.4 of the Staff Regulations.

120. See L. Gordenker, "United Nations' Use of Mass-Communications in Korea, 1950–51," 8 *Int'l. Org.* 331, 343 (1954).

them to discharge their mission effectively. However, here again the Secretary-General can waive the immunity if its exercise is likely to impede the course of justice.[121]

In the past even the Commissions of the United Nations have shown little enthusiasm in participating in the use of the ideological instrument. In the case of Korea, on the outbreak of hostilities, the United Nations Commission on Korea (UNCOK) took a bold step in denouncing on the radio the action of the North Korean authorities as a violation of the fundamental principles of the United Nations.[122] The Commission's appeal to the people of North Korea over the heads of their leaders was, however, short-lived. The successor commission to UNCOK was far less active in this field.[123]

The Secretary-General stands in a position which differs from that of other international civil servants, as he has important political functions to discharge under the Charter.[124] Any statement he might make before the Security Council under Article 99 of the Charter, bringing to the notice of the Council any threat to the peace, breach of the peace, or act of aggression, may have coercive effect on the states against which it is directed by virtue of his status.[125] However, the exercise of the functions attached to his office involves extreme delicacy; and the experience of Mr. Trygve Lie, who had to resign because of the hostile, though uncalled for, attitude adopted by the delegation of the U.S.S.R. toward him because of the part he played in the Korean affair, brings out too well the hazards involved in the exercise of the functions attached to that office.[126] And Dag Hammarskjöld, too, had it not been for his tragic, untimely death, might have had to follow the example of his predecessor and resign from office in the face of Soviet hostility generated by the turn of events in the Congo.[127] The pronouncements made by Hammarskjöld before the U.N. organs and elsewhere in connection with the Congo crisis have brought out fully the

121. See Secs. 22 and 23 of the Convention.

122. See Gordenker; Report of the United Nations Commission on Korea to the Fifth Session of the General Assembly (U.N. Doc. A/1350, 1950).

123. Gordenker, p. 335.

124. For an account of his political functions, see S. M. Schwebel, *The Secretary-General of the United Nations* (Cambridge, Harvard University Press, 1952), p. 19; F. R. Scott, "The World Civil Service," *Int'l Conciliation*, No. 496 (Jan. 1954), pp. 272–73; H. Kelsen, *The Law of the United Nations* (New York, Praeger, 1950), pp. 302–07; Goodrich and Hambro, *Charter of the United Nations*, p. 497; J. P. Lask, "Dag Hammarskjold's Conception of His Office," 16 *Int'l. Org.* 542 (1962); L. M. Goodrich, "The Political Role of the Secretary-General," ibid., p. 720.

125. See Schwebel, p. 26. Other occasions when the Secretary-General might by his statements influence public opinion are when he makes reports to the General Assembly or makes a statement before any organ of the organization.

126. See Trygve Lie, *In the Cause of Peace* (New York, Macmillan, 1954), Chap. 23.

127. See Goodrich, p. 729.

political role of the Security-General. Indeed Hammarskjöld claimed that he had a responsibility to act according to his own convictions and the principles of the Charter in the absence of positive advice from the U.N. organs.[128] The Secretary-General can hardly escape from making utterances unpalatable to some members, especially when conflicts, violent or otherwise, engage the attention of the Organization. He can do so only if he chooses to abdicate his political functions. But, having regard to the stature of the person who comes to the office, and the pressures to which he is generally subject, it may be expected that he will take a line different from that of the members most directly affected.

The Secretary-General, no doubt, enjoys diplomatic immunities and privileges under the Convention on Privileges and Immunities of the United Nations. But that circumstance does not guarantee unrestricted participation. The immunities are declared to have been granted for the benefit of the Organization and not for his personal benefit and the Security Council has the power to waive them.[129]

It may be noted from the above that the regime to which international civil servants are subject does not permit them to participate in the ideological operations of the elites in the world arena. In conformity with the general character of the service, the Secretariat refrained from participating even in the psychological warfare operations in connection with the Korean enforcement action. The Secretary-General, in his public pronouncements, cannot be expected to take a stand which is completely identical with that of any elite in the world arena.

The Secretariat, it has become clear in recent years, has an important role in the enforcement of the U.N.'s policy of maintaining peace and security in the world in general, and of preventing the "escalation" of local conflicts into major ones. "Preventive diplomacy," interposition of forces between the fighting parties, and using forces to attain limited objectives, are the chief instruments by which "escalation" is to be prevented. At this juncture the Secretary-General and his top aides should have full control over the activities of the staff, so that effective conduct of "preventive diplomacy" and discreet use of the ideological instrument against a recalcitrant elite are not interfered with by the activities of the staff. The staff regulations now give the Secretary-General the necessary control.

128. See "Secretary-General's Reply to U.S.S.R.," *U.N. Review* (November 1960), pp. 39–40; also see S. D. Bailey, *The Secretariat of the United Nations* (New York, Carnegie Endowment, 1962), p. 40.

129. See Sec. 20 of the Convention.

6

Audience

Traditional doctrines of international law, by implication, provided for a variation in community policy as the expectations created by communications to internal or external audiences vary. Before we proceed to state these doctrines and the deductions that follow from them, it may be noted that none of the traditional doctrines is absolute. No legal doctrine can perhaps ever be so; each has indeed its counterpart.[1] And neither can an inference drawn from any traditional doctrine ever be absolute. It has to be taken in juxtaposition with the deductions from the counterpart of the main doctrine.

The doctrine of sovereignty of states permitted the elite in each state to exercise a high degree of control, and therefore allowed a high degree of freedom in the use of any instrument of policy to exercise, maintain, or strengthen that control. In particular, the officials of each state could prescribe what symbols might be circulated, propagated, or manipulated within the territory. However, the traditional prescription that required each state to respect the sovereignty of others was matched by the prescription that permitted adoption of measures of self-defense. Intervention by one state in the internal affairs of another was generally prohibited, but was permitted under certain circumstances, especially when self-defense was involved. Inferentially, while the elites, generally speaking, were free to use the ideological instrument to influence internal groups, if—from the objective of the strategists, the intensity of the use of the instrument, the techniques and tactics employed, and the situation in which it was employed—an expectation was created on the part of government of another state that it would be attacked, that government was entitled to adopt measures designed to meet the anticipated danger.[2]

1. See Benjamin N. Cardozo, *The Paradoxes of Legal Science* (New York, Columbia University Press, 1928), p. 8.

2. See the remarks of Creasy, *First Platform of International Law*, p. 285, expounding the doctrines of Vattel on sovereignty and self-defense. "If a preponderant power

By virtue of the doctrine of nonintervention, an external elite was prohibited from employing any coercive process to interfere with the system of order and control established in a state by its ruling elite. Coercive use of the ideological instrument with respect to an external audience was generally open to objection, but the doctrine of permissible intervention sometimes rendered it legitimate. Traditional law, it will be presently seen, did not prohibit communication as such with an external audience. In other words, the legitimacy of propaganda addressed to a foreign audience depended partly upon its outcome, actual or expected.

In respect of communications addressed to audiences in third states, under traditional law, the officials of the aggrieved state were either to invoke the prescription allegedly violated and the doctrine of state responsibility, and demand that the officials of the state from which the strategy was operated stop the activity,[3] or to call upon the officials of the audience's state to exercise, in discharge of their responsibility stemming from their territorial control, their power to restrain the activity.[4] Such a demand was presented only when the outcome of the activity was expected to be harmful to the elite of the state presenting it, and the response depended upon the receiver's expectations of the outcome of the activity, and of noncompliance with the demand.

What has been stated so far may be questioned on two grounds: (1) one may doubt whether there is freedom of transnational communication under traditional law; and (2) one may doubt the utility of the doctrines of intervention and nonintervention in present international law.[5] We shall deal very briefly with these two issues before we take note of the trend of decisions in regard to audience.

. . . by arrogance of its pretensions, *the tone of its public despatches and manifestoes,* or by any other manner of conduct beyond the mere increase of its strength, clearly threatens to attack or suppress its neighbors, then other States are justified in combining together and in making war on it" (emphasis supplied).

3. Thus the British government in its notes of September 7, 1921, and of May 29, 1923, protested to the Soviet Union over Soviet official representatives in Persia and Afghanistan carrying on propaganda prejudicial to British interests in those countries. See *A Selection of Papers Dealing with the Relations between His Majesty's Government and the Soviet Government,* 1921–27, cited in Chap. 5, note 82. In the note of May 29, the British government demanded that the Soviet government disown their activity. On these occasions the Soviet government denied either the fact of propaganda or the connection of the participants with the Soviet government.

4. On representation by India in 1962, the Polish government asked the Chinese Embassy in Warsaw to stop the circulation of a brochure containing the Chinese version of the Sino-Indian border dispute. See *New York Times,* Nov. 20, 1962.

5. See e.g. Briggs, *The Law of Nations,* p. 960.

PERMISSIBILITY OF TRANSNATIONAL COMMUNICATION

Traditional doctrines merely gave formal power to the elite of each state to control the events occurring within its territory, and consequently to regulate the use of the ideological instrument within it. On the other hand the doctrinal writings of earlier publicists affirmed the permissibility of communication by external elites. And further, the environmental conditions which existed till the rise of the totalitarian regimes was such that the elites could not have thought of using that power to interfere seriously with transnational community processes in order to cut off all communications from outside to their peoples. They did not in fact attempt to do so.

Among the early publicists, the Spanish jurists, Vittoria, Suarez, and Ayala maintained that the Spaniards had a right to preach the Christian doctrine to all nations. In order to appreciate this assertion, we have only to remember the important place occupied by the symbols of Christianity in the ideologies of the European communities of the sixteenth and seventeenth centuries. Vittoria maintained that as members of the "natural society and fellowship" of human beings in general, Spaniards had a right to travel into the lands of the Indians and stay there, provided they did no harm to the natives. He went on to say,

> If the Spaniards have a right to travel and trade among the Indians, they can teach the truth to those willing to hear them, especially as regards matters pertaining to salvation and happiness, much more than as regards matters pertaining to any human subject of instruction . . . because brotherly correction is required by the law of nature, just as brotherly love is.[6]

Suarez and Ayala were positive in their assertion of the right to wage war against a people who might obstruct the preaching of the Christian doctrine.[7] What has to be particularly noted in this context is the fact that the arguments advanced by these jurists, especially by Vittoria, were not merely those based on religious dogma but included some secular in character, based on the cognizance that human society as such constitutes a larger society that transcends national boundaries.[8] Even Grotius, who at-

6. See Vittoria, *De Indis,* sec. iii, in J. B. Scott, *Spanish Origins of International Law,* Appendix, pp. xxxi, xlii.

7. For the statement of Suarez see his *On Faith, Selections From Three Works of Francisco Suarez* (Washington, D.C., Carnegie Endowment, 1944), p. 756. For Ayala's, see Balthazar Ayala, *Three Books on the Law of War and on Duties Connected with War and on Military Discipline* (Washington, D.C., Carnegie Endowment, 1942), p. 21.

8. Vittoria uses the expressions "natural society and fellowship," "brotherly correction," and "brotherly love." Suarez, too, takes a nonreligious stand to support his thesis.

tempted to give the law of nations a secular framework,[9] said that infliction of punishment on those preaching Christianity would give rise to a just cause of war.[10]

The Peace of Westphalia, however, brought the principle of territorial sovereignty to the forefront. The objective sought by the elites of states in accepting the principle was to bring down the ideological conflict, which in the course of the Thirty Years' War had destroyed a good portion of Europe, to a low level of intensity. There arose after the treaty a need to reformulate preexisting doctrines concerning the freedom to preach the Gospel, in the light of the new principle. The eighteenth-century jurists, Wolff and Vattel, restated the pre-Westphalian doctrines, keeping intact the right to preach the Christian doctrines but giving power to the elite of each state to regulate such activity within its territory. Wolff maintained that every nation had a natural duty to humanity to persuade others to accept the doctrines but was not entitled to compel, and therefore the latter might refuse to admit missionaries or religious literature into their respective territories.[11] Vattel, after stating that, by virtue of the principle of sovereignty of states, intervention by one state in the government of another was not permissible, proceeded to formulate the principle with reference to interference in religious affairs thus:

> But it is an office of humanity to endeavor, by lawful and gentle means, to persuade a Nation to receive a form of religion which it is believed is the only true and proper one. Missionaries may be sent to instruct the Nation, and the act is entirely in keeping with the interest which every Nation should have in the advancement and happiness of other Nations. But in order not to act in contempt of the rights of the sovereign, the missionaries should refrain from preaching, secretly and without his permission, a new doctrine to his subjects. He may refuse their services, and, if he orders them away they must obey him.

He says, "this tolerance [of preaching the Gospel] is obligatory under the *jus gentium* and it cannot be impeded without just cause" (p. 756). It may be noted that *jus gentium*, according to Suarez, is not natural law but man-made law (p. 343). Quincy Wright has pertinently pointed out that these writers did not recognize the right of infidels to preach in Christian lands. See his "Freedom and Responsibility in Respect to Trans-National Communication," 1950 *Proc. Am. Soc. of Int'l. Law*, pp. 95, 97. But this question did not arise for them. If it had, it is reasonable to believe that they would have denied the right more on the ground that those doctrines were harmful to mankind than on the ground that infidels as such did not possess the right.

9. See A. Nussbaum, *A Concise History of the Law of Nations* (rev. ed. New York, Macmillan, 1954), p. 109.

10. *De Jure Belli*, Bk. ii, Chap. xx, Sec. 49.

11. Christian Wolff, *Jus Gentium, Methodo Scientifica* (Washington, D.C., Carnegie Endowment, 1934), 2, 133–35.

About the manner in which foreigners should preach religious doctrines Vattel stated:

> Be ever ready to share your knowledge; set forth simply and sincerely the principles of your belief to those who desire to hear you; instruct them, persuade them by an appeal to reason; but do not seek to win them over by the ardor of enthusiasm.[12]

Vattel thus placed in juxtaposition the right of foreigners to disseminate by methods of persuasion principles of religion and the right of the territorial sovereign to set limits to such activity in order to protect his state from dissension and disintegration. But the important point to be noted is the fact that Vattel upheld the permissibility of the external elites communicating with the people of a state, using methods of persuasion, to gain acceptance of their ideological symbols. The writings of Vattel do not seem to be gratuitous assertions. The conditions which prevailed in many Germanic states in the pre- and post-Westphalian period formed the basis of his writings.[13]

Before examining the attitude of the governments of states toward transnational community processes which occasion communication across state boundaries, we should recall that the chief means of communication available before the advent of radio were human agents and printed and written materials.

Among European countries in the last century, except during war, movement of persons across state boundaries was largely unrestricted.[14] In 1848, when the British government, irked by the activities of sympathizers with the Irish revolutionists, decided to take certain measures against all American citizens who might travel to Ireland, such as arresting them and examining their baggage and papers, the United States Ambassador to Britain protested, pointing out that such measures were contrary to the usages of nations. Viscount Palmerston, the British Foreign Secretary, in reply assured him that extreme care would be taken by the British government not to cause any inconvenience to innocent travelers.[15] In 1852, when the European governments threatened to take similar measures against British citizens who might travel to their countries, because of the failure of the

12. See *The Law of Nations*, 3, 133, 134.

13. See ibid., and cf. the account given in *Cambridge Modern History* (Cambridge, Cambridge University Press, 1906), 4, 411–12.

14. It may be noted that about 1867, all the European countries, with the exception of Russia and Turkey, had practically eliminated the passport requirements; see G. H. Stuart, "Safeguarding of the State through Passport Control," 12 *Dept. of State Bull.* 1066 (1945).

15. See the letter of Mr. Bancroft to Viscount Palmerston, cited in Chap. 5, note 29; and Palmerston to Bancroft, Sept. 30, 1848, *British and For. State Papers*, 1852–53, p. 412.

British government to restrain the activities of political refugees in England, Earl Grenville, then British Foreign Secretary, declared: "it would be in the highest degree unjust, and unworthy of the enlightened character of any European Government . . . to put vexatious impediments in the way of unoffending travelers, by way of retaliation for the acts of foreign refugees in England." [16] No doubt, the right to exclude aliens or any class of them had been frequently asserted by governments,[17] but as Westlake remarked, "Between the States of white races, the entire exclusion of the subjects of any from the territory of another at peace with the former has scarcely been attempted within historical times." [18]

The reason for such restraint in the exercise of the territorial power is not difficult to find. In an environment in which officials of states exercised limited functions, peoples of different states depended for mutual exchange of values upon the effort and enterprise of private persons. Movement of persons across state boundaries was a matter of necessity. A state that refused to admit aliens had necessarily to risk deprivations resulting from retaliatory action by the affected states. Practical necessities restrained governments from putting forward extravagant claims on the basis of the doctrine of territorial sovereignty, in the matter of exclusion of aliens.[19]

When men moved across the state boundaries they must have functioned at least to some extent as carriers of information and symbols. In regard to printed materials, it was no doubt considered permissible for the government of a state to exclude from its territory materials which it might consider prejudicial to the internal order of the state.[20] But even here governments had to use the power with the expectation that its arbitrary exercise would evoke an adverse response from the states prejudiced by such action. In fact, the officials of states were quite ready in the past to protest whenever any book or periodical published in their country was subjected to arbitrary exclusion or discrimatory treatment in any foreign country.[21]

16. See the letter of Earl Grenville cited in Chap. 5, note 36.

17. See Hackworth, *Digest*, 3, 717.

18. J. Westlake, *International Law*, Part I, *Peace* (2d ed. Cambridge, Cambridge University Press, 1910), p. 215.

19. It is interesting to note that all the leading writers maintain that a state has the right to exclude even all aliens, but at once proceed to state that the right of exclusion has to be exercised with restraint, and that total exclusion is not a measure to which states can ever resort without facing deprivations. Even partial exclusion, they indicate, should not be resorted to except on reasonable grounds. See in this connection the remarks in Hall, p. 224; Borchard, *Diplomatic Protection*, p. 46; T. Baty, *International Law* (London, John Murray, 1909), p. 26; Moore, *Digest*, 6, 57–58; Fenwick, *International Law*, p. 267.

20. As early as 1802, the British government conceded this right. See Lord Hawkesbury's letter to Mr. Merry, cited in Chap. 5, note 27.

21. See Hackworth, *Digest*, 2, 143: "The American government has on several occasions made representations to foreign governments in regard to the treatment ac-

As for written materials, long before the establishment of the International Postal Union there was a huge network of treaties among states for the transnational carriage of mails.[22]

The acceptance of the doctrine of territorial sovereignty, we thus observe, by no means led to an abandonment of the idea of human society being a "natural society and fellowship." Apart from practical needs growing out of expanding commerce, the fact that the European nations shared a common civilization militated against any such abandonment. Nor did it give the rulers of each state a handle to prescribe the extent of permissible intercourse between their people and the peoples of other states according to their whims and fancies.[23] It gave them in effect only the power to prescribe policy regarding such intercourse in terms of three factors: the practical needs and the demands of their people for such exchanges, similar demands of other states, and the safety of their own value position.

Thus the traditional law did not proscribe communication with external audiences. It prohibited, however, external elites from interfering with internal arrangements regarding the circulation of ideological symbols within the state as a means of sociopolitical control. And such arrangements could never have included rigorous exclusion of all communications from outside.

THE DOCTRINE OF INTERVENTION

There are three important points made by writers who doubt the usefulness of intervention as a legal concept. First, in the past, not only military invasions but mere tendering of diplomatic advice were all characterized as intervention.[24] To regard tendering diplomatic advice as intervention, a violation of law, is preposterous. Further, a legal concept which places military invasions and diplomatic advice in the same category will be as little useful as a medical diagnosis which treats fleabites and plagues all in the

---

corded to periodicals published in the United States"; see also Moore, *Digest, 4,* 335–36, about the representations made by the United States in 1882–83, when Russia imposed restrictions on the sale of copies of the Bible by the American Bible Society. When it came to light that the British Bible Society was allowed full freedom, Mr. Frelinghuysen, Secretary of State, considered that there was definite ground for complaint inasmuch as the American Society was subjected to discrimination.

22. See K. Clark, *International Communications* (New York, 1931), p. 17.

23. We may note that Western powers did not admit Japan and China as formal members of the international community until they opened their ports for commerce. Fenwick, "Freedom of Communication Across National Boundaries," 1950 *Proc. Am. Soc. of Int'l. L.*, p. 107. Anglo-American writers deny the right of mutual intercourse between states, but admit that such intercourse must exist factually as an incident of community life.

24. See the remarks of Winfield in "*The History of Intervention in International Law*," p. 130; H. W. Briggs, p. 960.

same category of scarlet fevers.[25] Second, if proscription of intervention is the rule, the exceptions mentioned by statesmen and writers in the past as to when intervention is permissible are too many, and they defy any attempt at reducing them to a principle.[26] Finally, under the traditional system states were at liberty to initiate hostilities at any time they wished; in that situation, doctrinal assertions about interference with the freedom and independence of states in their internal or external affairs did not carry with them any air of realism.[27]

"Intervention" in traditional legal terminology covered a wider range of cases of application of transnational coercion, falling mainly into three classes. First, when two states were engaged in mutual violence, a third that took one side or the other might claim that it was merely "intervening" in the conflict.[28] The second class covered cases of similar character. When the governments of two states were about to arrive at some arrangement by mutual consent with a view to achieving any desired objective, the government of a third state might step forward opposing the contemplated arrangement because of possible adverse effects on its state. Or when two states were engaged in mutual application of nonviolent means of coercion in pursuit of their respective objectives, the government of a third state might interest itself in the matter and apply nonviolent means of coercion against either or both of the governments of the first two states. According to traditional legal terminology, in such cases the third state was said to intervene. Intervention in these cases stood for interfering with the freedom of governments in their interaction by means of nonviolent instruments of coercion.[29] The third class included cases in which the elites in a

25. Sir William Harcourt, *Letters by Historicus on Some Questions of International Law* (London, 1863), p. 41, uses the expressions "fleabite," "plague," and "scarlet fevers." He considers that intervention is not a principle of international law but only a matter of national policy.

26. See Winfield, "*Intervention in International Law,*" 5 *B.Y.B.I.L.* 149, 150 (1924).

27. See Brierly, *The Law of Nations* (5th ed. 1955), p. 309: "there was a certain unreality in attempting to formulate a law of intervention and at the same time admitting, as until recently it was necessary to admit, that a state might go to war for any cause or no cause without any breach of law"; see also his *The Outlook for International Law* (Oxford, Oxford University Press, 1944), p. 21, where he points out the logical impossibility in asserting the duty of states to respect each other's mutual independence (which is none other than the doctrine of nonintervention) while saying that they are free to attack each other.

28. Thus Italy claimed when it entered World War I that it was "intervening" in the war; see F. Grob, *The Relativity of War and Peace* (New Haven, Yale University Press, 1949), pp. 224–25.

29. See A. V. W. Thomas and A. J. Thomas, *Non-Intervention, The Law and Its Imports in the Americas* (Dallas, Southern Methodist University Press, 1956), p. 70.

state attempted to control the events in another by applying varying means and degrees of coercion against the state as a whole, against its officials, or against one section of the state for the benefit of another.[30] Such instances were also referred to by the word "intervention."

When used in the context of the first group, "intervention" carried only limited significance under the traditional system. There was no question of permissibility or otherwise of such intervention, for a third state was always free to join a war in progress between two others and to take any side it pleased.[31] "Intervention" used in connection with the second and third groups of cases carried more significance. Intervention was doctrinally prohibited in these cases. Under the conditions of multipolarity of power that had emerged on the disintegration of the medieval order of European society, it was thought that outbreaks of violence in the community could be avoided only if the elites refrained from using transnational coercive processes. The doctrine of nonintervention postulated the proscription of all transnational coercion between states which were not engaged in formal hostilities.

It was impossible, however, that such a proscription could then be absolute. It ran counter to the realities of world community life, and the behavior of states at the time of its formulation,[32] and indeed at all times. The elites in many states will always be attempting to control the conduct of the governments of other states in respect to internal or external affairs,

30. In the past, application of coercion by a state in order to obtain satisfaction of the claims of its nationals was termed "intervention." One such example was the British intervention in Greece in connection with the claims of Don Pacifico. Taking sides in civil wars is generally referred to as intervention. It is not necessary that the taking of sides should be by giving military assistance. Premature recognition of a rebel government is generally considered intervention; see H. Lauterpacht, *Recognition in International Law* (Cambridge, Cambridge University Press, 1947), p. 11; "lending open approval, as by relaxing an arms embargo, to a revolutionary group headed by individuals ready to accept the political or economic dominance of the intervening state" is also considered intervention; see Phillip C. Jessup, *A Modern Law of Nations, An Introduction* (New York, Macmillan, 1952), pp. 172–73. Aiding an existing regime to prevent its overthrow by revolutionary movements is also generally treated as intervention. The policy of the Holy Alliance Powers during the early part of the last century is referred to, in accordance with that usage, as one of "intervention." We had recently the Soviet "intervention" in Hungary.

31. Viscount Palmerston, for example, stated in 1848 in Parliament, in answer to the remark of Disraeli that France had no right to intervene in the dispute between Austria and Sardinia, "It was objected that France had no right to intermeddle; but there could be no question, whatever might be the justice of interference, that, when two nations were at war, it was competent for a third to take whichever side it pleased, if it chose to engage in the contest." 90 *Annual Register* 173 (1848). See also, Winfield, "The History of Intervention in International Law."

32. See Winfield, "History of Intervention in International Law"; Butler and Maccoby, *The Development of International Law*, p. 69.

using methods ranging from persuasion to coercion. Apart from being out of unison with the facts of community life, the proscription did not square with the pattern of world community regulation which existed at the time of its formulation. When there was no centralized control over the processes of transnational coercion, and the officials of states assumed the triple role of agents who put forward claims, prescribers of community policy with respect to those claims, and agents who enforced the policy, the occasions when they might have to resort to the use of transnational coercion to enforce community prescriptions were many. The doctrine of nonintervention, which implied the extreme position of proscribing all transnational coercion, had necessarily to be qualified by other prescriptions which permitted resort to transnational coercive processes under prescribed conditions as a sanctioning measure.

Under the traditional community regulations it is no wonder that, apart from the use of violence after formal declaration of hostilities, states were permitted to use a great variety of transnational coercive processes. They could make coercive use of any instrument of policy, or any combination of them, subject to prescribed conditions. In traditional legal terminology, states might resort to retortions, which are returning *damnum sine injuria* for such *damnum*. They might impose embargoes (a coercive use of the economic instrument), take reprisals (coercion applied mostly by using the economic and/or military instrument and involving what would otherwise be a violation of community prescriptions), enforce blockades, or engage in bombardment operations, in order to obtain satisfaction of their claims. Apart from these, permissible intervention formed another category of sanctioned application of transnational coercion (partly overlapping the others mentioned above).

Claims were put forward by states in the past, inclusive as well as exclusive, maintaining that it was permissible to intervene for the purpose of self-defense,[33] for the protection of interests other than the safety of the entire state as such,[34] and for the preservation of certain humanitarian

33. The claims of the Holy Alliance during the last century to suppress revolutions wherever they might occur were based on this ground. It was maintained that a government that came to power after a revolution would necessarily be hostile to legitimate governments; see T. W. E. Lingelbach, "The Doctrine and Practice of Intervention in Europe," 16 *Annals of the Am. Academy of Political and Social Science* 1, 11 (1900).

34. The intervention of Britain, France, and Russia in favor of the Greek rebels in 1827 is generally justified by writers on humanitarian grounds (see Stowell, p. 126); but the British based it on their right to protect their commercial and shipping interests. See the State Paper cited in this regard in Sir Robert Phillimore, *Commentaries upon International Law*, 1, (3d ed. London, Butterworth, 1879), 571; Westlake, *International Law*, 1, 319n., considered that it was designed for protection against piracy in the Levant. The intervention by the U.S. in Cuba was partly based on the claim to protect the commercial and other interests of American citizens, partly on the ground of alleviation of a menace to the peace of the United States, and partly on humanitarian

values.[35] It was further claimed that it was permissible to intervene in accordance with treaty rights, or, if necessary, to counteract intervention by another.[36]

The policy decisions of the past with reference to claims based on permissible intervention and nonintervention doctrines become intelligible, in spite of their diversity and lack of principle, if two facts are borne in mind: (1) the instruments of coercion are not merely military, but include all the four instruments of interaction; (2) decision-making under the traditional pattern of regulation being decentralized, the invocation of the proscription of coercion had to be done by none other than the officials of the victim state themselves in the first instance, and when they invoked depended upon when the process of coercion applied by external elites created an expectation on their part that it would cause deprivation of their values, and not upon the particular instrument used. That explains why the doctrine of nonintervention was invoked in the past even when only the diplomatic instrument was used,[37] or the ideological instrument.[38] Similarly, application of the prescription had to be done by none other than the officials of the state applying coercion. Their decisions depended for obvious reasons on their own demands and expectations. Sanctions against improper application of coercion under the guise of permissible intervention had to be

---

grounds; see the "Annual Message of President McKinley to Congress, 1898," *For. Rel. of U.S. 1898*, p. liii.

35. Thus the Russian attack on Turkey in 1877 was claimed to be for the protection of the Christian population in Bulgaria; see "The Russian Manifesto, April 19, 1877," *For. Rel. of U.S. 1877*, p. 585; see the "Annual Message of President Roosevelt, 1904," *For. Rel. of U.S. 1904*, p. xli, in the course of which he said, "If a nation shows that it knows how to act with reasonable efficiency and decency in social and political matters, if it keeps order and pays its obligations, it need fear no interference from the United States. Chronic wrongdoing, or an impotence which results in a general loosening of the ties of civilized society, may in America, as elsewhere, ultimately require the intervention of some civilized nation."

36. E.g. the United States claimed justification for intervention in Panama under treaty rights; see C. C. Hyde, *International Law*, 1 (3d ed. Boston, Little, Brown, 1945), 248, 260.

37. Thus Dr. Ramon Grau San Martin, the Provisional President of Cuba from Sept. 1933 to Jan. 15, 1934, held that nonrecognition by the United States of his government amounted to a new type of intervention in the internal affairs of Cuba, intervention by inertia; see *New York Times*, Oct. 29, 1933, cited in Grob, p. 227.

38. Thus in 1831, Austria, partly in reaction to propaganda appeals by the leaders of the rebel governments in the Papal States calling upon the peoples of Lombardy and Naples to rebel, and partly in reply to the request of the Pope and other deposed rulers, intervened militarily to put down the rebellion in those states; see 73 *Annual Register* 453–55 (1831). More recently, President Eisenhower's 1955 Christmas Message to the peoples of Eastern Europe, broadcast by Radio Free Europe, was called by Russian leaders "crude intervention" (see *New York Times*, Dec. 31, 1955), and was considered by the Hungarian Prime Minister to be "interference" (ibid., Jan. 2, 1956).

applied by officials of the victim state and of third states. The response of the officials of third states depended upon diverse factors including their expectations of the effects of the "intervention" on their own state, and not merely on whether or not the coercion was applied for justifiable reasons. The community policy with reference to claims advanced in relation to any particular situation depended upon the perspectives and response of the decision-makers to the particular factual situation.

The doctrines of nonintervention and permissible intervention did not merely prescribe a few permissions and prohibitions. The two formed a pair of legal formulas, polar and complementary, which decision-makers under the traditional system used to prescribe policy with reference to certain types of situations in which transnational coercion was applied in support of inclusive and exclusive claims. The policy prescribed by them varied from time to time depending upon a multiplicity of factors.[39]

The traditional doctrines of nonintervention and permissible intervention stand at present modified by the prescriptions of the U.N. Charter regarding the use of force.

TRENDS

The question as to which audience is addressed has not received direct attention in decision-making in the past, perhaps because of the expectation that what is communicated to one audience will be transmitted to others in due course. There have been, however, a few instances when the audience variable figured significantly.

In 1930, the Soviet Union started to broadcast communist propaganda in German on a high-power transmitter from Moscow. When Germany protested, the reply was that the transmissions were meant for the German settlers in the Volga basin, and that they were made in the German language with a view to giving the intended audience an opportunity to listen in their own language.[40] In 1934, when Austria protested over the inflammatory propaganda addressed from radio stations in Germany apparently to German nationals in Austria, the reply of the Nazi government was that the broadcasts were intended for the audience in Germany, to explain to them the events occurring in Austria.[41] Claims that the broadcasts were

39. That the doctrine of intervention and nonintervention never represented a fixed policy but a policy that changed from time to time was pointed out by Lingelbach. He stated that the policy varied with "the prevailing thought and institutions of different periods of history." He added, "It must be borne in mind that the doctrine and practice of intervention has gone through a process of evolution; that the causes justifying intervention at any period may be entirely out of accord with the standards of another, and yet be, historically, perfectly just and legal."

40. See S. S. Biro, "The International Aspect of Radio Control," 2 *Journal of Radio Law* 45 (1932).

41. See *New York Times*, Feb. 3, 1934.

intended for an internal and not an external audience, it may be pointed out, have to be examined in the light of all the other variables involved, and the assertion that the objective is to enlighten the internal audience should not form the conclusive factor in determining legal policy. However, in view of the developments that have taken place since 1930—with broadcasting to foreign audiences becoming common, and freedom of information coming to be recognized as a human right—it is doubtful whether such claims will be presented in the future. It is more likely that the claim will be that the transmission is made to enlighten the foreign audience.

The fact that under certain circumstances the operation of the strategy to influence an internal audience may be open to objection by virtue of the expectation it creates is brought out by some of the claims put forward before the United Nations General Assembly. The United States representative to the Assembly, Mrs. Roosevelt, in her speech before the Third Committee of the Assembly in 1947 stated: [42]

> The threat to international peace and security is indeed grave when behind these walls of contrived ignorance governments persistently slander governments and official propagandists work to poison the wells of international friendship—without the possibility of effective reply.

A similar note was struck by the Australian representative, Mr. Forsyth, in 1954.[43] In its response to the allegations of the Soviet Union that war propaganda was being carried on the Western countries, the General Assembly pointed to the need to promote freedom of information, in addition to condemning propaganda in favor of war.[44]

42. The statement was made during the debate on the proposal of Yugoslavia that members should take measures to prevent dissemination of false and distorted statements, slanderous to foreign states, and harmful to good relations. U.N. Doc. A/C.3/162, Oct. 4, 1947. See 17 *Dept. of State Bull.* 874, 876 (1947). The statement does not appear in the official records of the Third Committee.

43. G.A.O.R., 9th Sess., Ad. Hoc Comm. (1954), pp. 183–84. He said: "The real danger [to peace] was found not where there was discord, contention and debate, but where there was enforced uniformity and mass indoctrination. An excess of information was preferable to information selected and cut to pattern. Attempts to restrict or prohibit information must inevitably lead to a dangerous situation in which Governments could dictate to peoples without contradiction." See also in this connection, Quincy Wright, *A Study of War*, 1 (Chicago, University of Chicago Press, 1942), 180; Martin, *Collective Security*, p. 93.

44. The resolutions adopted during the Second, Fifth, and Ninth Sessions in response to Communist complaints were Resolutions 110(II), 8 November 1947, 381(V), 17 November 1950, and 819(IX), 11 December 1954. These resolutions, while generally condemning "all . . . propaganda, in whatsoever country conducted, which is either designed or likely to provoke or encourage any threat to the peace, breach of the peace or act of aggression" [110(II) and 819(IX)], also condemned "measures tending to

Between the two World Wars, some states entered into bilateral treaties with a view to avoiding the development of such situations as might embitter relations between them. These treaties may be divided into two broad categories: the first, among other things, prohibited the parties from disseminating certain specified types of propaganda within their respective territories,[45] and the second prohibited specified types of propaganda irrespective of the audience.[46] The reason for this variation will be apparent when one looks at what the parties intended to prohibit by these treaties. In the first group of treaties the parties were concerned with movements initiated from the territory of one against the other, but not inspired by any new ideology. Hence the obligation was limited to internal audiences. In almost all the second group of treaties the concern was about the spread of a revolutionary ideology from Soviet Russia, and hence external audiences were also included. This variation emphasizes that the relevancy of the audience factor is intimately connected with other factors, particularly the character of the symbols whose circulation is intended to be restricted. In the process of decision we find no attention explicitly given to the predispositions of the audience.

---

isolate the peoples from any contact with the outside world, by preventing the Press, radio and other media of communication from reporting international events, and thus hindering mutual comprehension and understanding between peoples." Further in its Resolution 290(IV), 1 December 1949, on "Essentials of Peace," the Assembly called upon every nation "to remove the barriers which deny to peoples the free exchange of information and ideas essential to international understanding and peace."

45. In this category are: Preliminary Agreement as to the Resumption of Relations between Germany and Latvia, Berlin, 1920; the Treaty of Neutrality and Non-Aggression between Persia and Turkey, 1932; and Agreement between Italy and Yugoslavia for Consolidating the Relations of Friendship, 1937, all cited in Chap. 5, note 97.

46. Agreement between the Republic of China and U.S.S.R., 1925, cited in Chap. 5, note 89; Russo-German Treaty, Rapallo, 1922, ibid., note 88; Exchange of Letters between President Roosevelt and M. Litvinov, 1933, ibid., note 93; Provisional Treaty of Friendship and Commerce between Russia and Czechoslovakia, 1922, ibid., note 88; Franco-Russian Non-Aggression Pact, 1932, ibid., note 94; Protocol Concerning the Reestablishment of Diplomatic Relations between Bulgaria and U.S.S.R., 1934, ibid., note 89; Agreement between the U.S.S.R. and Rumania, 1934, ibid., note 89; Indo-Pakistan Agreement, 1948, ibid., note 69. The Trade Agreement between the United Kingdom and U.S.S.R., 1921, ibid., note 90, however, confined the obligation to external audiences. The Provisional Agreement of Commerce between Norway and Russia, 1921, and the Provisional Agreement between Denmark and Russia, 1923, both cited in ibid., note 88, obligated the diplomatic representatives of the contracting parties only to refrain from carrying on propaganda in the receiving country.

7

Objectives

CLAIM THAT IT IS PERMISSIBLE TO USE THE INSTRUMENT FOR PERSUASION

It has always been regarded as permissible to influence events in a foreign state by persuasion. Diplomatic practice, which is predominantly persuasive, is a widely favored instrument of policy from historic times. The doctrine of nonintervention in theory prohibited only coercive interference but not persuasion. Wolff, Vattel, and G. F. von Martens,[1] who were early exponents of the doctrine of intervention, maintained that it was permissible for a sovereign to use his good offices to settle any difference between a foreign sovereign and his subjects, or to persuade them to adopt a particular course of conduct. Besides doctrinal writings, we have the assertion by Lord Palmerston in 1849 in the House of Commons, in reference to the Hungarian civil war then in progress, that though the British government was not entitled to interpose in any manner which would involve England in those hostilities, they could legitimately express their opinion on the subject and communicate it to the parties.[2] The objective of such a course of conduct could only be to persuade the parties to accept the British government's view as to how the conflict might be ended. While such was the position regarding external use of the instrument, there could never have been any objection to internal use for the same purpose.

CLAIM THAT IT IS NOT PERMISSIBLE TO USE FOR DELIBERATE COERCION

Major Coercion

In this century, the Covenant of the League of Nations, the Briand-Kellogg Pact, and the United Nations Charter have progressively imposed

1. *Jus Gentium*, 2, 131; *The Law of Nations*, 3, 132; *The Law of Nations* (trans. W. Cobbet, 4th ed. London, 1829), p. 77.

2. 91 *Annual Register* 148 (1849).

restrictions on strategies of violence. The collective security system set up by the League failed, and the proscriptions of violence contained in the Covenant and the Briand-Kellogg Pact had little effect on the march of events which culminated in World War II. Their effect, however, insofar as individual criminal responsibility was concerned, came up for examination in the postwar trials of the former leaders of Germany and Japan. It was at these trials that the question was at issue whether participation in the use of the ideological instrument as a means of preparation for initiating a war of aggression, or for accomplishing aggression, is criminal.

The Trial by the Nuremberg International Military Tribunal[3]

The International Military Tribunal at Nuremberg was constituted by an agreement entered into in 1945 between the United States, the United Kingdom, the U.S.S.R., and the Provisional Government of the Republic of France.[4] The agreement was later adhered to by 19 other nations.[5] Though the entire responsibility for the conduct of the trial was assumed by the above four major powers, the principles of the Charter by which the Tribunal was constituted and the principles it laid down received the approval of practically the whole of the world community.[6]

The London Charter of 1945 by which the Tribunal was constituted invested it with jurisdiction in respect to three categories of offenses, crimes against peace, war crimes, and crimes against humanity. A crime against peace was defined in the Charter as follows:

> Art. 6(a). Crime against Peace: namely, planning, preparation, initiation, waging a war of aggression, or a war in violation of international treaties, agreements, or assurances, or participation in a common plan or conspiracy for the accomplishment of any of the foregoing.

Article 6(b) and (c) defined war crimes and crimes against humanity. The second paragraph of Article 6 declared:

> Leaders, organizers, instigators, and accomplices participating in the formulation or execution of a common plan or conspiracy to commit any of the foregoing crimes are responsible for all acts performed by any person in execution of such plan.

The defendants were charged under four counts: first, conspiracy to wage a war of aggression, to commit war crimes and crimes against human-

3. For citation see Chap. 3, note 74.
4. For the text of the Agreement and the Charter of the Tribunal, see I.M.T., Nuremberg, *Trial of Major War Criminals, 1,* 8 et seq.
5. For a list of those countries, see ibid., p. 9.
6. The U.N. General Assembly approved the Charter and the Judgment in its Resolution 95(I), 11 December 1947.

ity; second, participating in planning, preparation, initiation, and waging of a war of aggression; third, commission of war crimes; and fourth, commission of crimes against humanity.

The first was, by and large, the most comprehensive of the charges in the indictment. It charged the defendants with being parties to a common plan or conspiracy which had as its objective to circumvent the territorial arrangements prescribed by the Treaty of Versailles and to conquer new territories. With a view to putting into operation their plans, the indictment charged, the defendants disseminated the Nazi ideology in order to induce people to join their conspiracy, or to give their support to the plan. The defendants gained control over the German community, seized power and consolidated their hold. They then made the necessary military, economic, and psychological preparation for war, and put into operation their plan by annexing Austria and Czechoslovakia, and attacking Poland and other countries. In the course of execution of the plan, they were charged with having committed war crimes and crimes against humanity. The prosecution claimed that each of the defendants should be held liable for all acts committed by any person in execution of the common plan or conspiracy.[7]

Individually, the indictment charged the following defendants with activities connected with the use of the ideological instrument, in addition to acts of a different character. Hess was charged as having participated in the "psychological preparations for war." [8] Rosenberg was accused of having "developed, disseminated and exploited the doctrinal techniques of the Nazi conspirators," and "promoted the psychological preparations for war." Von Schirach was charged with having "promoted the psychological and educational preparations for war." Fritzsche was alleged to have used his official and nonofficial influence "to disseminate and exploit the principal doctrines of the Nazi conspirators." Von Papen was charged with having engineered Nazi propaganda in Austria, while he served as Ambassador there, with a view to accomplishing *Anschluss*. Among the organizations which, the prosecution claimed, should be declared criminal, the SA was alleged to have been used as "an instrument for the physical and *ideological* and military training of the party members" (emphasis supplied).

The conspiracy charge in the indictment, it may be observed, was based on the concept of conspiracy as it obtains in the common law systems of jurisprudence. The extent to which the Tribunal made use of the evidentiary facts relating to the use of the ideological instrument in preparation for aggressive wars as a basis for convicting the defendants was, however, very slight. That was because the Tribunal preferred to adopt the concept

7. See the "Indictment Presented to the Tribunal," *Trial of the Major War Criminals*, 1, 27.

8. Ibid., p. 69 et seq.

of conspiracy in the civil law systems and to reject the common law concept.

One of the criticisms urged against the common law concept of conspiracy is in regard to the high degree of laxity allowed in the mode of proving the crime at a trial for conspiracy.[9] In most cases direct evidence of the agreement might not be forthcoming, and therefore indirect proof is permitted. The evidence produced might consist of a wide range of acts committed by the defendants at different times and places. If the court infers a conspiracy from this mass of facts, it may thereafter treat the evidence against any one conspirator as evidence against all. In other words, in a conspiracy trial a court may use a large bulk of facts against any defendant which it is not permitted to use if the defendant is tried independently. But this feature is, by and large, incidental to any trial in which the principals and accessories are jointly tried. Compared with civil law systems, perhaps the position is not too unfair to the defendant, for under those systems the courts are not bound by any exclusionary rule of evidence and consequently enjoy a wide discretion in the choice of evidence to support their decisions.[10] There is, however, one important point of difference between the common and civil law systems which makes the latter more advantageous to the defendant. In the matter of proof of criminal intent the common law systems follow an objective principle of evidence, while the civil law systems follow a subjective principle.[11] Under the latter, criminal intent will not be so readily inferred from facts adduced in evidence as under the former. In a trial for conspiracy under the latter, guilt will be based more on evidence showing direct participation in the planning or the knowledge and adoption of it, rather than on inferences drawn from facts placed before the court not directly indicating such participation.

The Nuremberg Tribunal adopted the civil law principle and limited the conspiracy charge to the crime against peace only. Conspiracy, according to the view adopted by the Tribunal, was participation in a concrete plan to commit a specific crime and intended to be executed in the proximate future.[12] Its existence was not to be inferred from the general declarations of party programs and the like. For all practical purposes, the Tribunal took the first secret conference held by Hitler on November 5, 1937, with some

9. For a description as to how proof of a charge of conspiracy is permitted in the common law system, see J. W. C. Turner, ed., *Kenny's Outlines of Criminal Law* (Cambridge, Cambridge University Press, 1952), pp. 343–44. For a criticism of the method of proof permitted in the common law system, see G. W. Paton, "The War Trials and International Law," 3 *Res Judicatae* 192 (1946).

10. See Stone, *Legal Controls of International Conflict*, p. 361 n.

11. See H. D. De Vabres, "Les Proces De Nuremberg devant Les Principes Modernes du Droit Pénal International," 70 *Hague Recueil* 530, 581 (1947). The author was a member of the Tribunal.

12. *Trial of Major War Criminals*, 1, 225, 226.

of the top German officials to discuss his plans of conquest as the starting point of plans to wage wars of aggression. The steps taken earlier by the Nazis to consolidate the position of their party or its political control were not regarded as criminal.[13] Only eight of the defendants were held guilty of conspiracy,[14] but they were all persons intimately associated with Hitler and attended some of Hitler's secret conferences. The rest were acquitted on this count as no proof was found that they were aware of the plans of aggression of Hitler, or were his close associates.

The Tribunal did not use the evidence of participation in psychological preparations to establish the guilt of any of the defendants on the charge of conspiracy. Of the defendants charged with participation in the use of the ideological instrument, Rosenberg was convicted both under count one and count two, but his guilt was founded more on his activity in connection with the invasions of Norway and Eastern European countries than on the use of the ideological instrument.[15] Von Schirach and Fritzsche were charged only under count one, and were found not guilty. The Tribunal remarked with reference to von Schirach that "it did not appear that [he] was involved in the development of Hitler's plans for territorial expansion by means of aggressive war, or that he participated in the planning or preparation of any wars of aggression." In the case of Fritzsche the Tribunal's conclusion was that there was no evidence that he was aware of the plans, or that he had ever occupied a status where he could have formulated governmental policies.[16] Hess was convicted under counts one and two, and it is only in his case that the Tribunal had the following remarks to make: [17]

> Hess was an active supporter of preparations for war . . . Throughout the years he supported Hitler's policy of vigorous rearmament in many speeches. He told the people that they must sacrifice for armaments, repeating the phrase, "Guns instead of butter."

On the other hand, Schacht's "violently pro-Nazi speech," the activities of the SA, which consisted of dissemination of Nazi ideology, the doctrine of "Lebensraum," propaganda urging revision of the Versailles Treaty and demanding return of colonies, were regarded as innocent because they were

13. Ibid., p. 225.

14. They were Goering, Hess, Ribbentrop, Keitel, Rosenberg, Raeder, Jodl, and Neurath.

15. *Trial of Major War Criminals,* 1, 293.

16. Ibid., pp. 317, 336.

17. Ibid., p. 293. In the case of Schacht, however, the Tribunal stated that rearmament was not by itself a crime under the Charter. The difference between the cases of Hess and of Schacht, which the Tribunal took into account in acquitting the latter, was that Schacht had no knowledge of the aggressive plans of Hitler. See ibid., p. 309.

not related to the implementation of Hitler's plans of aggression.[18] Von Papen was acquitted on the ground that he was not proved to have been a party to any plan under which *Anschluss* was conceived as a step toward initiating a war of aggression. Funk, who served as an Under-Secretary in the Ministry of Propaganda for some time, and was a leading figure later in the Nazi organizations which were used to control the press, film, music, and publishing houses, was held guilty under count two, not by virtue of these activities but because of his economic planning for the war.[19]

Perhaps the Tribunal adopted a very narrow concept of conspiracy to give effect to the principle it had laid down that "mass punishments should be avoided." It wanted to confine the application of penal sanctions only to those who had exercised the power to formulate and influence directly the policies of the state leading to aggressive war. Out of nineteen defendants only eleven were convicted for a crime against the peace, but all of them did participate some time or other in the policymaking at the highest level. In the case of Fritzsche the Tribunal explicitly mentioned the fact that he had always occupied an inferior status in the German official hierarchy, having little control over the policymaking, as a reason for his acquittal.[20] To give effect to this policy of confining the administration of penal discipline only to those who had formulated or influenced the policies of aggression, the Tribunal had to adopt a restricted concept of conspiracy.

It is not unreasonable, however, to infer from the judgment of the Tribunal that if any of the defendants had exercised policymaking functions and had participated, even exclusively, in the use of the ideological instrument to prepare for aggressive war, he would have been held guilty. If Fritzsche, for example, had been in Hitler's inner circle, it is reasonable to believe that he would have been convicted. If Goebbels had been one of the defendants, it is hard to believe that he would have been acquitted.

THE MINISTRIES CASE[21]

This is one of the twelve war crime trials held before the United States Military Tribunals in Nuremberg under Law No. 10 of the Allied Control Council in Germany. That law authorized the zonal commanders in the United States, British, French, and Soviet occupation zones to arrest and bring to trial persons suspected of commission of crimes against peace, war crimes, or crimes against humanity, if the commission of such crimes was

18. Ibid., and the Judgment in reference to the SA, ibid., pp. 274–75.
19. Ibid., pp. 304, 325.
20. Ibid., pp. 256, 337.
21. Judgment dated Nov. 4, 1948, *Trials of War Criminals before Nuremberg Military Tribunals under Control Council Law No. 10*, 14, 314.

not confined to any specific geographical locality. Of those twelve trials, only in four the prosecution alleged the commission of crimes against peace.[22] The substantive definitions of crimes against the peace, war crimes, and crimes against humanity adopted under Law No. 10 being substantially the same as those given in the Charter of the I.M.T., Nuremberg, a conspiracy charge was put forward in all four cases. The tribunals, however, were guided to a large extent by the judgment of the I.M.T., Nuremberg, and confined the conspiracy charge to the crime against peace only. Further, in none of the cases was anybody held guilty of conspiracy. It was only in *The Ministries Case* that three of the defendants [23] were held liable for participation in planning and preparation for aggressive invasions. But their activity did not involve the use of the ideological instrument. The decision of the tribunal in regard to the case of the defendants Dietrich and von Weizsaecker alone are of interest to us here.

Dietrich was the Press Chief of the Reich and of the Nazi party during the entire period when aggressive wars were planned and initiated. He had full control of the entire German press. Before and after the initiation of every invasion, he was shown to have directed the propaganda operations carried out to influence the German people in favor of war. He was, however, acquitted. The tribunal found that it was not proved beyond doubt that he had knowledge of the plans of aggression of Hitler.[24] In regard to Baron von Weizsaecker, the Tribunal considered whether his giving support to the Nazi propaganda in Austria could form a basis for conviction. It found that the defendant, as the State Secretary in the German Foreign Office, did finance the activity, but observed:

> In the absence of treaty obligations, one may encourage political movements in another state, consort with the leaders of such movements, and give them financial or other support, all for the purpose of strengthening the movement which has annexation as its ultimate purpose without violating international law. It is only when these things are done with knowledge that they are part of a scheme to use force and to be followed if necessary by aggressive war or invasion that an offense cognizable by this Tribunal comes into being. There is no evidence that von Weizsaecker at the time knew that Hitler intended to invade Austria.[25]

22. The four trials were, *The I.G. Farben Trial*, 1948, *U.N. War Crimes Cases*, 10, 1; *The Krupp Trial*, 1948, ibid., p. 69; *The German High Command Trial*, 1948, ibid., 12, 1; and *The Ministries Case*.

23. They were Keppler, Lammars, and Koerner. Weizsaecker and Woermann were convicted for crimes against peace, but their conviction was later set aside; see ibid., pp. 959 and 966.

24. Ibid., p. 417.

25. Ibid., p. 343.

We may only add that if there had been evidence, for example, that these defendants had been present at one of the secret conferences of Hitler, the result would probably have been different.

The Trial by the International Military Tribunal for the Far East (The Tokyo Trial)

The Tribunal was constituted by a proclamation issued by the Supreme Commander of the Allied Forces in conformance with the terms of the Japanese surrender. The jurisdiction vested in the Tribunal was similar to that vested in the I.M.T., Nuremberg.

In this trial the presiding Tribunal gave greater importance to the facts relating to the use of the ideological instrument as a means of preparation for aggression than in the Nuremberg trial. That was because the Tribunal adopted a concept of conspiracy which was in many respects similar to the common law concept.

The Tribunal considered only two charges in reference to the crime against peace—conspiracy to wage an aggressive war, and actual waging of it. The charges dealing with the planning and preparation stages of the crime were omitted as the Tribunal considered that they were included in the charge of conspiracy.[26] In its view the original parties to the agreement to wage a war of aggression and all later adherents who worked for its execution were guilty of the offense of conspiracy itself. That is to say, any person who with guilty knowledge participated in the preparation or planning stages of the crime was also guilty of conspiracy itself.

Just as any court in a common law system would do, the Tribunal considered diverse evidential facts and arrived at the conclusion that a conspiracy was formed, about the years 1927–29, to wage a war of aggression. All but two of the defendants were held to be either the original parties to it or later adherents. Among the facts the Tribunal took into account in finding the existence of conspiracy were those relating to the use of the ideological instrument to prepare the Japanese people psychologically for an aggressive war. They included imposition of censorship and stringent control over the press, indoctrination of youth in militarist doctrines, manipulation of symbols like "Kodo," "Hakko Ichiu," [27] "Anti-Communnism," "New Order," "Life Line," the use of the press, radio, and film to disseminate propaganda which would create attitudes in favor of aggressive

26. Justice Jarnilla, the Philippine member of the Tribunal and Justice Bernard, the French member, dissented from the majority decision to merge the conspiracy charge and the charges of participation in planning and preparation into one. See S. Horwitz, "The Tokyo Trial," *Int'l. Conciliation*, No. 465 (1950), p. 533.

27. These expressions have varied meanings, but in the propaganda of the 1930s, "Kodo" meant benevolent imperial rule or the imperial way, and "Hakko Ichiu," bringing the four corners of the world together under one roof.

war, and the preparation of propaganda blueprints to be used during the contemplated military campaigns.

In establishing the connection of some of the defendants with the conspiracy, the Tribunal took into account their participation in the use of the ideological instrument, besides their other activities. Thus Araki was held guilty because among other things the Tribunal found against him:

> After its early years it was mainly as a propagandist that he figured in the execution of the conspiracy by inciting the appetite of the Japanese people for the possessions of Japan's neighbors, by inflaming Japanese opinion for war to secure these possessions, by his advocacy of an alliance with Germany and Italy which were bent on similar schemes of expansion . . . his fervent support of the agitation for great increase in the armaments of Japan so that she might secure these aims by force or threat of force.[28]

Itagaki was found guilty of conspiracy and one of the circumstances relied on against him was that "he was one of the coiners of the term "anti-Communism" to serve as a pretext for Japanese aggression in North China." Kodo was held guilty because, among other things, as Minister of Education he applied himself to the development of a strong warlike spirit in Japan. Against Kiroshi the Tribunal cited his articles in newspapers and magazines supporting the war. Sato's knowledge of the conspiracy and participation were inferred from his speeches. Shiratori's articles advocating a totalitarian government, his propaganda activities advocating the objectives of the conspirators, and his use of the symbol "New Order," were taken as some of the facts which established his participation in the conspiracy. The propaganda activities of Dr. Okawa were referred to by the Tribunal many a time but his mental unfitness to stand trial saved a decision.

This manner of evaluation of evidence to establish guilt on a conspiracy charge is typically the one which a court in the common law system adopts in conspiracy trials. The Tribunal applied the objective principle of appreciation of evidence in establishing the fact of conspiracy and the fact of participation of the defendants in it. Agreement to commit the crime, or adherence to it later, was liberally inferred from objective facts. The Tribunal found 23 out of 25 defendants to be guilty of conspiracy to wage a war of aggression. At Nuremberg, out of 19 defendants only 8 were found guilty of conspiracy and 4 for participation at the stage of planning and preparation. But it should be remembered that both tribunals were not fettered by any technical rules of evidence.[29] They had complete freedom with respect to the manner of appreciation of evidence.

28. See the judgment of the Tribunal, dated Nov. 4, 1948, Chap. 9.

29. See Art. 19 of the Charter of the I.M.T. Nuremberg and Art. 13(a) of the Charter of the I.M.T. Tokyo.

Some authors have criticized the Tokyo Tribunal's judgment in regard to the manner in which the conspiracy charge was dealt with.[30] It is true that the Tribunal departed from the Nuremberg precedent in certain respects. The Far East Tribunal followed the Nuremberg precedent in confining the charge of conspiracy to the crime against the peace, [31] but differed on the manner in which the two charges—the charge of conspiracy and of planning and preparation—were merged into one, and in adopting a different set of principles of proof of the crime of conspiracy to wage a war of aggression. It is difficult to see how the exercise of discretion by any international tribunal in this regard may be questioned unless the discretion has been limited by clear rules of evidence; and the Tokyo Tribunal's discretion was in no way limited.

The above trials, the provisions of the charters constituting the tribunals, and the world community response which at least the Nuremberg judgment has received, lead us reasonably to expect that in future trials for crimes against peace, not only the use of transnational violence for purposes of aggression would be regarded as wrongful but also preparations for its use in furtherance of a plan or conspiracy of aggression. It may also be expected that the use of the ideological instrument to further plans of aggression by violence will be regarded as wrongful. It may further be expected that a person who, having power to shape or influence the policies of his state, plans or conspires to use a strategy of violence for purposes of aggression, or joins such conspiracy, and participates in the operation of the ideological strategy—whether to make the necessary psychological preparations at home, or to undermine the will to resist of the people of the state which is intended to be or is actually the victim—will be held guilty of a crime against peace.

However, as the use of violence for self-defense has not been proscribed either under the League Covenant, the Kellogg Pact, or the U.N. Charter, intensive use of the ideological instrument to promote a strategy of defense even by violence remains permissible.

From the point of view of policy, in order effectively to control the use of transnational violence, punishment should extend not only to actual use of the military instrument but also to all acts done with the intention of promoting, and capable of contributing substantially to the success of, the military strategy of aggression. Intensive psychological preparations for military aggression, and intensive use of the ideological instrument to destroy the will to resist of the intended victims of aggression, must be included within the range of punishment. On the other hand, in a world in which the expectation of violence is very high, preparations for self-defense

30. See C. A. Pompe, *Aggressive War, An International Crime* (The Hague, Nijhoff, 1953), p. 255; Horwitz, p. 532.

31. See the judgment, Chap. 2; see also Keenan and Brown, supra, notes 46, 89, et seq.

even by violence cannot be prohibited.[32] Nor can the use of the ideological instrument to prepare internal audiences to resist aggression, and to influence external audiences to restrain an external elite from committing military aggression, or to counteract the psychological preparations which an elite is making, be prohibited.

Aggression v. Self-Defense, Ideological Aggression, etc.

The above trials have primary reference to the determination of criminal responsibility of individuals for crimes against peace. It is now necessary to turn attention to those modalities of controlling transnational strategies of coercion whereby preventive or repressive action is taken by international organs entrusted with maintenance of peace and security in the world, or any region of it, as well as measures taken by the officials of the affected state or states to counter the coercion applied. There are two concepts central to these methods of regulation, *aggression* and *self-defense*. Much has been said and written on these two concepts, and an elaborate discussion cannot be undertaken here.

The term *aggression* has been in use since very early times as an expression employed in international propaganda and politics.[33] Before the establishment of the League of Nations it had little legal significance.[34] With the establishment of the League some wars came to be re-

32. Whitton and Larson in specifying their concept of war propaganda point out, "First, this term does not apply to wartime propaganda of psychological warfare between combatants. It is intended here to include the kind of propaganda that *leads* to war. Second, the term would not apply to preparing people for use of force when under the United Nations Charter the use of force is a legitimate one. This can occur generally in only two cases: genuine self-defense and use of force under actual authorization by the United Nations" (p. 65).

33. See Quincy Wright, "The Prevention of Aggression," 50 *A.J.I.L.* 514, 519 (1956).

34. Early writers indeed made a distinction between "aggressive war" and "defensive war." See Suarez, *On Faith*, pp. 804–05; Vittoria, *De Indis*, Appendix F., p. cxvi; Grotius, De Jure Belli, Bk. ii, Chap. ii, Secs. 2–3, 16; Vattel, *The Law of Nations*, 3, 246. A "defensive war" was, according to them, a *just* war, except when the opponent had a just cause; see Grotius, Bk. ii, Chap. i, Sec. xviii; Vattel, 3, 246. But the just and unjust war distinction never gained legal significance; see A. Nussbaum, "Just War, A Legal Concept," 42 *Mich. L. Rev.* 453 (1943). The term *aggression* was frequently employed to indicate that the opponent was pursuing a policy of attacking other states, and therefore must be met by resistance. See e.g. the message of the British King to the House of Commons on Feb. 11, 1793, in which he accused France of acts of "wanton and unprovoked aggression" and called upon the Commons and the people to contribute effectively to prosecuting a "just and necessary war"; 36 *Annual Register, Public Papers* 79 (1793); also the King's Message to Parliament in 1803 on the withdrawal of the British Ambassador from France, in the course of which he charged France with "violence, aggression and aggrandizement," of "views of ambition and acts of aggression" as reasons for the step; see 45 *Annual Register* 734 (1803).

garded as illicit, and others licit, and the attempt in the days of the League was to give aggression a meaning relative to the public order established by that organization,[35] and during recent years, relative to the public order established by the United Nations.

There is fairly precise indication in the Charter of the permissible and impermissible categories of transnational coercion under the present system of world public order. In the light of Article 2(3) and (4) and Article 51, the following categories of transnational coercion are permissible: (1) coercion of low intensity, which may be expected to be always present as a normal incident of community interactions across state boundaries and has to be tolerated, or which neither endangers the maintenance of international peace and security nor constitutes an international deliquency; (2) coercion, even highly intense and extensive, including the use of violence, used as a measure of self-defense against impermissible coercion applied, or threatened to be immediately applied, by others; and (3) peace enforcement measures sanctioned by authoritative international organs in accordance with the provisions of the Charter, of whatever degree of intensity or extensiveness. The impermissible categories are: (1) coercion of low intensity, which, though incapable of threatening the "territorial integrity or political independence" of a state, the realms protected by Article 2(4) of the Charter, constitutes an international delinquency; and (2) coercion, intense, extensive, destructive, the exercise of which is liable to be met by inforcement actions contemplated in the Charter.[36]

The main problem that arises in connection with defining aggression is the identification and definition of the second category of impermissible coercion and the differentiation of it from the second category of permissible coercion. The polar and complementary character of aggression and self-defense is widely recognized.[37]

During the discussions in the United Nations on the question of defining aggression, members have taken the following broad positions: Some favored an "enumerative" definition,[38] while some others preferred a

35. See Komarnicki, "*Definition de L'Agresseur,*" pp. 14–15. He says that the concept of aggression, after the establishment of the League of Nations, became related to the juridical order represented by the international organization.

36. See McDougal and Feliciano, *Law and Minimum World Public Order*, pp. 123–27.

37. See Pompe, *Aggressive War, an International Crime*, p. 55. Shotwell, *War as an Instrument of National Policy*, p. 57; H. Lauterpacht, "The Pact of Paris . . . ," 20 *Trans. Grot. Soc.* 178, 199 (1935); Julius Stone, *Aggression and World Order* (Berkeley, University of California Press, 1958), p. 75.

38. For a definition of this type, which specifies the various acts that should be regarded as acts of aggression, see the draft definition submitted by the Soviet Union to the Special Committee of the U.N. General Assembly on the Question of Defining Aggression, *Report of the Special Committee on the Question of Defining Aggression*,

definition in general and abstract terms;[39] a third group preferred a "mixed" definition,[40] and others were opposed to any defining of the concept.[41] According to one view the concept should be limited to military attack only while according to another it should also include the concepts of "indirect," "ideological," and "economic" aggressions.[42]

The Principle of Priority of Use of Coercion

In the first place, it may be noted that the principle of priority of use of impermissible coercion is central to the concept of aggression.[43] During the debates in the United Nations on defining aggression, there was much discussion on the principle of "First Act," by which the state that first commits one of the acts specified will be deemed to be guilty of aggression. This principle, on which was based the Soviet definition of aggression, met with strong criticism. It was pointed out, in particular, that every one of the acts mentioned in the Soviet definition as constituting aggression may in a given context be legitimate self-defense.[44] However, while a single,

---

1953, G.A.O.R., 9th Sess., Supp. No. 11 (1954), p. 13, and *Report of the 1956 Special Committee on the Question of Defining Aggression,* G.A.O.R., 12th Sess., Supp. 16 (1957), p. 30.

39. See *Report of the Special Committee of 1953*, p. 4, and *Report of 1956 Special Committee*, p. 8, and for examples of such definitions, ibid., p. 28. For instance, the definition proposed by Mr. Cordova in the International Law Commission during its third session runs thus: "Aggression is the direct or indirect employment by the authorities of a State of armed force against another State for any purpose other than national or collective self-defense or execution of a decision by a competent organ of the United Nations."

40. Many in the 1956 Special Committee favored this type of definition. See the "*Report of the 1956 Special Committee*, para. 65.

41. The United States and United Kingdom are the chief among those that take this position, which may be summed up thus: "A general definition would be of little value as it would be too vague, an enumerative definition would be dangerous because it might contain too much or too little, and a mixed definition was apt to combine the disadvantages of the other two types." *Report of the 1956 Special Committee*, para. 133. Professor Julius Stone has argued at length against definition in his *Aggression and World Order*

42. For the position that the concept of aggression should be limited to armed attack, see the speech of Sir G. Fitzmaurice, British representative in the Sixth Committee of the U.N. General Assembly during the Ninth Session, G.A.O.R., 9th Sess., Comm. VI, pp. 48, 79. In the view of the British government, "force" in Art. 2(4) of the Charter refers only to armed force, but includes indirect as well as direct use of force. See the proposal submitted by the United Kingdom to the Special Committee on Principles of International Law concerning Friendly Relations and Cooperation among States, *Report of the Special Committee*, U.N. Doc. A/5646, 16 November 1964, p. 20. Among scholars, Professor Quincy Wright favors limitation of the concept of aggression to armed attacks. See his "The Prevention of Aggression," p. 526.

43. McDougal and Feliciano, p. 168.

44. See Stone, *Aggression and World Order*, pp. 69–72; it may be noted that the

precisely defined act may as well be an act of self-defense as an act of aggression, depending upon the context in which it occurs, the idea of priority in the use of coercion is indeed central to the concept of aggression. Self defense is indeed the response, under the expectation of deprivations, to operation of coercive instruments on the part of another.[45] Aggression may be termed prior use, without legal justification, of destructive coercive process.

When international decision-makers such as the Security Council and the General Assembly, entrusted with the task of maintaining peace and security in the world community, are confronted with a situation involving mutual application of destructive transnational coercive processes, and are called upon to determine which of the participants has committed aggression, and to deal with the aggressor, or to regulate the situation otherwise, they must take into account the sequence of events concerning the conflict. They may also consider the following factors,[46] having due regard for the necessity of dispatch in reaching a decision:

1. The character of the participants in the process of mutual application of coercion, their posture—of *self-extension* or *self-conservation*—and their

---

"first shot" rule has been rejected even from the time of French Revolution. Early revolutionaries developed the theory that "aggressive war" constituted a crime, but they rejected the first shot rule as a test of aggression; see R. Redslob, *Histoire des Grand Principes du Droit des Gens* (Paris, 1923), p. 282. During the time of the League of Nations, the Permanent Advisory Commission and a Special Committee of the Temporary Mixed Commission considered the question of definition of aggression and both rejected the first shot principle; see the opinion of the Commission regarding the *Assembly Resolutions XIV and XV, L.O.N., Official Journal*, Spl. Supp. No. 16 (1923), pp. 114, 115–18, and "Commentary on the Definition of a Case of Aggression" drawn up by a Special Committee of the Temporary Mixed Commission, ibid., pp. 183–85. It was pointed out that though the manner of use of the military instrument by the parties involved in a conflict might indicate who the aggressor was, it would not supply an infallible test in many cases. Aggressive wars could be initiated without crossing any fronter (e.g. by attacking ships at sea); and invasion of the territory of another state might under certain circumstances be only a measure of self-defense. Neither priority in military attack nor priority in the crossing of a frontier would furnish a satisfactory test as to who the aggressor was, though in some cases suddenness of the attack, its intensity, and the nature of the weapons used might afford a clue. See also in this connection Shotwell, pp. 213–14; S. de Madariaga, *Disarmament* (New York, Coward-McCann, 1929), p. 126.

45. "Self-defense" here refers to the launching of a large-scale, destructive, coercive process against a foreign state, as distinguished from resistance offered to stray attacks, on one hand, and the adoption of measures under the plea of self-preservation to meet possible harmful threats or moves in the future. See in this connection McDougal and Feliciano, pp. 209 et seq., for the necessity to distinguish between measures of self-defense taken for varied objectives, and between different degrees of intensity and comprehensiveness, and the necessity to adopt different policies in different contexts.

46. The variables here are based upon what has been suggested by McDougal and Feliciano. For a fuller and detailed account the reader is referred to their work.

propensities to commit aggression or to conform to the world public order.[47]

2. The nature of the *objectives* of the participants: The reference here should be not to the self-proclaimed objectives but to those determined from observed facts. The most relevant questions to be investigated here are: is the objective of the participant "self-extension" or "self-conservation," and is it, or its consequentiality, so comprehensive as to cause deprivation to the opponent of "territorial integrity" or "political independence," the values to which Article 2(4) of the Charter affords protection.[48] Pursuit of objectives of negligible consequence call for no intervention by decision-makers on behalf of the community. It is also necessary to observe whether the objective is an inclusive or exclusive one, and whether it is compatible with world public order. Pursuit of objectives which are inclusive or compatible with world public order has to be tolerated to a greater extent than pursuit of the others.[49]

3. The *conditions* under which the participants employ coercive processes are also relevant for the determination of the aggressor. It is not probable, for instance, that an extremely weak state commits aggression on a strong one.[50] The relative military capabilities of the parties, along with those of their allies, indeed throw some light on who is the aggressor. The level of expectation of timely intervention by collective security agencies to stop aggression is a relevant factor, for when the level is low relatively hasty reactions by way of self-defense may have to be condoned.[51]

4. *The instruments of coercion used and intensity of coercion:* As it is now widely felt that nonmilitary instruments of coercion possess efficacy comparable to that of the military instrument in undermining the political independence of a foreign state or compelling it to surrender territory, especially when the military instrument is kept in readiness as a threat, or to be used if necessary, a definition of aggression which is confined to the use of the military instrument only is not likely to receive wide support. This is clear from the persistent pressure exerted, during the debates in the United Nations on defining aggression, for the inclusion of "ideological," "economic," and "indirect" aggression in the definition. The

47. It is generally posited that states having a constitutional and democratic form of government are less prone to aggression than those having an authoritarian government. See ibid., p. 173, and the works cited therein.

48. "Political independence" generally signifies the freedom of the government of a state to take policy decisions concerning the state without coercion by the government of another; see ibid., p. 175; Goodrich and Hambro, *Charter of the United Nations,* p. 105; Pompe, p. 106.

49. The relevance of these questions to the use of the ideological instrument for realizing self-determination, etc. will be observed later.

50. However, the weaker may sometimes launch attacks of nuisance value.

51. McDougal and Feliciano, p. 183.

proposal to include these concepts was opposed partly due to the fear that it would suggest the legitimacy of the initiation of large-scale use of violence in "self-defense" against alleged nonviolent aggressions.[52] However, when self-defense is limited by the principles of necessity and proportionality, the fear has no substantial basis. It is suggested here that decision-makers must take into account the coercive process employed as a whole, whatever instruments or combinations of them are used, and not the use of any single instrument of coercion alone.[53]

The level of intensity of coercion that should be reached before it may be regarded as aggression presents some difficulty. Flagrant aggressions such as the Nazi aggressions, and instances of application of negligible coercion, present no difficulty indeed. Cases that fall between these two extremes require consideration. In order to amount to aggression, the coercion applied must be at least of such intensity and proportion that it releases the target state, under the principle of self-defense, from the obligations imposed by Article 2(4) of the Charter not to use force against the "territorial integrity" or "political independence" of a state.[54] A reasonable expectation must be created on the part of the target that nonviolent countermeasures would not suffice to protect its essential values of political independence and territorial integrity, and only violence would meet the demands of the situation.

5. The outcome secured by the participant as a result of applying coercion, as distinguished from the objectives sought, needs also to be noted. When practically negligible consequences are produced for the target state, no collective enforcement action is necessary, and the determination of the aggressor might not be needed.

52. See *Report of the Special Committee on the Question of Defining Aggression, 1953*, p. 7; *Report of the 1956 Special Committee*, p. 8.

53. It may be noted in this connection that the Permanent Advisory Commission of the League of Nations and the Special Committee of the Temporary Mixed Commission, whose reports were cited in note 44 above, discussed the facts which might indicate in general an *intention* to initiate a war of aggression. According to them, the manner in which the government might operate the diplomatic, ideological, and economic strategies, in addition to the military strategy, would more likely manifest the intention. The signs which indicate the intention, they stated, appear in the following order: "1. Organization on paper of industrial mobilization. 2. Actual organization of industrial mobilization. 3. Collection of stocks of raw materials. 4. Setting-on-foot war industries. 5. Preparations for military mobilization. 6. Actual military mobilization. 7. Hostilities." Further, in the absence of any indisputable test, intention could be inferred on the basis of an *impression* gathered from factors such as "the political attitude of the possible aggressor; his propaganda; the attitude of his press and population; his policy on the international market, etc." See also McDougal and Feliciano, p. 190.

54. Ibid., pp. 200–01; Pompe, p. 111. Dr. Pompe limits reference to the use of the military instrument only.

6. *Response to the decisions or recommendations of decision-makers:* The response of the participants to the decisions or recommendations of the decision-makers to stop the hostilities has to be taken into account to a certain extent.[55] In general, the participant who remains impervious to such recommendations is more likely to be the aggressor and merits to be adjudged as such. However, where the initiator of hostilities gains some significant strategic or tactical advantage, and does not show willingness to give it up, and the expectation is that cessation of hostilities would result only in freezing the situation, it is not reasonable to expect the loser to stop immediately, on call, its efforts to recover the lost ground.

7. *Expectations about the effects of the decision:* The decision-maker should have regard to the expediency of branding a participant as an aggressor. He cannot overlook the prevailing pattern of distribution of power in the world arena, the alignments of powers, and the probable effects of declaring a participant an aggressor. If the situation is such that the decision is likely to be disapproved by a large number of significantly powerful states, it is not realistic to expect that the decision to brand a state as aggressor will be taken. If, in the face of the impracticability of taking further steps to suppress aggression, such a decision is taken, it will only bring the decision into contempt. However, if the expectation is that the mere passing of the judgment will bring about a cessation of fighting and of aggression such a decision may be taken. But this is rarely possible.

Under present conditions, especially due to the fear of nuclear war, if fighting on a limited scale breaks out, international decision-makers en-

55. The Report of the Special Committee of the Temporary Mixed Commission of the League of Nations, cited in note 44 above, and the Committee on Arbitration and Security of the Preparatory Commission for the Disarmament Conference, in its report based upon the Memorandum of M. Rutger on Arts. 10, 11, 16 of the Covenant (L.O.N. Pub., Disarmament. 1928. IX. 3, p. 24), suggested that the attitude adopted by a government during the negotiations preceding and succeeding the outbreak of violence might be taken into account in the determination of the intention to commit aggression. Further, the two Committees and the Permanent Advisory Commission in its report cited in note 44 above, considered that the government's response to the recommendations that the League Assembly or Council might make to prevent the outbreak or expansion of violence might be taken into account in the determination of the aggressor. Under Art. 40 of the U.N. Charter, the Security Council must take into account the response of the parties to the provisional measures recommended. See in this connection, *Repertory of the Practice of the United Nations* (New York, 1955), 2, 340–41; Goodrich and Hambro, p. 364; L. M. Goodrich, *Korea, A Study of the U.S. Policy in the United Nations* (New York, Council on Foreign Relations, 1956), p. 106. See also the General Assembly's resolution on "Duties of States upon the Outbreak of Hostilities," Resolution 378(V), 17 Nov. 1950, according to which the Assembly has to take into account the compliance of the parties with the resolution and the recommendations of the Assembly. About the limited utility of this factor, in the present age of thermonuclear weapons, for the purpose of determining the aggressor, see Stone, *Aggression and World Order*, p. 109.

trusted with the maintenance of peace and security are more likely to try to bring about a cessation of the fighting. When the immediate objective of the decision-maker is to prevent the expansion of hostilities, to stop them and restore normal conditions, it is more expedient to invoke the formula of "breach of the peace" than "act of aggression." [56] Branding a state as an aggressor seems to be useful only when it can form the starting point of a successful enforcement action, or can at least serve as a means of rallying world public opinion against the aggressor who is impervious to the restraining influence of international decision-makers.

Further, it has been suggested that the decision-makers have to take into consideration the possible effect of the decision that a state has committed aggression and the consequential adoption of suppressive measures, on the promotion of the values of human dignity.[57] Indeed the decision-makers are practically certain to be influenced by their perspectives, their demands, expectations, and identifications.

Taking the above factors into account, and the sequence of events, the decision-makers may decide which of the participants has committed aggression, which one has resorted to legitimate self-defense, provided, of course, that expedience does not demand that they should refrain from such a decision and adopt other available alternatives such as the invocation of the formula of "breach of the peace." Inasmuch as decision-makers act under the immediate impact of events, as promptly as possible, there is bound to be a lack of precision in their determinations. There cannot indeed be such precision as may be found in the determinations by an international tribunal trying a crime against peace. Realistically speaking, trials of that nature can take place only after the aggressor is completely vanquished. Such a tribunal can take more time, carry on more elaborate inquiry, and obtain more evidence, possibly from the secret archives of the aggressor state as the Nuremberg and Tokyo Tribunals were able to do, than can international decision-makers entrusted with the maintenance of peace and security.

Among other decision-makers,[58] the officials of the state subjected to coercion are likely to decide about the commission of aggression on the

56. See in this connection ibid., p. 160; also McDougal and Feliciano, p. 206.

57. See ibid., p. 259.

58. Regional organizations may be expected to act, with respect to conflicts between their respective members, more or less in the same manner as the U.N. Organs do in reference to conflicts brought before them; and in respect of an attack by an outsider on one of the members, in the same manner as an individual state. The respective spheres of competence of the U.N. organs and the regional organizations in relation to intraregional conflicts are somewhat controversial, but it seems clear, by virtue of Arts. 51 and 53 of the U.N. Charter, that the Security Council possesses competence to review the decisions of a regional organization. See in this connection the study by Garcia Amador, G.A.O.R., 5th Sess., Supp. No. 14, Appendix (1950).

basis of their expectations of the effects of the coercive process on their state—whether it will cause deprivation of "territorial integrity" or "political independence." The officials of other states will decide on the basis of the facts that come to their knowledge, their identifications, expectations of the probable outcome of the conflict and its effects on their state, and their demands. Their decisions are, under the system of the public order of the U.N., reviewable by the Security Council or the General Assembly.

Ideological Aggression

In recent times claims have been put forward for recognition of "ideological aggression," and definitions have been suggested. Here we may examine the suggested definitions and their limitations, and suggest some special indices by which the commission of the "ideological aggression" may be determined. The reference will be to situations in which the ideological instrument of coercion is used with great intensity and as the chief instrument of policy.

THE SOVIET DEFINITION OF "IDEOLOGICAL AGGRESSION"

The definition runs thus:

> That State shall be declared to have committed an act of ideological aggression which:
> (a) Encourages war propaganda;
> (b) Encourages propaganda in favor of using atomic, bacterial, chemical and other weapons of mass destruction;
> (c) Promotes the propagation of fascist-nazi views, of racial and national exclusiveness, and hatred and contempt for other peoples.[59]

Apart from these acts, the Security Council will have the power to regard any other act to be an act of aggression of whatever pattern, military, indirect, economic, or ideological. The definition further contains a catalogue of circumstances which might exist in a state and which should not form a justification for "ideological aggression." The enumerated circumstances comprise a variety of social, political, and economic events occuring within a state, and events which either manifest or occasion strain in the relations between states, such as adoption by a state of diplomatic or economic measures against another, and frontier incidents.

It is not difficult to point out the absurdities in this definition. It purports to proscribe all "war propaganda," and does not on the face of it exclude propaganda calling upon the people of a state to prepare for any

59. See the draft definition of aggression submitted by the Soviet Union, *Report of the Special Committee on the Question of Defining Aggression*, 1953, p. 13; *Report of the 1956 Special Committee*, p. 30.

expected military aggression. The expression "war propaganda" is so vague that it may take within its net even discussions in the national press about that country's defenses.[60] The definition purports to prohibit "war propaganda," but does not mention a variety of techniques which could be employed to develop attitudes of hostility among the people of a state against the people of others without ever mentioning the word "war," such as strict censorship, intensive indoctrination of youth, exposure of people to a one-sided version of events. Once predispositions of hostility against the people of another state are developed by slow processes stretching over a long period of time, it would then not be difficult, nor would it take long, to convert that hostility into a sentiment favoring aggression.

With reference to the second clause of the definition, one may point out that it seeks to proscribe even warnings addressed to the elite and people of a foreign state that a resort to the weapons mentioned in that clause would be followed by retaliation in kind, when the only safeguard against the use of such weapons at the present day is the fear of retaliation. The third clause seeks to proscribe propaganda of "fascist-nazi" views of national or racial hatred, and the expression "fascist-nazi" is again too vague to be used in a definition like this.[61] If the idea is to proscribe propagation of views of racial hatred in order to protect the target racial groups from deprivations, the issue has to be considered in the context of the techniques of the strategy that ought to be prohibited, and not prevention of aggression. On the other hand, if the intention is to prohibit development of perspectives among the audience in favor of aggression against other nations, a formula having a more comprehensive reference to the strategy of coercion must be adopted, rather than one that merely refers to circulation of certain symbols, which may occur also in a situation not connected with aggression. Another important point is that the enumerated circumstances which are declared to be insufficient to justify "aggression" are so sweeping as to cover practically every aspect of the life of a state. Some of these aspects might legitimately and as a normal incident evoke comment, protest, remonstrance, or expressions of resentment and moral indignation from the people of other states. Adoption of the Soviet definition might result in

60. See in this connection the criticism of Mr. Vallat, the representative of the U.K. in the Special Committee on the Question of Defining Aggression, at the 9th meeting of the Committee, U.N. Doc. A/AC.66/SR.9 (1953); see also the speech of the U.S. representative in the same committee at its 12th meeting, U.N. Doc. A/AC.66/SR.12 (1953).

61. See the criticism of Mr. Christenson, the delegate of Norway, in the U.N. Sub-Commission on Freedom of Information and the Press, at its 14th meeting, U.N. Doc. E/CN.4/Sub. 1/SR.14 (1948), on the use of the expression "fascist" in the statement of general principles of freedom of information proposed by the Soviet Union. He pointed out that the expression was ambiguous, and therefore could not be used in the statement of general principles.

the officials of a state using it to charge the government of another with "ideological aggression" even for simple toleration by the latter of comments in the press of that country about such events.

From the point of view of policy, it may be noted that the Soviet definition does not contribute much. The definition purports to proscribe certain types of propaganda only. Whether or not such proscriptions will serve any purpose may be observed later.[62] If the objective is to prevent armed aggression, and with that end in view it is desired to facilitate community intervention even at the stage when the prospective aggressor is making psychological preparations, community prescriptions and procedures should be suitably patterned to achieve that purpose—in fact, to restrain all activity found to be preparation for aggression. A definition of the type given by the Soviet Union will not serve such a purpose.

THE CHINESE DEFINITION OF AGGRESSION

The Chinese delegation proposed before the First Special Committee on the Question of Defining Aggression, 1953, a definition of aggression which ran thus: [63]

> [Aggression] consists of the employment of force, open or under cover, armed or unarmed, by a State for the violation, impairment or destruction of the territorial integrity or political independence of another State, or for the subversion of its political and social order, or in the case of dispute with another State, for the coercion of that State in the place of pacific settlement. Among other acts it includes: . . .
> (c) Planting fifth columnists or subversive agents in a victim state
> (d) Inciting civil strife in a victim State by propaganda

During the second session of the International Law Commission, when the Draft Code of Offenses Against the Peace and Security of Mankind was discussed, the Chinese member proposed that "the fact of a State carrying on subversive propaganda against another State" should be regarded as a crime against the peace and security of mankind.[64] The Commission did not accept the proposal, considering the expression "subversive propaganda" to be a vague one.[65]

The main defect of the Chinese proposals insofar as they relate to incitement to civil strife and subversive propaganda is that they tend to stretch

62. See below, Chap. 11.

63. See *Report of the Special Committee on the Question of Defining Aggression,* 1953, p. 14.

64. See International Law Commission, Summary Rec., 58th meeting (U.N. Doc. A/CN.4/SR.58, 1950).

65. See proceedings of the International Law Commission, 6th sess., 269th meeting, Summary Rec. (U.N. Doc. A/CN./4/SR.269, 1954).

the concept of aggression to such an extent that it covers "fleabites" as well as "plagues." The definition, it may be noted, does not mention the degree of intensity the propaganda activity should reach before it might be characterized as aggression. It specifies what must be the objective of the activity if it is to be regarded as aggression: either the impairment or destruction of the territorial integrity or political independence of the victim state, subversion of its social or political order, or coercing that state to accept any particular settlement of an existing dispute between the two states.[66] But the statement of the objectives, instead of circumscribing the definition, so expands the concept that it facilitates its invocation even in cases when the instrument is used to apply a low degree of coercion. And the proposal that "planting of fifth columnists or subversive agents in a victim state" must be regarded as aggression, insofar as it pertains to the use of the ideological instrument, seeks to characterize the mere establishment of covert channels of communication as aggression.

THE DRAFT CODE OF OFFENSES AGAINST THE PEACE AND SECURITY OF MANKIND

The claim that indirect forms of aggression, and the use of the ideological instrument to promote such aggression, should be regarded as serious offenses, was pressed before the International Law Commission during the discussion on the Draft Code of Offenses against the Peace and Security of Mankind, and the code recommended by the Commission was based upon an acceptance of some of these claims.[67] Article 2 enumerates the various offenses that the Commission recommended be regarded as offenses against the peace and security of mankind. Clauses (4) and (9) of the article mention acts that some states regard as acts of aggression, although they do not consist of an open military attack by one state on another. Clause (5) of the Article runs thus: "The undertaking or encouragement by the authorities of a State of activities calculated to foment civil strife in another State, or the toleration by the authorities of a State of organized activities to foment civil strife in another." Clause (9) makes intervention in the internal or external affairs of a state by coercive economic or political measures an offense. Clause (13) condemns conspiracy, direct incitement, complicity, or any attempt to commit any of the offenses enumerated in the article.

Clauses (5), (9), and (13) are far from satisfactory. In effect, they tend to impose an absolute and far-reaching prohibition on any type of foreign interference in the internal affairs of a state, while, as has been mentioned before, even the traditional doctrine of nonintervention did not lay down

66. The first paragraph of the definition mentions these objectives.

67. For the text of the Code, see the Report of the International Law Commission, 6th sess. (U.N. Doc. A/2693, 1954).

any such absolute prohibition. The imperfections of the clauses were brought to light fully during the discussions in the Commission. During the third session, for example, when Judge Hudson raised the question whether clause (5) would prohibit publications in the press of any country calling for help to any seditious movement in a foreign country, the reply of Mr. (now Judge) Spiropoulos, the rapporteur on the Draft Code, was in the affirmative.[68] He went on to explain that just as incitement to genocide was a crime, incitement to civil war in a foreign country was also a crime. When it was pointed out by Judge Hudson that genocide was recognized as an international crime while civil wars had not been so regarded, the answer of Mr. Spiropoulos was that the practice in the United Nations had been to regard it as an international crime—a statement for which it is not possible to find support. Even the "Peace Through Deeds" resolution [69] of the General Assembly only declared that "aggression, whether committed openly or by fomenting civil strife in the interest of a foreign power" is a crime against peace and security, but did not say that activity likely to foment civil war was a crime. The Code as a whole indeed has received serious adverse criticism inside [70] as well as outside the Commission.[71] The chances that it will ever become the law seem now to be extremely remote.[72]

68. See International Law Commission, Summary Rec., 3rd. sess., 56th meeting (U.N. Doc. A/CN.4/SR.56, 1950).

69. Resolution 380(V), 17 November 1950.

70. The Code was adopted by the Commission, 6–4, with five abstentions. See Summary Rec. of 280th meeting of the Commission (A/CN.4/SR.280, 1954).

71. See C. G. Fenwick, "Draft Code of Offenses Against the Peace and Security of Mankind," 46 *A.J.I.L.* 98 (1952); P. B. Potter, "Offenses Against the Peace and Security," ibid., p. 101.

72. The General Assembly discussed the draft Code of Offenses Against the Peace and Security of Mankind during its Ninth Session, and as there was little agreement on the concept of aggression, the Assembly decided to postpone further discussion on the Code until the Second Special Committee on the Question of Defining Aggression submitted its report in 1956. See Resolutions 895(IX) and 897(IX), 4 December 1954. The idea was to include in the Code any agreed definition of aggression which the Special Committee might evolve, but the Special Committee failed in that task. During its Twelfth Session, the Assembly decided to defer the consideration of the Code till it took up again for consideration the question of defining aggression. See Assembly Resolution 1186(XII), 11 December 1957.

The last time the General Assembly considered the question of defining aggression was during its Twelfth Session. By Resolution 1181(XII), 29 November 1957, the Assembly constituted a committee, comprising the members of the General Committee during that session, to consider the comments of the newly admitted members on the question of defining aggression, and to report to the Secretary-General that the item should be placed on the agenda of the Assembly when the committee "has determined that time is appropriate" for the consideration of the question, setting forth the reasons that led the committee to such a conclusion. The resolution also directed that the item should not be brought before the Assembly in 1958. The committee, in 1959, found

It is, however, worth noting that the General Assembly's "Peace Through Deeds" resolution referred to above marks a recognition by the General Assembly that "fomenting of civil strife in the interests of a foreign power" might under certain conditions fall into the general category of "aggression."

A SUGGESTED CONCEPT OF IDEOLOGICAL AGGRESSION

In line with what has been stated above in regard to aggression it may be possible to suggest a concept of *ideological aggression*—that is, a coercive process of a character designed to cause and capable of causing deprivation of the values of "territorial integrity or political independence" of the target state.[73] It is indeed possible to doubt that the ideological instrument can cause such a deprivation. But in deciding upon the legitimacy of the use of a coercive process by the officials of a state, allegedly in response to ideological aggression launched by the elite of another state, the structure of reasonable expectations on the part of the officials of the first state has to be appraised. The appraisal should be based upon the demands, intentions, and capabilities of those operating the ideological strategy, the conditions under which the operations are carried out, rendering them more or less effective, and the intensity with which the operations are carried on. The following factors may then be taken into account in making the appraisal:

1. *The Participants*: Here the inquiry has to be into the character of the elite operating the strategy, its posture of self-conservation or self-extension, and its propensities to conform to the world public order. The extent to which the participants are regarded as credible by the audience is also a factor to be taken into account.

2. *Their Objectives*: The most relevant questions are (a) is the objective one of self-conservation or self-extension; is it a minor objective such as withdrawal or abstention or is it the more comprehensive one of recon-

---

that the comments received were not encouraging and decided to postpone the consideration of the question till April 1962. See the *Yearbook of the U.N.*, 1959, p. 420. In April 1962 the committee met again, but decided to adjourn till April 1965, to meet earlier only if the majority of the committee "in the light of the views and comments received and the situation prevailing in international relations considers it desirable for the committee to meet at an earlier date." See *U.N. Review* (May 1962), p. 14. In 1965 consideration of the issue was postponed until 1967, when again the Committee adjourned without decision. 2 *U.N. Monthly Chronicle* 26 (May 1965); 4 ibid. 51 (May 1967); 4 ibid. 79 (June 1967).

73. Reference may be made in this connection to the definition of "force" proposed by Ghana, India, and Yugoslavia in the U.N. Special Committee on Principles of International Law concerning Friendly Relations and Cooperation Among States, 1964 (U.N. Doc. A/AC. 119/L. 15, 1964), which included "other forms of pressure, which have the effect of threatening the territorial integrity and political independence of any State."

struction; (b) what is its consequentiality, is it so comprehensive as to cause deprivation of the "territorial integrity or political independence" of another state; (c) is the objective inclusive or exclusive; and (d) is it in conformance with world public order? Some specific objectives in reference to which the last two considerations become material will be discussed later.[74]

3. *The Audience:* What are the predispositions of the audience in relation to the demands of the strategists, including any willingness to believe in and act according to what is communicated? If there are favorable predispositions, the strategy is more likely to succeed than otherwise. It is also necessary to find out whether the predispositions have been developed by the strategists themselves, for, if such be the case, the use of the instrument under examination may be taken to be part of an overall strategic design.

4. *Conditions:* It is important to observe whether any tensions are prevailing among the audience, in acute form, that can increase the efficacy of the instrument. Inquiry may also have to be made whether the strategists themselves have been responsible for development of those tensions, in which case an idea may be obtained of the design of the strategists.

5. *Relative Capabilities of the Parties:* Their capabilities with regard to all the instruments of policy should be examined. It is inconceivable, for example, that a militarily powerful state will fall victim to an attack by a weak state by means of the ideological instrument. A state which has resources and personnel to operate an ideological strategy is very unlikely to be seriously troubled by the ideological stragegy of the opponent. It can easily fight back with the same weapons. A state which is economically strong and well organized can, without much difficulty, counteract the ideological strategy of an external elite.

6. *Operations:* Under this head inquiry is directed to the character of the symbols communicated, the intensity of the communication, the media by which the symbols are disseminated, and indeed all the variables relevant to estimating the probable effects of the operations. In this context attention has to be given also to the covert channels of communication which the strategists have been able to establish and make use of. If there is large-scale infiltration of agents into groups within the attacked state, that is a very significant factor.

In the light of the above variables, if it can be said that any activity of the strategists which is not justifiable as a measure of self-defense is capable of creating a reasonable expectation on the part of the government of the attacked state that deprivation of the state's territorial integrity or political independence is fairly imminent, unless the coercive process is stopped or substantially reduced in its intensity, it seems reasonable to infer the existence of ideological aggression.

74. See below, pp. 175–81.

In thus delineating the concept of ideological aggression, the coercive activity designated as ideological aggression must, in respect of the intentions and purposes with which the instrument is employed and probable effect of the use of the instrument, be a near approximation to military aggression. Unlike the Soviet and Chinese definitions of ideological aggression, which sought to characterize as aggression certain specified types of activity—such as encouraging a particular type of propaganda, planting subversive agents, or incitement to civil strife by propaganda—the concept suggested here facilitates an examination of the impugned use of the instrument in the total context in which it occurs.

Minor Coercion

Impermissible Minor Coercion

The reference here is to coercion which is less intense than that employed with the objective of depriving a state of its territorial integrity or political independence, and capable of accomplishing that objective. Under traditional, imprecise doctrines of nonintervention and permissible intervention, governments objected to the use of the ideological instrument whenever they felt or expected coercive effects. Thus in 1804 when the Spanish Ambassador in the United States attempted to bribe a newspaper to adopt an attitude favorable to Spain, the United States censured his conduct, and later, when he justified his action in public statements, demanded his recall.[75] In 1924 the British government reacted sharply to the circulation of the Zinoviev letter, which called upon the Communist party in England to carry on propaganda among British workers to bring pressure on the British government to ratify the Anglo-Soviet treaty.[76] In 1927, the same government severed diplomatic relations with the U.S.S.R. upon discovering the telegram dispatched to Moscow by the Russian chargé d'affaires seeking factual material to carry on a propaganda campaign in England, with the objective of influencing the British public to put pressure on their government to adopt softer policies toward the U.S.S.R.[77]

By way of contrast one may look at the response of the United States government under somewhat similar circumstances. In 1934–35, the Japanese Ambassador in the United States made a number of speeches suggesting that the United States government should alter its policy toward Japan.[78] His objective was indeed to develop popular sentiment in the United States in favor of a change of policy, but the Department of State

75. Moore, *Digest*, 4, 509.
76. See Brit. Parl. Papers, Cmd. No. 2993 (1927), cited in Chap. 5, note 68.
77. See the letter of Sir Austen Chamberlain to M. Rosengolz, May 26, 1927, ibid.
78. See B. Akzin, "Propaganda by Diplomats," 5 *International Law and Relations*, No. 7 (1936).

did not take any action. This difference in response of the two governments to the activity, motivated in both cases by the same objective, can be explained only if one looks at the likely difference in the expectation of the two governments about the outcome of the activity in the respective situations. The British government had more to fear from propaganda carried on through the local Communist party seeking to influence labor groups than the American government from speeches made in public by an ambassador of a foreign state. In 1930, the British government protested to the Italian government over the Italian broadcasts to Arab peoples from Bari, which were apparently designed to modify the perspectives of the audience toward the British.[79]

Juristic writings tended to take the position in relation to transnational propaganda designed to bring about *reconstruction*—a highly coercive objective—that such propaganda is impermissible if reconstruction is intended to be effected by violent means. Thus, according to Vattel, to call upon the subjects of another state who are actually obeying their sovereign to revolt is a clear violation of the law of nations.[80] F. de Martens asserted the right of each state to require that foreign powers "*do not incite the people of its territory to rise against it,* to separate from it, or to migrate." [81] Even among modern writers, Hall considered impermissible only the fomenting of revolution abroad.[82] Sir Hersch Lauterpacht, however, went a little further and maintained that "revolutionary propaganda," that is, propaganda designed to bring about a radical change in the institutions of a foreign state, if carried on by officials of a state, was illegal.[83]

Many of the bilateral treaties entered into between the two world wars, however, prescribed a much wider obligation than that inferred from juristic opinion. In general, all proscribed propaganda activity designed to reconstruct the social, political, and governmental systems and institutions of the contracting parties.[84] Some proscribed propaganda activity directed

79. See R.I.I.A., *Documents on International Affairs,* 1938, *2* (1943), 91.

80. The Law of Nations, 3, 131.

81. *Traité De Droit International,* *1* (trans. A. Leo, Paris, 1883), 393 (emphasis supplied).

82. See Hall, p. 339.

83. See his "Revolutionary Propaganda by Governments."

84. The treaties adopt a wide variety of formulas but they contain something in common. They are in the main designed to protect the political order or the territorial integrity of the contracting states, which practically amounts to insuring against reconstruction of the decision-making process in all or part of a contracting state. In the Agreement Revising the Convention of December 18, 1923, Relating to the Organization of the Statute of Tangiers zone, 1928, cited in Chap. 5 note 97, the expression used was "established order"; in the Rapallo Treaty, 1922, between Germany and the U.S.S.R., ibid., note 88, what was prohibited was propaganda "directed against the political and social systems of either contracting party"; in the Russo-Japanese Treaty, 1925, ibid., note 92, the formula used was "to endanger the order and security in any

against the territorial integrity of the contracting states,[85] which amounted to saying that the objective of reconstruction, even if confined to any portion of the territory of a contracting state, was impermissible. Only a few of the treaties limited the prohibition to the objective of accomplishing reconstruction by violent means.[86] Among the multilateral conventions, the Broadcasting Convention of 1936 proscribed all broadcasts inciting the population of any contracting state to acts incompatible with internal order or security of that state (Art. 1). The South American Regional Agreement on Radio Communications (revised), Rio de Janeiro, 1937, proscribed transmissions by radio which might threaten the sovereignty or territorial integrity of any contracting state.

While one may maintain that traditional law prohibited coercion across state boundaries, it is not possible to infer with any precision, from the practice of states, treaties, and juristic writings, what degree of coercion constituted the minimum that was prohibited.

Under the U.N. Charter, it might appear at first sight that, before a situation involving the use of ideological instrument may be brought before the Security Council or the General Assembly, it should be of such nature as "might lead to international friction or give rise to a dispute"

part of the territories" of Japan or the U.S.S.R.; in the U.S. and the U.S.S.R. exchange of letters, ibid., note 93, the formulas used were "violation of the territorial integrity of the United States or its territorial possessions," and "bring about by force a change in the political or social order of the whole or any part of the United States, or its territories or possessions"; in the Treaty of Neutrality and Non-Aggression between Persia and Turkey, ibid., note 97, propaganda having the purpose of "fighting the government of the other party" was prohibited; in the Italo-Yugoslav Agreement of 1937, ibid., the formula employed was "territorial integrity or existing order"; in the Provisional Agreement between Denmark and U.S.S.R., ibid., note 88, propaganda directed against "the institutions" of either contracting party was prohibited; the Provisional Agreement of Commerce between Norway and Russia, ibid., adopted the formula "not to interfere in internal affairs"; so also the Bulgaria-U.S.S.R. Treaty of 1934, and the Rumania-U.S.S.R. Treaty of 1934, both cited in ibid., note 89; the Treaty of Peace, Riga, 1921, between Poland and the U.S.S.R. and Ukraine, ibid., mentions "intervention"; the Czechoslovakia-U.S.S.R. Treaty, 1922, ibid., note 89, obligated the parties "not to propagate against the social or political system of the other party or to intervene in social or political troubles of the other"; the Franco-Russian Non-Aggression Pact, 1932, ibid., note 94, prohibited activity directed against "the territorial integrity of the other or to change by force the political and social regime in the territories of the other party"; the Additional Treaty of Friendship, Neutrality, and Conciliation between Greece and Turkey, 1933, ibid., uses the formula "subverting the other state by propaganda"; the Indo-Pakistan Agreement, 1948, ibid., note 97, obligated the parties to discourage propaganda carried on with the objective of "amalgamation of Pakistan and India or parts thereof."

85. Treaties falling within this category are the U.S.-U.S.S.R. Agreement, the treaty between Italy and Yugoslavia, and the Franco-Prussian Non-Aggression Pact referred to above.

86. The U.S.-U.S.S.R. Agreement, the Franco-Russian Non-Aggression Pact, and the treaty between Greece and Turkey belong in this category.

(Art. 35). Perhaps the position is more liberal than that. The actual practice of the Council and Assembly in placing most questions brought before them on the agenda, and of the Assembly in making recommendations of a general character to all members,[87] apparently permit even situations less serious than indicated by Article 35 to be considered and action of a persuasive character to be taken against those alleged to be using coercion.

In the context of deciding upon a claim that impermissible coercion has been used, initially or in retaliation, it seems useful to have a working formula to identify the impermissible minor coercion. It may be defined as the first use, deliberately and without justification, of such degree of coercion, brought to bear by using any combination of instruments of policy, as creates a reasonable expectation on the part of the target of coercion (reasonableness being determinable by an objective, third party appraisal) that the target will suffer deprivation of values unless it resorts to coercive measures to protect its own values. Admittedly, this formula does not precisely specify the level coercion should reach in order that it may be impermissible, but it may be used as a guide in the process of decision-making. Coercion of a level of intensity lower than this may be regarded as something which has to be tolerated as an incident of community interaction.

Permissible Minor Coercion

Under the rubrics of retortion, reprisal, embargo, pacific blockade, permissible intervention, and self-defense, traditional international law permitted states to have recourse to coercion, including the use of violence. As we are concerned here with the processes of coercion which involve the use of the ideological instrument, we may leave out of consideration embargoes and pacific blockades. And retortions, being acts conforming to community prescriptions, may also be ignored here.

The impermissibility of the use of violence by way of reprisal seems to be more or less definitely established at present. A reprisal presupposes a breach of a community prescription, a demand for redress, and failure on the part of the delinquent to afford redress.[88] The sanctioning objective in reprisal is mostly *rehabilitation*. Article 2(3) of the Charter, which obligates recourse to peaceful means for settlement of claims, excludes the use of violence by way of reprisal.[89] However, a reprisal may sometimes serve the sanctioning goal of *restoration*; that is to say, it may help create conditions under which illegal acts causing deprivations would not continue. In-

87. See below, Chap. 12.

88. See the *Naulilaa* arbitration, Briggs, *The Law of Nations, Cases and Materials*, p. 951; Oppenheim-Lauterpacht, 2, 142.

89. The Security Council has on more than one occasion disapproved armed reprisals. In 1964, in relation to the British bombing of Harib in Yemen, the Council referred to Art. 2, Clauses (3) and (4) of the Charter, and declared that it "condemns reprisals as incompatible with the purposes and principles of the Charter." See S.C.O.R., 19th

sofar as reprisal serves this objective it can be assimilated to self-defense and regulated by the same principles as are applicable to the latter.[90]

A reprisal by nonviolent means is presently open to no objection. In many instances in the past the legitimacy of the use of the ideological instrument for reprisal has been asserted.[91] And indeed, whenever reprisal by violence is permissible, the use of the ideological instrument, either singly or in combination with the military instrument, cannot be open to objection in view of the far less destructive character of the former instrument. The coercion employed in reprisal, however, should be proportional to the objective sought.[92]

In a community where centralized institutions of third-party settlement of claims and enforcement of decisions are not well developed, the participants must be conceded the right to have recourse to regulated, nonviolent coercion to obtain settlement of claims.

The grounds on which intervention by force is permissible under the present law are highly controversial,[93] and a discussion of the various suggested bases of permissible intervention cannot be attempted here. If in any situation intervention by force is permissible, it can be reasonably maintained that the use of the ideological instrument in that situation is

---

Year, 1111th Mtg. (1964). Twice earlier, in relation to Israeli attacks on Lake Tiberias and on Syria, the Council expressed disapproval of reprisals. See S.C.O.R., 10th Year, 707th Mtg. (1956); ibid., 17th Year, 1006th Mtg. (1962).

90. Sir Patrick Dean, the representative of the United Kingdom, explaining during the 1109th Meeting of the Security Council that the British bombing of Harib was not a reprisal but self-defense, pointed out: "It [bombing] has no parallel with acts of retaliation or reprisals, which have as an essential element the purposes of vengeance or retribution. It is the latter use of force which is condemned by the Charter, and not the use of force for defensive purposes such as warding off future attacks," S.C.O.R., 1109th Mtg. (1964), para. 31. The Council, however, did not regard the bombing as a defensive operation.

91. For example, in 1803, the French government claimed that a report by a colonel in the French army, one Sebastiani, to the First Consul—which the British government complained contained unjustified insinuations and charges against it and British army officers in Egypt—was a refutation and a reparation for the statement of a colonel in the British army which contained calumnies against the French army. See 45 *Annual Register* 700, 707 (1803). Also ibid., p. 682, for the British claim that what was stated in the British press, to which the French government objected, was "national retaliation" for what was published in France. See ibid., p. 660, for the French threat that if the British government did not stop publications in the British press that were offensive to the French government, the former would retaliate. The threat was apparently carried out, and enabled the British government to take the position later that the publications in the British press were "national retaliation."

92. For the principle of proportionality, see the *Naulilaa* arbitration; also Oppenheim-Lauterpacht, 2, 141.

93. See Ian Brownlie, *International Law and the Use of Force by States* (Oxford, Clarendon Press, 1963), generally, and pp. 432–33 in particular; Thomas and Thomas, *Non-Intervention*, Chap. 4.

quite permissible.[94] And a reference to traditional customary law also becomes necessary where the use of the ideological instrument is claimed to be legitimate by virtue of the permissibility of intervention in the particular context, even though intervention by violence on that ground is impermissible under modern law. It was noted earlier that the traditional doctrines of nonintervention and permissible intervention formed a complementary set which facilitated prescription of policy suitable to each particular context. Decision-makers should in each case decide about the legitimacy of the use of the instrument having regard to the factual context and basic policies postulated.

The concept of self-defense as employed in the past had more than a single reference.[95] At one level it was contraposed to impermissible major coercion or aggression. At another level it referred to the legitimate response when subjected to, or in anticipation of, impermissible use of force on a limited scale, which is not regarded as aggression. The leading case on self-defense, an offshoot of the *Caroline* incident, was about the use of violence to meet anticipated danger from armed rebels operating from the territory of the United States but not alleged to have been aided by the United States government.[96] Self-defense is claimed in respect of attacks on ships at sea,[97] and such attacks of limited magnitude cannot be regarded as impermissible major coercion. The doctrine of self-preservation, from which the doctrine of self-defense was evolved to prescribe relatively precise limits to the use of violence as a measure of self-protection,[98] referred also to situations when a state expected harm from another, not immediately but at a remote time. The doctrine permitted diplomatic and other measures designed to minimize the danger or to meet it when it actually emerged.[99]

94. Stowell, *Intervention in International Law*, p. 353, raises the question whether it is a violation of law to cause disaffection among the people of a neighboring state "when a just ground for war exists and this milder measure with hostile intent may achieve the result without an invasion of the territory by foreign troops." The answer suggested is in the negative. See also Hall, p. 339. He states that when a government threatens hostilities which may be averted by its overthrow, it is permissible for the menaced state to safeguard its security by necessary measures, including causing the overthrow of the threatening government.

95. See McDougal and Feliciano, pp. 207 et seq.

96. For a detailed discussion of the *Caroline* incident, see R. Y. Jennings, "The Caroline and McLeod cases," 32 *A.J.I.L.* 82 (1938).

97. See Brownlie, p. 305.

98. See Jennings.

99. See T. Twiss, *The Law of Nations*, 1 (London, Oxford University Press, 1861), 145; Phillimore, *Commentaries upon International Law*, 1, 313. In these and other treatises written in the last century it is generally stated that if a state menaces another's security by sudden increase of its armed forces, the latter may seek explanations through diplomatic channels and take other measures of protection. The conditions in a totally

Whenever it is permissible to resort to violence as a measure of self-defense, it can be maintained that the less destructive ideological instrument of coercion can be legitimately employed for the same purpose. This principle applies equally in the contexts of impermissible major and minor coercions which occasion the exercise of self-defense. The policy of minimization of coercion, however, demands that the use of the ideological instrument should be regulated by the same principles that apply to the use of violence—the principles of necessity and proportionality. Necessity, in this context, may not pass the strict test laid down in the *Caroline* case in connection with armed incursion into another's territory, of being "instant, overwhelming, leaving no choice of means and no moment for deliberation"; and the criterion may be limited to the existence of a reasonable expectation, on the part of the target of initial impermissible coercion, that it will suffer appreciable deprivations if countermeasures to bring about restoration are not taken.[100] And the use of the ideological instrument as a countermeasure should not be so intense as to result in greater deprivations than the permissible use of violence in the particular circumstances. The application of this test with precision is indeed difficult, and it may be used only as a guiding tool by decision-makers in projecting the policy of minimization of coercion in the community.

It is difficult for any legal scholar at present to support a claim on the basis of self-preservation, because of the vagueness generally associated with it, which can give legal cover to any action taken by one state against another.[101] However, with relative ease scholars and statesmen have put forward, despite its vagueness, the doctrine of intervention to impugn the legitimacy of any transnational, nonviolent coercive process employed by a state.[102] It may be remembered that the doctrine of nonintervention has its counterpart, the doctrine of permissible intervention for self-preservation. In recent years legitimacy has been claimed for the use of the ideolog-

---

disorganized arena necessitated each state taking measures designed for its security, and it was apparently recognized that the state need not wait to take measures of self-protection till the threat assumed serious proportions. At each stage in the development of the threat appropriate measures were permissible.

100. See McDougal and Feliciano, p. 231, for a discussion of *necessity* in relation to the military instrument.

101. As self-preservation came to be distinguished from self-defense, the former came to be rejected as a legal right. See Westlake, *International Law*, 1, 310–11; Brierly, *The Law of Nations*, Chap. 9, Sec. 2, for the thesis that "self-preservation is not a legal right but an instinct"; Brownlie, p. 252. See Brownlie, pp. 46–47, for the evolution of the doctrine of self-defense from the doctrine of self-preservation.

102. See Chap. 6, note 38; Thomas and Thomas, p. 274; Quincy Wright, "Subversive Intervention," 54 *A.J.I.L.* 521 (1960), wherein the author notes the protests over the proclamation of "Captive Nations Week" by the President of the United States in 1959; Whitton, "Propaganda and International Law," p. 579; Whitton and Larson, *Propaganda*, p. 96.

ical instrument of coercion to reduce the possibility of a state initiating major coercion in the future. Transmission of the "Voice of America" broadcasts to Eastern Europe,[103] broadcasts by "Radio Free Europe,"[104] and the observance of "Captive Nations Week"[105] have been claimed to serve the objective of reducing the possibility of expansionist moves by the Soviet elite. If, as generally alleged, some propaganda can be impugned as impermissible intervention, it is difficult to deny that other propaganda can be justified as a legitimate measure to counteract the psychological preparations an elite is making for eventual aggression against its neighbors, or to prevent aggression with far less harmful means than violence. With the policy of minimization of coercion in view, we recommended that transnational use of coercion beyond a certain level should be regarded as impermissible, a recommendation that accords with the basic policy underlying the doctrine of intervention. The policy of minimization of coercion also calls for an imposition of reasonable limitations, in terms of necessity and proportionality, on the transnational use of the ideological instrument, allegedly made to meet anticipated impermissible coercion.

CLAIM THAT COERCION IS JUSTIFIED BY COMMUNITY POLICY

Public opinion has always been considered one of the sanctions of international law.[106] In order to create public opinion in favor of conformance

103. Senator Karl E. Mundt, speaking on the Voice of America in 1951, stated that its strategy was to drive a wedge between the people and the ruling elite of the U.S.S.R., thus restraining them from embarking upon any aggression. *Congressional Record*, 97 (March 30, 1951), A1763–64, extracts reproduced in R. E. Summers, ed., *America's Weapons of Psychological Warfare* (New York, H. W. Wilson, 1951), pp. 77–78.

104. Speaking on the mission of Radio Free Europe, President Eisenhower said in 1955, "While we maintain our vigilance at home and abroad, we must intensify the will for freedom in the satellite countries behind the Iron Curtain. These countries are in the Soviet backyard, and only so long as their people are reminded that the outside world has not forgotten them—only that long do they remain as *potential deterrents to Soviet aggression*" (italics added). 32 *Dept. of State Bull.* 298 (1955).

105. The Joint Resolution of both Houses of Congress authorizing the President to proclaim "Captive Nations Week" declared among other things, "It is vital to the security of the United States that the desire for liberty and independence on the part of the peoples of these conquered nations should be steadfastly kept alive," and that "the desire for liberty and independence by the overwhelming majority of the people of these submerged nations constitutes a powerful deterrent to war and one of the best hopes of a just and lasting peace." The reference to the conquered nations was to twenty-two nations specified in the resolution and said to have been enslaved by Soviet communism since 1919. See Quincy Wright, "Subversive Intervention," for a full discussion of this resolution and the subsequent proclamation by the President. Also Whitton, " 'Subversive Propaganda' Reconsidered," 55 *A.J.I.L.* 120 (1961).

106. See Grotius, *Freedom of the Seas*, p. 3; the Permanent Court of Arbitration in the *North Atlantic Fisheries Arbitration, Hague Court Reports*, 1 (J. B. Scott, ed.,

to community policy it is considered permissible to use the ideological instrument and to openly denounce treaty violators.[107] Recently, the People's Republic of China claimed, while demanding from the Soviet Union an apology and punishment of Soviet officials who allegedly dealt with Chinese student demonstrators in Moscow in a brutal fashion, that it was entirely legitimate for the students to demonstrate as they did in view of the wanton bombing by the United States in North Viet Nam.[108]

Claim that Ideological Coercion Is Permissible for Promoting Self-Determination, Rights of Minorities, and Human Rights

It is a common incident of world community life that the people of any state find various bases of identification with people living outside the boundaries of their state, such as common religion, culture, racial origin, and if nothing else, at least humanity. They may proceed further and present demands for values on behalf of those with whom they identify. In the past demands have been presented to other governments for the protection of religious minorities in the foreign state, and for self-determination of groups belonging to the nationality of the demanding state.

The presentation of such demands may stem from a genuine wish to obtain a wider sharing of values for those on whose behalf the demands are presented; or it may stem from motives of self-aggrandizement. For example, the exercise of the right of self-determination by a foreign group may hold out the prospect of territorial acquisitions to a state and also an increase in its population; and these considerations might induce the elite of that state to press forward the demand for self-determination. Irredentist movements are always motivated by the prospect of such gain, by the hope of bringing into existence a new ally, or weakening an opposing state.

During the last century, in Europe, governments helped national groups in foreign states to exercise their right of self-determination, intervened by diverse means for the protection of religious minorities, especially in Turkey, and claimed the right to intervene in the internal affairs of a foreign state for humanitarian reasons. In recent years claims have been frequently put forward that it is right to use nonviolent instruments of policy—in particular, the ideological instrument—to promote self-determination of

1916), 146, 167, mentioned the following among the sanctions of international law: "appeal to public opinion, publication of correspondence, censure by parliamentary vote, demand for arbitration and the odium attendant on a refusal to arbitrate." See also the discussion on "Public Opinion as a Force Toward Compliance," 1964 *Proc. of Am. Soc. of Int. Law*, p. 143.

107. See Quincy Wright, "Denunciation of Treaty Violators," 32 *A.J.I.L.*, 520 (1938).

108. See *New York Times*, March 14, 1966. But the Chinese note ignores the obligation incumbent upon a state to give protection to foreign embassies.

groups in foreign states, to protect the rights of groups threatened with deprivations of values by the majority groups in those foreign states, and to promote human rights in general.

Thus, in 1956, Greece claimed justification for radio broadcasts from Greek radio stations to Cyprus, about which the United Kingdom frequently protested, asserting that the struggle in Cyprus was for Greece a struggle for self-determination and a "national and sacred one." [109] Hitler claimed before World War II the right to take whatever measures were necessary to protect the German minorities in other countries.[110] The Egyptian government claimed in 1966, when the British and the French governments objected to the radio broadcasts from Cairo to neighboring countries, that its objective was only to establish closer contact between all the Moslems of the world and to attract them to Cairo, the center of Islamic culture.[111] For a long time the United States openly professed a policy of "peaceful liberation" of Eastern European countries from Communist domination, and of enabling the people of those countries to regain their individual freedom and political liberty.[112] The State Department justified, without accepting responsibility for, the activities of organizations like the "Free Europe Committee," claiming that they were designed to help the peoples of Eastern European countries to obtain recognition of the human rights assured to them under the peace treaties entered into after World War II.[113]

The ground on which these claims might be objected to is not difficult to see. The logical consequence of the exercise of the right of self-determination by any group is the breaking up of a state or an empire, and the government of that state or empire will object to any activity directed toward establishing self-determination as unjustifiable interference in its internal affairs. Activity designed to promote the interests of any minority group in a foreign state, or even the promotion of the human rights of the group, is likely to be met with similar objections.[114]

109. See *New York Times*, Feb. 1, 1956.

110. See the speech of Adolf Hitler on March 23, 1933, to the Reichstag, in the course of which he said, "The fate of Germans outside the frontiers of the Reich, who have the special task of struggling for the protection of their language, culture, manners, and religion, will always move us to intercede, with every means at our command for the rights guaranteed to German minorities." See R.I.I.A., *Documents on International Affairs*, 1933, pp. 404–05.

111. See *New York Times*, March 1, 1956.

112. *American Foreign Policy* 1950–55, 2 (U.S. Dept. of State Pub. No. 6446, 1957), 1959.

113. See the U.S. reply to the protest of Hungary over the leaflet drop operations, 32 *Dept. of State Bull.* 14 (1955).

114. Thus the Ethiopian Emperor protested over the Egyptian broadcasts to the Moslem minority in his country (*New York Times*, Feb. 16, 1957), the British and the French protested over the Egyptian broadcasts to Moslem populations in their possessions

Self-Determination

Self-determination as a general principle of world community policy is now disputed by few. The origin of this principle dates back to the time when the theory of divine right of kings came under challenge. In the initial stages of its evolution the principle meant freedom of peoples to choose their own form of government.[115] Thus conceived, the principle was designed to uphold human dignity, and to facilitate a wider sharing of values. But at the hands of later German theorists the principle came to mean the right of a group united by certain ties (other than political) to choose the state or political organization in which it would like to live. The movement for self-determination after the advent of this theory took the form of converting "cultural nations" into "state-nations." [116] After World War I, Eastern Europe was split into states created on the principle of nationality. After World War II, the principle of self-determination found recognition at the time of framing of the U.N. Charter. Article 1(2) mentions the development of "friendly relations among nations based on respect for the principle of equal rights and self-determination" among the basic objectives of the Organization.[117]

Since the advent of the Organization the principle has been invoked, by member states that gained independence from colonial rule after World War II, to bring about a liquidation of the remnants of the overseas empires of some of the Western European countries. Their efforts were also directed to converting the general principle laid down in Article 1(2) into a more concrete legal prescription. This is not the place to trace their efforts, the opposition they have met, and the trends of development.[118] It is sufficient to note that the principle has been affirmed in some impor-

---

in Africa (ibid., March 1, 1956), Hungary protested over President Eisenhower's 1955 Christmas message promising "peaceful liberation" of the peoples of Eastern Europe (ibid., Jan. 2, 1956), and the U.S.S.R. also protested over the same message (ibid., Dec. 31, 1955).

115. This was the underlying idea of "self-determination" as put forward at the time of the American Revolution and the French Revolution. See A. Cobban, *National Self-Determination* (London, Oxford University Press, 1945), p. 53.

116. Ibid., pp. 7–9, 50.

117. There is a difference of opinion among writers as to the effect of this provision. Kelsen considered that "self-determination" as used in the article means only "sovereignty of states"; see his *The Law of the United Nations*, pp. 51–53. For an opposite view, see Quincy Wright, "Recognition and Self-Determination," *Proc. Am. Soc. of Int'l. Law*, 1954, p. 22.

118. For a detailed account of these facts, one may refer to B. Rivlin, "Self-Determination of Dependent Areas," *Int'l. Conciliation*, No. 501 (1955), pp. 195–271. See also C. E. Toussaint, "The Colonial Controversy in the United Nations," *Year Book of World Affairs*, 1956, p. 271; M. K. Nawaz, "Colonies, Self-Government, and the United Nations," *Indian Year Book of International Affairs*, 1962, p. 3.

tant resolutions of the General Assembly,[119] and incorporated in the Covenants on Human Rights.[120] One other point that deserves notice is that, at the time of the drafting of the Charter, it was not intended that Article 1(2) should supply legal authority for demands for secession from existing states or empires.[121]

Although the principle of self-determination has long been recognized by the world community, in operational terms policy has differed from time to time. Inherent in the principle is the idea of wider sharing of power and other values by peoples; and also the idea of dividing people who are presently united under a set of symbols and regrouping them under a different set of symbols of identification.

The problem of regulating transnational coercion cannot be ignored while dealing with the strategy of an elite directed to promoting the self-determination of a foreign group. As a symbol, "self-determination" conveys the idea of wide sharing of human values, and so it remains a convenient one to manipulate at all times in ideological strategy. By using the symbol, at one and the same time a new basis of identification can be put forward, attractive promises of value accretions can be made to the groups addressed, and a demand can be presented for something which the community has long regarded as a major principle of community policy. When an external elite professes to operate its strategy to promote self-determination, it becomes necessary to question whether its real objective is promotion of a wider sharing of human values by permissible means, or whether it is using the symbol to promote a strategy of self-extension by highly coercive means. If the latter happens to be the situation, a stage might be reached when community intervention becomes necessary to regulate the use of transnational coercion.

In the U.N. General Assembly's Special Committees on the Principles of International Law concerning Friendly Relations and Cooperation among States, Czechoslovakia proposed, among the permissible uses of force, mention of its use in "self-defense of nations against colonial domination in the exercise of the right of self-determination." The joint proposal of Ghana, India, and Yugoslavia also provided for declaring, among other things, "the right of peoples to self-defense against colonial domination in the exercise of their right of self-determination." [122] If the proposals merely

119. See Resolution 545(VI), 5 Feb. 1952; Resolution 1188(XII), 11 Dec. 1957; and the Resolution on Colonialism of Dec. 14, 1960.

120. In both the Covenants the very first article deals with the principle of self-determination.

121. See Goodrich and Hambro, p. 95.

122. See the *Report of the Special Committee on the Principles of International Law concerning Friendly Relations and Cooperation Among States,* U.N. Doc. A/5746 (16 Nov. 1964), paras. 27 and 31; and *Report of the 1966 Special Committee* (U.N. Doc. A/6230, 27 June 1966), paras. 25 and 26. No consensus was reached on these

reiterate the general rule that permits the people of a territory to rebel and establish a state of their own, it is submitted that the proposals are unnecessary. If they imply that a state can use force, in the name of self-determination, across its boundaries for effecting a change of authority in a foreign territory, the tenability of such a proposition has to be examined in light of the provisions of the Charter.

It seems that the question whether the use of the ideological instrument to promote self-determination is permissible cannot be answered by a straight yes or no. As "self-determination" implies wider sharing of human values, and has long been recognized as one of the policy principles of the community, the use of the ideological instrument to promote self-determination has to be regarded as permissible. On the other hand, because it is possible to use "self-determination" as a symbol in a strategy of aggression, the professed use of the ideological instrument in any situation to promote self-determination may have to be restrained if the community policy of maintaining peace and security so requires. The policy in reference to any situation should be predicated upon promoting both contemporary high policy objectives of the world community: maintaining peace and security and promoting human rights. If there happens to be a conflict between the two objectives, emphasis should be upon balancing them. As situations that might arise in this context are likely to be of differing complexions, it seems impractical to make more specific suggestions. What has been stated in regard to self-determination applies to strategies motivated by irredentism also.

Protection of Minorities

As a general principle of community policy, protection of minorities has received recognition for a long time. The earliest treaty on the subject dates back to 1606.[123] A number of treaties have been entered into from time to time with a view to securing to minorities protection of their rights. The most important of the last century was the Treaty of Berlin which obligated Bulgaria, Montenegro, Serbia, and Rumania not to discriminate against groups on the ground of their religion.[124] After World War I, a number of treaties were entered into at the Paris Peace Conference for affording protection to the national minorities in the newly created states in Eastern Europe, and the League of Nations was given the

proposals. The proposal of Ghana, India and Yugoslavia was sponsored in the 1966 Special Committee also by Algeria, Burma, Cameroon, Dahomey, Kenya, Madagascar, Nigeria and U.A.R., Dahomey and Nigeria having opposed in the 1964 Special Committee.

123. See J. Robinson, "From Protection of Minorities to Promotion of Human Rights," *The Jewish Year Book of International Law*, 1948, pp. 115, 116.

124. Ibid. See also I. L. Claude, Jr., *National Minorities, An International Question* (Cambridge, Harvard University Press, 1955), p. 6.

function of supervising enforcement of these treaties. After World War II, though the general approach toward the problem has changed from one of protecting minorities as such to promoting human rights in general,[125] the General Assembly has twice declared the interest of the United Nations in protecting minorities,[126] and has evinced interest in safeguarding them against unjust discriminations.[127] The Assembly adopted in 1948 the Genocide Convention. Article 20(2) of the recently adopted International Covenant on Civil and Political Rights obligates the parties to prohibit by law any advocacy of national, racial, or religious hatred which constitutes incitement to discrimination, hostility, or violence.

Since world community policy is in favor of protection of the interest of minorities, the use of the ideological instrument to promote those interests in foreign states may be regarded as permissible. However, external elites often find minority groups in foreign states handy instruments in causing disintegration of those states. Hitler used the German minority groups successfully in implementing his plans of extending the frontiers of Germany. By means of propaganda carried on among German minorities in neighboring countries by radio, movies, the domestic and bribed foreign press, local Nazi organizations, and human agents, he made of the minorities "human dynamite" [128] that he could detonate when he found conditions propitious, and thus create at will situations in those countries which appeared to warrant outside interference. He made use of the minorities to dismember Czechoslovakia and to build up "fifth columns" in all the countries he overran with his military machine.

In shaping the community policy, therefore, with reference to any strategy professedly directed to promote a wider sharing of values by minority groups in foreign states, one will have to take into account not merely the human rights aspect of the problem but also the aspect of regulating transnational coercion. A policy recommendation along the lines suggested in relation to strategies to promote self-determination may be made in this case as well.

Promotion of Human Rights

During the previous century, liberal democratic doctrines did not completely penetrate the façades of absolutist monarchies, and hence the idea that the rights of the individual are a matter of concern for the entire

125. See Robinson, "Protection of Minorities."

126. See the Resolution on "Persecution and Discrimination," 103(1), 19 Nov. 1946, and the "Fate of Minorities" Resolution, 217(III)C, 10 Dec. 1948.

127. As early as 1947 the Commission on Human Rights set up a Sub-Commission on Prevention of Discrimination and Protection of Minorities.

128. See Wolfe, *Human Dynamite, The Story of European Minorities,* pp. 73–92. Robinson, p. 134.

world community, and not merely for the territorial sovereigns, did not gain a high degree of acceptance. Though the right to intervene on humanitarian grounds was frequently asserted by writers,[129] very rarely did governments claim that right; and in the instances when they did, they supported their claims by other weighty reasons, such as protection of the interests of their state, protection of their citizens, etc.[130]

With the advent of the United Nations the traditional position has undergone change at least to the extent that, under the Charter, the member states are obligated to accept promotion of human rights as one of the basic policies of the world community. The adoption of the Universal Declaration of Human Rights by the General Assembly marked another important step in the direction of acceptance by members of promotion of human rights as high policy. The progress made by the Western European powers in the matter of giving recognition to, undertaking obligations in respect of, and providing international machinery for the enforcement of, human rights is even more noteworthy.[131] Under these conditions, a strategy designed to promote human rights cannot be open to objections unless it runs into conflict with the policy of maintenance of peace and security in the world community. One may reasonably make, therefore, the same recommendation on a policy to be adopted in regard to strategies operated by elites for the purpose of promoting human rights as has been made in the two previous cases.

129. See Stowell, *Intervention in International Law*, pp. 126–27; Phillimore, 1, 571; Oppenheim-Lauterpacht, 1, sec. 137.

130. See Chap. 6, note 34; see also Winfield, "The Ground of Intervention in International Law," p. 149; Oppenheim-Lauterpacht, 1, sec. 137.

131. See in this connection A. H. Robertson, "The European Convention on Human Rights," 27 *B.Y.B.I.L.* 145 (1950); his "Legal Problems of European Integration," 91 *Hague Recueil* 109, 155 (1957).

8

Situation and Capability

SITUATION

GEOGRAPHICAL

The importance of the geographical situation of the parties from the point of view of formulation of community policy was well brought out in the letter of the U.S. Ambassador, Mr. Bancroft, to Viscount Palmerston, in 1849, in which he stated that conditions in Ireland were not likely to be changed "by rebellions organized at public meetings at three thousand miles distance from the scene of action." [1] Professor Whitton emphasizes the importance of the geographical factor in his reply to the thesis of Professor Quincy Wright that the U.S. Presidential Proclamation of July 17, 1959, of "Captive Nations Week," and the joint congressional resolution on the Proclamation, constituted illegal intervention in the internal affairs of Eastern European countries.[2] Whitton points out that the proclamation was "a mere manifestation of sympathy, officially inspired, it is true, *several thousand miles from the scene* where millions of captive people live in oppression." [3]

TEMPORAL DURATION

It is not necessary to labor the point that there is a difference between isolated or chance utterances and sustained use of communication as an instrument of strategy. It is illustrated by the difference in the response of governments to publication of libels affecting heads of states and governments and to sustained propaganda activity. We may compare the response of the British government in 1803 to the publication in a Hamburg gazette of a libel on the government and the King by the French minister

1. See Chap. 5, note 29.
2. See Quincy Wright, "Subversive Intervention," and Whitton, " 'Subversive Propaganda' Reconsidered."
3. Whitton, p. 122 (emphasis supplied).

in Hamburg, when the British government demanded "some satisfaction," [4] with the French declaration of war against Britain in 1792, giving as one of the causes of the war that "the English minister . . . was employing all possible means, both in parliament and out of it, to cover the French republic with ignominy, and to draw upon it the execration of the English nation, and of all Europe." [5] A recent example may be noted in connection with the complaint of Lebanon in 1958 to the Security Council against the United Arab Republic. The Lebanese representative pointed out that vehement attacks had been carried on in the U.A.R. press and by radio "for two years with mounting crescendo," and that long before the disturbances broke out in Lebanon on May 9, 1958, "there were unmistakable preparations for them in the press and radio of the United Arab Republic." [6] In reply to the suggestion of the U.A.R. representative that the Council should ignore the allegations relating to propaganda, the British representative pointed out that the Council "surely cannot expect that the Government of any country shall submit passively to *persistent* threats from the press and radio of a more powerful neighbor without seeking redress." [7]

INSTITUTIONALIZATION

While stray communications should be differentiated for policy purposes from sustained activity, a communication pattern which has become institutionalized has to be treated in a manner different from a new pattern of sustained use. The response pattern of the audience to an institutionalized pattern is predictable to a high degree, but it is not so with respect to a new pattern. Hence a new pattern of activity may create greater expectations of adverse effects on the values of the target elite than an institutionalized pattern, and calls for differential treatment. For instance, the practice of public information agencies generally is to interpret intelligence and disseminate it in a manner that will accord with the prevailing climate of relations between their state and other states.[8] A habitual and expected bias in the press of a country, having regard to the nature of its relations with others, must be distinguished from deliberate initiation of such practice against a particular participant. During election campaigning, and debate on the floor of legislatures and organs of international organizations, some rhetorical flourishes, some polemics and heated exchanges must be expected, and communications in such contexts have to be dealt with differently from those in noninstitutionalized situations.

4. *Annual Register*, 45 (1803), 713–14.
5. 36 *Annual Register, Public Papers*, 105, 106 (1793).
6. See S.C.O.R., 13th Year, 823rd Mtg. (1958), para. 62.
7. Ibid., 824th Mtg., para. 278 (emphasis supplied).
8. See Lasswell, "The Climate of International Action," pp. 339, 350.

CRISIS

The policy to be adopted in situations when violence has not broken out has been indicated in Chapter 4. Here we shall discuss the issues relating to situations when violence has broken out.

Traditional writers on international law divide community prescriptions into three broad groups: those applicable in peace, those applicable during war, and those applicable between a belligerent and a neutral state. This classification is rational to the extent that it separates the community prescriptions designed to regulate the relations between states—with a view to preventing the outbreak of violence between them—from those designed to regulate the use of the instruments of violence, and also from those to regulate the relations between a state using the military instrument, and therefore pressed by the exigencies of that situation, and a state remaining outside the conflict. Community policies laid down with reference to each of these situations had different objectives. The traditional manner of presentation of the community prescriptions in a threefold division, however, suffers from the defect that it conveys the impression that war, peace, and neutrality are three absolute relationships between states with clear lines separating them. It obscures the fact that the peace and war dichotomy covers a continuum of relations between states, ranging from situations involving the application of no pressure to those involving the use of violence,[9] and that nonparticipation in a war may be anything from the highest degree of abstention to a situation which lacks only a formal characterization of belligerency.[10] It does not attempt an intelligible description of how policies are prescribed, invoked, and applied by decision-makers in a manner suitable for the occasion, as mutual application of coercive process between states reaches different levels of intensity. For convenience, however, we shall divide the following discussion into two parts, the first dealing with the relations between states engaged in mutual application of violence, and the second with relations between a state so engaged and a third state remaining out of the conflict.

Between States Engaged in Mutual Application of Violence

The traditional prescriptions relating to war did not discriminate between the aggressor and the victim, and applied equally to both. As the

9. For amplification of the thesis, see McDougal, "Peace and War, Factual Continuum with Multiple Legal Consequences," 49 *A.J.I.L.* 63 (1955).

10. Titus Komarnicki remarks about the positions adopted by states which did not assume the formal status of belligerency during World War II: "In the course of the war many states adopted positions differing from both neutrality and belligerency, the term non-belligerency covering different attitudes and various measures short of war." See his "The Place of Neutrality in the Modern International Law," 80 *Hague Recueil* 399, 463 (1952).

United Nations Charter has proscribed resort to force for aggressive purposes, it has been suggested that, in any enforcement action taken in accordance with the United Nations procedures against an aggressor state, the traditional laws of war should not apply but rather a different set of rules which discriminate against the aggressor. Quincy Wright has developed this thesis at considerable length.[11] However, his suggestion amounts only to saying that individual participants on either side should have the same rights and duties, but the aggressor state should not have belligerent rights. His proposal has bearing only on the settlement of reparations at the termination of hostilities.[12] It has not been suggested so far by anybody that all who participate on the side of an aggressor in war should be deemed criminals.[13] The traditional prescriptions that determine permissible and nonpermissible participants in the application of coercion by a belligerent state will remain unaffected even if Wright's suggestion advocating discrimination is adopted.

When the rules of war are broken, sanctions may be applied in either of two principal ways. The individual who has violated the prescriptions may be held criminally liable. The offender may be tried before the tribunals of his own state; failing that, before the tribunals of the injured state, if he falls into its hands; or before any international tribunal that might be set up on the termination of hostilities. Or collective responsibility may be attributed to the state to which the guilty participant belongs. Taking reprisals and collecting reparations at the close of a war are important means by which the collective responsibility is enforced. However, collective responsibility for violation of prescriptions by participants cannot be attributed to a belligerent state unless the violations were authorized by responsible officials of that state, or were so widespread in their incidence that a presumption of such authorization could be drawn.[14]

We shall mention the relevant prescriptions and policies regarding the use of the instrument with respect to participants, audience, objectives, strategies, and outcome-effects.

11. "The Outlawry of War, and the Law of War," 47 *A.J.I.L.* 365 (1954).

12. See H. Lauterpacht, "The Law of War," 30 *B.Y.B.I.L.* 206, 242 (1953).

13. In the post-World War II trials, it has been observed, only the top leaders responsible for policymaking were held responsible for the crimes against peace. In only one of these trials was a conviction given for mere participation in an aggressive war; see the *Trial of Takashi Sakai, U.N. War Crime Cases,* 14 (1946), 1.

14. In the *Trial of General Yamashita, U.N. War Crime Cases,* 4 (1946), 1, the presiding U.S. Military Tribunal observed, "It is absurd . . . to consider a commander a murderer or a rapist because one of his soldiers commits a murder or rape. Nevertheless, where murder and rape and vicious, revengeful actions are widespread offenses, and there is no effective attempt by a commander to discover and control criminal acts, such a commander may be held responsible, even criminally liable, for the lawless acts of his troops, depending upon the nature and circumstances surrounding them." (Ibid., p. 35.) The same principle applies in connection with the attribution of responsibility to the belligerent state.

Participants

It needs no special mention that the responsibility of a state in relation to an enemy state differs from its responsibility toward one with which it is not at war. Prescriptions which apply during peacetime, such as the one making a state responsible for applying remedial measures against those who might publish, within its jurisdiction, libels directed against the heads or other dignitaries of foreign states, do not apply as between belligerents.[15] Belligerents allow enemy aliens procedural access to their domestic tribunals only under exceptional circumstances.[16] The responsibility of a belligerent state toward an enemy state is determined solely by the laws of war.

The official non-official dichotomy which assumes considerable importance in ordinary times has, in view of what has been stated above, less importance during belligerency. It may be relevant only insofar as the violation of any prescription by officials may, apart from engaging their individual responsibility, afford a stronger basis for attributing responsibility to the belligerent state to which they belong than when the participants happen to be non-officials.

According to contemporary prescriptions, members of field psychological warfare units, whether they be military men or civilians, are entitled to be treated on capture as prisoners of war.[17] Civilians, whether they be officials or non-officials, who participate in propaganda activities to further the war effort at home or to reduce the power of the enemy by weakening the loyalties of the people toward their elites, cannot be arrested or prosecuted by the enemy in the event that the territory falls under belligerent occupation.[18] When it is permissible, as we shall presently observe, for a belligerent to use the ideological instrument for the purpose of obtaining military success, and when it is accepted as a normal fact that in a modern war civilian contribution to the war effort is as important as the military's,

15. In 1802, on the complaint of the French government, the British government prosecuted one Peltier for publication of libels on Napoleon and other French officials. A verdict of guilty was obtained but, as war broke out in 1803, the accused was not called upon to serve any sentence. See R. *v. Peltier, State Trials*, 28 (1802), 529.

16. See Oppenheim-Lauterpacht, 2, 310; Sir A. D. McNair, *The Legal Effects of War* (Cambridge, Cambridge University Press, 1948), pp. 44–45.

17. See Art. 4(4) of the Geneva Convention Relative to the Treatment of Prisoners of War, 1949. In referring to civilians who might follow the armed units and be entitled to the privileges of prisoners of war on capture, this article does not specify those who might be engaged in psychological warfare operations. But the specific enumeration of the classes in the clause does not limit the preceding general statement which covers all "persons who accompany the armed forces, without actually being members thereof."

18. See Art. 70 of the Geneva Convention Relative to the Protection of Civilians in Occupied Territory. It provides that unless the act in question amounts to a violation of the laws and customs of war, a belligerent occupying power cannot arrest, prosecute, or convict the person who committed it.

there is no policy consideration which calls for discriminating between one class of belligerent population and another in the use of the ideological instrument. Certainly there is no reason why any participant should be asked to put on a uniform like a soldier,[19] possess an official designation, or be a non-official.

Audience

The question whether a person who participated in the internal use of the ideological instrument to promote the war effort during the progress of hostilities can be punished, assuming that the leaders of the state have been found guilty, was considered and answered in the negative by the Nuremberg tribunal in the case of Fritzsche.[20] This appears to be a reasonable position. If those who participate in the use of the ideological instrument are to be regarded as criminals, then every soldier who fights and every laborer who works in a war industry should be regarded as a criminal. That would result in imposition of punishment on a mass scale.

Prior to World War I, some writers held the opinion that incitement of enemy troops to treason or of civilians to revolt was impermissible. Bluntschli, representing this view, held that it was impermissible to incite enemy troops to disloyalty for two reasons.[21] First, he said, it was opposed to the laws of honor to incite enemy soldiers to treason, and second, the interest of states in military discipline ought not to be jeopardized by permitting such incitement. Both reasons appear to stem from a conception of war as an engagement between professional armies carried on in accordance with the rules of chivalry. It can hardly be said that the first reason holds good at the present day. As regards the second, military discipline cannot be said to be a value that calls for protection by the community. A breakdown in the military discipline of the state that has committed aggression will certainly benefit the community.

Spaight and Pillet took a view opposite to that of Bluntschli,[22] holding that inciting enemy troops to treason was permissible but not inciting civilian populations to revolt. Spaight, however, later took the view that inciting both is permissible.[23] The reason given by Pillet was that incitement of the civilian population would constitute an attempt on the very

19. Even in the case of those who participate in violence, the policy of rigidly insisting upon the wearing of distinctive emblems has met with criticism. See R. R. Baxter, "The So-Called 'Unprivileged Belligerency': Spies, Guerillas and Saboteurs," 28 *B.Y.B.I.L.* 323, 343 (1951).

20. *I.M.T., Nuremberg, Trial of Major War Criminals, 1*, 337; the defense specifically pleaded that his speeches in support of the war effort should be regarded as innocent. See ibid., 19, 352.

21. See J. M. Spaight, *War Rights on Land* (London, Macmillan, 1911), p. 147.

22. Ibid.

23. See J. M. Spaight, *Air Power and War Rights* (3d ed. London, Longmans, 1947), p. 319.

life of the enemy state. This reason might have been valid under the conditions obtaining in the seventeenth and eighteenth centuries when wars were no more than military engagements between rival professional armies, and caused minimal disturbance to civilian life, and when an aggressor could escape with minimal deprivation of power within his own state. Under modern conditions, when civilian industrial production adds enormously to the military potential of a belligerent, an attempt to dislocate civilian life seems to be open to no objection. A breakdown in civilian morale may bring hostilities to a speedy termination. When the officials of an aggressor state may be tried criminally for adopting the policy of aggression, it would be paradoxical to maintain that the loyalties of the subjects of that state to its officials should be regarded as an interest that ought to be protected by the community.

Despagnet considered that all incitement to disloyalty to enemy subjects was objectionable.[24] The reason he gave was that since treason was an offense punishable by all states, incitement of its subjects would not be tolerated by any belligerent power and therefore should be regarded as impermissible. This seems hardly a tenable reason, for during war the enemy commits acts which would be far less tolerated by a belligerent during peacetime.

Since World War I, the practice of states has confirmed the permissibility of the use of the ideological instrument to incite an enemy population to revolt against their government.[25] During that war the Germans claimed that such incitement constituted a war crime, but when the British threatened reprisals they gave up their claim.[26] During the Second World War the permissibility of the use of the instrument was never questioned.[27]

Objectives

Traditional prescriptions place no restriction on the right of the elite of a belligerent state to compel the people of the state to render services for the war, and consequently the use of the propaganda instrument internally for coercion is not open to objection. While violence is being employed against the opponent, to speak of the impermissibility of coercion by the ideological instrument would be meaningless. The legitimacy of the use of the instrument coercively in the territory under belligerent occupation may also be examined. Community policy in regard to belligerent occupation

24. See F. Despagnet, *Cours De Droit International Public* (4th ed. Paris, 1910), p. 845.

25. See Spaight, *Air Power and War Rights*, Chap. 14; Wheaton, *War*, Vol. 2 of *International Law* (7th ed. by A. B. Keith, London, Stevens, 1944), 353–54; H. Lauterpacht, "Revolutionary Propaganda by Governments."

26. See Spaight, *Air Power and War Rights*, p. 330 et seq.

27. For an account of World War II practice, see ibid., p. 334 et seq.

has been formulated with reference to two conflicting claims: the claim of the belligerent occupant that it should be permissible for him to use his power—flowing from effective control of the people and the territory—to satisfy military necessity; and the claim of the community that the power should not be used in disregard of all principles of humanity.[28] The policy of the world community has been arrived at by balancing these two conflicting claims.

According to traditional law a belligerent occupant is permitted to change the laws in force in the territory if it is necessary for the maintenance and safety of his forces in the prosecution of war. He is entitled to demand obedience to such laws.[29] The Geneva Convention Relative to the Protection of Civilian Persons, 1949, has imposed certain limitations on this power only in respect of sanctions which might be attached to such laws.[30] Under such conditions, it follows, it is quite permissible for the belligerent occupant to use the instrument intensively to insure that the population will abstain from taking any attitude hostile to him.

According to traditional law a belligerent occupant cannot demand allegiance from the people in the area.[31] While the issue of arms is not finally settled and the general duty of allegiance of the people to their government has not come to an end, it is not consistent with the principle of humanity that the belligerent occupant should be permitted to demand allegiance to himself. Change of allegiance would, at the least, expose the people to the risk of punishment in case the territory is recovered by the original ruler. However, there does not seem to be any restriction implicit in the traditional doctrines which prevents the occupying power from intensively manipulating symbols and words to create among the people sentiments hostile to their former rulers, and to change their predispositions and their attitudes toward the pattern of value shaping and sharing prevailing in the area before occupation.

According to traditional law a belligerent occupant is prohibited from compulsorily enlisting the inhabitants in the occupied territories into his forces.[32] But it is permissible for him to take volunteers. During World War II the Germans resorted to intensive propagandizing to secure voluntary enlistment, as in French Alsace where they attempted to induce French nationals to enlist in the German army. In the *Trial of Robert Wagner and others,*[33] a French Permanent Military Tribunal in Stras-

28. See R. R. Baxter, "*The Duty of Obedience to the Belligerent Occupant,*" 27 *B.Y.B.I.L.* 235 (1950).
29. See Oppenheim-Lauterpacht, 2, 437.
30. See Art. 68.
31. See Spaight, *War Rights on Land,* p. 323.
32. Ibid.
33. See Judgment (1946), *U.N. War Crime Cases,* 11, 23.

bourg held that such propaganda constituted a war crime and convicted three German officers who carried it on. Article 51 of the Geneva Convention Relative to Civilian Persons, 1949, expressly proscribes pressure or propaganda by the occupying power to procure voluntary enlistment. The use of the ideological instrument, therefore, with the object of obtaining cooperation in the form of voluntary enlistment is not permissible. Even the slightest amount of psychic coercion seems to be prohibited in this context.

A belligerent occupant is permitted to requisition the services of local inhabitants for certain types of civilian jobs, but not for other types.[34] Even the Geneva Convention of 1949, however, does not prohibit intensive use of the instrument to procure "voluntary" cooperation of civilians for doing the latter category of jobs. When a belligerent occupant is prohibited from requisitioning services for certain types of civilian jobs for humanitarian reasons, it seems to be necessary to prohibit him from using the ideological instrument with a high degree of intensity to coerce civilians to take up those jobs.

Strategies

The limitations on the techniques and tactics of a user of the ideological instrument during hostilities stem from the traditional rules of warfare which, on the one hand, permit the use of ruses and stratagems and, on the other, prohibit perfidious and treacherous killing.[35] The demarcation line between the two is often not identifiable.

Disseminating false information to reach the enemy and induce him to make disadvantageous moves, or to obtain a modification of the potentialities of any of the instruments of strategy in his hand is quite permissible.[36] It is obviously permissible to disseminate false statements to compel the enemy to disclose any information he is suppressing, whether such disclosure weakens the enemy or gives an advantage to the strategists. Thus during World War II, on the eve of the Allied landings in Italy, the Allies broadcast the terms of the secret armistice agreement entered into with Marshal Badoglio. The Marshal had agreed to broadcast the terms himself but he backed out of the arrangement because of fear of the Germans. The Allies nevertheless transmitted it from Algiers by radio, saying, contrary to fact, that the arrangement entered into with Badoglio was that the announcement should come from Algiers to avoid its possible obstruction by

34. See Geneva Convention Relative to Civilian Persons (1949), Art. 51.

35. The Hague *Reglement*, Arts. 23(b) and 24; U.S. Department of the Army, *Field Manual, The Law of Land Warfare* (Washington, 1956), Rule 50.

36. See in this regard, Spaight, *War Rights on Land*, p. 154; also J. Westlake, *International Law*, Part II, *War* (Cambridge, Cambridge University Press, 1913), p. 80.

the Germans. The broadcast from Algiers compelled the Marshal to disclose the agreement shortly thereafter.[37]

We may attempt here to distinguish between a permissible and an impermissible ruse. Oppenheim adopts the distinction formulated by Halleck: "Whenever a belligerent has expressly or tacitly engaged, and is, therefore, bound by a moral obligation, to speak the truth to an enemy, it is perfidy to betray the confidence, because it is a breach of good faith." [38] Westlake adopts the same distinction,[39] and says that a communication of false reports in breach of such faith as should exist between combatants is wrongful. A communication by a commander intended to be acted upon by the enemy commander, he says, must be truthful. He mentions as an example of an impermissible communication a false statement that an armistice has been concluded. Oppenheim seems to adopt the same view but Spaight disputes it.[40] Spaight's contention is that it is the responsibility of the commander of an army not to be taken in by the lies of his opponents.

Perhaps the true line of distinction can be formulated by reference to the main policy underlying the laws of war. Certain symbols and signs may have come to carry special significance according to the rules and customs of warfare, and when a belligerent uses these symbols the opponents may be under a legal obligation to adopt a certain course of conduct, the policy underlying the obligation being one of humanity. If such symbols are abused as ruses, the opponent cannot be expected to respect the obligation further and suffer military disadvantage. Abuse of symbols of that character may be regarded as impermissible.[41]

In this light, a false statement by a commander that an armistice has been concluded seems permissible, for a commander to whom it is made need not accept it until he gets a verification from his own authentic sources. Under the modern conditions of communication it is not difficult for him to obtain such confirmation.

Outcome-Effects

Whenever it is impermissible and criminal for a belligerent to commit a particular act, it may be said that it is equally impermissible to accomplish the result by inciting the civilian population to commit the crime. Thus in

37. The incident is related by R. H. S. Crossman in his supplementary essay, in Lerner, *Syke War*, p. 323.

38. See Oppenheim-Lauterpacht, 2, sec. 165.

39. Westlake, *War*, pp. 80–81.

40. Spaight, *War Rights on Land*, p. 155.

41. See Spaight, *Air Power and War Rights*, p. 170; U.S., *The Law of Land Warfare*, pp. 22–23.

the *Essen Lynching Case,*[42] a captain in the German army gave instructions to his men to escort three Allied war prisoners to a certain place. He gave his orders in such a loud voice that a crowd gathered nearby could hear and know exactly what was going to happen. The three airmen were later killed by the crowd. A British Military Court held that the captain was guilty of inciting the killing of the prisoners of war and sentenced him to death.

The draft Code of Offenses Against the Peace and Security of Mankind contains provisions which make direct incitement to act in violation of laws and customs of war a crime.[43] The recommendation is consistent with our preferred policy.

Between a State Using Violence and a Nonparticipating State

The relations of such states are in general governed under traditional law by the prescriptions known as the laws of neutrality, which to some extent modify prescriptions applicable in peacetime. According to the traditional doctrines a state which is not participating in the hostilities in progress between others has to observe certain duties. These duties may be broadly summed up under the headings of abstention and prevention.[44] The officials of a nonparticipating state should refrain from participating in the hostilities and prevent the use of the resources of their state, human and material, by either of the belligerents. Some authors mention the duty to adopt an attitude of impartiality and act in accord with such an attitude.[45] Perhaps, in describing the duties and rights of a neutral state, it would be safer to detail the relevant prescriptions than to refer to them by shorthand expressions such as impartiality, abstention, and the like; for, as Quincy Wright has rightly pointed out, though these expressions have given general direction to the development of the law, they in themselves were merely generalizations of specific rules arrived at by practice and compromise.[46]

Castrén, the Finnish author on the laws of war and neutrality, states

42. *U.N. War Crime Cases, Judgment, 1* (1948), 88; U.S., *The Law of Land Warfare,* pp. 22–23; see also the case of Brigadefuhrer Kurt Meyer, *U.N. War Crime Cases, 4,* 97. See also Spaight, *Air Power and War Rights,* p. 333; *Report of the Commission of Jurists to Report upon the Revision of Rules of Warfare,* The Hague, 1923 (British Parliamentary Papers, Cmd. 2201 of 1924), p. 25.

43. Art. 2, clauses (11), (12).

44. See Hyde, *International Law, 3,* secs. 848–49. E. Castrén, *The Present Law of War and Neutrality* (Helsinki, Suomalaisen Tiedeakatemian, 1954), p. 439; Fenwick, *International Law,* p. 646.

45. See Oppenheim-Lauterpacht, 2, 673; Titus Komarnicki, "The Place of Neutrality in the Modern International Law," p. 406.

46. See "The Present Status of Neutrality," 34 *A.J.I.L.* 391 (1939); see also P. C. Jessup and F. Deák, *Neutrality, Its History, Economics and Law, 1* (New York, Co-

that the officials of a state owe the same duty of respect and of nonintervention by hostile propaganda toward a belligerent state as toward a state at peace. The officials of a neutral state may, however, express sympathy for either of the belligerents, and criticize the policies and methods of either belligerent with restraint, avoiding insulting expressions. It is also permissible for them to protest against the violations of international law by either of the belligerents whether harmful to their state or not.[47]

Before World War I, when the law of neutrality was at its zenith,[48] it may have been considered by governments that there was a duty on the part of the officials of a neutral state not to express any opinion adverse to either of the belligerents. At the time of the Spanish-American War, the French government reprimanded the cadets of a French Marine Corps for communicating a resolution to Madrid, expressing their sympathy for Spain.[49] President Wilson appealed to the people of the United States, in 1914, to be "impartial in thought as well as action," while declaring the neutrality of the United States in the war.[50] In these instances, perhaps, restraint of a degree not required by the community prescriptions was assumed. President Roosevelt's assertion in 1939, "Even a neutral has a right to take account of facts. Even a neutral cannot be asked to close his mind or his conscience,"[51] indicates the traditional position more accurately.

Even if the traditional doctrine required the abstention of the officials of a neutral state from expressing opinions adverse to the belligerents, insistence upon strict adherence to it at present would be devoid of rationality. If the government of a state resorts to the use of violence against another, under the provisions of the United Nations Charter their conduct may become immediately a subject of discussion before the United Nations organs. The officials of the member states, while they participate in the deliberations of the United Nations organs, need not be under restraint in expressing their opinions, inasmuch as a major principle of the United Nations is to facilitate free discussion within its organs.[52] If

---

lumbia University Press, 1935), xii; C. Eagleton, "The Duty of Impartiality on the Part of a Neutral," 34 *A.J.I.L.* 99 (1940).

47. *The Present Law of War and Neutrality*, p. 452.

48. Quincy Wright, "The Future of Neutrality," *International Conciliation*, No. 242 (1928), p. 367.

49. See Hyde, *International Law*, 3, 2230; Moore, *Digest*, 7, 867.

50. See C. G. Fenwick, *American Neutrality, Trial, and Failure* (New York, New York University Press, 1940), p. 108; it is, however, considered that the President went beyond what was in fact required under the law existing at that time. See Fenwick, *International Law*, p. 656; Hyde, *International Law*, 3, 2313.

51. Radio address by President Roosevelt, Sept. 3, 1939, 1 *Dept. of State Bull.* 201–02 (1939).

52. See Chap. 9.

officials may express their opinions freely before United Nations organs, there should not be any objection against expression of those opinions before any other forum, if the fact that a different forum is chosen does not substantially alter the effects produced on the belligerent concerned. Apart from what effect the community policy of facilitating free discussion before international forums may have on the assumed position, one may also point out the anachronism involved in demanding strict compliance with the traditional doctrines of neutrality when the concept of neutrality has broken down as a result of developments which have taken place in this century. This aspect of the question will be examined later.

The traditional prescriptions did not require that a neutral state should prevent expressions of opinion by non-officials.[53] Castrén states the position as comparable to what the prescriptions applicable during peacetime require.[54] During the years of World War II, some German writers maintained that a neutral state should observe ideological neutrality as well, but the view was rejected by writers of Switzerland and Norway.[55] Goebbels at one time vaguely demanded that public opinion in a neutral state be neutral, but at the same time he asserted that he did not desire any limitation of the freedom of expression.[56] During both world wars, however, Switzerland adopted internal censorship of the press, and during World War II of radio broadcasting also. At the beginning of World War II it prohibited the opening of propaganda bureaus within its territory for the benefit of any of the belligerents.[57] The rights of a neutral state, it should be remembered, after all depend on the ability and willingness of its government to exercise and defend them.

While it is thus permissible for the officials of a neutral state to express, and permit private persons to express, their opinions about the policies of the official elites of a belligerent state, the question poses itself whether sustained and intensive use of the ideological instrument against those elites stands to be treated in the same manner as expression of opinion. We have already noted the statement of Castrén that the officials of a neutral state should refrain from carrying on hostile propaganda. Justice Pal, one of the members of the International Military Tribunal for the Far East, indicated in a dissenting judgment that a belligerent affected by such activity coming from a neutral state would be justified in treating it as a violation of neutrality duties, in view of the potential inhering in such ac-

53. See Fenwick, *American Neutrality, Trial and Failure,* p. 121; the same author, *International Law,* p. 655; Hyde, *International Law,* 3, 2312–13; A. Verdross, "Austria's Permanent Neutrality and the United Nations Organization," 50 *A.J.I.L.* 61 (1956).

54. *The Present Law of War and Neutrality,* p. 485.

55. For references to those works see A. Verdross.

56. See Fenwick, *American Neutrality, Trial and Failure,* p. 122.

57. See Castrén, p. 486.

tivity in the present age of developed means of mass communication.[58] There may indeed come a stage when propaganda activity will be regarded by the affected belligerent state as something more than the exercise of freedom of expression. In the case of *Lothar Eisentrager and others*,[59] a United States Military Commission in Shanghai considered that the activities of the accused, who were formerly employees of the German diplomatic mission in Japanese-occupied China—consisting of, among other things, the writing and transmission of propaganda to the troops of the United States—constituted war crimes, inasmuch as they amounted to "military activities" undertaken in violation of the German armistice agreement. It might be possible to conclude, by analogy, that when the propaganda activity launched from the territory of a neutral state, directed against a belligerent, creates an expectation on the part of the officials of the latter that it will have a substantial effect on their war effort, they will have sufficient basis to claim that the activity should be stopped; and if they fail to obtain compliance with their demand, to consider that a breach of neutrality has been committed. This will especially be the case if such activity is carried on by officials.

It may thus be observed that, while prescriptions of the traditional doctrines of neutrality are very similar to the prescriptions applicable during peacetime, by virtue of developments in mass communication it is likely that in the future belligerent states will claim that the officials of nonparticipating states should refrain from, and should restrain private persons within their states from engaging in, an intensive use of the ideological instrument of coercion. But the policy issues which arise in connection with the relations between a belligerent and a nonparticipating state differ from those arising in relations between states not engaged in mutual application of transnational violence. The policy underlying the traditional neutrality doctrine is to permit a state to take any side it pleases in an armed conflict in which others are engaged, or to keep out of the conflict with little concern about its outcome. The neutrality doctrines provided an arrangement by which a state could so keep out, and the belligerents re-

58. *International Military Tribunal for the Far East, Dissenting Judgment of Justice R. B. Pal*, 125 (Calcutta, Sanyal & Co., 1953). He stated thus: "Apart from any other matter, the question how far a neutral has the right to make hostile comment upon the actions of a belligerent is decidedly a grave one, remembering that today, besides the power of the press, the radio carries the spoken word to all the corners of the earth in a moment. The effect of a nation's broadcasting may do more harm to a combatant than the destruction of any army corps; so that if a combatant feels that the broadcasting and the press utterances of a nation which owed a duty of remaining neutral are sufficiently damaging to him, he may be within his right to demand discontinuance of such utterances." This, no doubt, is an extreme statement, but is quoted here only to spotlight the contemporary issue.

59. *U.N. War Crime Cases*, 14 (1947), 8.

spect the abstention. Contemporary community policy, on the other hand, as it finds expression in the provisions of the United Nations Charter designed for maintaining peace and security in the world community, presents an altogether different perspective on nonparticipation. That policy is to promote collective application of the means of coercion against an aggressor, and to see that no assistance is rendered to an aggressor, and all assistance is given to the victim. This change in community policy, and the legal formulas which seek to give effect to it, have necessarily to be taken into account in evaluating the claims that a belligerent may present in future to a nonparticipating state in regard to the use of the ideological instrument by its officials and private persons.

Neutrality and the U.N. Charter

In the first place, if the functioning of the Security Council is facilitated by the absence of the veto of any of the permanent members, and the Council determines under Article 39 the existence of any "threat to the peace, breach of the peace, or act of aggression," it may further decide to take measures of coercion, nonviolent under Article 41 and violent under Article 42, to restore peace and security. If the Council calls upon the members to apply against the delinquent state nonviolent means of coercion, the members are under an obligation by virtue of Article 25 to comply with the direction of the Council. The Council may decide to take military measures also. The agreements contemplated under Article 43, by which members were to enter into agreements with the Council, undertaking to make available, on its call, military units and other facilities, have not yet materialized. Nevertheless, the Council has competence to call upon the members to contribute military forces, on an ad hoc basis, to be used against the guilty state.[60] Members who fail to contribute military units for the enforcement action, for some reason or other, will at least be bound to participate in the application of the nonviolent means of coercion, if the Council so directs them. It is possible, therefore, in certain situations that a member state may, without participating militarily in the enforcement action, be applying economic and/or ideological instruments of coercion against the delinquent state in discharge of its obligations under the Charter.

But, it has to be conceded that under present conditions this is largely a theoretical possibility. Because of the cleavage that exists between the Western and the Soviet blocs, proposals for armed action in the enforcement of peace are more often than not likely to be met by the veto of one or the other of the permanent members. The very special circumstances

60. See L. M. Goodrich and A. P. Simmons, *The United Nations and the Maintenance of Peace and Security* (Washington, D.C., Brookings Institution, 1955), p. 437.

that existed at the time of the North Korean aggression, resulting from the absence of the Soviet representative from Security Council table, are not likely to recur. At present what may be expected in most cases is that the Council will adopt methods of persuasion and nonviolent pressure,[61] calling upon the parties to adopt "provisional measures" (contemplated in Article 40) to prevent the aggravation of the situation and to stop the fighting.[62] There may consequently occur intervals, even fairly long, during which fighting proceeds, and other member states and nonmembers remain outside the conflict. Such states are likely to take the position of neutral states under traditional law.[63]

When there is a breach of peace or act of aggression,[64] and unanimity of the permanent members does not obtain, the General Assembly can take action under the "Uniting for Peace" resolution,[65] recommending that the members cooperate in adopting collective measures against the aggressor. The Assembly may recommend, according to the suggestion made by the Collective Measures Committee set up by the Assembly under the resolution, political, economic, and military measures.[66] It is quite conceivable that when the Assembly recommends the application of all the means of coercion, some member states which are unable to contribute military units may at least cooperate in the application of the economic and political instruments.

Again it must be stated that, under the present conditions, it is unrealistic to expect the Assembly to recommend the use of force to restore peace. Because of the present composition of the Assembly, it is not easy to secure

61. See in this connection L. M. Goodrich, *The United Nations* (New York, Thomas Y. Crowell Co., 1960), pp. 164–66, 167.

62. This is not to deny that in suitable cases the Council might decide to use forces for peacekeeping purposes.

63. A qualification may be added here that the neutrality so assumed would be besides what the states might do as members of the U.N.

64. The Collective Measures Committee appointed by the U.N. General Assembly in its first report stated that the General Assembly would not recommend military measures unless there was a breach of the peace or act of aggression, while the Security Council might recommend or decide upon such measures even in the case of mere threat to the peace. See Collective Measures Committee, *Report*, G.A.O.R., 6th Sess., Supp. No. 13 (1951), p. 3.

65. Resolution 377(V), 3 November 1950. There are indeed doubts regarding the legal competence of the Assembly to do the various things contemplated in this resolution. For a discussion of the difficulties involved, see Kelsen, *The Law of the United Nations*, pp. 959–84; also Stone, *Legal Controls of International Conflict*, pp. 268–72. However, in view of the Communist Chinese, Suez, Lebanon, and Congo precedents, the competence of the Assembly appears to have been well established, at least to the extent to which the Assembly went in those cases.

66. Collective Measures Committee, *Report*, p. 3. What the Committee mentions as political measures are in fact the diplomatic and ideological measures of coercion.

a majority for such a recommendation.[67] Furthermore, due to the fear that the use of force might escalate into a nuclear conflagration, such a recommendation is most unlikely to receive the requisite majority.[68]

The General Assembly indeed can only recommend action against an aggressor or disturber of peace, and compliance with a recommendation per se is not, technically speaking, obligatory. However, viewing the question from a broader perspective, we can say that the fulfillment of the obligations undertaken by the members under the Charter calls for a high degree of respect for the recommendations made by the Assembly under the "Uniting for Peace" resolution. By becoming a member the state has undertaken the general obligation arising from the purposes and principles of the Charter to act as best it can for maintaining peace and security in the world community.[69] That obligation requires respect for a determination made by the most representative principal organ of the Organization about the existence of a breach of the peace or an act of aggression, and for the recommendation that members participate in the application of collective enforcement measures. The members, no doubt, will have discretion as to the extent to which they would carry out the recommendation. But the discretion is one which the members are bound to exercise in good faith. A member state which flouts the recommendation may find at some stage, as Judge Lauterpacht remarked with reference to recommendations made by the Assembly to the Administering Powers of Trust Territories, that "it has overstepped the imperceptible line between impropriety and illegality . . . and has exposed itself to consequences legitimately following as a legal sanction." [70] A recommendation of the General Assembly acting under the "Uniting for Peace" resolution is not devoid of legal effect, even though it is not technically binding. It carries at least such formal authority as gives to conduct in accordance with it the legal clothing of permissibility.[71]

67. For an account of the impact of the new members on the Assembly, see Goodrich, *The United Nations*, p. 180.

68. This fear is likely to be present more often than not. Apparently it restrained more serious action in the case of Hungary in 1956. Ibid.

69. See Beckett, *The North Atlantic Treaty, the Brussels Treaty and the Charter of the United Nations*, p. 35.

70. Judge Lauterpacht considers that a recommendation of the General Assembly to an Administering Power in regard to the administration of a Trust Territory is one which, no doubt, leaves to the Administering Power's discretion whether to give effect to it or not, but the discretion has to be exercised by the Power in good faith. See *Advisory Opinion on the Question of Voting Procedures on Questions Relating to Reports and Petitions Concerning the Territory of South West Africa*, Advisory Opinion of June 7, 1955, I.C.J. Rep., p. 120. The statement applies equally well to recommendations made under the "Uniting for Peace" resolution.

71. This view at any rate is likely to prevail if the Assembly develops into an effective instrument of collective security.

The Charter provisions thus make it permissible for a member state to apply any nonviolent instrument of coercion against a belligerent in compliance with a decision of the Security Council or recommendation of the General Assembly, even though that state is not participating in the military operations initiated in pursuance of such decision or recommendation.[72] This, needless to say, is a great departure from what the traditional doctrines of neutrality prescribed; a legal consequence of any collective security system would seem to be at least a risk of involuntary abandonment, by any of those who participate in that system, of a policy of impartiality toward contestants and of strict non-participation. Indeed, writers have maintained even during the period between the two world wars that the traditional neutrality doctrines lost their importance by virtue of the League Covenant and the Kellogg Pact, and that it was permissible for a non-participant by virtue of those two instruments to discriminate against the aggressor.[73] Actions have been persuasive, even more than doctrinal writings. In 1935, during the Italo-Abyssinian War, when Italy protested that the application of economic sanctions in pursuance of the resolution of the League Council would amount to commission of hostile acts against Italy, justifying the latter to resort to countermeasures, Britain and France replied that they were bound to act in accordance with their obligations under the Covenant and no other attitude was open to them.[74] However, the thesis that the traditional neutrality doctrines have become obsolete by virtue of the League Covenant, the Kellogg Pact, and finally, the Charter, and that it is permissible for a non-participant to discriminate between the belligerents, has met with some criticism.

Komarnicki, for instance, has pointed out that such a doctrine will be found unworkable, for the belligerent discriminated against cannot be expected to respect the neutrality of the discriminating state.[75] Nor would it help collective security by eliminating neutrality, because the threat of reprisals would deter many states from applying discriminatory measures. But this is no more than stating the obvious. The possibility of an aggressor

72. Apart from Art. 2(6) of the U.N. Charter, the policy of the United Nations in the past has been to enlist the cooperation of non-members freely. Thus during the Korean War, non-members participated in the enforcement action. Resolution 503 A(VI) of the General Assembly, adopted on 12 January 1952, contemplates enlisting the cooperation of non-members in any enforcement action which might be organized in pursuance of a resolution of the General Assembly. Further, even under traditional law there was nothing to prevent a neutral from engaging in discriminatory actions against one of the belligerents provided it accepted the risk of involvement in war; see Eagleton, "The Duty of Impartiality on the Part of a Neutral," p. 130.

73. For a presentation of all such views see Titus Komarnicki, Chap. 3; see also "Harvard Research on the Rights and Duties of States in the Case of Aggression," 33 *A.J.I.L.* Supp. 827 (1939), comment on Art. 10 and Art. 11.

74. See R.I.I.A., *Documents on International Affairs* 1938, 2, 216, 219–21.

75. See his "The Place of Neutrality in Modern International Law," Chap. 2.

state responding with countermeasures of coercion against those applying discriminatory and coercive processes is inherent in the consideration of any policy of collective security.[76] And the degree to which any state will cooperate in any system of collective security depends to a great extent upon the degree to which the elite of that state expects that its security will be promoted by such participation. A state which chooses to participate in the application of nonviolent means of coercion against an aggressor, without participating in the military operations, has to look for protection against retaliation to the collective security system itself and not the traditional doctrines of neutrality. The aggressor state will, of course, be committing a fresh act of aggression by attacking such state. The significant point to be noted is that, so long as the collective security system under the Charter remains functioning, it will be permissible for a state to apply discriminatory coercive measures against a state which is determined, in accordance with the prescriptions and procedures of the United Nations, to be one subject to restraint by collective action.

In addition to permitting a state which is not participating in military operations to apply nonviolent measures of coercion against the aggressor, the Charter prohibits the members from rendering any assistance to the latter when the United Nations is taking any enforcement action against it (Art. 2[5]). If the Security Council is taking the action, there is no doubt about it. If the action is initiated in pursuance of a resolution of the General Assembly, the obligations of the members under the Charter would appear to require of them respect for the decision of the Assembly, at least to the extent of refraining from giving assistance to the state against which the action is being taken.

Even nonmembers are bound to refrain from assisting a belligerent state against which the Security Council is taking an enforcement action. The discussions at San Francisco at the time of framing the Charter disclose that one of the objects the framers had in view in including Article 2(6) was to insure that nonmembers would refrain from obstructing the functioning of the collective security mechanism of the United Nations.[77] Further, the discussions in the United Nations make clear the view of a large majority of the members that nonmembers should refrain from rendering any assistance to a state against which the United Nations is taking an

76. See the report of the Collective Measures Committee, cited above, p. 20.

77. See U.N. C.I.O., Documents, 6, *Summary Record of the 12th Meeting of Committee 1/1, June 5, 1945*. During the discussion on the clause which now stands as Art. 2(6), the delegate of Belgium stated that he considered it to be a most important provision, for the Organization should not be allowed to be paralyzed by any state invoking the Hague Agreements, neutrality laws, and the like. He stated that the Organization could ignore any claim which a non-member might make. His statement was not challenged and the clause was adopted unanimously.

enforcement action.[78] It may be expected that an enforcement action taken under the "Uniting for Peace" resolution will be considered by the members, at least those who participate in it, as an enforcement action taken by the organization.[79]

It appears from the above that when a collective enforcement action is being taken, a state which remains outside the conflict should not permit within its territory such use of the ideological instrument as creates a reasonable expectation on the part of the concerned U.N. organ that its outcome will be a violation of Charter obligations. For example, intensive activity appealing to the people to volunteer for the aggressor's armed forces, if it creates an expectation that it will be effective, may have to be restrained. Similarly action can be taken if the activity creates an expectation that it will force the government to go to the assistance of the aggressor. On the other hand, it seems quite permissible to allow such activities if their purpose happens to be to mobilize opinion against the aggressor.

If the General Assembly is also unable to act due to a failure to secure the necessary two-thirds majority for determining aggression and recommending collective action, this amounts to a collapse of the collective security mechanism of the United Nations. In that event, the only obligation which states will have to comply with is that which they have undertaken under any of the regional or other collective defense arrangements entered into under Article 51 or 52 of the Charter. They may indeed go to the assistance of the victim under Article 51 even before the Security Council or the General Assembly has determined who the aggressor is, their decision being, however, reviewable by either of the two bodies. When it is permissible for a state to use even violence under Article 51, there is no reason why it should not be permissible to use nonviolent means of coercion alone. But in the absence of centralized determination of who the aggressor is, each regional or defense organization will have to arrive at that determination in accordance with its prescriptions and procedures. Uncommitted nations may choose to keep out of the conflict. Traditional neutrality doctrines may prove to be of some use in that event, to afford a basis for adjusting the relations between those who desire to keep out and the belligerents who respect their abstention.

It is in the light of these prescriptions that the claims which may be presented in the future by belligerents to the officials of nonparticipating states—that the latter should refrain from, and restrain private persons

78. For an account of those discussions, see H. J. Taubenfeld, "International Actions and Neutrality," 47 *A.J.I.L.* 377, 387–90 (1953).

79. It may be noted that the Resolution of the Assembly of February 1, 1951, branding the People's Republic of China an aggressor in Korea, called upon "all States and authorities to refrain from giving assistance to the aggressor in Korea."

from, using the ideological instrument of coercion, as distinguished from expression of facts and opinions—should be evaluated.

RELATIVE CAPABILITIES

The relevancy, for the formulation of community policy, of the relative capabilities of the parties to employ the ideological instrument was brought to sharp focus during the debate in the Security Council on the complaint of Cuba, of March 13, 1962,[80] over the resolutions adopted at the Eighth Meeting of Consultation of Ministers of Foreign Affairs of American States, held at Punta del Este in January 1962. These resolutions, expelling Cuba from the Organization of American States and imposing an economic boycott, it was urged, were null and void; their validity should be referred to the opinion of the International Court of Justice, and until the opinion was received the resolutions must be suspended.

Speaking in justification of the resolutions, the United States representative pointed out that facts were brought to the attention of the Punta del Este conference which showed that the Castro regime of Cuba, with the assistance of local Communist parties, was employing a variety of techniques and practices to overturn democratic institutions in Latin America. The practices included: bringing people from other countries to Cuba for indoctrination and sending them back to their respective countries to carry on agitation and subversion; building up dissident groups in those countries; distributing propaganda literature and transmitting propaganda by a powerful short-wave transmitter calling upon the people of some Latin American countries to overthrow their regimes; and imparting training in guerilla warfare to people brought from foreign countries and sent back. It was further pointed out that the Cuban government got a large supply of arms from the Communist bloc and was prepared to use them, and in fact did use them in the Caribbean states, for overthrowing existing regimes.[81]

In the course of his reply the Cuban representative pointed out:

> The United States representative spoke of subversive activity by our Government throughout America, as if that were feasible, as if it were logically possible for a small country blockaded by the Government of the world's second greatest military Power to subvert a whole continent. . . . There has been talk of ideological aggression against countries of the hemisphere, as though Radio Havana and our publications could compete in resources with the United States press, radio and television with their powerful networks and subsidiaries throughout the world.[82]

80. U.N. Doc. S/5088.
81. See S.C.O.R., 17th year, 993rd Mtg. (1962), paras. 96–98.
82. Ibid., 994th Mtg. (1962), paras. 11, 12.

But earlier the United States representative pointed out that what was involved was not an encounter between Cuba on the one hand and other American states on the other, but that "Cuba represents a bridgehead of Sino-Soviet imperialism in the Western Hemisphere and a base for communist aggression, intervention, agitation and subversion against the republics." [83]

Again, during the discussion in the Council on the complaint of Yemen, April 1, 1964, that the United Kingdom had illegally bombed Harib, the representative of the United Kingdom invited attention to the propaganda activity and border shootings on the part of Yemeni authorities against the Federation of South Arabia, which he maintained justified the bombing, and stated,

> The representative of the Yemeni authorities likes to portray his country as being weak and defenseless, torn by civil war and menaced from without. We should none of us forget that this is not the true picture. The Yemeni authorities are supported by enormous numbers of United Arab Republic troops, and the successive reports of the Secretary-General bear ample witness to this fact.[84]

These examples illustrate two significant factors which ought to be given attention in the process of deciding on community policy. First, what are the relative capabilities of the parties, in terms of their possession of base values, to operate the ideological and other instruments? Second, when considering capability, it is necessary to take into account not only the capability of the state from which the strategy is being operated but also of all the sympathetic states that may be expected to employ the base values at their disposal in furtherance of the strategy.

83. Ibid., 993rd Mtg. (1962), para. 99.

84. Ibid., 19th year, 1109th Mtg. (1964), para. 12. The outcome of the discussion is not of interest here.

9

Strategies

RELEVANCY OF THE OTHER INSTRUMENTS OF STRATEGY EMPLOYED

Quite often, when authority is invoked regarding the use of coercion, a reference is made to all the instruments of policy employed, and not any one singly. We may cite a few instances for illustration. The declaration of war by the French National Assembly against England and Holland on February 1, 1792, cited a number of reasons: continued British coalition with other monarchical regimes in Europe, directed against France; refusal to recognize the French republican government and have official relations; preventing commerce between England and France and imposing an embargo on the ships laden with cargo bound for France; considerable increase of naval and armed forces while there was peace in Europe; and employment of all means by the British government to defame the French republic and rouse the hatred of the English nation and other nations of Europe against France.[1] Very recently, during the debate in the Security Council on the Syrian complaint of March 20, 1962, against Israel's armed attack, the Israeli representative contended that the attack was a measure of self-protection:

> All our land borders are sealed. The Suez Canal remains barred to our ships and cargoes in an eleven-year defiance of the Security Council resolution of 1 September 1951. An elaborate boycott organization has been built up to disrupt our normal commercial ties with other countries. Third-party States are threatened with reprisals for maintaining diplomatic relations with Israel. And from Arab leaders, Arab radio stations and Arab propaganda officers there pours forth a vicious stream of threats and hostile propaganda preaching the doctrine that the State of Israel must be liquidated.[2]

1. See 36 *Annual Register, Public Papers,* 105 (1793).
2. S.C.O.R., 17th year, 999th Mtg. (1962), para. 88.

Similarly, in 1964, during the debate on the Yemeni complaint of armed attack by the United Kingdom, the representative of the United Kingdom maintained that the armed action was a defensive measure to protect the Federation of South Arabia, which had requested assistance, against activity designed to destroy it by "incessant propaganda, subversion and armed attacks." [3] On the occasion of the Cuban quarantine crisis, the Venezuelan representative accused Cuba of "clandestine introduction into [other American republics] of weapons to equip guerilla forces" as well as propaganda activity.[4]

In 1962, presenting the Lebanese case of "illegal and unprovoked intervention" by the United Arab Republic in the internal affairs of Lebanon, the Lebanese representative alleged, firstly, supply of arms to Lebanese subversives by the U.A.R., training of Lebanese nationals in subversive activities and sending them back to Lebanon, and participation of U.A.R. officials and non-officials in subversive and terrorist activities to promote rebellion, and secondly, propaganda by the press and radio. The representative of Lebanon stated that he was placing the facts relating to propaganda before the council as they would establish the U.A.R.'s objective to undermine the independence of Lebanon. He alleged cultivation among the people of the U.A.R. of a mood of expectancy of revolt in Lebanon, and when disturbances broke out, propaganda was employed to uphold, inflame, direct, and guide subversive activities.[5] The contention of the U.A.R. that the allegations deserved no attention and the disagreement of the representative of the United Kingdom on this point have already been noted.[6] The U.K. representative's contention regarding the propaganda was that "it is internationally wrong that this kind of warfare on the air should be employed," and "it is in such media of public communication that intentions are revealed." [7]

The decisions that were actually arrived at in the above cases are not material here. We wish only to emphasize that in the phase of invoking authority in the decision process, reference is made to all the instruments of policy that are being employed in the strategy, and such reference will not fail to affect the prescription and application of policy, even though it may not be apparent on the surface.

3. Ibid., 19th year, 1109th Mtg. (1964), para. 4.
4. Ibid., 17th year, 1023rd Mtg. (1962), para. 6.
5. Ibid., 13th year, 823rd Mtg. (1958), pp. 4, 20.
6. See Chap. 8.
7. S.C.O.R., 13th year, 824th Mtg. (1958), para. 281.

RELEVANCY OF THE TECHNIQUES AND TACTICS OF THE IDEOLOGICAL STRATEGY EMPLOYED

Symbols and Words Circulated

Although decision-makers in general note significant portions of the propaganda material disseminated, the material is not subjected to systematic analysis. In pursuing the policy objectives suggested here—promoting freedom of information and protecting other community values from destruction—the first question is to what degree the particular communication is likely to generate a stress toward action. If overt acts are not to be expected immediately in consequence of the communication, the undesired effects may be avoided by remedial measures such as dissemination of information to neutralize the impact of the communication. On the other hand, if the stress is intense, remedial measures likely to be ineffective, and the expected effects of overt response to the communication likely to be detrimental to community values, restrictive regulation of the communication will have to be considered and, if feasible, adopted.[8]

The importance of the element of feasibility requires particular notice. With regard to some of the techniques employed, there is virtually no restrictive regulation that can be thought of, short of complete suppression of communication by pre-censorship or by deterring communication, threatening severe penalties for offenses that can in the nature of things be only very imprecisely defined. The only measure that would not unduly jeopardize enlightenment would seem to be a program of information and education. We may note here particularly such techniques as selection of suitable facts or events for reporting, giving a slant, and distracting attention from some facts by mentioning or emphasizing others. In relation to communications prepared by employing such techniques, the plea may be advanced that the facts selected were those genuinely believed by the reporter to be the more important ones—it being indeed practically impossible for anybody to report all the facts in any case—that the language used conveys the reporter's interpretation of facts genuinely believed by him to

8. The development of some techniques of propaganda—such as "subliminal projection," "depth manipulation"—especially in consumer advertising, and their gradual extension on a limited scale to political campaigning, have given rise to calls for prohibition of such techniques in national contexts, in the interest of preservation of democratic values. See, e.g., Aldous Huxley, *Brave New World Revisited*, p. 136. These techniques consist of appealing to some deep-seated and universal human desires, or of associating an irrelevant message which appeals to such desires with the main communication intended to influence the audience. But the real protection against such techniques, it is pointed out, is their exposure, and education of the audience in facts and values. See Vance Packard, *The Hidden Persuaders* (New York, McKay, 1957), pp. 265–66; Huxley, p. 129.

be objective, or is designed to impart such liveliness to reporting as is generally done in literary or journalistic practice; and he may contend that other facts were mentioned to avoid making the communication one-sided. When such techniques are at issue, it would appear that policy should be directed, firstly, to maintenance of minimum order, and secondly, to facilitating the dissemination of different versions of events. And in pursuing the policy of minimum order, the techniques and tactics adopted may be examined in the light of all the relevant variables and the expected outcome and effects.

To find out whether the communications in question are such as are likely to create a stress toward action, it is necessary to observe to what extent the symbols disseminated are likely to alter the expectations of the audience to a degree not warranted by actual changes in the environment, foster emotionally charged identifications and demands, rouse the anxiety of the audience to widen the frame of attention, and appeal to the nonrational element in human personality. Even here, it may be noted, the essential elements of the policy that can be meaningfully adopted are maintenance of minimum order and exposure of the "pathic" character of the symbols.[9] Suitable restrictive regulation may be thought of if the policy of maintenance of minimum order or protection of other community values such as the well-being of target groups demands it.

Communications likely to produce the response of panic on the part of the audience are to be treated in a similar manner. Here the inquiry ought to be to what degree the symbols circulated induce among the audience such fear as is capable of producing a disorganizing effect on human personality, having full regard to the degree of organization and other features obtaining among the audience which protect from panic.

Centers of Dissemination

According to traditional law, the center of dissemination becomes material, first, in the determination of the responsibility of the state for the dissemination. Disseminations from the official centers of the state are prima facie attributable to the state, while those from nonofficial centers are not so attributable. Since what is disseminated from an official center will ordinarily be regarded as more authentic than what is disseminated from nonofficial centers, a discrimination between the two types is justified on policy grounds.

Secondly, the law shows considerable tolerance to disseminations made from some centers, and subjects them to a special regime for certain policy reasons. These centers are: (1) legislatures and judicial tribunals within states, and (2) international forums.

9. For the meaning of "pathic," see p. 30.

Legislatures

Generally utterances made on the floor of a legislature are not liable to be called into question before any body except the legislature itself, and the constitutions of many states accord them immunity from the jurisdiction of the courts.[10]

If a legislator makes a statement on the floor of the legislature offensive to a foreign government, and that government protests, the question arises whether the utterance engages the responsibility of the speaker's state. If it does, the government of that state should restrain its legislators from making remarks offensive to foreign governments. In 1920, the Spanish Ambassador to the United States complained about certain reports, which had appeared in the press, of speeches made in the House of Representatives which he considered derogatory to the Spanish nation and government.[11] The response of the United States was that by virtue of Article 1, Section 6, of the United States Constitution the utterances could not be questioned anywhere except before the House and hence no action could be taken against the members in question. The justification put forward seems to be no justification at all, for a state cannot avoid its international responsibility by merely relying upon the provisions of its constitution. The true justification seems to be that it is a general principle recognized in the municipal legal systems of many states that legislators should be allowed immunity in respect of their utterances before the legislatures. This policy has been adopted to facilitate the efficient functioning of democratic government. It is not as though the indiscretions of the legislators are left entirely unchecked, because the house will have power to restrain its members. It may be taken that the world community accepts such a regulation of the utterances of legislators by the house itself as measuring up to the standards demanded by the community. If the house judiciously exercises its functions, the responsibility may be regarded as having been discharged.

The policy of regulating transnational coercion does not in general call for the adoption of a different position. Speeches made in the legislature by a legislator may not produce effects substantially different from his statements made outside the house. In respect of the latter category of speeches, it has been observed, the law attributes no more responsibility to the state than in the case of utterances by private persons.[12] Furthermore, a speech made on the floor of a legislature is likely to receive an instant reply from other legislators, if two or more parties are represented in it. The expectations produced in the elite of the opposing state are, in many cases, likely to be that the speeches are made for domestic consumption. In

10. See A. J. Peaselee, *Constitutions of Nations* (2d ed. The Hague, Nijhoff, 1956).
11. Hackworth, *Digest*, 2, 144.
12. See Chap. 5.

a very unlikely situation, however, if the legislature is used persistently and in an organized form to influence the attitudes of the people of the state and the activity menaces the security of another state, the latter state may invoke appropriate procedures. But it does not seem necessary to hold states responsible for speeches of individual legislators made during the normal deliberations of the legislature.

Judicial Tribunals

Generally, utterances before judicial tribunals having reference to the subject matter of the inquiry are regarded as privileged,[13] in order to facilitate full and free disclosures before the tribunals. On several grounds it appears to be good policy not to limit immunity in any manner to satisfy the claims, if any, put forward by external elites. First, the expectation that the statement will reach a wide audience will not be generally very high. Second, a person making statements is subject to the regulatory rules of the forum. Third, the benefit to the community by virtue of freedom of disclosure before the tribunal far outweighs the loss which the external elite might possibly incur.

International Forums

Here attention will be devoted only to intergovernmental conferences because the participants are the authorized representatives of states, and therefore their utterances will be attributed to their respective states.

Since such conferences will take place within the territory of a state, one question that may be raised is to what extent the government of the territory can take punitive measures related to speeches made at those conferences. Until the founding of the League of Nations, the practice of states was to accredit delegates to intergovernmental conferences as envoys extraordinary within the meaning of the Vienna Protocol.[14] Under the League system the representatives of members, too, were given diplomatic immunities and privileges (Article 7 of the Covenant).

Under the United Nations Charter, the Convention on the Privileges and Immunities of the United Nations, and the Convention on the Privileges and Immunities of the Specialized Agencies, the position of the representatives is more specifically defined. One of the objectives sought in prescribing the privileges and immunities was to facilitate free discussion in the organs of the U.N. and the Specialized Agencies. With this end in view, Article 105 of the Charter has provided that the representatives of

13. See P. H. Winfield, *A Textbook of Law of Tort* (London, Sweet and Maxwell, 1946), p. 277; W. L. Prosser, *Handbook of the Law of Torts* (3d ed. St. Paul, West Pub. Co., 1964), p. 797.

14. Josef Kunz, "Immunities of International Organizations," 41 *A.J.I.L.* 828 (1947).

the member states should enjoy such privileges and immunities within the territories of member states as are necessary for the independent exercise of their functions connected with the organization. Under the conventions referred to above the representatives are allowed immunity from legal process in respect of words spoken or written or acts done in that capacity.[15] The United Nations convention further provides:

> In order to secure, for the representatives of Members to the principal and subsidiary organs of the United Nations and to conferences convened by the United Nations, complete freedom of speech and independence in the discharge of their duties, the immunity from legal process in respect of words spoken or written and all acts done by them in discharging their duties shall continue to be accorded notwithstanding that the persons concerned are no longer the representatives of Members.[16]

The privileges are allowed during the journey of the representatives to and from the place of meeting.[17] However, the privileges are granted not for the benefit of the individuals but in the interests of the organization. A member state is declared to be under a duty to waive the privilege in case its exercise is likely to impede the course of justice.[18]

The conventions have not been ratified by the United States and have no force there. The immunities and privileges allowed in the United States are those provided for under the Headquarters Agreement[19] and the International Organizations Immunities Act.[20] Under the Headquarters Agreement, only some specified classes of representatives and their staff are allowed immunities and privileges.[21]

15. U.N. Convention, Sec. 16. In addition to delegates, deputy delegates, advisors, technical experts, and secretaries of the delegations are also entitled to the privileges.

16. Sec. 12; Specialized Agencies Convention, Sec. 14, runs along practically the same lines.

17. U.N. General Convention, Sec. 11; Specialized Agencies Convention, Sec. 15.

18. U.N. General Convention, Sec. 14; Specialized Agencies Convention, Sec. 16.

19. U.N. Doc. A/427 (1947).

20. 59 Stat. 665, Pub. Law 291, 79th Congress.

21. See Sec. 15 of the Agreement. The representatives and their staff specified therein are: principal resident representative of a member to the U.N.; resident representative with the rank of ambassador or minister plenipotentiary; such resident members of the staff of the representatives as are agreed upon between the Secretary General of the U.N., the U.S. government, and the government of the member; principal resident representative of a member of a specialized agency with the rank of ambassador or minister plenipotentiary at the headquarters of such agency in the United States; such other principal resident representatives and resident members of their staff as are agreed upon between the principal executive officer of the agency, the U.S. government, and the government of the member, residing within or outside the headquarters district. These are accorded the privileges and immunities of diplomatic envoys.

During their participation in the deliberations of the organs, however, the representatives will remain subject to the regulatory processes of the organs.[22] During the Fourth Session of the General Assembly, for instance, at one stage the exchange of abuse between the delegates of the Soviet bloc and the Western countries reached a high level, evoking the intervention of the President of the Assembly, who warned that the use of such language was derogatory to the dignity of the United Nations, and if such remarks were to be repeated he would order the expunging of those remarks from the records.[23] During the 1960 Session of the General Assembly, the President ordered the expunging of the offensive remarks made by Premier Khrushchev and President Castro.[24]

During the past few years the forum of the United Nations has been used quite frequently for mutual vilification to such an extent that the confidence generally held earlier that conferences of representatives of states will further the settlement of international disputes has sagged. Writers have come to express the opinion that the debates at such conferences will rather increase international tensions than reduce them.[25] These writers affirm their faith in the traditional form of diplomacy in preference to diplomacy by conference or parliamentary diplomacy.[26]

It is hardly within the scope of this study to discuss the relative merits of traditional diplomacy, diplomacy by conference, and parliamentary diplomacy. Before condemning the debates in the U.N. as an additional source of international tension, positive evidence should be available that speeches made before the United Nations forum produce substantially different effects on the audiences than those made outside. So far no definite evidence is available to that effect. On the other hand, it is believed that the debates serve some useful purposes.[27] Further it must be remembered that in the United Nations forum a member faces an audience of a mixed character, consisting of friends, opponents, and the nonaligned, possessing opportunities of instant reply. Such an environment is hardly

22. See, e.g., rules 70, 35 and 36 of Rules of Procedure of the General Assembly. The effect of these rules is that the President and the General Assembly have powers to keep any speaker in order.

23. See G.A.O.R., Plenary (1949), p. 263.

24. See *The Hindu*, Sept. 26, 1960, Oct. 3, 1960.

25. See F. Honig, "The Cold War As an Instrument of Policy," 7 *The Year Book of World Affairs* 45, 53 (1953); Harold Nicolson, "The Faults of American Diplomacy," *Harper's* (Jan. 1955), pp. 52, 57; see also P. C. Jessup, "Parliamentary Diplomacy," 89 *Hague Recueil* 185, 238–40 (1956).

26. The expression "parliamentary diplomacy" was first coined by Mr. Dean Rusk; see "Parliamentary Diplomacy—Debate v. Negotiation," 26 *World Affairs Interpreter* 121–22 (1955), for the meaning of the expression as given by Mr. Rusk.

27. See C. M. Eichelberger, *The U.N., The First Ten Years* (New York, Harper, 1955), p. 10.

suited for the kind of effective propaganda campaigning from which a menace to international peace can be expected.

In reference to the anti-Western propaganda disseminated at the ILO conferences by Communist delegations, a United States congressional committee suggested that the United States delegations to the International Labor Organization explore the possibility of adopting amendments to the procedural rules which would secure strict adherence to the rules of procedure applicable to the deliberations, limiting discussion to the technical matters under consideration and thereby reducing the opportunities for propaganda.[28] This suggestion is worth considering, though it should be added that just as in a national legislature the party in power ought not to shy from the criticism of the opposition, in an international forum a delegation should be prepared to face the propagandistic utterances of the delegations of opposing states, and the policy bases applicable to free discussion in national legislatures apply at least in equal measure to international conferences.

Channels of Communication

It may be expected that in the future no differentiation will be made, in the decision-making, between overt and covert channels of communication. The observations of the United States Military Tribunal, Nuremberg, in *The Ministries Case* convey the opinion of the tribunal that propaganda engineered through covert channels by an external elite to promote a strategy of aggression by violence is as blameworthy as propaganda transmitted by overt channels,[29] and these observations may be expected to influence future decisions. This is consistent with policy inasmuch as it is more difficult to counteract propaganda by covert channels than by overt channels.

The medium of communication employed is indeed worthy of attention, inasmuch as the high expectations of effectiveness of propaganda at the present time proceed partly from the highly refined character of modern media. It appears from the trend since the 1930s that the employment of radio broadcasting will be regarded with more serious concern than other media. The reason for this can be gathered from the statement of Dr. Raestad cited above,[30] which summarized the general opinion obtaining in the 1930s and perhaps even now. He mentioned that the state affected cannot stop radio communication at the frontiers, and the political effects of the communication "are not easy to foresee or control or canalize at need." Under the influence of this line of thinking the Broadcasting Con-

28. See Committee on Foreign Relations, Sub-Committee on International Organizations, *Report on Hearings on U.S. Participation in International Labor Organization*, pursuant to H. Res. 55, 88th Congress, 1st Sess. (Washington, D.C., 1963), p. 8.

29. See the judgment cited in Chap. 7, note 21, p. 343.

30. See p. 109.

vention of 1936 was adopted. Whitton and Larson also consider that radio broadcasting should be regarded as potentially more dangerous than other means of communication and should be subjected to restrictive regulation to a greater degree than communication by other media.[31]

It is perhaps necessary to guard against views which assign an absolute superiority to one medium over others, regardless of other factors involved in the situation. Radio broadcasting possesses indeed certain advantages: [32] it can be used to reach the audience that cannot read, it approximates preson-to-person communication, and it facilitates instantaneous transmission of the material. However, these advantages are counterpoised by the following factors: (1) Those who can read prefer the medium of the printed word, and group-leaders—those who influence opinion in groups —may almost invariably be expected to be capable of reading. (2) Communication of the message by radio is dependent upon the audience selecting it for listening, and if what is transmitted does not accord with the predispositions of the listener, he may just not listen to it. (3) The interpretation that people may give to a matter after listening to the radio can be easily corrected later by providing further information.[33] (4) Radio broadcasting has now become quite common and its impact may be expected to be less intense than it was when the practice had just started. As a matter of fact each medium has its own advantages and shortcomings,[34] and the most effective means to influence the opinions and attitudes of people are communication by a mass medium followed by communication in person.

We may recommend consequently that no channel of communication should be regarded as possessing an undisputed, all-time efficacy superior to others, and should hence be subjected to greater restrictive regulation than others. On the other hand, all the various channels employed in a particular context should be taken into account, and the probable outcome should be estimated only after considering all the relevant variables involved.[35]

31. See their *Propaganda*, pp. 160–62.

32. See Klapper, "The Comparative Effects of the Various Media," for a discussion of the relative advantages and disadvantages of radio broadcasting; in particular, pp. 101 et seq.

33. Ibid., p. 101.

34. See pp. 53–56.

35. Reference may be made in this connection to the 1958 statement of the Lebanese representative in the Security Council, presenting the case of U.A.R. intervention in Lebanon, specifying why importance should be attached to propaganda by radio in that context. He said, "The radio differs from the Press in two crucial respects. Not everybody can read, but except for the deaf, everybody can hear; and in the East, in general, I think it is a fact that more people listen to the radio than read the newspapers, and the living voice is more effective in the dissemination and impression of opinion than the printed word. Secondly, whatever the relationship between the Press and the Government of some countries, that between the radio and the Government is at

Because of the controversy it has given rise to in recent years, we should devote some attention to the permissibility of leaflet-drops by plastic balloons. In reply to the Hungarian protest over such operations by the Free Europe Committee in 1955, the United States claimed that the use of this unconventional method of communication was permissible in view of the barriers raised against all channels of communication by the Hungarian government, including the jamming of radio broadcasts from Western countries.[36]

The West German government was reported to have claimed justification for the operations on another basis—that there was no German law which prevented the owner of property from using his land to release balloons.[37] This contention, if it was in fact put forward, is too naïve to be given any weight. It is inconceivable that the permissibility of the operation could be judged without reference to what was transmitted by the balloons. Nobody could contend that it would be permissible if some explosive were transmitted. One has to take account of the contents of leaflets and the physical damage the balloons are likely to cause to men and property in the country to which they are flown.

The Soviet Union complained that the balloons endangered aviation and that the floating of balloons into a foreign country constituted a violation of the air space of that country, and was therefore illegal.[38] According to one view, the balloons did not endanger aviation at all.[39] The balloons, undeniably, did float in air space which was under sovereignty of another state.[40] Their release further amounted to a violation of Article 8 of the

least as close. Thus, while it is conceivably possible for some to hold that in the United Arab Republic the Press is free, no one will deny that in the United Arab Republic the radio is controlled by the Government. The evidence of the radio, then, so far as the actuality and aim of intervention are concerned, is the highest and most authentic." S.C.O.R., 13th year, 823rd Mtg. (1958), para. 50.

36. See 32 *Dept. of State Bull.* 14 (1955).

37. See *New York Times*, Oct. 30, 1955.

38. Ibid., February 11, 1956. One view was that the Soviet objection to the legality of the balloon releases was confined to meteorological balloons only and did not extend to the propaganda ones; see Bin Cheng, "International Law and High Altitude Flights: Balloons, Rockets and Man-Made Sattelites," 6 *Int'l. and Comp. L.Q.* 487, 501 (1957). See the same for a general discussion of the legality of balloon flights, p. 498 et seq.

39. It was stated that the balloons traveled at a height of 40,000 feet, quite out of the path of air traffic. Further, the total weight of the device and leaflets did not exceed 8 pounds, so if a balloon was hit by a plane the balloon would be shattered and the plane would not be endangered. It was also pointed out that according to U.S. Civil Air Regulations, balloon loads of 10 pounds or less were not a menace to aircraft. See *New York Times*, Feb. 11, 1956.

40. Speaking about the release of balloons in general, those flown for meteorological as well as propaganda purposes, the former U.S. Secretary of State, Mr. Dulles, said at a press conference on Feb. 7, 1956, that the ownership of upper air and of the ether above the air was disputable. He conceded that it was a recognized practice to avoid

Chicago Convention of 1944 on aerial navigation, which prohibited the flying of pilotless aircraft over the territory of another state without authorization by that state, but the U.S.S.R. and Eastern European states, with the exception of Czechoslovakia, were not parties to it. But the issue was whether the policies of violation of human rights, of forcing out refugees in large numbers, and of raising an "iron curtain" justified the refugees and their sympathizers using this particular means of communication with the people behind the "iron curtain," violating thereby the air space of the state adopting such policies. A policy of promotion of human rights and maintenance of peace does not supply an unequivocal answer to this question. However, the fact that these operations were suspended in the autumn of 1956,[41] following Soviet protests, and have not been subsequently resumed, would indicate that apparently the United States had some doubt about the permissibility of the operation. If the balloons do in fact endanger aviation, then the well-being of the aviation personnel and passengers must be given a definite priority over the possible enlightenment resulting from the leaflet-drops.

---

putting into the air anything which could interfere with the normal use of air space by anybody else, but he pointed out that the balloons traveled at a height far above that of commercial flights. He further stated that he could not say how high a balloon had to go in order to get above the bounds of state sovereignty. See *New York Times*, Feb. 8, 1956. The balloon operations were, however, suspended in the autumn of 1956 in response to the Soviet protests and have not been resumed since.

The question how far into the air the exclusive domain of a state extends, and from what point the inclusive rights of other states come into force is not now an easy question to answer. The U.N. Ad Hoc Committee on the Peaceful Use of Outer Space, set up by the General Assembly in May 1959, reached the conclusion that fixation of the precise limits between outer and air space was not an immediate problem and could be postponed for the present without prejudice to activities connected with the exploration of outer space. See P. C. Jessup and J. Taubenfeld, "The United Nations Ad Hoc Committee on the Peaceful Use of Outer Space," 53 *A.J.I.L.* 877, 880 (1959). See McDougal and Leon Lipson, "Perspectives for a Law of Outer Space," 52 *A.J.I.L.* 407, 421–29 (1958), for some suggestions put forward in the past regarding the fixation of the limit and the inadequacy of the suggestions. See also the remarks of John A. Johnson, General Counsel, National Aeronautics and Space Administration, made at the 55th Annual Meeting of the American Society of International Law, 1965 *Proc. of Am. Soc. Int'l. Law*, p. 165, regarding the fixation of the limit. He suggested that the upper limit of state sovereignty be set at 30, 50, or 100 miles, taking into account that the maximum ascent of aircraft up to then had been about 25 miles, and that a satellite designed to accomplish a useful space mission should reach a minimum altitude of 100 miles in order not to encounter appreciable atmospheric drag. Further, see the comment of Professor Myres McDougal during the ensuing discussion, ibid., p. 183, that the flight of Gary Powers (the incident of the U-2 plane flying at a height of 68,000 ft. when Soviet rockets brought it down) "had apparently been in the area historically regarded as of the most comprehensive, exclusive competence of States."

41. Holt, *Radio Free Europe*, p. xii.

10

Outcome

DEPRIVATION OF POWER OF THE EXTERNAL ELITE

In relation to communications transmitted from the territory of a state to another, claims are frequently presented that their outcome, whether or not enlightenment, will be or may be expected to be deprivation of power of the elite of the latter state, and so the communication must be stopped. As against such claims it is asserted that the communications intrinsically are not such as to produce that outcome, but if from the internal conditions of the state in question the communications are likely to have such an outcome, suppression of the communications cannot be demanded. Thus in the controversy between the United States and Hungary over the leaflet-drop operation by Radio Free Europe and Crusade for Freedom referred to above, the Hungarian government claimed that the leaflets contained incitement to sedition against the government, while the United States asserted that the operations were a permissible process of enlightenment carried on by private agencies.[1] In 1956, the British and French governments claimed that the Egyptian broadcasts to neighboring countries constituted incitement of the nationalist elements against the governmental authorities in those countries, while the Egyptian officials claimed that the broadcasts consisted merely of unbiased news,[2] and that it was the political situation in those countries that was inflammatory and not their broadcasts. We have observed in the previous chapters the claims presented in the last century that the propaganda activity of refugees directed against the government in home countries should be stopped and the counterclaim that the activity was a permissible exercise of freedom of expression.

In relation to such claims and counterclaims, the question arises what communications should be restrained because of their expected outcome of

1. 32 *Dept. of State Bull.* 14 (1955).
2. See *New York Times,* Feb. 1, 1956.

deprivation of power to the external elite, and what should be regarded as permissible, in the absence of such an expectation, at any rate in an appreciable degree. Apparently in order to make this differentiation, some formulas have been suggested and may be examined.

The Broadcasting Convention of 1936, which obligated the signatory states to prevent transmission from their territories of certain types of broadcasts, provided in Article 1 that broadcasts "of such character as to incite the population of any country to acts incompatible with the internal order or security" of the territory of any contracting state should not be permitted. The South American Regional Agreement on Radio Communication (Revised), Rio de Janeiro, 1937, obligated the parties to insure, among other things, that broadcasts which "might threaten the sovereignty and integrity" of the contracting states are not transmitted from their territories (Art. 2). The formulas used in these conventions help very little in distinguishing the permissible from the impermissible communications. The criteria offered are in the form of legal conclusions, and no attempt is made to furnish the indices by which one may reach the conclusions.

We have noted the proposals made by the Chinese representative in the International Law Commission and before the Special Committee on the Question of Defining Aggression, 1954:[3] that "the fact of a state carrying on subversive propaganda against another state" should be regarded as a crime against the peace and security of mankind; and that "inciting civil strife in a victim state by propaganda" with the objective specified in the proposal should be regarded as aggression. But the formulas suggested in these proposals, too, give little assistance in solving the problem by supplying us with any operational indices.

Mention has been made of the "Peace Through Deeds" Resolution of the United Nations General Assembly which recognized that "fomenting of civil strife in the interests of a foreign Power" could be a pattern of aggression; and also of Article 2(5) of the Draft Code of Offenses Against the Peace and Security of Mankind which characterized activities calculated to "foment civil strife in another state" as a crime against the peace and security of mankind.[4] The expression "fomenting civil strife" gives no useful indication as to how permissible communications might be distinguished from the impermissible. In fact, during the discussions on the Draft Code in the International Law Commission, Mr. Amado, one of the members of the Commission, wanted to know the purport of the expression "foment," whether it meant supply of arms and the like only, or whether it included dissemination of propaganda also,[5] and he received no

3. See p. 162.
4. See ibid.
5. See International Law Commission, 3rd sess., Summary Rec., 56th meeting (U.N. Doc. A/CN.4/SR.56, 1956).

answer. The formulas used in the resolution and the code can be of little value to the present purpose.

Professor Quincy Wright, who has developed the thesis that "war-mongering" including "civil-war-mongering" constitutes an international crime according to contemporary world community prescriptions,[6] has given a definition of the crime of war-mongering: "Propaganda designed and likely to provoke or encourage any threat to the peace, breach of the peace, or act of aggression." And he has further suggested that this definition has to be interpreted in accord with the "clear and present danger rule," which was first formulated by Mr. Justice Holmes in *Schenck v. United States*.[7]

The "clear and present danger" rule, it may be pointed out, is not a talismanic appellation which opens up clues to all problems of distinguishing between permissible and impermissible utterances, even when one is dealing with problems which arise in the limited context of determining the extent to which the First Amendment of the United States Constitution protects freedom of speech. Judge Learned Hand stated about this doctrine, in *United States v. Dennis et al.*, as follows: [8]

> It is not a vade-mecum; indeed from its very words it could not be. It is a way to describe a penumbra of occasions, even the outskirts of which are indefinable, but within which, as is often the case, the courts must find their way.

A decision-maker has to give the rule a meaningful content with reference to any utterance made in any particular situation, by appraising the conflicting policy considerations involved in the situation and determining the policy to be prescribed in regard to the utterances. According to Judge Hand, a court has to ask itself, in reference to any utterance, whether the magnitude of the evil resulting from the utterance, discounted by its improbability, justifies the limitation of freedom of speech in the particular case, and to arrive at a decision.[9]

According to Quincy Wright, "civil-war-mongering" must be prohibited because such propaganda might provoke the government of the state to which it is directed to respond by an attack of violence to obtain a cessation of the activity, or the propaganda might weaken that state and in consequence a third state might be tempted to commit aggression against it. In applying Wright's definition, along with the clear and present danger

6. "The Crime of War-Mongering," p. 135.

7. 242 U.S. 47 (1919).

8. 183 F. 2d 201, 212 (2d Cir. 1950).

9. Ibid.; this view of Judge Hand was approved in the Supreme Court by Vinson C. J.; see *Dennis et al. v. United States*, 341 U.S. 494 (1951). On the present status of the "clear and present danger" rule, see Emerson, "Toward a General Theory of the First Amendment," p. 910.

rule, the evils which have to be taken into account, consistently with his thesis, are the possibility of the government of the state to which propaganda is directed responding by recourse to violence, or of the government of a third state launching aggression. Neither of these two likely evils, it is submitted, can exclusively form an index of reference, for provocability of the government of the state to which propaganda is addressed or the aggressive disposition of the third state cannot be the sole basis for determining the permissible limits of transnational communication—and by extension of Wright's thesis, a basis for making persons criminally liable.

We have noted the thesis of Garcia-Mora that a state is under a duty to restrain "revolutionary activities and hostile propaganda" of private persons against foreign states, and its incompleteness.[10] Whitton and Larson define "subversive propaganda" as consisting of "communications calculated to overthrow the existing internal political order of a state." The government of a state "is under a duty to refrain from spreading subversive propaganda hostile to a foreign country in the time of peace." If the propaganda is that of private persons, such activity "which goes to the extreme of terroristic activity, and most clearly incitement to assassination," gives rise to the responsibility of the state to restrain. The state is also under an obligation to suppress the propaganda of private persons if it is directly connected with a hostile expedition directed from the territory of the state against a foreign state and is manifest as an overt act. The state, further, has a duty not to permit its territory to be used to transmit subversive propaganda by radio.[11] Besides reiterating the traditional position, with good documentation, with a modification added to make allowance for the modern development of radio broadcasting, the authors indicate the core of the contemporary problem when they state: [12]

> But we must admit that to draw a line between mere "moral support" [to a subversive movement in a foreign country] and psychological pressures which risk grave injury to a foreign state is becoming more and more difficult in modern times, due to the invention of redoubtable techniques of mass persuasion, and to the skill of clever agitators in the pay of some dictatorship bent on world conquest.

If the propaganda in question is that of private persons, but disseminated by the radio, the question arises as to how the decision-makers should differentiate between permissible "moral support" and impermissible "subversive propaganda." And by reference to what indices should decision-makers say whether the propaganda is "calculated" to overthrow the existing internal political order of the state.

10. See p. 113.
11. *Propaganda,* pp. 83, 95, 166.
12. Ibid., p. 136.

As already noted, propaganda disseminated within or across the boundaries of a state is likely to create varied levels of expectation of different degrees of deprivation of power to the external elite against which the propaganda is directed. All the varied situations cannot be brought within the scope of a single verbal formula. The formulas we have noted above refer, more or less, to a situation in which there is an expectation of overthrow by overt or covert violence of the established government of a foreign state; in the terminology employed herein, major coercion.[13]

Traditional law, it may be recalled, afforded means for varied regulation of the use of propaganda depending upon the nature of the expectations created by the activity. If it was official propaganda, the doctrines of nonintervention and permissible intervention were invocable. If nonofficial propaganda, at the stage when an expectation that the proximate outcome of the activity was an attack of violence on the foreign state or violent overthrow of a foreign government, the state was required to take restraining measures to prevent initiation of the attack from its territory. If there was no such expectation, and minor deprivations were expected, it was open to the affected state to close its frontiers to prevent transmission of propaganda and to resort to measures like retaliation.[14]

In reference to any situation, the expected outcome is to be ascertained —with such accuracy as the nature of things permits—by reference to the participants, the audience, the objectives, the characteristics of the situation, the base values at the disposal of those operating the strategy, and the various strategies employed.[15] And community regulation must vary according to whether the expected outcome is major or minor coercion, and whether it is permissible or impermissible coercion.[16]

It is necessary to mention here something about the statement generally made that a state is not responsible for propaganda by private persons. The

13. Ibid., p. 85. The authors classify subversive propaganda, without showing its relevance to legal regulation, into ordinary subversive propaganda, irredentist subversive propaganda, and social-revolutionary subversive propaganda. The first apparently refers to propaganda disseminated in a strategy of overt violence and the third in a strategy of covert violence. The second is distinguishable from the other two in that the consequentiality of the objective is limited to a part of the territory of the target state.

14. See pp. 97–99 and Chap. 7, note 91.

15. The criteria mentioned here are mostly those already adopted by national courts. In England, for instance, in distinguishing permissible free expression from seditious utterances, with a view to preventing incitements which cause resort to force, the courts advised the juries to take into account the intention of the person making the utterance (whether he intended to provoke violence), the character of the audience (whether excitable or not), the "state of public feeling" (that is, the character of the situation), the language used, and the place and mode of dissemination. See *R. v. Sullivan* and *R. v. Piggot*, 11 Cox C.C.44 (1869); *R. v. Burns*, 16 Cox C.C.355 (1886); and *R. v. Aldred*, 22 Cox C.C.1 (1909).

16. It needs no explanation here that the expectation of deprivation of power produces the outcome of coercion.

analysis in Chapter 5 has shown that under traditional law the state was required to adopt restraining measures when the activity of private persons in its territory gave rise to an expectation that its outcome would be an attack of violence on a foreign state. In the nineteenth century such attack was capable of precipitating a war. At the present time, if there is a reasonable expectation that the proximate outcome of the activity of private persons is an impermissible major coercion on a foreign state, the state becomes responsible to restrain such propaganda activity and to prevent such coercion. The obligation under Article 2(4) of the Charter applies to the state as a whole and obliges the government to refrain from the activity prohibited by it, and to exercise due diligence to prevent private persons from using its territory to commit a breach of the prescription. The aid which private persons may receive from the government, the base values at their disposal to operate a strategy of coercion, and the extent to which they have access to the resources at the disposal of the government, are very material in estimating the probable outcome of the strategy.

If the expected outcome of private persons' activity is only impermissible minor coercion, the government subjected to it, if desirous of maintaining cordial relations with the government of the state from which the propaganda is being disseminated, may ignore the activity on the basis of the traditional doctrine which does not in general attribute private persons' activity to the government. On the other hand, if the target government feels that it must adopt countermeasures to obtain a cessation of the coercive action, and is prepared to sacrifice the cordiality, it may apply countermeasures against the state from which propaganda is being disseminated. Under contemporary conditions, when some states have a free and privately owned press and others a government-owned or controlled press, if the latter desire to take retaliatory action, they can do so by means of the government-owned or controlled agencies. Such retaliations will indeed involve in due course the government of the state from which propaganda was first disseminated. The traditional doctrine that a state is not responsible for the propaganda of private persons is difficult to apply between states of these two varieties.[17] But if the mutual application of coercion escalates in intensity, and presents a threat to peace, the authority of the United Nations or an appropriate regional agency becomes invocable. It is, however, desirable not to surrender the prescription that a state is not responsible for the utterances of private persons, for a contrary position would require the state to impose a strict control on all utterances of private persons, to the detriment of freedom of information.

17. This should not cause surprise, for, as noted in Chap. 7, note 91, even in 1803 the prescriptions did not work between England and France. The French governmental press took to retaliatory publications in response to the publications in the privately owned British press, which the British government refused to suppress.

DEPRIVATION OF RESPECT

We shall first examine the prescriptions and policies relating to communications which occasion loss of respect to the elite, and then examine those relating to the defamation of institutions of the state. Individuals and groups among foreign elites who are likely to be the objects of attack and in consequence sustain a loss in respect belong to the following categories: heads of foreign states, accredited ambassadors to the state of the strategists, heads of foreign governments, private citizens, and groups in foreign states unified by common symbols of identification.

Heads of Foreign States

Traditionally libels on the heads of foreign states are regarded as impermissible.[18] The origin of this prescription may be traced back to the practice of states during the time when monarchy was the predominant form of government; the personal honor of monarchs was of great importance,[19] and could not be allowed to be invaded because of its significant function as a means of control of the population. Many states, probably influenced by this tradition, even now give complete protection to heads of foreign states against libelous attacks.[20] In some states the protection is expressly limited to the heads of "friendly powers." [21]

The policy of the British government was originally influenced more or less by the same consideration. Libels on the head of a foreign state were regarded as punishable at common law because they were presumed likely to disturb relations with that state.[22] The libel was not punishable if the object of attack in question happened to be the head of an enemy state or if a war broke out with that state.[23]

There had been, however, in common law, a gradual shift to another

18. See Oppenheim-Lauterpacht, 1, 282.

19. See T. A. Walker, *The Science of International Law* (London, Clay & Sons, 1893), p. 118.

20. See Terrou and Solal, *Press, Film and Radio*, p. 323. In this list are Switzerland, Sweden, Portugal, Rumania, Yugoslavia, U.A.R., and Colombia. Van Dyke, in "The Responsibility of States for International Propaganda," examined the legislation of 51 countries, and stated that in 28 special protection is given to heads of foreign states in respect of libels, in 3 to sovereigns only, and in 20 the matter is ignored altogether.

21. Terrou and Solal, p. 323. Iran, Thailand, and Turkey are said to come in this category.

22. See Sir A. D. McNair, "Aspects of Sovereignty," 26 *B.Y.B.I.L.* 6, 27–28 (1949), where he mentions the 1779 opinion of a high law officer of the Crown in regard to a complaint by one Baron de Hompesch about a libel on his uncle published in the *Times*. See also the *Trial of George Gordon*, 22 State Trials 213 (1787), the *Trial of John Vint*, 27 State Trials 627 (1799); and *R. v. Peltier*, 28 State Trials 529 (1803), in which the judges mention that the main reason why libels on foreign sovereigns are punished is to preserve good relations with the sovereigns.

23. See the Peltier Case, cited in Chap. 8, note 15, above.

basis for punishing libels on heads of foreign states, and that was state responsibility. It was considered that a foreigner, including a foreign sovereign, could maintain an action in England in respect of libels published in that country.[24] If the object of attack happened to be the head of a foreign state, it was regarded as inexpedient to insist that the head or his agent should maintain an action for libel, and therefore the practice was adopted in appropriate cases of directing the Crown officers to initiate proceedings before courts.[25] But such a direction was given in a very limited number of cases because of the fact that the chances of successful prosecution before a jury depended upon the esteem in which the libeled sovereign was held among the British public.[26]

In the United States, in federal jurisdictions the common law does not apply, and there is no federal statute which punishes defamation of officials of foreign states.[27] In the state jurisdictions the common law applies, but ever since the 1797 *Trial of William Cobbett* [28] before the Pennsylvania Supreme Court, over a libel on the King of Spain, when the grand jury returned a verdict of discharge in spite of strong directions of Mckean, C. J., to the contrary, the state governments do not seem to have invoked the common law to initiate actions against libelers on foreign sovereigns. It is, however, considered that the head of a foreign state, by himself or by an agent, can maintain an action in the state courts in respect of any libel on him.[29]

In view of this position under internal law, the practice adopted by the United States government has been to accept responsibility and render reparation when the offender happened to be an official of the United States,[30] to disavow the attack when he was a state official,[31] or the official

24. See the reasoning in the *Trial of George Gordon*, cited above; also the letter of Lord Hawkesbury, British Foreign Secretary, to Mr. Merry, dated Aug. 28, 1802, 45 *Annual Register* 664, 665 (1803).

25. See McNair, "Aspects of Sovereignty," pp. 27–28; also the *Trial of George Gordon*, and the *Trial of Peltier*.

26. *Russel on Crime* (J. W. C. Turner, ed., 12th ed. London, Stevens, 1964), p. 1549, cites very few cases of this character. Apparently, *R. v. Peltier* was the last of such cases.

27. See E. D. Dickinson, "The Defamation of Foreign Governments," 22 *A.J.I.L.* 840, 843 (1928).

28. See F. Wharton, *State Trials of the United States* (Philadelphia, 1849), p. 322.

29. See Hackworth, Digest of International Law, 2, sec. 129.

30. See in this connection E. C. Stowell, "The General Smedley D. Butler Incident," 25 *A.J.I.L.* 321 (1931). The U.S. government expressed regret over the General's insulting remarks about Mussolini and apologized to the Italian government.

31. See the s.s. *Bremen* incident, 12 U.S. Press Releases 196 (1935); a New York magistrate's remarks in the course of his judgment occasioned a complaint by the German Ambassador that the remarks were derogatory of the German government. The Secretary of State expressed regret over the remarks, and disapproved the action of the magistrate, but stated that because the magistrate was not an instrumentality of the federal government, no action could be taken against him.

of a municipal corporation,[32] and to refuse to accept any responsibility, beyond allowing free access to the judiciary to pursue the remedies prescribed under the local law, if the offender were a private citizen.[33]

The proscription of libels of the heads of foreign states was at no time regarded as having the effect of prohibiting criticism of foreign sovereigns in respect of their policies, as in narration of contemporary events and comments thereupon made in a fair manner.[34]

Under traditional law, it may be observed, it is possible for the government of a state to adopt a flexible policy in regard to libelous attack on the heads of foreign states. The aggrieved head of the state, either of his own accord, or after obtaining affirmations from the officials of the state within which the publication has occurred that it does not represent their policy, may ignore it. If the officials of the state in which the libel has been published so desire, they may take corrective and remedial measures against the libeler in order to avoid any strain in relations with the government of the offended state. However, when the two governments find no basis for agreement there is nothing to prevent both of them from resorting to mutual application of coercion.[35]

Under modern conditions any contention that the head of a foreign state should be given greater protection from defamatory attacks than is given generally to private persons seems a little anachronistic. The heads of foreign states at the present day are not, in most cases, inheritors of a crown but persons who come to that office by popular consent—genuine or simulated. The claim that their reputation should be beyond comment, no matter what their past or present behavior might be, is outdated. The courts in Holland had to pass judgment on such claims during the pre-World War II days, and found no easy solution.[36]

32. See the incident over Mayor La Guardia's defamatory remarks about Hitler, Hackworth, *Digest*, 2, 145. The United States disclaimed the utterance and deprecated it. No further action was taken. See the comment of E. C. Stowell on this incident, "Attacks on the Heads of Foreign States," 31 *A.J.I.L.* 301 (1937).

33. See Hackworth, *Digest*, 2, sec. 129.

34. In the *Trial of John Vint* cited supra, and in R. v. *Peltier*, the defense raised these pleas, which were apparently conceded on behalf of the Crown. Oppenheim-Lauterpacht, 1, sec. 121, says "mere criticism of policy or judgment concerning past attitudes need neither be suppressed nor punished."

35. Thus in 1802 the relations between Britain and France steadily deteriorated after the British refusal to prevent the publication of libels on the French government in the British press; see 45 *Annual Register* 664 et seq. (1803); in 1947, Brazil severed diplomatic relations with the U.S.S.R. when the Soviet government refused to apologize for the publication of libels on the Brazilian President in the Soviet press. See *Survey of International Affairs*, 1947–48, p. 480.

36. Thus in *Public Prosecutor* v. G., *Annual Digest* 1935–1937, Case No. 11, a prosecution for insulting Adolf Hitler at a public meeting, the defendant claimed that he was merely criticizing him for his actions as the leader of the National Socialist Party. The District Court of Maastricht acquitted him. The Court remarked, "There

Ambassadors and Other Diplomatic Representatives of Foreign States

The municipal law of some states provides for special protection to the diplomatic representatives of foreign states against defamatory attacks.[37] In the United States, the United Kingdom, and some other states no protection other than what is granted to an ordinary foreign citizen is allowed.[38] There does not seem to be any world community prescription which makes it obligatory to grant special protection to such persons.[39] Article 29 of the Convention on Diplomatic Intercourse and Immunities, Vienna, 1961, requires the receiving state to take appropriate steps to prevent any attack on the dignity of the diplomatic agent.[40] It does not appear that the convention introduces a stricter standard than the one existing before.

Other Officials of Foreign States and Private Citizens

In some states, for instance, in France and Belgium, even heads of foreign governments are given special protection under the law against defamatory attacks,[41] but it does not seem to be obligatory to give such protection. Lower officials of foreign states are afforded no special protection anywhere.

Traditional international law prescribes that a state is responsible for affording a remedy to any foreigner for any injury sustained by him within its territory, and the remedy should be such as is generally granted under civilized systems of law in similar cases.[42]

---

was a legitimate doubt whether the accused had the intent to insult Herr Adolf Hitler as the Head of German Reich, the more so as the latter united in himself the qualities of Leader of the National Socialist Party and of Leader of the German People, and, at the same time, of the Chancellor of the Reich. In the first and in the last quality Herr Adolf Hitler is a political person whose actions are and must be, susceptible of criticism without being treated as an insult to the Head of the State." But in another case, the Court of Appeal at Arnheim arrived at a different conclusion and held that such a splitting of the capacities was not possible. Ibid.

37. Van Dyke in "The Responsibility of States for International Propaganda," says that the legislation of 37 out of 51 countries whose laws he had examined give special protection; see also Terrou and Solal, p. 323; "Harvard Research on Diplomatic Privileges and Immunities," 26 *A.J.I.L.* Supp. 19, 94 (1932).

38. See ibid.; also Van Dyke.

39. Ibid.; "Harvard Research on Diplomatic Privileges and Immunities," pp. 94–97.

40. For the text of the Convention, see 55 *A.J.I.L.*, 1064 (1961). Art. 29 runs thus: "The person of the diplomatic agent shall be inviolate. He shall not be liable to any form of arrest or detention. The receiving state shall treat him with due respect and shall take appropriate steps to prevent any attack on his person, freedom or dignity."

41. Terrou and Solal, p. 323.

42. See Chap. 5 above.

Libels on Groups

Under traditional doctrines there seems to be no responsibility on the part of a state to adopt any remedial measures to safeguard the reputation of foreign groups. The municipal laws of many states, no doubt, provide criminal sanctions against libels on groups, but the policy basis of such laws is to protect the respect value of ruling groups only; in the case of other groups they are meant more for the protection of well-being or for the preservation of public peace and other interests. In some states civil sanctions are provided for repression of group libels, but in those instances the value intended to be protected is the respect of ascertainable individuals but not of groups as such.[43] But there does not seem to be any world community prescription which obligates states to protect the reputation of groups such as "communists," "capitalists," "people of the Kremlin," and "Wall Street agents."

In order that communication between the elites of states—that is, the diplomatic process—may be facilitated, it is necessary that cordiality and respect be observed in the utterances of at least the officials of states. And the diplomatic process, being an important means of persuasion, requires encouragement and protection from irrelevant, extraneous factors. The traditional doctrine of the dignity of states [44] affords a means of pursuing this objective. And the consideration of reciprocity will generally induce officials to adhere to the norm of cordiality and respect. However, sometimes the advantages to be derived from discarding cordiality and respect outweigh the reciprocal courtesy. And there will be sufficient legal justification for so discarding when the government of the opposing state is violating community prescriptions and policies, and resort to the ideological strategy is necessary to create public opinion against such violations.[45] Open criticism and denunciation become inevitable and justifiable.

The utterances of private persons defamatory of a foreign head of state or government, if not subjected to corrective and remedial procedures, are likely to strain the relations between the governments. But observance of fair standards in the trial of libelers cannot be abandoned if human dignity is given due regard, and such observance can become difficult and troublesome. If freedom of expression as a means of enlightenment and democratic social control are given due regard, the defendant cannot be denied the defenses of fair comment on matters of public interest and justification by truth.[46] At present, when governments keep many things in secrecy, the

43. See David Riesman, "Democracy and Defamation, Control of Group Libel," 42 *Columbia L. Rev.* 727 (1942).

44. See Oppenheim-Lauterpacht, 1, 282.

45. See Chap. 7, notes 106 to 108.

46. On these defenses, see *Russel on Crime*, pp. 803–07; Whitton and Larson discuss the principle of "fair comment" as a defense, as it obtains in the leading legal systems

individual may not obtain adequate access to facts to defend himself, and a certain amount of arbitrariness is likely to be present in the trial. And sometimes juries, influenced by the state of public opinion, are likely to be overly lenient to the defendant. On the other hand, there is also the probability of the trial itself being converted into another occasion for defamation. It is necessary for statesmen in general, as suggested in 1803 by Lord Whitworth, the British Ambassador in Paris, to M. Talleyrand, to master their feelings so as to be indifferent to scurrility in publications in the press.[47] In times of tension, certain intemperate outbursts must be expected as ordinary incidents of the situation.

There is also the possibility of an elite using the ideological instrument to resort to defamation of individuals and groups as a technique in ideological strategy. The technique affords several advantages. The strategists might select a few persons or groups to be used as scapegoats on which to project all existing tensions arising out of internal troubles. They might under the guise of freedom of expression display violence in expression, hurl insults, and intensify tensions among the people. When strategy is operated through affiliated organizations in foreign states against the elite in power in that state, individuals and groups might be used as symbols to attack the institutions of power. It might even be possible by adopting this technique to eliminate some leading personalities from the political scene as the fascist and Nazi leaders did in the pre-World War II years in Germany and France.[48]

Community policy in reference to communications likely to cause deprivations of respect among a foreign elite cannot, therefore, be of an inflexible pattern. It has to be varied according to the factual conditions under which the utterances are made and the effects expected from them. A chance utterance might perhaps require no more than the traditional corrective processes. A sustained dissemination of libelous utterances may under some circumstances be expected to produce no more than catharsis of existing tensions, in which case also no special community measures of regulation need be adopted. On the other hand, the occasion might be one when the strategists are using the technique to heighten tension and to

---

of the world; see pp. 115–20. But curiously the authors put forward some provisions in the Sudanese penal code as representative of Islamic law. The provisions cited are a part of Sec. 499 of the Indian Penal Code, introduced by the British into Indian law, and later adopted by them into the law of some African colonies. They are common law principles introduced into India in a statutory form and are in no sense representative of Islamic law.

47. 45 *Annual Register* 683 (1803).

48. See David Riesman, "Democracy and Defamation: Fair Game and Fair Comment-I," 42 *Columbia L. Rev.* 1085, 1088, 1098 (1942). Thus the fascists in France were able to get rid of Salengro, the Interior Minister, who committed suicide. In Germany the Nazis drove many from public life by this technique.

channel all existing internal hatreds upon the external elite with a view to putting into operation a strategy of aggression; or the activity might create an expectation that its outcome will in fact be initiation of such a strategy. Or, the strategists may use the technique through human agents functioning as covert channels of communication, creating an expectation on the part of the elite against whom it is directed of severe deprivation of values. In the latter cases, world community measures suitably patterned to maintain peace and security have to be adopted. In other words, a contextual approach is necessary when making policy decisions, and the participants, audience, objectives, characteristics of the situation, base values, and strategies involved all require attention. The goals to be sought range from reinfusing cordiality and respect in the relations to maintaining peace, without sacrificing the values of a fair trial and freedom of expression.

Respect for the Institutions of a Foreign State

There seems to be no doctrine which proscribes communications that occasion deprivation of respect of a foreign state. Oppenheim, while denying the existence of any fundamental right of reputation of states, thought that a state "which has a corrupt Government and behaves unfairly and perfidiously in its intercourse with others will be looked down upon and despised." [49] He did not mention any duty to refrain from criticism of the institutions of foreign states even on the part of officials. However, Sir Hersch Lauterpacht introduced into the text of Oppenheim a statement to the effect that it was impermissible for the officials of a state to engage in such criticism.[50] He further added: "The principles of independence and non-intervention enjoin upon Governments and State officials the duty of scrupulous abstention not only from active interference, but from criticism of foreign laws and institutions." [51] In support of this statement he cited only the General Smedley Butler incident and E. C. Stowell's comment on it.[52] Neither of these support the main proposition. From what has been mentioned before about the doctrine of nonintervention it seems doubtful whether one can assert an absolute proposition such as the one above.

It is no doubt true that on considerations of reciprocity and of desire to avoid any strain in international relations officials of states generally refrain from criticizing the laws and institutions of other states. And if any criticism occurs the response of the officials of the aggrieved state will vary with

49. Oppenheim-Lauterpacht, 1, 282.

50. Sec. 127a, which contains this statement, was first introduced by Lauterpacht in 1935.

51. Oppenheim-Lauterpacht, 1, 293–94.

52. Stowell, "The General Smedley D. Butler Incident."

the factual conditions under which the criticism has occurred and the effects expected from it.[53]

Between the two world wars, a number of bilateral treaties were entered into which prohibited, in general, propaganda directed against the social and political systems of the contracting parties and their governments and institutions.[54] Most of these treaties were between the Soviet Union on one side and European countries on the other. The treaties were entered into with the objective of restraining the Soviet government from propagandizing the communist revolutionary ideology among people of the contracting states, but that objective was little realized. The Soviet elite did not stop their condemnations of the institutions of capitalist countries which invariably reached the peoples of those countries. Nor did the elites of liberal democracies stop expressing their disapproval of communist principles.[55] In a world in which the contestants in political struggles increas-

53. In 1858, following an unsuccessful attempt on the life of Emperor Napoleon III, strong feelings prevailed in France; England was denounced as a den of conspirators by some French officials, and these statements appeared in the *Moniteur*. There was considerable resentment over the publications in England, and the matter was raised in Parliament. But Lord Palmerston took the position that the British government should not lose its equanimity over the intemperate utterances on the other side of the channel. See 100 *Annual Register, History* 32 (1857). One may compare this with the recent trial of Mihajlov in Yugoslavia. The defendant, a writer, published an article, "Moscow Summer 1964," which the Soviet Union charged contained an attack on its reputation. On a demand by the Soviet Union, the defendant was prosecuted in Yugoslavia and convicted. The plea that the writer presented historical facts was not accepted. An intention to belittle the efforts to fight against Stalinism was attributed, and he was held guilty. See *New York Times*, May 1, 1965.

54. Among such treaties the following may be mentioned: Preliminary Agreement as to the Resumption of Relations between Germany and Latvia, 1920, cited in Chap. 5, note 97; Agreement Revising the Convention of 1923 Relating to the Organization and the Statute of the Tangier Zone, ibid.; The Russo-German Agreement, Rapallo, 1922, ibid., note 88; Trade Agreement between Great Britain and the U.S.S.R., 1921, ibid., note 90; Agreement between the Republic of China and the U.S.S.R., ibid., note 89; Exchange of Letters between President Roosevelt and M. Litvinov, 1933, ibid., note 93; Treaty of Neutrality and Non-Aggression between Persia and Turkey, 1932, ibid., note 97; Provisional Agreement between Denmark and Russia, 1923, ibid., note 88; Provisional Treaty of Friendship and Commerce between Russia and Czechoslovakia, 1922, ibid.; Franco-Soviet Non-Aggression Pact, 1932, ibid., note 77; Protocol Concerning the Re-establishment of Diplomatic Relations between Bulgaria and the U.S.S.R., 1934, ibid., note 89; Additional Treaty of Friendship, Neutrality, Conciliation, and Arbitration, 1933, ibid., note 97; Treaty of Peace between Poland, Russia and Ukraine, Riga, 1921, ibid., note 89.

55. In this connection one might refer to the comment of M. Litvinov in the course of his report to the Central Commissariat of the U.S.S.R. in 1929: "But it is not only the organs of the press which do this [anti-Soviet propaganda], but also the most respectable representatives of the State, past, present and future Ministers. Anti-Soviet sermons far from parliamentary in language are delivered in mushroom Parliaments.

ingly tend to convert them into ideological ones, it is unrealistic to expect that treaty obligations which foreclose all manipulations of ideological symbols will be faithfully adhered to over a length of time. Such treaties might be obeyed only so long as the elite of each of the two contracting states does not engage in active pursuit of power at the expense of the elite of the other.

DEPRIVATION OF WELL-BEING

Elimination of some of the leaders of the elite of a foreign state by such methods as assassination or threats of deprivation of their well-being might sometimes form the objective of strategists in a state. Or such elimination might result from an intensive use of the ideological instrument, whether intended by the strategists or not. We may consider here how far communications designed or likely to produce such results are permissible.

Incitements to assassination or to other forms of severe deprivation of well-being are punished in all legal systems, even though the incited acts are not actually committed.[56] The question of main interest to us here is whether it is necessary for governments to restrain by punitive measures incitements which might cause deprivation of the well-being of persons in a foreign state. In 1883, when the British government protested to the United States over publications that appeared in the United States press, alleged by the British government to be such as would prompt assassination and arson in England, Mr. Frelinghuysen, then Secretary of State, replied that though the United States government condemned such publications there was no law in the United States to punish them.[57] He doubted whether the law of any other country except Britain contained a provision covering such publications.[58] The publications complained about, it may be noted, were not in fact incitements but news reports of plans of certain Irish revolutionaries supposed to be contemplating the commission of such offenses in England.[59]

After the assassination of King Alexander I of Yugoslavia in 1934, on a complaint by Yugoslavia that Hungary had been tolerating irredentist activity within its territory directed against the former, and consisting of incitements to crime, the League Council adopted a resolution declaring it

You will even find these sermons contained in the conclusions and summing up judgments in foreign legal institutions which are famous for their objectivity. Isn't all this propaganda directed against the Soviet Union?" see R.I.I.A., *Documents on International Affairs*, 1929, p. 207.

56. See Terrou and Solal, p. 311.

57. See Wharton, *Digest of International Law*, 1 (2d ed. 1887), 265; Moore, *Digest*, 2, 170.

58. In England, under the Offenses Against Persons Act, 1863, such incitements were made punishable.

59. Moore, *Digest*, 2, 171.

the duty of every state to desist from encouraging or tolerating such activity.[60] A committee of experts was later set up by the Council to draft a convention prescribing the duties of states in regard to terrorist activities. The Convention for the Prevention and Punishment of Terrorism was drafted and opened for signature in 1937. It contained a reaffirmation of "the principle of international law in virtue of which it is the duty of every State to refrain from any act designed to encourage terrorist activities against another State and to prevent the acts in which such activities take shape" (Art. 1). Under the convention, conspiracies and incitements to terrorist acts which are successful are punishable (Art. 2). Twenty-three states signed the convention, but only one of them, India, ratified it in 1941. The convention never entered into force.

The Draft Code of Offenses against the Peace and Security of Mankind recommended by the International Law Commission contains two clauses, Article 2(6) and 2(13), which are of interest in this connection. Article 2(6) declares that the undertaking, encouragement, or toleration by the authorities of a state of organized activities calculated to carry out terrorist acts in another state is a crime. Article 2(13) declares that direct incitements, attempts, conspiracies, or complicity, in the commission of any of the offenses mentioned in Article 2 also are crimes. The combined effect of these two clauses seems to be to make incitement to terrorist acts in a foreign state a crime. But, as we noted before, the Draft Code is not likely to be adopted in the form of a treaty.

From the above it is possible to doubt the existence of any prescription which obligates states to punish incitements to commit crimes such as assassination in a foreign state. However, curiously, one finds that the laws of war proscribe incitement to assassination. Whatever might have been the degree of compliance with this prescription in the past,[61] it was referred to by Oppenheim as traditional.[62] The United States Field Manual, the Law of Land Warfare, 1956, prohibits the offering of a reward on the head of any enemy (Rule 31). The Commission of Jurists who prepared a Draft Code of Rules for Air Warfare at The Hague in 1923 were of the opinion that the incitements to murder or assassination were illegitimate forms of propaganda during a war.[63] If such incitements are impermissible during times of belligerency, it is difficult to deny their illegal character in ordinary times.

60. See A. Kuhn, "The Complaint of Yugoslavia Against Hungary with Reference to the Assassination of King Alexander," 29 *A.J.I.L.* 87 (1936).

61. See in this connection Spaight, *War Rights on Land*, pp. 86–87; Walker, *Science of International Law*, p. 331.

62. Oppenheim-Lauterpacht, 2, sec. 110.

63. See *Brit. Parl. Papers*, Cmd. No. 2201 of 1924; Spaight, *Air Power and War Rights*, p. 333.

However, it is not easy to say whether any particular transnational communication is an incitement to assassination or not. In 1956 the British government charged that Greek broadcasts to Cyprus contained incitements to murder, while the Greek officials asserted that they were merely disseminations of truth.[64] It is very likely that factual claims of a conflicting character will be put forward by the parties involved.

From the point of view of community policy, two questions present themselves: whether incitements to deprivation of well-being should be regarded as impermissible, and in what manner conflicting claims which might be presented about the character of any utterance should be determined. From the humanitarian point of view, it seems all incitements to assassination should be regarded as criminal. When they are so regarded during hostilities it is unreasonable to adopt a different prescription during the time of peace. The determination of the nature of the communication —whether or not it amounts to an incitement to assassination—has to depend upon a cognizance of all the relevant facts attending the communication. That is, the character of the disseminator, the environmental and predispositional factors of the audience addressed, the character of the language used, and the time and manner of communication should be taken into account; and if from those and other relevant factors it can be reasonably expected that the communications will influence members of the audience addressed to commit the crime, it might be regarded as incitement. However, the decision-makers will have to take into account not merely the humanitarian value protected by restraining the utterance, but also the values pursued by the disseminators. For that reason, perhaps, a greater degree of tolerance has to be shown toward activity pursued for the vindication of human rights brutally trampled upon by the elite against whom the activity is directed.

64. See *New York Times*, Feb. 1, 1956.

11

Effects on Community Values

MAINTENANCE OF MINIMUM PUBLIC ORDER

Since the days of the League of Nations some states have been claiming that propaganda activity which might lead to an outbreak of war should be prohibited by community prescriptions. It has been suggested that in the main the following five types of propaganda or disseminations should be prohibited: (1) war propaganda; (2) propaganda which might tend to develop hatred against a foreign state; (3) dissemination of false and distorted reports which might lead to disturbance of friendly relations between states; (4) disseminations which give offense to the people of a foreign state; (5) propaganda which incites the people of a foreign state to internal violence. The prescriptions applicable to the last category and the policy issues which arise in that context have been discussed already. We shall consider here the other categories of propaganda.

War Propaganda

The idea of moral disarmament was put forward during the days of the League of Nations as the Preparatory Commission to the Disarmament Conference was carrying on its deliberations. The Polish government presented a memorandum in 1931 to the League on the question of attainment of moral disarmament.[1] The Polish delegation also presented a draft convention to the Disarmament Conference, Geneva, 1932, which sought to obligate states to punish "any person guilty of public incitement to war." [2] The Committee on Moral Disarmament discussed the proposal, and its Legal Committee, headed by V. V. Pella, submitted a report

1. See Memorandum submitted by the Polish government to the League of Nations Concerning the Attainment of Moral Disarmament, *L.O.N. Doc.*, C.602.M.240. 1931.IX.

2. See Minutes of the Political Commission, Disarmament Conference (1933), *L.O.N. Pub.*, Disarmament. 1936.IX.8, p. 60.

proposing an international convention obligating states to prevent, by penal legislation, incitements of public opinion to aggression and certain other types of propaganda.[3] But these proposals were strongly opposed especially by Britain and the United States. In fact, a majority of the states represented at the conference strongly opposed any form of regulation of propaganda by methods amounting to censorship.[4] No convention was entered into on this question at Geneva as the main conference itself ended in failure.

The Soviet delegation revived the proposal and proposed a resolution during the Second Session of the General Assembly which called upon the governments of member states to punish "war propaganda" within their respective jurisdictions.[5] We have noted the Soviet definition of "ideological aggression" which contains as its first clause "war propaganda." The Soviet proposal in the form in which it was presented was opposed by the liberal democracies; their position was that the effects of the so-called "war propaganda" should be overcome by enlightenment processes and not by suppressive methods and censorship. As put by Mr. Herbert Evatt, representative of Australia, the most effective way to handle warmongers was not to suppress them but to expose them.[6] The Soviet proposals have fared no better than the Polish proposals of the 1930s. The Third Committee of the U.N. General Assembly, however, in 1960, in the course of its consideration of the draft Convention on Freedom of Information, adopted a draft of Article 2 of the Convention which permits the contracting states to prohibit within their territories "incitement to war." [7] Article 20 (1) of the International Covenant on Civil and Political Rights recently adopted by the Assembly obligates the parties to prohibit by law "any propaganda for war."

3. See *Report of the Legal Committee of the Committee on Moral Disarmament, 1933*, *L.O.N. Pub.*, Disarmament.1935.IX.4, 2, 701.

4. See the study by Arnold Raestad in *Broadcasting and Peace, Studies and Projects in the Matter of International Agreements* (Paris, International Institute of Intellectual Cooperation, 1933), pp. 155, 156.

5. See the draft resolution presented at the Second Session of the General Assembly (U.N. Doc. A/BUR/86, Sept. 18, 1947); see also in this connection the draft resolution submitted by the Czechoslovakian delegation at the Ninth Session of the General Assembly (U.N. Doc. A/AC.76/L.16, 1954).

6. See the speech on the Soviet draft resolution in the First Committee by Mr. Austin, representative of the U.S. (G.A.O.R., 2d Sess., Committee 1, 1947), pp. 188, 192.

7. The text of Art. 2 is as follows:

> 1. The exercise of the freedoms referred to in Article 1 carries with it duties and responsibilities. It may, however, be subject only to such necessary restrictions as are clearly defined by law and applied in accordance with the law in respect of: national security and public order (*ordre public*); systematic dissemination of false reports harmful to friendly relations among nations and of expressions inciting to war or to national, racial or religious hatred; attacks on founders of religions;

Under the Broadcasting Convention of 1936 the contracting states accepted the obligation not to permit within their jurisdictions transmission of any broadcasts inciting war against any of the parties to the Convention, or any acts likely to lead thereto.

At the Conference of the Eighteen-Nation Committee on Disarmament in 1962, an agreement was almost reached on war propaganda. On a proposal by the Soviet Union, the Committee of the Whole Conference unanimously adopted on May 24 the following declaration. The amendments later proposed by the Soviet Union indicate its demands and to what extent the Western powers were prepared to go.

> The Governments of states participating in the eighteen-nation Disarmament Committee in Geneva:
>
> Considering that in the preamble of the Charter of the United Nations the peoples express their determination "to practice tolerance and live together in peace with one another as good neighbors" :
>
> Considering that Article 2, Paragraph 4, of the Charter lays down the obligation that all members shall refrain in their international relations from the threat or use of force against the territorial integrity or political independence of any state:
>
> Recalling that the joint statement of agreed principles of disarmament negotiations affirms that it is important for the achievement of disarmament that all states refrain from any action which might aggravate international tensions:

---

incitement to violence and crime; public health and morals; the rights, honor and reputation of others; and the fair administration of justice.

2. The restrictions specified in the preceding paragraph shall not be deemed to justify the imposition by any State of prior censorship on news, comments and political opinions, and may not be used as grounds for restricting the right to criticise the Government. *U.N. Yearbook*, 1960, p. 336.

Cf. the provisions of Articles 19 and 20 of the International Covenant on Civil and Political Rights:

Art. 19. 1. Everyone shall have the right to hold opinions without interference.

2. Everyone shall have the right to freedom of expression; this right shall include freedom to seek, receive and impart information and ideas of all kinds, regardless of frontiers, either orally, in writing or in print, in the form of art, or through any other media of his choice.

3. The exercise of the rights provided for in the foregoing paragraph carries with it special duties and responsibilities. It may therefore be subject to certain restrictions, but these shall be only such as are provided by law and are necessary (1) for respect of the rights or reputations of others, (2) for the protection of national security or of public order ("*ordre public*"), or of public health or morals.

Art. 20. 1. Any propaganda for war shall be prohibited.

2. Any advocacy of national, racial, or religious hatred that constitutes incitement to discrimniation, hostility or violence shall be prohibited.

Convinced that the younger generation of today should be brought up in the spirit of peace, mutual respect and understanding among peoples:

Determined to promote by every means at their disposal friendly relations among states in accordance with the purposes and principles of the United Nations:

Recognizing that war propaganda in whatsoever form or country conducted which can provoke or encourage a threat to or breach of, the peace, is incompatible with the United Nations Charter and can lead to acts of aggression and war:

Recognizing that an end to such propaganda could facilitate the conclusion of an agreement on general complete disarmament:

1. Solemnly affirm their support for the United Nations General Assembly Resolution 110(II) which condemned "all forms of propaganda, in whatsoever country conducted, which is either designed or likely to provoke or encourage any threat to the peace, breach of the peace, or act of aggression":
2. Condemn appeals for war and for the settlement of disputes between states by the use of force, and also statements to the effect that war is necessary or inevitable:
3. Affirm their conviction that in our day, war can no longer serve as a method of settling international disputes and their desire to educate the younger generation in this conviction and to promote the ideas of peace, mutual respect and understanding among the peoples:
4. Undertake to promote by every means at their disposal the widest possible circulation of news, ideas and opinions conducive to the strengthening of peace and friendship among peoples, and to extend cultural, scientific and educational relations with a view to better dissemination of the ideas of peaceful and friendly co-operation among states, and general and complete disarmament:
5. Call upon all states to adopt, within the limits of their constitutional systems, appropriate practical measures, including measures in a legislative form in the case of states which consider such form appropriate, with a view to giving effect to this declaration against war propaganda:
6. Call upon all other states to support this declaration.[8]

But on May 29, when the declaration was brought before the plenary session for adoption, the Soviet representative, M. Zorin, read a statement of his government referring to the alleged West German demand for nu-

8. Eighteen-Nation Disarmament Committee Document, ENDC/C.I/20, May 25, 1962.

clear arms, revanchist propaganda for a change of frontiers, and the reported utterances of some statesmen and organs in the United States urging summary treatment of the "national liberation movements" of the peoples of Laos and South Vietnam, and demanded the following alterations in the declaration before it was adopted:

> For operative paragraphs 3 to 6, the following should be substituted:
> Resolutely condemn all appeals for a preventive nuclear war as aggressive acts which conflict with the purposes and principles of the Charter of the United Nations and with the interests of maintaining peace, and which are incompatible with the honor and conscience of mankind:
> Condemn propaganda for revanchism and for the revision of state frontiers in Europe which resulted from the Second World War as action conflicting with the interests of peace and creating a threat to the security of the peoples:
> Also condemn as being at variance with the United Nations Declaration on granting of independence to colonial countries and peoples, and as threatening universal peace, incitement to the use of force against peoples which have embarked on the course of national liberation and independent development:
> Undertake, within the shortest possible period and in any event not later than six months from the date of signature of this Declaration, to enact legislation, if it has not previously been enacted, declaring war propaganda in any form a grave crime against peace and humanity and providing for severe penalties against persons guilty of conducting such propaganda, including their immediate removal from all official posts, the loss of all ranks and titles and their criminal prosecution:
> Call upon all other states to accede to this Declaration and to take similar measures in accordance with it.[9]

These amendments, as might be expected, were rejected by the representatives of the West, and the discussion on war propaganda disappeared from the Committee's work thereafter.

Before the U. N. General Assembly Special Committee on Principles of International Law concerning Friendly Relations and Cooperation among States, Czechoslovakia submitted a draft proposal specifying in detail the prohibition of the threat or use of force in international relations contained in the Charter, paragraph 3 of which ran thus: [10]

9. ENDC/PV/44, May 29, 1962.

10. See *Report of the Special Committee of Principles of International Law concerning Friendly Relations and Cooperation among States*, para. 27. Cf. other proposals of a similar character made in the 1966 Special Committee. Ghana, India, Yugoslavia, and eight others: "Wars of aggression constitute international crimes against peace.

> Any propaganda for war, incitement to or fomenting of war and any propaganda for preventive war and for striking the first nuclear blow shall be prohibited. States shall take, within the framework of their jurisdiction, all measures, in particular legislative measures, in order to prevent such propaganda.

Among the twenty-seven members of the Committee, seven members, the United States, the United Kingdom, Nigeria, Italy, Australia, Sweden, and Venezuela, opposed the proposal and The Netherlands doubted its desirability. But the Soviet Union fully supported the proposal. The Committee was not able to reach consensus on the proposal.[11]

From the point of view of policy, it should be obvious that if any propaganda activity has to be restrained in this context, it is only the following three types: (1) propaganda activity organized by the key policy-makers in a state, designed as a preparation for initiating a strategy of violence for purposes of aggression; (2) activity organized by those policy-makers which creates a reasonable expectation that its outcome will be that the leaders will be compelled by the force of public opinion within their state to initiate such aggression. It has been noted before that an intensive use of the ideological instrument might cause power deprivations to the strategists, and therefore, when a reasonable expectation is created that those using the ideological instrument will lose power to such an extent that they would be compelled to initiate aggression of violence, there would be suffi-

---

Consequently any propaganda which encourages the threat or use of force against the territorial integrity and political independence or another State is prohibited." Chile: "The prohibition (of the threat or use of force) shall therefore include . . . propaganda for war or for the use of force in any of its forms." Italy and the Netherlands: "In order to ensure the more effective application of the foregoing principle (regarding abstention from the threat or use of force), the Members of the United Nations . . . should endeavor, to the extent compatible with their relevant constitutional provisions, to prevent propaganda for aggressive war, or incitement thereof." See the *Report of the 1966 Special Committee*, paras. 26, 28, and 29.

11. Ibid., para. 106, Annex B, section F, item no. 2. In this connection reference may be made to the remarks of Mr. Blix, representative of Sweden in the Committee, during the 10th meeting: "He saw greater difficulty in including a reference (in the principles relating to the use of force) to war propaganda; what might be regarded as a statement of fact in one State might be viewed as war propaganda in another. In a country like his, where freedom of the Press and freedom of speech were strongly protected by law and public opinion, the Government could not and would not introduce by legislation a vague restriction such as prohibition of war propaganda. If aggressive words were used in their Press, Swedes would feel confident that they would be contradicted and through free discussion the right course would be chosen. A simple condemnation of war propaganda coupled with a statement on the importance of the free flow of information for the preservation of peace was another matter; that incidentally was the subject of the General Assembly resolution 381 (V)." U.N. Doc. A/AC. 119/SR.10 (1964), p. 9.

cient justification to restrain the activity. (3) Propaganda by persons other than the key policy-makers may have to be restrained if it creates a reasonable expectation that its necessary outcome will be initiation of such aggression. In these instances world community measures designed to prevent aggression may be quite justifiably taken; and if the situation warrants the restraining of the propaganda activity, there could be no objection to such a step. The enlightenment value is not likely to suffer by restraining such activity.

The proposals made in the past by the Polish government and the Soviet government were not suitable to restrain effectively activities of the types mentioned above, and instead were likely to jeopardize unduly the enlightenment value. The Polish proposal was that states should enter into a treaty obligation to punish "incitement to aggressive war." Such a treaty obligation will do little to restrain psychological preparations to initiate a strategy of violence for purposes of aggression. If policy-makers so intend, they can carry out such preparations without ever mentioning the word "war," always professing peaceful intentions. Hitler professed to be a seeker of peace.

The Polish proposal did not provide for any machinery to enforce the treaty obligation against any government which carried on propaganda in violation of the treaty; therefore, the proposal contained no effective means to restrain activities of the second and third types mentioned above. Furthermore, it was likely to create one serious difficulty. Ordinarily if private persons in a state start intensive propaganda activity for an aggressive war and the government of the state disapproves, it will itself adopt suitable measures to restrain the activity. While normally it will have free choice to select appropriate measures of restraint, the suggested treaty would compel the government to adopt invariably one particular method—that is, initiation of criminal proceedings against the persons making the utterance, however unsuitable or inadequate the measure might be under the circumstances.[12] A treaty of the type suggested by the Polish government is vulnerable to criticism from other directions also. It could enable the elite of a state to charge the government of another with treaty violations and thus make gains in the ideological strategy. The Soviet Union has repeatedly contended that while she has prohibited war propaganda by legislation,[13]

12. See in this connection the very persuasive arguments of Raestad, cited above, against such a convention.

13. The law passed in the U.S.S.R. is the Peace Defense Act, 1951; for text see 46 *A.J.I.L.* Supp., 34 (1952). The main provision declares:

> 1. That war propaganda, in whatever form conducted, undermines the cause of peace, creates the danger of a new war and is therefore a grave crime against humanity.
>
> 2. That persons guilty of war propaganda shall be committed for trial as major criminals.

the Western powers are encouraging it, even though instances of invocation or application of the law, even when the cold war was intense, have been few.[14]

The Soviet conception of war propaganda was never clarified beyond specification of the types of utterances that the Soviet Union would like to be proscribed under all conditions, irrespective of the other variables involved in the context, and such specification did not proceed beyond reference to the activity desired to be prohibited by such shorthand expressions as "war propaganda," "incitement to a new war," and "propaganda for a preventive war or for striking the first nuclear blow."

The Polish proposal—and its revived version, the Soviet proposals—suffer from another infirmity. It is not necessary in the interest of peace in the world community that every "incitement to aggressive war" should be prohibited. It is not necessary to pay serious attention to soapbox orators who harangue for the initiation of an aggressive war, for it is not their audience that will initiate one. Propaganda activity of private persons need be prohibited, if at all, only when it reaches such a level of intensity that it can reasonably be expected to compel the policy-makers of the state to initiate such a war. The type of activity that may have to be restrained has been better indicated in the draft Convention on Moral Disarmament prepared by the Legal Committee of the Committee on Moral Disarmament: "Inciting public opinion by direct public propaganda with a view to forcing the State to embark upon a war of aggression."[15] But even this formula does not provide any qualification as to the level of intensity the activity should reach before community measures of regulation might be put into operation. No policy consideration calls for restraining activity of low intensity. But the Polish and Soviet proposals seek punishment of utterances which do not injure the interests of the world community at all.

Professor Quincy Wright's definition of the crime of warmongering as propaganda "which is designed and likely to provoke or encourage any threat to the peace, breach of the peace or act of aggression" taken along with the "clear and present danger" rule,[16] has the merit of indicating that only propaganda activity of a high degree of intensity, which creates a reasonable expectation that it will bring the evil of aggression in the proximate future, should be brought under restraint.

For similar laws in other Eastern European countries and Outer Mongolia see 46 A.J.I.L. Supp., 96–106 (1952). See also K. Grzybowski and M. Pundeff, "Soviet Bloc Peace-Defense Laws," 46 *A.J.I.L.* 537 (1952).

14. Ibid. In 1962, however, in East Germany one Harry Seidel was convicted under such a law, not for "war mongering" but for attempting to escape to West Germany; *See Bull. of Int'l Commission of Jurists*, No. 16 (1963), p. 1.

15. See the Report cited in note 3 above.

16. See "The Crime of War-Mongering," p. 135.

In the previous chapter it was noted that the post-World War II trials established that activity of the first type mentioned above is criminal. In the case of the activities of the second type, too, it may reasonably be expected that if aggression actually materializes the policy-makers of the state responsible for the commission of aggression will be punished, and the use of the ideological instrument would come within the range of the objectionable activity attributed to them. The fact of absence of intent to commit aggression at the beginning might not be accepted as a valid defense because the policy-makers who organized the activity would be charged at least with the knowledge of probable consequences of their acts, and thereby be taken to have intended them. In activities of the third type also, if aggression occurs, the same result may be expected to follow. The fact that the organizers were not persons of sufficient significance would not form sustainable grounds of defense, because if their activity had precipitated aggression they must at one stage have reached a position where they were able to influence the policies of their state. It can be expected that the three types of activity thus will be held criminal in the future before tribunals such as those of Nuremberg and Tokyo. And it is good policy to adopt suitable measures to prevent the precipitation of aggression, by restraining such activity.

It is suggested by some that incitements to war directed to the people of a foreign state also should be covered by the prohibition of war propaganda.[17] One can very easily see that it is only in very rare cases that the policy-makers of a foreign state would be influenced by such propaganda to initiate aggression, or the people of that state would be influenced to such an extent as to put pressure on their government to initiate war. In appropriate cases, however, world community procedures available to prevent aggression might be employed to restrain such activity.

In conclusion it may be suggested that, consistent with existing prescriptions, the following types of propaganda activity may be regarded by decision-makers as prohibited: (1) activity organized by the policy-makers of a state to promote a strategy of violence for purposes of aggression; (2) activity of those persons which creates a reasonable expectation that they will be compelled to initiate such a strategy; (3) activity of persons other than those belonging to the above category which creates a reasonable expectation that its necessary outcome will be the initiation of such strategy by the policy-makers of that state; (4) activity organized in one state which creates a reasonable expectation that its necessary outcome will be the initiation of such strategy by the policy-makers of a foreign state. The label used to refer to such propaganda may be "war propaganda" or something else.

17. Raestad, p. 184, discusses the suggestion.

Propaganda of Hatred

Suggestions put forward in the past for restraining the dissemination of material likely to create in the minds of the people of a state hatred against people of another covered two types of communications—those disseminated through the fast media of mass communication, and those disseminated through slow educational processes.

Hatred Propaganda through the Mass Media

The Polish government's memorandum referred to above suggested that states should amend their internal penal legislation and adopt severe measures "to deal with any person attempting to undermine the moral bases of world peace by a propaganda of hatred." [18] The recommendations of the Legal Committee of the Committee on Moral Disarmament contained a proposal that states should adopt measures to punish publications causing prejudice to a foreign state by attributing to it acts manifestly untrue and thus exposing it to public resentment and contempt.[19] We noted the Soviet definition of "ideological aggression" according to which "nazi-fascist propaganda of national or racial hatred" would constitute aggression. All these proposals met opposition from the liberal democratic states.[20]

The policy basis which may be suggested in support of suppression of the so-called "propaganda of hatred" is that it might create a predisposition among the audience to respond to events in general in a manner hostile to the people against whom it is directed. Given such a predisposition, the internal elite might at any time use the ideological instrument and obtain a favorable response to any of their policies of aggression. Or when such predispositions are created, even relatively small incidents might heighten tensions among the people, and bring forth a response favoring resort to violence against the objects of hatred. Such a response might compel the policy-makers of the state to initiate an attack.

Weighty as these considerations may be, the policy question remains as to how to regulate that type of propaganda activity. The method suggested by the Polish government is not at all satisfactory as it provides one rigid pattern of regulation to deal with a wide variety of situations that might arise in practice. It may be noted that utterances likely to develop hatred might be made by persons out of ignorance and prejudice, and in such cases enlightenment and not penal discipline would be the proper remedy.

18. See the memorandum cited in note 1 above.

19. See note 3.

20. But see note 7, the text of Art. 2 of the draft Convention on Freedom of Information adopted by the Third Committee of the U.N. General Assembly, which permits states to prohibit within their territories "national, racial or religious hatred; attacks on the founders of religions." See also Art. 20(2) of the International Covenant on Civil and Political Rights, the text of which is given in the same note.

A person might make such an utterance when the governments of the two states concerned enjoy cordial relations. In such a case it could be ignored or the matter might be left to the government within whose jurisdiction it was made to deal with it. A convention which obligates states to adopt penal measures in respect of such utterances will create difficulties similar to those noted in connection with war propaganda. The existence of a convention might not be effective in preventing such utterances, and indeed, it can be a source of further irritation in a situation where the statements are likely to produce no more than cathartic effects. If policy-makers in a state, with the intent to commit aggression, organize a campaign of hatred against another state, or persons other than policy-makers try to influence the people of their state to exert pressure on the policy-makers to initiate aggression, it becomes necessary to adopt measures of individual and collective security, and a convention of the suggested pattern will not be a substitute.

In order to indicate when community measures will be necessary to restrain hate propaganda activity within a state, in order to maintain peace and security without endangering the enlightenment value, the following may be suggested: If from the activity a reasonable expectation is created that the policy-makers of the state within which the activity is being carried on will be putting into operation a strategy of violence for purposes of aggression, or when it creates an expectation that the policy-makers will be compelled to initiate such aggression, community measures to restrain the activity and to prevent any possible aggression might be adopted. The government of the menaced state will, of course, be entitled under those conditions to adopt permissible measures of security.

Educational Processes

The liberal democratic tradition, perhaps the tradition of a major part of humanity, is that educational processes should not be directly controlled by those exercising formal and effective power within the body politic. The trend toward governments taking a direct interest in the promotion of the processes of education may be said to date from the time of the French Revolution.[21] The early revolutionists adopted this policy with the hope that it would strengthen the republic. Since that time the trend has been on the increase. At present governmental systems range from those that exercise complete control over educational processes to those that allow a high degree of freedom to educational institutions in discharge of their functions.

Under the traditional doctrine of sovereignty the manner in which the educational processes in a state are carried on is a matter of domestic concern. However, as the doctrine of domestic jurisdiction is not an absolute

21. See J. A. Lauwerys, *History Text-Books and International Understanding* (Paris, UNESCO, 1953), p. 13.

one, it is possible for the government of a state whose security might be threatened by such processes to demand that they be altered. Thus in 1914, on the assassination of the Archduke Ferdinand in Sarajevo by a member of an irredentist movement in Serbia, Austria-Hungary demanded that Serbia should "eliminate without delay from public instruction in Serbia, both as regards the teaching body and also as regards the methods of instruction, everything that serves, or might serve, to foment propaganda against Austria-Hungary," and Serbia undertook to comply, if definite proof of such propaganda was forthcoming.[22]

As the nineteenth century drew to its close "the progressive school" of thinkers began to search for causes which occasioned outbreaks of violence in international relations.[23] Before World War I some writers pointed to instruction given to children in schools and the attitudes developed there as one of the causes.[24] After the war the educational processes received greater attention with a view to preventing them from becoming contributory factors to international conflicts.

In 1925 "Casarès Resolution," adopted by the International Committee for Intellectual Cooperation of the League of Nations, called for cooperation of governments in eliminating from schoolbooks passages which might develop hatred or moral distrust among people. In the subsequent year several bilateral agreements, official and nonofficial, were entered into for the reform of school textbooks.[25]

At the Disarmament Conference in 1932, the Polish government proposed that states should by treaty undertake to adopt legislation to effect reforms in teaching, and to prohibit all activities of teachers intended to arouse hatred toward foreigners or to disturb good international relations.[26] This proposal was not accepted at the Conference, but in 1937 the League General Assembly adopted a Declaration on the Teaching of History.[27] The declaration was signed by seventeen countries, but they included none of the major powers. The declaration contained only an affirmation by the signatory governments that it was desirable to "endeavor to ascertain" the means by which, especially in connection with the choice of schoolbooks, school children might be put on guard against all allegations and interpretations of historical events which might arouse unjust prejudices against other states. In each signatory state an advisory body was

22. See *Collected Diplomatic Documents Relating to the Outbreak of European War* (London, H.M. Stationery Office, 1915), pp. 7, 34.

23. See W. Schiffer, *The Legal Community of Mankind* (New York, Columbia University Press, 1954), Chap. 12.

24. See, e.g., A. B. Hart, "School Books and International Prejudices," *Int'l. Conciliation*, No. 38 (1911).

25. See Lauwerys, Chap. 4.

26. Memorandum cited in note 1.

27. See Hudson, *International Legislation*, 7, 850.

set up to carry out the objectives outlined in the declaration. At the Inter-American Conference, Montevideo, 1933, a Convention on the Teaching of History was adopted,[28] under which the contracting governments undertook to have textbooks used in their respective countries revised to eliminate from them anything which might tend "to arouse in the immature mind of youth aversion to any American Country." The United States, while appreciating the spirit of the Convention, did not sign it.

At the trial of German major war criminals the prosecution produced evidence of the policies adopted by the Nazi government in regard to education, and toward youth organizations, with a view to developing a pro-Nazi outlook among the youth and to preparing them for programs of aggression.[29] The tribunal, however, did not convict any of the defendants for participation in making and implementing these policies. The response of the Tokyo tribunal, however, to similar evidence presented before it was different. Defendant Koichikodo, the Education Minister of Japan from 1937 onward, was convicted of a crime against peace. The tribunal charged, among other things, that he was responsible for policies necessary to develop a warlike spirit in Japan.[30]

We see from the above three distinct trends of decisions. Firstly, there has been an assertion of the right of each state to organize its internal educational processes as it might choose, but to accept that the process should not be operated in a manner that would promote hostility among its people toward another state to the point of menacing that state's security. Secondly, governments of states have refused to accept any treaty obligation in regard to the manner in which education is operated within their respective states, or have accepted only to the extent of subscribing to certain general principles of policy. Thirdly, where the process has been used to promote a strategy of violence for the purpose of aggression, such operation has been regarded as criminal.

Looking at the question from the perspective of policy, one may note that educational processes in any state are generally so patterned as to develop among the rising generation certain skills as well as demands, expectations, and identifications. The development of identifications is to a certain extent desirable, for it is indeed by that process that transmission of the cultural accomplishments of any group to the succeeding generation is facilitated.[31] On the other hand, if the identifications are built up to irrational levels, it might be possible for the elite to work upon the predispositions created to develop hostility toward peoples of other states. The edu-

28. See the "Proceedings of the 7th International Conference of American States," 28 *A.J.I.L.* Supp., 71 (1934).

29. See *I.M.T.*, *Nuremberg, Trial of Major War Criminals*, 1, 181.

30. See *I.M.T. for Far East, Judgment,* (cited in Chap. 7, note 27), Chap. 10.

31. Lauwerys, p. 57.

cational processes tend to develop generally expectations which favor adherence to the prevailing pattern of value shaping and sharing within the state in question,[32] and this is not open to objection, as conservation is essential to the stability and progress of any group. But the process of shaping expectations may be stretched so far as to develop intense feelings of national or other group superiority over other sections of mankind. Generally the educational processes are used to develop demands on self by self, or on others by self. Encouragement of patriotic feelings, a spirit of self-sacrifice, and abhorrence for deviant groups is not undesirable, but if carried to extremes it can bring evils in its train. In the determination of policy, therefore, here as elsewhere, the question is one of drawing the line between the permissible and the impermissible.

The processes of shaping demands, expectations, and identifications may have to be brought under the world community's corrective measures when they assume a form that jeopardizes the community's interests. The stage at which community intervention is necessary can be determined only by reference to the objectives of those who operate the processes, the attitudes being shaped, the intensity with which they are shaped, and the effects expected. Furthermore, as the educational processes produce results by slow degrees, they admit of correction by persuasive means to a much greater degree than intensive propaganda processes.

Dissemination of False and Distorted Statements

Detailed arguments in favor of the claim that publication of such statements should be prohibited were presented by the Polish government in 1931 in its memorandum to the League on moral disarmament.[33] It was argued that governments, having accepted the principle of outlawing war as an instrument of national policy, should not adopt policies internally which would conflict with that principle. Their policies toward the press and other associations within their respective jurisdictions, in particular, should not be in conflict with that principle. The memorandum then proceeded to point out that certain sections of the press might, during periods of international crisis, instead of calming the feelings of people and helping the League to settle international disputes, make its task more difficult by misrepresenting facts and stirring up feelings. Four remedies were suggested in the memorandum to regulate such activities. (1) States should

32. The conclusions arrived at after a study of history textbooks by a study group of the British Royal Institute of International Affairs, reprinted in "History Text Books in International Relations," 15 *International Affairs* 877 (1936), show that one persistent trend found in the books was defense of the status quo. It was stated that another dominant trend was to show that the Soviet experiment was a complete failure. A third tendency was to extol the benefits of British imperial rule.

33. See the memorandum cited in note 1; it is interesting to note that the memorandum refers to earlier proposals made by the Swedish government along similar lines.

amend their penal laws to punish persons guilty of publishing in the press false and tendentious reports on the international situation. (2) The "right of reply" available in many European countries should be adopted by legislation in all countries and be made available to foreign governments also.[34] (3) An international disciplinary tribunal for journalists should be set up with powers to try any journalist whose activities endangered the international peace and to expel him from the profession of journalism. (4) An international information bureau ought to be set up to publish its versions of international events. The accounts given by such a body, by virtue of the prestige it was likely to command, would very likely be accepted by all as accurate.

In the draft convention presented to the Disarmament Conference the Polish government included two articles that sought to obligate the states to punish within their jurisdictions "any broadcasting transmission likely to disturb international relations or to wound the national sentiments of listeners of another contracting country," and "the projection of any film, and in general, any public performance, likely to disturb good relations between the peoples or to arouse hatred of foreigners." [35] The idea underlying these proposals was that by prohibiting disseminations of this character it might be possible to remove one of the causes of violence between states.

After World War II, as the East-West tension began to rise, the communist states revived the case for punishing false and distorted statements. Before her rift with other communist countries, Yugoslavia presented during the Second Session of the United Nations General Assembly a proposal that the member states should adopt measures to prevent dissemination of "false and tendentious reports calculated to aggravate relations between the States, and provoke conflicts and incite to new war." [36] At the U.N. Conference on Freedom of Information, Geneva, 1948, and subsequently this proposal received support from many delegations.[37] The objection of the major liberal democratic powers to this proposal was based upon their traditional philosophy that truth could best be ascertained only in an environment in which there was free opportunity to learn all the different versions of events.

The remedies suggested against the publication of false and distorted

34. The suggestion was that the government of any state, which finds that false statements concerning it were published in a foreign country, should be able to communicate its version through the Ministry of External Affairs of that country, and the particular newspaper which published the false statement should be obliged to publish the correction.

35. See note 2.

36. See U.N. Doc. A/C.3/162 (1947) for the text of the draft resolution presented by Yugoslavia.

37. The Indian amendment for Art. 2, cited in Chap. 5, note 62, reflects this claim.

statements so far may be divided into two classes: preventive and corrective. Under the first head fall measures involving the imposition of punishment. The trend of response of states to each of the two categories of remedies will be examined separately.

Preventive Remedies

The suggestion that states should adopt punitive measures to prevent publication of false statements which might have a disturbing effect on international relations has received very poor response. At the time of the Geneva Disarmament Conference of 1932, the suggestion was opposed in respect to all types of propaganda. The proposals of the Legal Committee of the Committee on Moral Disarmament in this regard were opposed by many countries in the main Committee.[38] In 1932, the General Assembly of the League discussed the question how far the dissemination of false news by the press constituted a danger to the international peace, and adopted a report made by the Sixth Committee of the Assembly.[39] The Committee considered that publication of such reports did not constitute a serious danger. In its opinion there was greater danger in suppressing facts and views than in publishing falsehoods. The Committee noted that it was not expedient to adopt coercive measures to prevent suppression of facts, and far less expedient to adopt coercive measures to prevent false and distorted versions. As a matter of general policy, the Committee considered that governments should not be encouraged to interfere with the freedom of the press.

The proposal of the Yugoslavian delegation to the Second Session of the United Nations General Assembly, referred to above, was discussed by the Assembly during the same session, but a decision was deferred to the Conference on the Freedom of Information which was to be convened shortly thereafter at Geneva.[40] At the Conference the view expressed by all the delegations outside the Soviet bloc was that, though freedom of information had to be exercised with responsibility, the fulfillment of the responsibility should be sought in the processes of self-regulation among the personnel engaged in the operations of public information agencies. The Conference, however, condemned by a resolution the tendency on the part of journalists to publish false and willfully distorted statements,[41] and also adopted the "Indian amendment" to Article 2 of the draft Convention on the Freedom of Information. We may recall the fact that this amendment constituted one of the most controversial matters in the project attempted

38. See Raestad, p. 156.

39. See Report of Sir Cecil Chelwood, cited in Chap. 5, note 70, above.

40. See Resolution 127 (11), 15 December 1947.

41. See Resolution No. 2 adopted by the Conference, Final Act (E/Conf.6/79, 1948).

at Geneva.[42] In the Broadcasting Convention of 1936, however, it was provided by Article 3 that the contracting parties should

> Prohibit and if occasion arises, . . . stop without delay within their respective territories any transmission likely to harm good international understanding by statements the incorrectness of which is, or ought to be, known to the person responsible for the broadcast.

Corrective Measures

At the Conference on the Freedom of Information, Geneva, the French delegation sponsored a proposal to institute an international right of correction.[43] The Conference adopted a draft Convention Concerning the Institution of an International Right of Correction, the salient features of which were contained in the French proposals. Under this draft convention, when any news report likely to injure the relations of a state with another is published in a foreign country, which in the opinion of the government of the former state is false or distorted, that government may submit its version of the event in question to the government of the state in which the publication was made. The latter government must, irrespective of its opinion about the facts, make the submitted version available to the news publishing agencies within its territory, and also within five days facilitate its dissemination through the channels generally used by that government to publish information to the public. If the government should fail to give such publicity, the corrected version may be submitted to the United Nations Secretary-General who would have to give it publicity within five days. The Convention was adopted by the United Nations General Assembly during its Seventh Session by a narrow majority of 25 to 22 and opened for signature in 1953. It came into force in 1962 when the required six ratifications were received.[44] None of the major powers has become a party.

It may be recollected that one of the Polish proposals of 1931 was the setting up of an international tribunal with disciplinary powers over journalists. The proposal was revived by the French delegation at the Geneva Conference on Freedom of Information. The proposal put forward at the Conference was that an International Information Council should be insti-

42. See Chap. 5. Art. 2 of the draft Convention on Freedom of Information, adopted by the Third Committee of the U.N. General Assembly, cited in note 7 above, however, provides this as a permissible ground of restraint on freedom of information.

43. The French law provides for the right of reply and the right of correction. The former gives an individual the right to require publication in a newspaper or journal of his own explanations or protest whenever that paper or journal publishes any account concerning him. The latter is the right of a person vested with public authority to have his version published in a newspaper or journal in which his official activities are not reported accurately. See Terrou and Solal, p. 338.

44. The parties are Cuba, El Salvador, Guatemala, U.A.R., Yugoslavia, and Sierra Leone.

tuted with power to issue something like professional cards to those who intend to work as journalists. The proposal received very little support at the Conference. On the recommendation of the Conference to consider the matter further, however, the Economic and Social Council entrusted to the Sub-Commission on the Freedom of Information and the Press the task of drafting an International Code of Ethics for Information Personnel. The Code was drafted, and the General Assembly during its Seventh Session requested the Secretary-General to assist in calling a conference of representatives of news agencies, the press, and other publicity organizations to adopt the Code. As the response of those organizations was poor, the Assembly during its Ninth Session decided to take no further action.[45]

We may note in this connection that the South American Regional Agreement on Radio Communications (Revised), Rio de Janeiro, 1937, contains a very moderate corrective remedy against dissemination of false reports. It is an obligation on the part of the contracting states to insure that when political news is broadcast from any radio station within their territories the broadcasters give accurately the source of the news (Art. 2 [1]). The contracting states should insure that news the source of which is not absolutely certain, or the publication of which has not been authorized, is not transmitted by radio.

The trend on the part of governments has so far been to refuse to accept any obligation to prevent within their jurisdictions the dissemination of false and distorted statements. The only exceptions which might be mentioned in this connection are the Broadcasting Convention of 1936 and the South American Agreement on Radio Communications referred to above. It may be useful now to examine the policy questions which arise in this context.

To start with, the proposal that states should by treaty undertake to prevent by penal legislation the dissemination of false statements does not merit acceptance. A treaty of that kind exposes foreign journalists, working in a country and sending reports outside which its officials do not like, to the risk of being accused of dissemination of false or distorted reports. The laws passed in pursuance of the treaty may be used by the officials as a means to compel all foreign journalists to dispatch only reports which the officials approve. The treaty may thus be turned into an instrument of punitive censorship.

The hardship that a treaty of this type might cause to journalists is easily seen. The experience of some states, which have laws punishing publication of false news causing public alarm or undermining the loyalty of people to the state, shows that such laws will be either ineffective or oppres-

45. J. F. Green, *The United Nations and Human Rights* (Washington, D.C., Brookings Institution, 1956), pp. 81–83; *U.N. Yearbook, 1954*, p. 236.

sive.[46] If such is the experience at the national level, it is not difficult to imagine the hardship which an international treaty might produce on working journalists. If a journalist is tried in one country for publishing a false statement about events in a foreign country, the court as well as the accused will be put to enormous difficulty and expenditure in summoning witnesses from abroad, having their evidence interpreted by experts, etc.[47] Furthermore, although courts generally possess a high degree of authority to order production of evidence and make factual investigations within their own state, in regard to foreign matters the range of factual inquiry they could make will necessarily be limited. Courts would either have to convict persons in many cases on very little evidence or not punish at all.

It may be noted that several reasons contribute to the appearance of false and distorted statements in the press and in the disseminations of other agencies of public information. Apart from commercialism on the part of those who operate the agencies, the following causes, which do not involve culpability on anyone's part, may be mentioned. Firstly, those engaged in modern journalism have to perform two essential but contradictory functions. They have to place facts before the public as soon after their occurrence as possible and report them accurately. Speed may be sacrificed if they care too much for accuracy, and accuracy can suffer if they concentrate on speed. They are obliged to make a compromise between speed and accuracy and it is but natural that sometimes inaccuracies enter their reports. But this is an incident of the high speed operations of modern agencies of public information. Further, it is impossible to present, in any version of an event, all the details of it, and a selection necessarily has to be made. The selection may appear to some to be quite natural and reasonable, and to others as an exercise in deliberate distortion.

Secondly, accounts given by journalists are generally intended to reach a wide audience whose level of sophistication to understand complicated accounts of facts and interpretations of facts is not sufficiently high. Materials disseminated to the large undereducated audience have necessarily to be simplified and "predigested." These accounts might appear to those scrupulous of accuracy as falsehoods and distortions. But the publication of such oversimplified accounts is one of the incidents of modern journalism.

Thirdly, elites at present tend to interpret the flow of events, as far as possible, in a manner to sustain their own ideologies and to show that those of the opponents have no factual basis. In such a situation, an account of events given by a person predisposed to one ideology will in many cases appear as falsehood or distortion to another predisposed to a different ideology.

46. See, in this regard, Terrou and Solal, pp. 288–89.

47. See Z. Chafee, Jr., "Legal Problems of Freedom of Information in the United Nations," 14 *Law and Contemp. Problems* 545, 579 (1949).

Faithful reporting under present conditions can convey no definitive meaning of an objective character, but only a somewhat subjective evaluation by whoever judges the character of the report in question.[48] In a world of competing ideologies, a system which seeks to punish a person for what he publishes as being "contrary to facts" or "distorted" can hardly be satisfactory.

We may now examine the *corrective* measures suggested in the past and try to appraise their underlying policy. The South American Convention of 1937 prescribes an obligation to ascertain the source of the information broadcast and disclose it. The disclosure of the source of information may indeed help the audience to evaluate the degree of its authenticity. Within a state or in a limited geographical area the disclosure of source may serve as a corrective to the dissemination of false or distorted reports. But at the global level, a convention which obligates states to compel all information agencies within their territories to disclose the sources of the information published may not improve the existing situation substantially.

One should not overlook the fact that spreading of canards may sometimes serve a useful purpose. It may compel an elite suppressing information to disclose it. It is a tactic which may be employed in the strategy for nonobjectionable purposes. But the existence of an obligation to disclose the source will exclude the possibility of using the tactic even for legitimate purposes. It also precludes policy-makers from using the "trial balloon" technique to study the probable response of the public to the policies under contemplation before they finally make their policy choices.

A convention on the right of correction at the international level is also open to many criticisms. Such a convention will be useless unless there is provision for compelling the agency which has published an alleged false report to publish the correction. Under the present convention no compulsion is possible. All that an aggrieved government could do is to compel the government of the state within the territory of which the statement is disseminated to publish the correction through the channels which the latter generally uses for its own publicity purposes. Or the aggrieved government may have it published by the United Nations Secretary-General. Even if there were no convention, an aggrieved government can have access to a number of avenues of publication under present conditions. What the convention gives by way of additional benefit seems to be very little. If the convention provides for compelling the agency which has published an alleged false report to publish a correction, there will be difficul-

48. See Karin Dovring, *The Road of Propaganda, Semantics of Biased Communication* (New York, Philosophical Library, 1959), p. 134. As a postscript to her essay the author remarks that many people would like to believe that it is not true that we are the subjects and objects of biased communication, while we are both.

ties of a different character. The press in most countries might be flooded by corrections sent by foreign governments.[49]

It seems from the above that the treaty arrangements suggested so far to control the dissemination of so-called false and distorted statements, by punitive, preventive, or corrective measures, are not likely to prove desirable from the point of view either of promoting freedom of information or of preventing outbreaks of violence in international relations. A treaty may at best remain superfluous, or at worst a source of controversy between states or justification for governments to impose undue restrictions on freedom of the press and of information.

On the other hand, the argument of adherents to the traditional liberal democratic philosophy—that truth will ultimately prevail in a free forum—does not seem to hold good under all conditions. The argument presupposes that masses of people in general are capable of weighing the various versions of contemporary events and ascertaining the truth. This assumption is not true. One of the widely known but least talked about features of contemporary societies—highly industrialized countries are no exception to this rule—is the degree of ignorance of large masses of people, even though they are literate, or their pseudo-sophistication.[50] This makes it possible for the elites to use intensively the means of mass communication and produce a public opinion which is "color-blind, and fact-blind; blind, it may be, to a yawning gulf beneath our feet." [51]

But the merit of the theory is that it keeps freedom of discussion uninhibited and contributes to the promotion of the enlightenment value. The harm against which the community must guard itself is the use of the technique of false and distorted statements by elites to prepare the people of their states psychologically to put into operation a strategy of aggression; and a reckless use of the technique is likely to influence the audience to put pressure on the policy-makers of their state to initiate such a strategy. Where there is a free forum the latter situation is not likely to arise. It is against these two uses of the technique of falsification and distortion that the community must guard itself, and not mere exhibitions of bad journalism.

A reasonable recommendation, in view of the above, is that world com-

49. It was for this reason that the United States opposed the original French suggestion to make the publication of reply compulsory. S. De Palma, "Freedom of the Press—An International Issue."

50. See in this regard significant statistics collected and given in J. A. R. Pimlott, *Public Relations and American Democracy* (Princeton, Princeton University Press, 1951), p. 256; M. Kriesberg, "Dark Areas of Ignorance," Lester Markel and others, ed., *Public Opinion and Foreign Policy* (New York, Harper, 1949), p. 56.

51. Sir Norman Angell, quoted in T. Baty, *International Law in Twilight* (Tokyo, Tuttle, 1954), p. 41.

munity intervention to prevent the use of the technique of falsification and distortion of information, and to maintain peace and security, should take place in the following cases only: when the policy-makers are using the technique under conditions which create a reasonable expectation that they will put into operation a strategy of aggression; or when its use creates a like expectation that the policy-makers of a state will be led as a result of it to initiate such a strategy.

The disadvantages which underdeveloped countries feel that they labor under at the present time, because of their less developed media of communication, cannot be ignored. Their feelings, voiced many a time during the discussion on freedom of information, found expression in the words of Mr. Farhadi, the representative of Afghanistan, in the Third Committee during the Fifteenth General Assembly session: "it was the underdeveloped and still little known countries which suffered from the excesses of sensational newspapers." [52] Coercion occasioned thereby, mostly minor, calls for corrective measures to enable presentation of the views of the peoples and governments of such countries.

Communications Giving Offense to Foreign Peoples

The fourth broad category of communications which, it was claimed, should be prohibited with a view to preventing outbreaks of violence are communications which might be offensive to peoples of foreign states. The Polish Draft Convention presented to the Disarmament Conference, Geneva, 1932, contained a provision that obligated states to prohibit the broadcasting of transmissions of this character and the projection of any film of like nature.

An international convention providing for an obligation along those lines has so far been adopted only among the South American states. The South American Agreement on Radio Communications, 1938, provides that the contracting parties should insure that no news or comment which might disturb good relations with other contracting states, or injure the national sentiments of those countries, is broadcast by radio from their respective territories.

As a matter of broad policy it is perhaps desirable that information agencies in states publish balanced statements, and statements which do not give needless offense to foreign peoples. But when one begins to think of converting the broad policy into a definite legal prescription, several difficulties arise. Every day somebody is likely to say something in one state which might be regarded as offensive by the people of a foreign state. Also,

52. G.A.O.R., 15th Sess., Comm. III (1960), p. 235; see also the remarks of the representative of Yugoslavia (ibid., 14th Sess., Comm. III, 1959, para. 59), who said that the draft Convention on Freedom of Information "must take into account that lack of balance and ensure protection of the under-developed countries."

an obligation to refrain from disseminating statements offensive to foreign peoples does not admit of precise phraseology. In addition, where the statements alleged to be offensive are nationalistic from the point of view of the disseminator, there is no reason why those statements should be suppressed to placate the nationalism of the people of another state.[53]

The objective of maintaining the peace cannot be secured by the mere avoidance of provocative utterances. To secure that objective one has to look to the building up of an effective collective security system. Aggressions cannot be prevented by the mere avoidance of statements in which aggressors are likely to find provocations; if aggressors so desire they will be able to find provocation in any statement whatsoever. Further, it is the responsibility of the policy-makers of a state not to succumb to the provocations of the moment.

EFFECT ON WELL-BEING

The effects of the ideological instrument on the values of *power* and *enlightenment* have received attention throughout. The jeopardy to *respect* was considered in the previous chapter. It remains now to discuss the effect on *well-being*. The jeopardy to well-being of the elite having been discussed already, we will confine attention here to communications that might cause deprivations to groups used as objects upon which hatreds are displaced. The group assigned the role of "scapegoat" may be foreigners residing within the territory of a state, may be its own nationals, or may be a group in a foreign state.

A state is responsible for the protection of foreigners residing in its territory according to traditional law, and therefore has to exercise due diligence to restrain utterances which might jeopardize their safety. In 1889 when a book entitled *Death Blow to Corrupt Doctrines* was published in China, the United States considered it proper to demand its suppression, as the publication was likely to incite people and put the lives and property of American nationals in China in jeopardy.[54]

If the group consists of the state's own nationals the situation is different. Under traditional law the doctrine of sovereignty gives the elite of a state a high degree of freedom in shaping internal policies. The doctrine of humanitarian intervention might theoretically serve as a restraining influence but, as has been noted earlier, the doctrine has rarely been invoked by governments for exclusively humanitarian reasons.

The Nazi policy of persecuting the Jews formed the subject-matter of indictment before I.M.T., Nuremberg.[55] The use of the ideological instru-

53. See in this connection "Major C. F. Atkinson's Study," in *Broadcasting and Peace*, p. 76.

54. See Moore, *Digest*, 2, 167.

55. See the indictment cited in Chap. 7, note 7.

ment to commit crimes against the Jews was the basis of specific accusations against defendants Streicher and Fritzsche. The Tribunal, however, adopted the view that it had no jurisdiction to try the accused for crimes against humanity committed before the commencement of the war, as such acts were not connected with the waging of the war of aggression, the main offense committed to the Tribunal's jurisdiction. Against Streicher, however, it was found that his writings and published articles incited the people in the occupied territories to exterminate the Jewish population of that area.[56] He was held guilty of the crime against humanity.

The case of Fritzsche[57] throws more useful light on the point under consideration. One of the charges leveled against him was that he caused the dissemination of false news to incite people to commit atrocities against the Jews. The Tribunal held that there was no proof that he knew that the news disseminated was false and acquitted him of the charge. It may be reasonably assumed that the Tribunal would have held him guilty if it had been found that he had deliberately caused the dissemination of the false news in order to incite the atrocities.

The decision of the Tribunal to limit its jurisdiction only to offenses committed in connection with the initiation and waging of war caused much disappointment among those who expected sterner treatment to be meted out to the perpetrators of the crimes. With a view to obtaining express recognition of the criminality of acts involving mass killing of groups, the recommendation that such acts should be regarded as international crimes was put forward in the United Nations. The General Assembly during its Third Session adopted the Convention on the Prevention and Punishment of the Crime of Genocide[58] which entered into force on January 12, 1951. The Convention makes genocide as well as direct and public incitement of it an international crime and also seems to proscribe direct and public incitements against a national, ethnic, racial, or religious group as such, even though the group in question is in a foreign state.

The International Law Commission has recommended the inclusion of a provision in the Draft Code of Offenses Against the Peace and Security of Mankind which makes the commission of, or direct incitement to commit, acts designed to destroy any national, ethnic, racial, or religious group, any inhuman acts such as murder, extermination, enslavement, and deportation, and persecutions committed against any civilian population on social, racial, religious or cultural grounds, a crime against the peace and security of mankind.[59]

The U.N. General Assembly, in its Declaration on the Elimination of all

56. *I.M.T. Nuremberg, Trial of Major War Criminals,* 1, 302–04.
57. Ibid., p. 338.
58. Resolution 260 (111), 9 December 1948.
59. Art. 2(10), Art. 2(11), and Art. 2(13).

Forms of Racial Discrimination, devoted an article (Art. 9) to propaganda.[60] The article condemned propaganda against a race or group of persons of one color or ethnic origin, declared incitements to violence against a race or a colored or ethnic group to be an offense against society and punishable under law, and called upon states to adopt immediate and positive measures, including legislative measures to prosecute and/or outlaw organizations which promote or incite racial discrimination, or incite or use violence for the purpose of discrimination. During its Twentieth Session, the Assembly adopted a Draft Convention on the Elimination of All Forms of Racial Discrimination, which obligates the parties to adopt, with due regard to principles embodied in the Universal Declaration of Human Rights, legislation to punish dissemination of ideas based upon racial superiority or hatred, incitement to discrimination or violence against any racial, colored, or ethnic group, and financial or other assistance to such activities. It also requires prohibition of organizations or organized activities devoted to propaganda for promoting or inciting racial discrimination. Public authorities and institutions should refrain from such activities. The parties should also take measures in the fields of teaching, education, culture, and information, to combat prejudices leading to racial discrimination, and to promote understanding, tolerance, and friendship among nations and racial or ethnic groups.[61] Article 20(2) of the International Covenant on Civil and Political Rights aims at protection of national, racial, and religious groups against discrimination and violence.[62]

60. Resolution 1904 (XVIII), 20 November 1963; Art. 9 of the Declaration gave rise to considerable debate. Some delegations were opposed to clause (3) which required enactment of penal laws. See *U.N. Yearbook*, 1963, p. 336. See also Natan Lerner, *The Crime of Incitement to Group Hatred, A Survey of International and National Legislation* (New York, World Jewish Congress 1965), especially pp. 12 and 33 which show the opposition of the Western powers to Art. 9(3) for its likely impact on freedom of speech, and Chap. 2 on the undesirability of having laws punishing group libels.

61. See Resolution 2106 (XX), 21 December 1965, and articles 4 and 7 of the convention.

62. See note 7 above.

12

Decision Process

INCLUSIVE DECISION

Claims Relating to Competence

The discussion here relates to the competence of the U.N. organs, Specialized Agencies, regional organizations, and states to participate on behalf of the community in inclusive decisions concerned with situations of coercive use of the instrument.

The United Nations

Whenever internal or external use of the instrument presents a threat to the security of another state, the matter can be brought before the Security Council under Article 36 or Article 39 of the Charter, or before the General Assembly under Article 10 or Article 14. In the case of internal use, the main claim that can be put forward is that the matter falls within the domestic jurisdiction of the member, and Article 2(7) of the Charter is applicable. But how little this article could help to balk United Nations action in such situations may be observed very briefly. The article runs thus:

> Nothing contained in the present Charter shall authorize the United Nations to intervene in matters which are essentially within the domestic jurisdiction of any State or shall require the Members to submit such matters to settlement under the present Charter; but this principle shall not prejudice the application of enforcement measures under Chapter VII.

This article purports to preserve intact the protective ring around the state afforded by the traditional doctrine of internal sovereignty against outside interference. But a break is made in the ring by virtue of the exception provided in the last part of the clause. Additionally, the two words, "essentially" and "intervene," employed in the article, provide considerable scope for interpretation; and U.N. organs possess competence to interpret an article and decide its applicability to situations brought before them.[1]

When a situation such as the one under consideration here is brought before the Security Council or the General Assembly, a discussion of it can be prevented only if the member opposing the discussion is able to muster sufficient votes to prevent the inclusion of the subject in the agenda.[2] Even during the discussion on the question of inclusion in the agenda, strict exclusion of references to merits is indeed neither possible nor insisted upon. In practice, the U.N. organs have so far, more often than not, included the items proposed in the agenda, and later ruled on their competence in the light of Article 2(7), in most cases only indirectly by a pronouncement on merits, and in a few cases directly.[3]

The decision whether a matter is "essentially within the domestic jurisdiction" of a state, it may be noted, is a matter to be judged by the U.N. organs in the light of all the treaty and other community prescriptions, of which the most important to mention are the provisions of the Charter.[4]

1. Much has been written on the competence of the U.N. organs as against the member states to decide upon the interpretation of Art. 2(7) and its application to concrete cases. Writers are quite divided on this matter. For a short account of the various views, see Marek St. Korowicz, *Introduction to International Law, Present Conceptions of International Law in Theory and Practice* (The Hague, Nijhoff, 1959), pp. 165–70. The author thinks that only the member claiming the exception of domestic jurisdiction has that power. He cites Alf Ross, Judge Lauterpacht, Georg Scelle, and Paul Guggenheim, among those holding the view favoring the competence of the organs. See in this connection also M. S. Rajan, *United Nations and Domestic Jurisdiction* (Bombay, Asia Publishing House, 1958), pp. 109–18; H. Lauterpacht, "International Protection of Human Rights," 70 *Hague Recueil* 5, 31–33 (1947); A. W. Rudzinski, "Domestic Jurisdiction in the United Nations Practice," 9 *India Quarterly*, 313, 318 (1953); L. Preuss, "Article 2, Paragraph 2 of the United Nations and Matters of Domestic Jurisdiction," 74 *Hague Recueil* 553, 620 (1949); C. B. H. Fincham, *Domestic Jurisdiction* (Leiden, Sijthoff, 1948), p. 162. In practice the U.N. organs have been exercising the power of interpretation and application whenever the objection of domestic jurisdiction is raised before them, if not always directly, by implication—dealing with the main question involved without answering the preliminary question regarding competence. See Goodrich, *The United Nations*, p. 76; Quincy Wright, "Is Discussion Intervention," 50 *A.J.I.L.* 102, 105 (1956).

On the interpretation of "essentially," see Rajan, p. 102, Rudzinski, p. 332, Lauterpacht, "International Protection of Human Rights," pp. 23–30; and on the interpretation of "intervene," see Lauterpacht, ibid., pp. 18–23, Rajan, p. 86, Korowicz, pp. 170–71.

2. The inclusion in the agenda is, of course, by a simple majority vote in the General Assembly, and by a vote of any nine in the Security Council.

3. See Rudzinski, pp. 320–22; Rajan, Chap. 4.

4. The Permanent Court of International Justice held in the *Nationality Decrees in Tunis and Morocco* case that what matters should be regarded as within domestic jurisdiction was a relative question, and its answer would depend upon the development of international relations; see *P.C.I.J.*, Ser. B., No. 4 (1923). Matters covered by

Matters which menace peace and security in the world community are not likely to be regarded by the organs as matters "essentially within the domestic jurisdiction." Indeed the practice of the United Nations so far has been to regard situations which give rise to even *potential* threats to peace as being outside the scope of Article 2(7).[5] When the complaint is that the alleged use of the ideological instrument is part of a design directed against peace in the world community, it is reasonable to expect that the plea of domestic jurisdiction will not be allowed to prevail and to preclude United Nations action.[6]

Article 2, Clause 7, bars "intervention." There is indeed wide agreement on the proposition that mere discussion does not constitute intervention.[7] The General Assembly as a matter of fact put upon its agenda and discussed on three different occasions the complaints of countries of the communist bloc that war propaganda was being carried on in the Western countries and their desire that the Assembly should recommend the adoption of legislation to prohibit war propaganda.[8] In appropriate cases the organs may investigate the truth of the complaint, and Article 2(7) is not a bar against investigations designed to examine whether the issue presented to them is essentially within the domestic jurisdiction or not.[9] Such inves-

---

treaties are generally regarded as outside domestic jurisdiction; see Fincham, p. 35; E. A. Gross, "Impact of the United Nations on Domestic Jurisdiction," 18 *Dept. of State Bull.* 259 (1948).

5. See Rudzinski; Preuss, p. 634. Also Goodrich, "The United Nations and Domestic Jurisdiction," 3 *Int'l Org.* 14 (1949); Lauterpacht, "International Protection of Human Rights," pp. 33–47, 53.

6. Lauterpacht thought that the racial and political persecutions such as those in Germany before World War II would be proper subjects to invoke U.N. action "under both Chapter VI and Chapter VII of the Charter, inasmuch as they caused international friction and difficulties through forced emigration and otherwise and *inasmuch as they were a link in the vast ramification of the design against the peace of the world*" (italics supplied). Ibid., p. 36.

7. See Quincy Wright, "Is Discussion Intervention"; Rudzinski, p. 330; Lauterpacht, "International Protection of Human Rights," p. 20; Rajan, p. 484; Korowicz, pp. 175–80, and cf. his view, pp. 180–81. There have been indeed a few instances wherein the plea of domestic jurisdiction was raised and discussion was successfully prevented at least for a time (e.g. Tunisia, Morocco, Cyprus, Algeria) and the responses of the concerned organs in these cases were more influenced by the desire not to jeopardize the chances of bilateral amicable settlement of the issues involved than by the consideration of domestic jurisdiction.

8. During the Second Session of the General Assembly, the Soviet draft resolution (U.N. Doc. A/BUR/86, Sept. 18, 1947); during the Fifth Session, draft resolution by the same delegation (U.N. Doc. A/C.1/595, 1950); during the Ninth Session, the draft resolution presented by the Czech delegation (U.N. Doc. A/AC.76/L.16, 1954); see Chap. 6, note 44 regarding the resolutions of the General Assembly on these occasions.

9. See Rajan, p. 484. Lauterpacht, as early as 1947, expressed doubt whether "an enquiry would amount to intervention, so long as it does not take place in the territory of the state concerned against its will." See his "International Protection of Human Rights," pp. 21–22.

tigations and discussions might by themselves, apart from throwing light on the truth of the charges, help to enlighten public opinion in the world about the conditions in the state complained against. They might also reach the people in the "accused" state and mitigate the effects produced by the intensive use of the instrument by the internal elite.

The U.N. organs may, without infringing Article 2(7), make recommendations of a general character,[10] request, call upon, or give advice to the parties concerned to desist from conduct which might jeopardize peaceful relations, and offer the good offices of the U.N. to help the parties to settle their outstanding differences.[11] When it is found that the situation is one which presents a threat to the peace and demands something more than these mild measures, the Security Council is competent to adopt such measures as might seem appropriate, and Article 2(7) is not a bar against such measures.[12] In such situations the provision does not constitute an obstacle even for the General Assembly to make recommendations that are considered necessary.[13]

Even if an internal use of the instrument does not present a threat to the security of another state, if freedom of information is severely violated in the operation of the strategy—and intensive use of the instrument is most likely to occasion such violation—the matter can be brought before the Assembly as one pertaining to human rights.

10. See Goodrich, *United Nations*, p. 79. "There would seem to be some basis in the United Nations practice for believing that a recommendation addressed to all Members, though it is intended to apply to only one or two, does not constitute intervention." See also Rudzinski, p. 330; Lauterpacht, "International Protection of Human Rights," p. 20.

11. Goodrich, ibid., says, "Nor does a recommendation addressed to the states directly involved in a dispute or situation, so long as it is limited to calling upon them to settle their differences in accordance with Charter principles and offering the services of the United Nations as a friendly intermediary." See also Rudzinski, p. 331.

12. It may be noted that in 1946 the Sub-Committee on the Spanish Question (a question dealing with a typically domestic matter—the internal regime of a state) pointed out that the situation came within the scope of Chapter VI of the Charter, and since it was a potential menace to internal peace it was one not essentially within the domestic jurisdiction of Spain, and the Council was competent to act under Art. 36(1). See *Report of the Sub-Committee on the Spanish Question*, S.C.O.R., 1st year, Special Supplement (S/75, 1946), pp. 2, 5–6. The Sub-Committee suggested the breaking of diplomatic relations by member states, but on a recommendation to be made by the General Assembly. This suggestion, if it had not been defeated with the Soviet veto, would very likely have been accepted by the Council. See Rajan, p. 148.

13. The Assembly, in regard to the Spanish Question, recommended in its Resolution 39(I) of 12 December 1946, that the members should recall their Ambassadors and Ministers Plenipotentiary from Madrid. While this measure, or the breaking of diplomatic relations, is a very mild one and does not amount to violation of any international prescription, under different conditions, if there is sufficient unity of purpose in the Security Council or the General Assembly to remove any existing threat to the peace, it is not unreasonable to expect the adoption of more coercive measures.

In relation to external use it may be claimed that the organs lack competence because the outcome to be expected from the use is negligible coercion, or coercion not of that degree of intensity as would affect international peace and security and render the jurisdiction of the organs invocable. The stand taken by the U.A.R.'s representative, in relation to the Lebanese allegations of propaganda presented to the Security Council in 1958, was that the alleged propaganda activity was inconsequential, did not affect the peace and security, and hence was not within the jurisdiction of the Council.[14] The Lebanese and United Kingdom position in reply to this stand was that the activity was relevant, as indicative of the intention behind the subversive operations which the U.A.R. was alleged to have been conducting then.[15] It is within the clear competence of the organs to determine whether there is a threat to, or to the maintenance of, international peace and security,[16] and to proceed to take further measures in the situation or dispute under consideration.

Regional Organizations

Regional organizations have procedures of comparable flexibility which can be invoked in the event of intensive use of the instrument affecting the security of a member state, whether the use is by a member of the organization or an outside state. For instance, under Article 25 of the Charter of the Organization of American States (OAS) and Article 6 of the Inter-American Treaty of Reciprocal Assistance, 1947, it is possible for a member to bring before the organization, among other situations, an aggression of a nonmilitary character, or any fact or situation endangering the peace of America. Article 4 of the North Atlantic Treaty Organization (NATO) provides for consultation among the members whenever, in the opinion of any one of them, the territorial integrity, political independence, or security of any of them is threatened. According to a resolution adopted by the NATO Council in 1956, conciliatory procedures within the framework of the or-

14. See S.C.O.R., 13th year, 823rd Mtg. (1958), Para. 114. He said, "To tell the truth, I do not think that the Security Council should have to concern itself with this question. Indeed, if it gave its attention to all the radio transmissions and radio campaigns going on in the world today, it would no longer be able to examine the important problems which are placed before it and which are a threat to international peace and security. If we consider even the juridical aspect of this question of the press, we cannot but agree that these problems are not likely to threaten international peace and security and they are consequently not within the jurisdiction of the Council. Indeed, I do not see which provision of the Charter would give the Council authority to consider radio and press campaigns.'

15. Ibid., para. 62; ibid., 824th Mtg., paras. 278–83. The U.K. representative contended that continuance of the situation was likely to endanger the maintenance of international peace and security.

16. See Goodrich and Simons, *The United Nations and the Maintenance of International Peace and Security*, passim, and p. 168.

ganization can be invoked, as provided in the resolution, in cases of disputes between members. Article 4 of the South East Asia Treaty Organization (SEATO) and Article 3 of the Security Treaty between Australia, New Zealand and the United States (ANZUS) Treaty contain provisions similar to Article 4 of the NATO Treaty. The Baghdad Pact does not contain any such explicit provision, but its Council acted in 1959 to condemn propaganda directed against Iran, disseminated from the territory of the Soviet Union, from the so-called "National Voice of Iran." [17]

Specialized Agencies

The constituent treaties of the Specialized Agencies do not contain provisions investing them with competence to deal with complaints relating to propaganda, but these agencies may conceivably reserve for themselves competence, in agreements entered into when aid is given to individual states for development of mass media of communication, to prevent deliberate utilization of such aid for impermissible coercive purposes.

Unorganized Arena

In the unorganized arena states may exercise inclusive competence, a notable example being the indictment of Fritzsche before the International Military Tribunal, Nuremberg, for acts consisting of operating the Nazi propaganda agencies, incitement to war crimes, and crimes against humanity.[18] As indicated before, our preference is for decisions reached in the organized arena, in accordance with authorized procedures, in case they are to be followed by appreciably coercive sanctions. Except when there is a breakdown in such procedures, a claim for inclusive decision to apply such sanctions should not be exercisable in the unorganized arena. Otherwise, there is the danger of states resorting to arbitrary action under the guise of inclusive decision.

SANCTIONING PROCESS

We shall discuss the sanctioning measures adopted with the following objectives: *prevention, deterrence, restoration, rehabilitation, reconstruction,* and *corrective measures against individuals.*

Prevention

The whole variety of programs currently undertaken by the United Nations and Specialized Agencies, and in pursuance of bilateral arrangements, to improve the social, economic, and educational conditions and technological skills in the global community may be said to serve the goal of prevention. Such programs contribute to the promotion of an optimal public

17. See R.I.I.A., *Documents on International Affairs,* 1959, p. 358.
18. *I.M.T., Nuremberg, Trial of Major War Criminals,* 1, 79.

order and to prevention, elimination, or reduction of tensions that occasion resort to coercive use of the ideological instrument. More directly related to the present discussion are programs designed to improve the access of peoples to information, inasmuch as such access reduces the coercive impact of the instrument. Although a brief reference to such programs will be made here, an exhaustive account cannot be attempted within the scope of this study.[19]

The efforts of the United Nations and its Specialized Agencies which are pertinent to our inquiry may be described under two heads: (1) improvement of the means by which information may be conveyed to audiences, and (2) the evolution of a community policy of promotion of freedom of information. The magnitude of the task involved at present in the improvement of facilities for dissemination of information is indicated in a report of the Director-General of UNESCO to the Economic and Social Council in 1961. He drew attention to the fact that "nearly 70 per cent of the world's peoples, living in over 100 countries, lack the barest means of being informed of events in their own lands, let alone others." [20] These countries form the underdeveloped part of the world. But the task is not confined to the development of the media of communication alone. The interrelationship which exists between general economic and technical development and the development of the media of communication deserves notice. As the report of the Director-General pointed out,[21]

> There is, in fact, a reciprocal relationship between development of the media and economic and technical development. On the one hand, a society must reach a certain level of wealth and technological advancement before it can establish and maintain services of mass media. On the other hand, the media can markedly stimulate the capacity to create further wealth and can spur technical progress by

19. An idea of the range of the problems involved may be obtained from two reports prepared on the authorization of the Economic and Social Council: the first, in 1953, by the rapporteur of the Council on Freedom of Information, Ambassador Salvador P. López (Philippines), *Freedom of Information,* E.S.C.O.R., 16th Sess., Supp. No. 12 (E/2426, 1953), hereafter cited as *López Report;* and the second, *Report on Developments in the Field of Freedom of Information since 1954,* by Dr. Hilding Eek, consultant of the Secretary-General, cited in Chap. 4, note 12. An account of the U.N. activities is given in these two reports. The endeavors of UNESCO, especially in the area of the development of information media in underdeveloped countries are described in "Development of Information Media in Under-Developed Countries: Report of the Director General of UNESCO," ibid., Agenda item 10 (Part I), hereafter cited as UNESCO *Director General's Report.* Reference may also be made to W. H. Laves and C. A. Thomson, *UNESCO, Purpose, Progress, Prospects* (Bloomington, Indiana University Press, 1957), pp. 116–21; *Food For Life—Food For Thought* (New York, Oceana Library on The United Nations, 1962), Chap. 12.

20. UNESCO *Director General's Report,* para. 295.

21. Ibid., para. 297.

enlisting human factors, such as improved skills and better education, more directly in efforts for economic and social expansion.

A matter allied to this development relates to news agencies. There are presently only five news agencies, belonging to four major powers, which gather and distribute news in the majority of countries.[22] The manner in which this affects the dissemination of news was pointed out thus: [23]

> Every country in the world depends on the [five] world agencies for getting its national news brought to the attention of the outside world; second, every country in the world depends on the [five] world agencies for its supply of foreign news; and third, many of the countries which as yet do not have national agencies depend to a large extent on the world agencies for the supply of even their own national news.

One of the complaints frequently raised by underdeveloped countries in debates on freedom of information is that news concerning their countries is not satisfactorily presented in advanced countries, with the result that a public opinion is created that is adverse to their interests.[24] In other words, the governments of these countries feel that the operations of the news agencies have a coercive impact on them, and they seek to minimize the impact by restrictive regulation in relation to dissemination of information and transmission of news abroad. In 1954, the U.N. Secretary-General, in a report to the Economic and Social Council, considered the feasibility of establishing a world news agency, and was of the opinion that the creation of such an agency would present serious financial and organizational problems.[25] The Director-General of UNESCO, in 1961, recommended that assistance should be furnished for expanding the existing na-

22. See *Eek's Report*, p. 21. The agencies are the American AP and UPI, the British Reuters, the French APF, and the Russian TASS.

23. See *López Report*, p. 38.

24. In a report by Mr. Eduardo Espinosa y Prieto of Mexico to the Committee on Freedom of Information, established by the Commission on Human Rights, emphasizing the importance of establishing independent news agencies, it is urged, "Equality must be sought at the very source of this activity, which is the gathering and distribution of news. The great cultural groups that are not at present engaged in this work must participate in it by means of an economic effort of important proportions, but one which is surely within their capacity and is obviously indispensable to their cultural survival. They must now enter this arena in the same manner in which nations from Latin America, Asia and other regions have moved openly into the fields of steel mills, navigation, air lines, moving pictures and other first class activities, on occasion against the bitter and logical opposition of interests which had previously held these fields alone." E/CN.4/762, annex D, para. 38, cited in *Eek's Report*, para. 126.

25. *Encouragement and Development of Independent Domestic Information Enterprises, Report of the Secretary-General*, E.S.C.O.R., 17th Sess. (1954), Annexes, Agenda item 12, pp. 24, 26.

tional news agencies, for creating new ones where there are none.[26] He further recommended promotion of cooperative arrangements among the news agencies to increase the free flow of information. In 1963, UNESCO helped the formation of the Union of African News Agencies linking together the news agencies in twenty African countries.[27] The formation of such unions should be encouraged with the eventual goal of increasing the number of agencies that gather news on a worldwide basis.

In regard to the evolution of community policy to promote freedom of information, the greatest achievement has been the adoption of Article 19 of the Universal Declaration of Human Rights. This article, as expressed in the Preamble to the Declaration, "proclaims . . . a common standard of achievement for all peoples and all nations," in the area of freedom of information. The further endeavors to bring into existence covenants providing specific obligations have not progressed beyond the coming into force of the Convention on International Right of Correction in 1962. The draft Convention on the Gathering and International Transmission of News, prepared by the U.N. Conference on Freedom of Information, Geneva, 1948, was adopted by the Assembly in 1949, but was not opened for signature as many delegations were not prepared to accept it until the draft Convention on Freedom of Information was adopted.[28] The latter became involved in the controversy whether the Convention should include mention of grounds on which the parties should be free to impose restrictions on freedom of information; and this controversy was perhaps not really resolved by the Third Committee of the General Assembly when it adopted in 1960 the controversial Article 2.[29] However, the adoption of Articles 19 and 20 of the International Covenant on Civil and Political Rights by the Assembly in 1966 is an encouraging development in the direction of growth of conventional law. Whether these conventions come to be adopted or not, Article 19 of the Universal Declaration on Human Rights presently provides a touchstone on which the restrictive policies adopted by states could be tested by international decision-makers for their compatibility with general community policy.[30]

Perhaps it is not wise to aim at conventions alone. Freedom of infor-

26. UNESCO *Director General's Report*, p. 33.

27. *U.N. Yearbook*, 1963, p. 612.

28. *U.N. Yearbook*, 1948–49, pp. 560–61.

29. The text of this article was discussed by the Third Committee during the Fifteenth Session of the General Assembly from the 1028th to 1044th Meetings. For the text see Chap. 11, note 7. The final vote on the text was 50 to 5, 19 abstentions. The bulk of the Western powers abstained and the Scandinavian powers voted against.

30. Actually, it is not Art. 19 alone that can be taken to articulate the general community policy of promoting freedom of information, but the entire effort of the U.N. and its Specialized Agencies ever since their establishment.

mation, not being an absolute freedom,[31] admits of regulation, and what happens to be reasonable regulation under one set of circumstances may not be so under different conditions. It may be somewhat utopian to expect to include the whole pattern of regulation regarded as reasonable within a few articles. In addition to aiming at conventions, decision-makers may devote effort to evolution of reasonable standards which national decision-makers should observe within their respective jurisdictions, failure to do so being met with sanctions ranging from disapproval, condemnation, etc. to progressively more coercive ones.[32] A convention, it may be urged, which gives explicit authority to national decision-makers to impose restrictions, without obligation to observe reasonable standards, even if it be from the point of view of attaining a balance between the developed and underdeveloped countries, is fraught with dangers to the freedom; for there is the possibility of misuse of the authority, and the elite which comes to possess it may never be willing to surrender it, or do so only very grudgingly.

It is suggested, apparently as a measure to prevent coercive use of the instrument, that the United Nations Radio should expand its activities and facilities of transmission, to broadcast regularly information on events of transnational importance.[33] Dissemination of information by a non-national agency would be a useful addition to the process of communication in the world forum, and a means to counteract in a certain measure nation-oriented propaganda campaigns. It is also suggested that the U.N.

31. The European Convention on Human Rights, in Art. 11 which defines freedom of information—despite the fact that the parties to the Convention have long traditions of this freedom—mentions grounds on which restrictions may be imposed, viz., in the interests of national security, territorial integrity, public safety, prevention of disorder or crime, and protection of health or morals. The freedom can be suspended in cases of emergency to the extent required by the situation. Art. 16 of the Convention permits imposition of restrictions on political activities of aliens, which by implication include political propaganda.

While the United Nations Conference on Freedom of Information, Geneva, 1948, specified eight grounds on which the freedom could be restricted, the drafting committee of the U.N. Commission on Human Rights specified twenty-five other reasonable grounds. See Commission on Human Rights, Drafting Committee, Second Session, *Report* (U.N. Doc. E/CN.4/95L., 1948).

32. E.g. in 1951, when Czechoslovakia jailed William Oatis under its espionage laws, the United States brought the matter before the Economic and Social Council, which expressed disapproval of the practice of governments interfering with the functioning of journalists by invoking espionage laws. See the Resolution of the Council, 387B(XIII), 1 September 1951.

33. See Whitton and Larson, p. 222. At present the United Nations Radio prepares news and newsreel broadcasts weekly during the intersession period of the Assembly, and daily during Assembly sessions and when there are important meetings of other Organs. These broadcasts are supplied to national agencies for relay or rebroadcast. See *Eek's Report*, p. 44.

establish a system of monitoring radio broadcasts, so that whenever a complaint is made there would be authentic evidence bearing on the charges.[34] Availability of evidence apart, the existence of such an operation might have a restraining influence on potential delinquents. However, in order to keep the costs within limits proportional to the benefits expected, the operation may be confined to areas where tensions are high and disturbance of the minimum order is expected. The U.N. may enter into agreements with members whereby the latter undertake to place at the disposal of the organization, if so required, a part of the radio monitoring facilities they have.

Deterrence

The objective of deterrence has not apparently been sought so far. Two reasons may account for this. As the organized arena is not very strong, deterrence may be expected to provoke coercion rather than reduce the possibility of resort to it, and thus could result in increase rather than decrease of net coercion applied in the community. Secondly, since the use of the ideological instrument is intimately connected with the process of enlightenment, a measure of deterrence may appear to be one directed to curbing freedom of information rather than reducing the incidence of coercion. However, when the organized arena gains in cohesion and strength, and the criteria that distinguish the process of enlightenment and persuasion from impermissible coercive use come to be recognized and the two processes clearly identified, the objective of deterrence may be pursued.

Restoration

There has so far been no instance of invoking the concept of ideological aggression, that is to say, impermissible use of the ideological instrument alone in such intensity as is capable of depriving a state of its "territorial integrity or political independence." In the United Nations, whenever a complaint alleging the use of the military as well as the ideological instrument is made, the tendency has been to concentrate attention on prevention of an outbreak of violence or to stop an existing conflict, and practically to ignore propaganda.[35] When charges of war propaganda, or of internal propaganda intended to produce hostility against foreign govern-

34. Whitton and Larson, p. 223.

35. A typical case is that of the Lebanese complaint in 1958 against the U.A.R., referred to earlier. See S.C.O.R., 13th year, 822nd Mtg. (1958), seq. In connection also with the Syrian complaint against Israel in 1962, and the Yemeni complaint against the United Kingdom in 1964, the allegations of propaganda put forward by Israel and the United Kingdom do not appear to have palpably affected the decisions of the Security Council. See ibid., 17th year, 1000th Mtg., seq., and ibid., 19th year, 1109th Mtg., seq.

ments, are leveled, the response has usually been condemnation or recommendations of a general character.[36]

In the OAS, however, considerable attention is given to the propaganda component of transnational coercion. Thus in 1950, Haiti charged the Dominican Republic with acts affecting its sovereignty, political independence, and territorial inviolability and requested the Council to convoke the Organ of Consultation. Before the Council, the Dominican Republic leveled countercharges against Haiti, Cuba, and Guatemala of similar acts directed against it. The Council constituted itself as the Provisional Organ of Consultation and appointed a Committee to conduct an on-the-spot investigation of facts. On the report of the Committee, the Council reached a number of decisions, calling upon the parties to take varied steps, including cessation of systematic and hostile propaganda against one another and against any American state.[37] In 1962, the Inter-American Peace Committee expressed the opinion that the activities of Cuba, viewed in light of the background of the subversive activities of the Sino-Soviet bloc in America, constituted "political aggression" or "aggression of a non-military character" as contemplated in the system of political defense of the western hemisphere introduced by the Inter-American Treaty of Reciprocal Assistance. This report formed a basis for the resolutions adopted at the Conference of Foreign Ministers at Punta del Este expelling Cuba from the OAS.[38]

When one of its members, Iran, was affected by the propaganda of a state outside the organization—the Soviet Union—the Council of the Baghdad Pact, in 1959, condemned such propaganda.[39]

The trend noticeable in the U.N., to concentrate on prevention or stopping of violence, is quite justifiable. Often in the process of preventing

36. E.g. during the debate on the U.S.S.R.'s proposal in the Second Session of the General Assembly, which resulted in the adoption of Resolution 110(II), 8 November 1947, the U.S.S.R. demanded condemnation of "the criminal propaganda for a new war carried on by reactionary circles in a number of countries and, in particular, in the United States, Turkey and Greece," and there was a countercharge of violent propaganda in the Soviet Union and Eastern Europe directed against the U.S. and other Western powers. The Assembly condemned "all forms of propaganda, in whatsoever country conducted, designed to encourage any act of aggression or the use of any measures for the purpose of aggression," and also "all forms of propaganda, in whatsoever country conducted, which falsely imputes to officials or other responsible persons of any nation the desire of encouraging any act of aggression or the use of any measures for the purpose of aggression." The pattern repeated itself during the Fourth, Fifth, and Ninth Sessions, the complaining state on the last occasion being Czechoslovakia. See the proceedings connected with Resolutions 290(IV) (Essentials of Peace), 1 December 1949; 381(V) (Peace Through Deeds), 17 November 1950; and 819(IX), 11 December 1954.

37. See 3 *Annals of the* OAS 22–23 (1951).

38. See 46 *Dept. of State Bull.* 119–120, 281 (1962).

39. See R.I.I.A., *Documents on International Affairs,* 1959, p. 358.

or stopping violence, the underlying conflicts may be resolved, leading to a cessation of the use of nonviolent coercion. And if violence is threatened or employed, it would be unwise to give more attention to the use of the ideological instrument than to the military instrument, even though, in the process of decision, attention should be given to all the instruments of policy employed by the parties. In the OAS, which has a higher degree of cohesion than the United Nations, more notice is given to propaganda. The general trend has been to use the diplomatic instrument to appeal to the governments involved to stop harmful propaganda. In the condemnation by the Baghdad Pact Council of anti-Iranian propaganda, we have an instance of the use of the ideological strategy. There is apparently no instance of the use of economic strategy to restrain propaganda activity.

Professor Whitton and Dr. Larson have recommended four coercive sanctions which may be adopted within the framework of international organizations to obtain a cessation of impermissible propaganda activity.[40] The first is suspension, by a simple vote of the General Assembly, of the right of the delinquent to address the Assembly till such time as compliance with community prescriptions is secured. The measure, involving as it does denial of access to an important, organized arena of diplomacy, and coercive application of ideological strategy by open, more than verbal, condemnation of the activity, is likely to have considerable effect. The competence to so suspend, according to the authors, stems from the Assembly's competence to make its own rules of procedure under Article 21 of the Charter. It seems doubtful, however, whether this power would give the Assembly competence to suspend the substantive rights of participation of a member in the Assembly's proceedings. Nor would it appear that the general power of the Assembly to regulate its own proceedings gives it the power to deny a member participation for some cause not connected with the proceedings of the Assembly. Before the suggested sanction is applied, a strong unity of purpose must obtain among the Members in support of curbing the activity, sufficient to attribute to the Assembly power so to suspend.[41]

The second suggested sanction is exclusion of the utterances of the delinquent from the records of the United Nations. If offensive utterances are made in a forum of the United Nations, there are precedents which authorize the concerned organ to order their expunction. If they are not offensive, apart from legal technicalities, expunction jeopardizes enlightenment. Above all, the effectiveness of these two suggested sanctions depends upon the value the delinquent attaches to the particular benefits of partici-

40. *Propaganda*, pp. 223–26.

41. The experience in connection with the Expenses for Peacekeeping controversy does not encourage a belief that such move for suspension would receive widespread support.

pation in the United Nations, of taking part in the proceedings of the Assembly, and appearing on U.N. records; the authors' recommendations are based upon the assumption that a high value is attached by the members to these benefits.

The third method is authorizing other states to jam the delinquent's propaganda broadcasts by radio. This may be done only where the effects of the propaganda broadcasts cannot be countered by a positive program of transmission of different versions of events to the audience. Otherwise the Assembly will be setting a bad example. The fourth suggested sanction is deprivation, within the framework of the International Telecommunications Union, of the delinquent state's right to use certain radio frequencies. This suggestion, it is submitted, is not workable, because in the ITU the allocation of frequencies is made to services and not states, and each member is free, on the basis of the principle of sovereignty, to use any frequency allotted to a service for that service, provided that it does not cause interference to the stations operated by other members. However, an action on the suggested lines may be possible with respect to the Communications Satellite System (COMSAT), for therein the space segment of the radio communications is internationalized, and by prescribing and applying appropriate procedures a delinquent state may be denied access to the use of the system.[42] However, this sanction will not be effective against states like the U.S.S.R. which have their own communication satellites and against nonmembers of the COMSAT.

At this stage of development of the organized arena, it may be suggested that the first objective to be sought toward the goal of restoration is maintenance of minimum order, and all the four instruments of strategy may be employed to bring to bear, on the actual or potential disturber of order, persuasion and progressively increasing coercion to desist from such disturbance. When the possibility of disturbance of minimum order is remote, but exchange of intensive propaganda is on a high scale, international organs may employ diplomatic and ideological strategies to bring about a reduction in the level of intensity of propaganda. Within the organs and in the lobbies diplomatic communication may be utilized to apply persuasion and pressure. Open discussion of the situation, appeals to the parties, expression of disapproval of certain patterns of propaganda, even though included in general recommendations, may be employed to reduce the level of intensity. The parties may be induced to submit their outstanding differences to peaceful procedures of settlement. The real difficulty arises when a "scapegoat" group is immediately threatened with deprivations as a result of internal propaganda. Even in such a situation, at

42. See the *Agreement Establishing Interim Arrangement for Global Commercial Communications Satellite System, between the U.S.A. and other Governments*, Washington, D.C., 1964, which provides for internationalization of the space segment.

the present time, open discussion in the organs and use of persuasion and pressure seem to be the principal strategies available. When the organized arena gains in strength and is able effectively to maintain minimum order, efforts may be directed toward more effective regulation of minor coercions.

Rehabilitation

Because the enlightenment value would have been affected as a result of the use of the instrument and the attitudes of the audiences would have been altered correspondingly, rehabilitation may sometimes require a program of information and education to restore realistic attitudes, though in many cases the lapse of time alone will accomplish the change in attitudes. If respect has been affected, expression of complimentary sentiments in the forums of international organizations will help to repair the loss. Where the alleged loss is well-being or wealth, it is difficult to establish conclusively the causal connection between the alleged loss and transnational propaganda said to have occasioned it, and claims for reparations are very difficult to sustain. Further, at the present time, when reparations for impermissible use of violence are recovered only very rarely, it is not practicable to aim at realization of reparations in respect of propaganda. When the legal organization of the world community improves, it might be possible.

Reconstruction

The goal of reconstruction being distinguishable from prevention only in that the sanction is applied to an established delinquent, and after restoration, all the policies adopted with the objective of prevention may be applied in the reconstruction process.

Corrective Measures Against Individuals

If the elite of a state initiates a strategy of violence for purposes of aggression and is completely defeated, the governments participating in the enforcement action against the aggressor may be expected to set up an ad hoc tribunal and try the persons responsible for the initiation of aggression, following the Nuremberg and Tokyo precedents. At such trials, persons who, being parties to the planning of the strategy of aggression, have participated in the operation of the ideological strategy to promote the strategy of violence may also expect to be tried for the offense of a crime against peace. However, the expectation which prevails at the present time is that unless the aggressor is completely beaten militarily, or the substitution of a new elite leads to a negotiated peace, the possibility of individuals being tried for crimes against peace is very remote. The Korean and the Chinese experiences amply justify such an expectation. It is unlikely that statesmen will insist upon the criminal trial of a few persons at the price of indefinite prolongation of the hostilities. Indeed, often it will not be in the interest of the world community to so insist. However, the judgment of the Tokyo Tribunal holds out the threat that if the aggressors should continue to pursue their policies of aggression and meet with defeat, they might well have to pay the penalty for crimes in respect of which they have at the moment escaped punishment.[43]

At a future post-hostilities trial for a crime against the peace, if the judgment of the I.M.T. Nuremberg should influence the presiding tribunal, it is likely that criminal liability will be limited solely to those who had knowledge of the plans of aggression, possessed the power to influence the policies of their state, and participated in the planning and promotion of the strategy.[44] On the other hand, if the judgment of the I.M.T. Tokyo should prevail, all those who had knowledge of the conspiracy and acted in furtherance of it are likely to be held responsible. But one may perhaps also expect that persons whose activity had not substantially contributed to the furtherance of conspiracy would not be subjected to any punishment. The Tokyo Tribunal, one may presume, would not have denied the applicability of the principle of *de minimis* in such cases. At any rate, a future tribunal will have *The Ministries Case* as a precedent for the application of the *de minimis* principle.[45]

From the point of view of policy, it is desirable to limit penal discipline to a few. Trials such as these are intended to serve mainly a deterrent purpose and to a certain extent a retributive purpose. To serve those purposes it is necessary to inflict punishment only on those who possessed the power to influence the policies of the aggressor state. And it is not good world community policy to punish any who did not have knowledge of the ag-

43. In reply to the contention that the Japanese aggressions against the U.S.S.R. in 1938 in the Lake Khassan area and in 1939 in the Nomohan area should not form the subject matter of a trial, as those matters had been settled by negotiation, and that the diplomatic relations continued between the two countries as before, the Tribunal stated, "In a matter of criminal liability, whether domestic or international, it would be against the public interest for any tribunal to countenance condonation of crime either expressly or by implication." See *I.M.T. for Far East, Judgment*, Chap. VII.

44. Reference may also be made in this connection to the judgment of the Nuremberg Tribunal in *The German High Command Trial* (1948), *U.N. War Crime Cases, 12*, 1, 69. The tribunal limited the liability for crimes against the peace only to those who possessed the actual power to shape and influence the policy of their state. See also the remarks in the *I.G. Farben Trial* (1948), *U.N. War Crime Cases, 10*, 1, 39.

45. The tribunal which reviewed *The Ministries Case* remarked in the case of Woermann, "To say that any action, no matter how slight, which in any way might further the execution of a plan of aggression, is sufficient to warrant a finding of guilt would be to apply a test too strict for practical purposes and the principle of *de minimis* should be considered." *Trials of War Criminals, 14*, 966. Reference may be made in this connection to the remarks of Judge Wilkins in the *Krupp Trial* (1948), *U.N. War Crime Cases, 10*, 130.

gressive character of the strategy and who contributed to its promotion only under the influence of coercion—governmental compulsion, or psychic coercion exerted by intensive use of the ideological instrument.

To limit the punishment thus, the concept of conspiracy which obtains in the civil law systems will be found to be more suitable than the concept in the common law systems. However, if carefully used by the presiding tribunal, having due regard to the broad policy issues which arise in this context, the latter concept is not likely to lead to any undesirable result. The main characteristic of the common law concept is its elasticity, which facilitates the extension of responsibility to a large number of persons. The elasticity stems from the fact that the concept admits of the use of less direct evidence than is generally required in the civil law systems. But a cautious tribunal may be expected to apply the concept with discretion.

At trials for a crime against peace, it does not seem likely that a defendant will be allowed to plead exemption from liability on the ground that he was only a non-official in the aggressor state at the time of the commission of the crime. The post-World War II trials indicate the improbability of acceptance of such a plea. In the *I. G. Farben Trial* and the *Krupp Trial* before the United States Military Tribunals in Nuremberg, the defendants accused of crimes against peace were non-officials. One of the defendants in the Tokyo trial, Dr. Okawa, was practically of the status of a non-official; He was an employee of the Southern Manchurian Railway, a corporation in which the Japanese government had only a partial interest. His writings promoting hatred against the Chinese and attitudes in favor of aggression received considerable attention from the Tribunal. A reading of the judgment would indicate that only his mental unfitness to stand trial saved him from conviction. Indeed, nonofficial status should not form a shield for the guilty.

It may be difficult for the prosecution to prove, if the defendant happens to be a non-official, the *mens rea* required, or that he influenced the policies of the aggressor state, but that is a different question.

When the offense of initiating a strategy of violence for purposes of aggression is in its inchoate stage, that is, at the stage of planning or preparation, the enforcement of world community prescriptions against individuals seems inexpedient at the present time. Within a state, unless the acts in question are opposed to the policies of the government, or a revolution throws out the offenders from positions of power, it is not likely that the prescriptions will be applied. And even in the above two cases, it is more likely that the state officials will choose to invoke some other prescriptions of municipal law to punish them rather than crimes against the peace.

The enforcement of the prescriptions prohibiting crimes against humanity, such as genocide, incitement to genocide, incitement to assassination, is attended with similar possibilities and difficulties. In most cases persons guilty of the crimes will be found to be those holding highly influential positions within the state in which the crimes are committed. Enforcement of the prescriptions is possible only if a successful military action is taken against that state.

As to communications affecting respect accorded to individuals, including high personages in states, community action to prosecute the offender before an international tribunal is not likely to be considered in view of the triviality of the loss to the community involved.

EXCLUSIVE DECISION

Competence

Under the system currently obtaining, the officials of each state are competent in the first instance to characterize a particular use of the ideological instrument directed against them or the state as impermissible, to adopt measures for the protection of their values or the values of the state, and to resort to reprisals to obtain cessation of the coercive use. As part of the measures of self-protection or self-defense they may employ their territorial power to counter the opponent's strategy. The decisions regarding the measures of self-defense or self-protection and reprisals are necessarily subject to questioning by other decision-makers in the arena in respect of the existence of the necessity that justifies them, or their proportionality. Even the decisions concerning the use of territorial power, it will be seen below, are open to similar challenge.

Sanctioning Process

We shall observe the strategies that governments are competent to adopt in regard to the particular uses of the instrument regarded by them as impermissible, pursuing the objectives of prevention, etc.

Prevention

With this objective, in the first place, diplomatic strategy may be employed. Bilateral or multilateral treaties may be entered into specifying the particular type of propaganda as impermissible. While such treaties might not be effective to restrain an elite when it is deliberately bent upon impermissible use of coercion, they might at least for a time influence the parties not to resort to coercive use. The danger inherent in them of jeopardizing enlightenment has been mentioned before. The elite may maintain cordiality in diplomatic communication to induce others to maintain a similar tone. Secondly, in employing the ideological instrument in the process of interaction, coercive use may be avoided and cordiality may be shown in speaking about other elites. This is likely to influence others, to a certain extent, to maintain similar restraint. Thirdly, economic advantages may be extended; the government of a state which gives economic aid is less likely to be an object of coercive use by the recipient than others. Fourthly, the military strength of the state may be improved. The probability of being an object of coercion is less in the case of militarily strong states.

Deterrence

When a potential user of coercive strategy is identified, warnings of retaliatory action may be communicated through diplomatic channels. Commitments may be obtained from third states that they would not encourage such propaganda either within their territories or outside. The internal and external audiences may be forewarned about the likelihood of the use of the instrument by the particular participant in the world arena, so that when the instrument is actually employed its impact may be less intense than otherwise. Coercive retaliation by economic means may be threatened. A military alliance which strengthens the menaced state might have a restraining influence on the prospective user of coercion.

Restoration

The government of the state which is the target of coercion may adopt diplomatic strategy to obtain its cessation. An agreement with the offending state might accomplish such a result, even though for a short period.[46] Recognition may be refused to the government that is carrying on propaganda.[47] If official relations exist between the two states, protest may be lodged, the doctrine of state responsibility may be invoked, and stopping of the activity may be demanded. If the response is not favorable, diplomatic relations may be severed.[48] Ideological strategy may be employed, either to reduce the effectiveness of the use of the instrument, or as a countermeasure of coercion to bring about cessation of the original coercion.

REDUCING THE EFFECTIVENESS OF THE OPPONENT'S USE OF THE INSTRUMENT

The strategy consists of blocking as far as possible the channels of communication available to the opponent to obtain intelligence necessary to

46. Thus, by the Tashkent Declaration, India and Pakistan agreed to "discourage any propaganda directed against the other country," and to "encourage propaganda which promotes the development of friendly relations." 5 *International Legal Materials* 320 (1966). After the declaration, both countries stopped propaganda against each other (*New York Times*, Jan. 22, 1966), but they resumed, though not with the same intensity as during the conflict in September 1965.

47. Thus the United States withheld recognition of the Soviet government of Russia till 1933 when an undertaking regarding propaganda was given. See Hyde, "Concerning a Russian Pledge," p. 658.

48. In 1927, Great Britain severed diplomatic relations with the Soviet Union. See R.I.I.A., *Survey of International Affairs*, 1927, pp. 256–71.

prepare the propaganda material and to disseminate it, and developing a sentiment of opposition among the audiences against the opponent. We may consider here briefly to what extent the various channels of communication—human agents, printed materials, mails, telecommunications, and movies—may be controlled in order to reduce the effectiveness of the opponent's strategy.

Human Agents. There are three methods of controlling this channel of communication: (1) by restricting freedom of movement across the state's boundaries, (2) by imposing restrictions on freedom of expression within the state, and (3) by strictly controlling the formation and functioning of groups within the state by imposing severe restrictions on freedom of association. The last measure helps to control intragroup communications, which have been observed to have a high degree of influence in the formation of opinions and attitudes. We have already discussed freedom of information, and we shall take up here the first and third methods.

Territorial power gives competence to states to exclude foreigners. The passport and visa controls may be so employed as to prevent one's own citizens from going out and foreigners from coming in.[49] The U.N. Conference on Freedom of Information, Geneva, 1948, adopted a very moderate draft Convention on the Gathering and International Transmission of News, referred to earlier, but it may take a long time before it is opened for signature and becomes a treaty.[50] Instead of refusing to grant a visa, a foreign journalist may be admitted, but subjected to harassment such as punitive action based on espionage charges.[51] It is not permissible, however, for a state to prevent foreigners leaving its territory if they have fulfilled the obligations under local law.[52] We have noticed, however, that the traditional law giving a state territorial power to control movement did not allow an absolute power of exclusion, and its underlying assumption was that some movement across boundaries must always be expected.

Regarding the formation and functioning of groups, the regimes obtaining under the municipal law of various states differ widely. In liberal democracies, as a general rule, a high degree of freedom is allowed to indi-

49. For an account as to how the visa procedures are used to render entry of foreigners into the territory difficult, see the *Memorandum of the U.N. Secretary-General to the U.N. Conference on Freedom of Information,* Geneva, 1948 (U.N. Doc. E/Conf. 6/13, 1948). In 1950, the United Kingdom prevented the holding of a World Peace Congress in England by refusing to grant visas to those desirous of attending the Congress. See R.I.I.A., *Survey of International Affairs, 1949–50,* p. 58.

50. The reason is, as has been noted, that it has come to be associated with the draft Convention on Freedom of Information.

51. Thus in 1951 Hungary jailed Vogeler on the charge of espionage. See 24 *Dept. of State Bull.* 723 (1951); and Czechoslovakia did likewise with William Oatis, ibid., 25 (1951), 290.

52. See Oppenheim-Lauterpacht, p. 690.

viduals to form into groups and act in pursuit of diverse objectives. Freedom of association is guaranteed under the constitutions of many liberal democratic states. But this freedom, as other freedoms, is subject to legal regulation in order to protect certain other values.[53] In communist states, this position is reversed. In the Soviet Union, for instance, all associations, including cultural, technical, and learned societies not limited in their operation to a local area, are to be formed only under a license from a governmental agency.[54] Further, all associations are subjected to the guidance of the party and governmental agencies in respect of their functioning.[55] Apart from such controls, one has to take into account that secret police and agents of the ruling party in a totalitarian or authoritarian state will maintain surveillance over the formation and functioning of groups.

International protection of freedom of association is presently in the initial stage of development. Article 20 of the Universal Declaration of Human Rights has provided that

> (1) Everyone has the right to freedom of peaceful assembly and association.
> (2) No one may be compelled to belong to an association.

The American Declaration of Rights and Duties of Man, Bogota, 1948, contains a similar provision (Article 22), and so does the European Convention for the Protection of Human Rights and Fundamental Freedoms, Rome, 1950. The International Labor Organization has been endeavoring to promote trade union freedom, and has succeeded in bringing into force the Right of Association (Agriculture) Convention, Rome, 1921, the Freedom of Association and Protection of the Right to Organize Convention, 1948, and the Right to Organize and Collective Bargaining Convention, 1949; a large number of states are parties to these Conventions. The procedures of the United Nations, the ILO, the Organization of American States, the European Commission on Human Rights, and the European Court of Human Rights, are available to deal with infringements of the freedom of association.[56] Significant as these developments are, the power elites in

53. In the United States, for instance, the Constitution guarantees freedom of association, but permits reasonable restrictions in the exercise of *police power*. In India, Art. 19 of the Constitution permits reasonable restrictions in the interests of public order or morality. In the United Kingdom, in the main, as well as in the U.S.A., the law of conspiracy prohibits formation of groups for illegal purposes, or to accomplish legal purposes by illegal means.

54. See J. N. Hazard, *Law and Social Change in the U.S.S.R.* (London, Stevens, 1953), pp. 82–83.

55. See V. Gsovski, *Soviet Civil Law* (Ann Arbor, University of Michigan Law School, 1948), pp. 391–92, 408–10.

56. See in this connection C. W. Jenks, *The International Protection of Trade Union Freedom* (London, Stevens, 1957), particularly Chaps. 1 and 10; see also Art. 22 of the International Covenant on Civil and Political Rights.

states now possess a high degree of freedom to control the formation and functioning of groups within their respective territories. But the general community policy of promotion of human rights may be utilized by community decision-makers as a basis for requiring the observance of standards of reasonableness in controlling the formation and functioning of groups.

Mails. Transnational carriage of mails is regulated at present by the Universal Postal Union Convention, Vienna, 1964. Article 1 of the Convention prescribes freedom of transit within the territory of the Union. A violation of the freedom by a member will entitle the other members to discontinue service with the offender.

Article 28.1(d) of the Convention, however, proscribes transmission in the mail of anything whose importation or circulation is prohibited in the country of destination. The government of a state may make use of this provision to prevent the transmission of any matter which the government desires to withhold from circulation. Further, the territorial power of a government gives it the power to censor incoming or outgoing mail to weed out any material the transmission of which the government desires to prevent.[57]

The contemporary trend to make use of postal stamps and cancellation marks as vehicles of propaganda has been noted earlier. In 1957, Hungary refused to transmit letters from the United States which bore the postal cancellation mark "Support Your Crusade for Freedom." [58] The Hungarian government invoked Article 1(2) of the Universal Postal Convention, which declares the purposes of the Union to be, "to assure the organization and improvement of the various postal services and to promote, in that sphere the development of international cooperation." The Hungarian government's contention was that the postmark was intended to incite further revolts by "counter-revolutionaries" in Hungary, an objective inconsistent with "international cooperation." The United States postal authorities denied the violation of the Convention and pointed out that on prior occasions the same mark had been used, with no complaint from Hungary.

The Hungarian argument based upon the purposes of the Union seems tenuous. It draws substance only from the fact that the government of a state will very likely prevent transmission of mails when they are used as a

57. But under municipal law, in respect of mails as other means of communication, citizens may enjoy a constitutional right of freedom of information which prevents imposition of unreasonable restrictions on transmission of mails. Thus in the United States, in *Lamont v. Postmaster General*, 381 U.S. 301 (1965), post office regulations which required an express request by the addressee for the delivery of materials containing "communist political propaganda" were held unconstitutional as violating the right of free speech guaranteed by the First Amendment.

58. See *New York Times*, March 27, 1957.

means of circulating revolutionary symbols and slogans, at the risk, however, of retaliations.

Printed Materials. The territorial authority in general gives the government of a state the power to control the export and import of printed materials. It has been noted, however, that the practice of states in the past has been to protest over abuses of this power.

Telecommunications. States by virtue of their territorial authority possess control over the centers of reception and transmission. It has been mentioned earlier that since 1885 governments have been asserting and exercising the right to control the matter transmitted. At this stage we need note only Articles 31 and 32 of the International Telecommunication Convention, Buenos Aires, 1952. Under Article 31 the members of the Telecommunication Union have the right to cut off any private telegraph or telephone communication if it is found to be dangerous to the security of their state, contrary to their laws, to public order, or to decency. Article 32 which gives a much wider right reads thus:

> Each Member or Associate Member reserves the right to *suspend* the international telecommunication service for an indefinite time, either generally or only for certain relations and/or for certain kinds of correspondence, outgoing, or incoming or in transit, provided that it immediately notifies such action to each of the Members and Associate Members through the medium of the General Secretariat.

In practice, some states are using this power in diverse ways to censor incoming and outgoing messages.[59]

The attempt on the part of the United States to persuade the members of the United Nations to surrender the power under Article 31 has so far not fructified. The effort was made during the discussions on the draft Convention on the Gathering and International Transmission of News referred to above. With a view to removing any possible conflict between that Convention and Article 31, the United States proposed that the members should undertake not to exercise the right under that article. The proposal was opposed by many members, including Belgium and Egypt, and was defeated.[60] Attempts made in this direction by the United States delegation and other delegations at the International Telecommunication Conference, Buenos Aires, 1952, were no more successful.[61]

59. See in this connection *Memorandum of the U.N. Secretariat on Censorship to the U.N. Conference on Freedom of Information* (U.N. Doc. E/Conf. 6/16, 1948).

60. See the *Proceedings* of the 204th meeting of the Third Committee, G.A.O.R., 3rd Sess., Comm. III, 204th Mtg. (1949). Art. 29 referred to in the International Telecommunication Convention, Atlantic City, 1947, differs in no way from Art. 31 of the Buenos Aires Convention.

61. See G. A. Codding, "Jamming and Protection of Frequency Assignments," 49 *A.J.I.L.* 384 (1955).

We may consider here to what extent jamming of foreign broadcasts is permissible. Article 47 of the International Telecommunication Convention, Geneva, 1961,[62] prohibits the operation of radio service by a member of the Telecommunication Union in a manner that causes interference with the radio services or communications of other members. Nor does Article 31 or 32 appear to permit such interference.

However, for a long time governments have asserted the right to disturb the reception of foreign broadcasts, in spite of the existence of a treaty obligation such as the one under Article 47. At the Intergovernmental Conference on Broadcasting in the Cause of Peace, Geneva, 1936, Dr. Arnold Raestad and Dr. M. Bourquin, representatives of Norway and Belgium, claimed the right of a state to interfere if the foreign broadcasting transmission threatens the security of that state.[63] They based this right on the general principles of international law. At the time of the signing of the Broadcasting Convention of 1936, Spain and the U.S.S.R. asserted this right. In 1956, the British government jammed the broadcasting transmissions from Greece to Cyprus.[64] Juristic opinion also seems to be in favor of the right.[65]

However, in 1948, when the U.S.S.R. started jamming the "Voice of America" broadcasts, the United States considered it to be a violation of the International Telecommunication Union Convention, Atlantic City, 1947, and lodged a protest with the Bureau of the Union.[66] During the Fifth Session of the United Nations General Assembly, the question of jamming was discussed. The Assembly by a resolution declared it to constitute a violation of the "principle of the freedom of information" and condemned it,[67] and further called upon the members to refrain from the practice. The resolution also called upon members to refrain from broadcasts that included unfair attacks or slanders against peoples anywhere. During the debate in the Third Committee on the resolution the delegation of the United States characterized jamming only as violation of freedom of information.[68] It was the delegation of Yugoslavia that maintained that it was a violation of an international obligation.

Thus in spite of Article 47 of the International Telecommunication Convention, governments in general seem to have taken the view that the legitimacy of jamming depends upon the content of the message broadcast.

As regards television, the advent of space satellites has not yet deprived

62. Montreux Convention, 1965, now in effect, continues this prohibition.
63. See 32 *A.J.I.L.* Supp. 113 (1938).
64. See *New York Times*, March 7, 1956.
65. Hyde, *International Law*, 1, 606.
66. 20 *Dept. of State Bull.* 638 (1948).
67. Resolution 424(V), 14 December 1950.
68. G.A.O.R., 5th Sess. Comm. III (1951), p. 279.

the territorial authority of its physical ability to control transmissions, for the ground stations from which the transmissions from the satellites are broadcast to the audience remain under the power of the territorial state. This control will be lost if technological advances make it possible to transmit broadcasts from the satellites straight to the receivers. In such an event television will present the same problems as radio broadcasting by shortwave.

Movies. In the absence of a treaty to the contrary, every state has, by virtue of its territorial authority, the power to control the importation of movies into its territory and their exhibition.

We may regard the exercise of territorial power by the government of a state, to restrict the flow of communications, as being within the reach of challenge by other decision-makers for several reasons. In the first place, some of the prescriptions noted above give the right of stoppage only if the content of the message happens to be of a particular character. In these cases, obviously, the territorial government's finding that the message is of such a character is open to questioning by others. Secondly, traditional doctrines which invest governments with territorial power presupposed transnational communication as a normal phenomenon of community life.[69] Thirdly, we have noticed the contention of governments that their security will be menaced if a government interferes with communication across its boundaries to a high degree. Finally, since the general community

69. At the present time, it may be said, even communist countries do not deny the permissibility of transnational communication as such. Thus at the Conference on Freedom of Information, Geneva, 1948, the U.S.S.R. delegation accepted Resolution No. 1 adopted by the Conference, which declared the basic concept to be freedom to seek, receive, and impart information "regardless of frontiers," though at the beginning they proposed the deletion of "regardless of frontiers" on the alleged ground that it infringes the principle of sovereignty of states. See the *Summary Record of the Proceedings of the Conference*, Committee I, 15th meeting (U.N. Doc. E/Conf.6/C.1/SR. 15, 1948). During the Fifth Session of the U.N. General Assembly, in the course of discussion on the resolution proposed by Chile condemning the jamming of broadcasts, the U.S.S.R. did not deny the general principle of freedom of communication across state boundaries but asserted the right to protect "their people against harmful effects of war propaganda," etc. See G.A.O.R., 5th Sess., Comm. III (1950), p. 281. See also the speech of Molotov at the Conference of Foreign Ministers of the U.S., the U.K., France, and the U.S.S.R., Geneva, 1955, in response to a proposal to promote free exchange of ideas between the peoples of the East and the West, *New York Times*, Nov. 15, 1955.

The scope for other states questioning a state's drastically cutting off communication from outside is indicated in the reply of the United States to the protest of Hungary over leaflet-drop operations organized from West Germany by private organizations—Radio Free Europe and the Free Europe Committee: "It is only natural that they [the private organizations] should take interest in the welfare of the Hungarian people and seek some means of communication with them. If unusual methods have been adopted, this is due solely to the action of the Hungarian government and those in and outside Hungary who may be responsible for the policy of erecting barriers against normal intercourse among peoples." See 32 *Dept. of State Bull.* 14 (1955).

policy is promotion of human rights and freedom of information, an exercise of territorial power which entails a blatant violation of this policy is liable to be questioned by other decision-makers. And we may recommend that such exercise of territorial power should always be within the limits of reasonableness, having regard to the harm expected from the use of the instrument by the opponent and the general community policy of promotion of freedom of information and human rights.

Ideological strategy may be used as a countermeasure against the opponent in order to induce him to reduce his coercion to a permissible level, and we have indicated earlier, consistently with our policy of maintaining the principle of economy in sanctioning coercion, that such use should be within the limits reasonably necessary for bringing about restoration. The economic instrument may likewise be used.[70]

In the course of history there have been instances of resort to the military instrument in response to propaganda. In 1831, for instance, the successful revolutionaries in the Papal States started issuing proclamations inciting the people of the Austrian dominions of Lombardy and Naples to revolt and throw off Austrian rule, and Austria responded by armed invasion.[71] In 1914, Austria-Hungary demanded that the Serbian government put an end to the irredentist propaganda carried on in Serbia, directed toward recovering Bosnia and Herzegovina from the former. The reply of Serbia, even though conciliatory, was regarded as unsatisfactory, and the armed invasion leading to World War I was initiated by Austria-Hungary.[72] But at present the use of force in pursuance of an exclusive decision is not permissible except as a measure of self-defense, and the onus will be on the state that uses force to show justification for it. Where the opponent has used only the ideological instrument, the onus may be expected to be almost impossible to discharge.

Rehabilitation and Reconstruction

If the opponent's strategy has affected enlightenment, and in consequence the attitudes of the audiences, the government which is the object of coercive use may institute a program of information to rectify the atti-

70. An example of the use of economic strategy in response to the use of the ideological instrument can be seen in the United States' action against Ghana. In view of anti-American publications in Ghana's press and other media, and the attacks on American overseas agencies in President Nkrumah's books, the United States "forcefully" protested, and expressed "displeasure" at those "continuing attacks on the United States" and further stated that the United States was not prepared to meet Ghana's request for food worth $127 million over a period of seven years. Other reasons were also reported for turning down the request. See *New York Times*, Nov. 24, 1965.

71. See *Annual Register*, 73 (1831), *History*, 453.

72. See W. C. Dennis, "Diplomatic Correspondence Leading up to War," 9 *A.J.I.L.* 402 (1915); *Collected Diplomatic Documents Relating to European War* (London, British Foreign Office, 1915), pp. 3–5.

tudes. If respect has been affected, diplomatic strategy may be employed to demand disowning the utterances, and in case the spokesman was an official, an apology.[73] If the response is not favorable, a more coercive diplomatic procedure such as severance of diplomatic relations may be adopted.[74] Since one mode of redress for defamation is repaying in the same coin,[75] when diplomatic strategy fails, ideological strategy may be adopted and the shortcomings of the opponents may be exposed openly. This procedure will not be useful where the manifest communicator is an inconsequential person. Economic strategy also may be employed to attain the goal of rehabilitation of injured respect. In view of Article 2(3) of the Charter, however, military strategy appears inadmissible for the purpose. To destroy values by violence, for the sake of the respect value, is unjustifiable from the viewpoint of policy as well.

All the strategies employed in pursuit of prevention may be used to achieve reconstruction.[76]

The Strategy of Corrective Measures Against Individuals

Generally the aggrieved government demands that the government of the state from which propaganda is disseminated institute criminal pro-

73. See Stowell, "The General Smedley D. Butler Incident." If the utterance is that of a diplomatic official, the receiving government may demand recall. Thus in 1952 the Soviet Union demanded the recall of U.S. Ambassador George Kennan because of a speech made in West Germany in which he compared the conditions in the Soviet Union with those in Nazi Germany, and suggested that the former were even worse. The U.S. government justified the remarks but recalled him. See 27 *Dept. of State Bull.* 557 (1952). If the remarks are of an official other than a diplomatic official, the government may, if it chooses, justify the utterances. Thus in 1938, the German government protested to the United States over the speech of Harold Ickes, U.S. Secretary of the Interior, at Cleveland, in the course of which he compared the Nazi treatment of Jews to that of a period of history when "man was unlettered, benighted and bestial," and added that it was an insult to the Middle Ages to compare the Nazi totalitarianism with conditions then. The State Department rejected the protest. See R.I.I.A., *Documents on International Affairs, 1938*, 2, 35–36. About that time the United States was making vain representations to the Nazi government in regard to the anti-Jewish policies in Germany, which also affected some citizens of the United States. See *Foreign Relations of the United States, 1938*, 2, 369.

74. Thus Brazil severed diplomatic relations with the Soviet Union in 1948 when the latter refused to apologize for a libelous publication on the President of Brazil. R.I.I.A., *Survey of International Affairs, 1947–48*, p. 480.

75. Chafee, *Free Speech in the United States*, p. 553 n.

76. In the armistice agreements with Finland, Hungary, Bulgaria, and Rumania after World War II, the Allies required the party concerned to dissolve organizations in its territory conducting propaganda hostile to the Soviet Union or to any of the United Nations. See Art. 8 of the Peace Treaty with Finland, 1947; Art. 8 of the Peace Treaty with Bulgaria, 1947; Art. 4 of the Peace Treaty with Hungary, 1947; and Art. 5 of the Peace Treaty with Rumania, 1947. For these treaties, see 42 *A.J.I.L.* Supp. 203, 179, 225, 252 (1948).

ceedings against the disseminator. This happens especially in the case of libels. But in view of the difficulties involved in prosecuting individuals in accordance with fair standards of justice, we may suggest that the government affected by the libel should demand only disavowal of the utterance, or disapproval and apology (in case the utterance is that of an official), from the responsible government. By these means, the injured respect, or even the value of power, will be rehabilitated, and prosecution of the communicator can be left out as insignificant. Such a course will be in accord with the general trend of decisions observed here.

If the government which is asked to institute criminal proceedings fails to do so, the aggrieved government itself may institute proceedings invoking an appropriate principle of jurisdiction. The principles of jurisdiction with respect to crime are generally stated to be territoriality, nationality, passive personality, universality, and protective principle.[77] In respect of crimes which involve the inclusive interests of all states, such as crimes against peace, incitement to assassination, etc., the principle of universality can be invoked, but with respect to communications affecting the power or respect of the elite of a state, only the exclusive interest of that elite is affected, and the principles invocable are those other than universality. We may recommend, with a view to promoting freedom of information, that jurisdiction should not be exercised over non-nationals in respect of utterances made by them outside the territory of the state, in the enjoyment of the freedom of expression guaranteed in the place of utterance.[78]

77. Harvard Research, "Jurisdiction with Respect to Crime," 29 *A.J.I.L.* Supp. 466 (1935); McDougal et al., *Law and Public Order in Space,* Chap. 6.

78. For similar recommendations, see "Jurisdiction with Respect to Crime," p. 543; "Report of J. L. Brierly, Rapporteur of the Committee of Experts for Progressive Codification of International Law, League of Nations, on Criminal Competence of States in Respect of Offenses Committed Outside their Territory," 20 *A.J.I.L.* Supp. 253, 256 (1926).

13

Final Appraisal and Recommendation

The ideological instrument, in the hands of an elite managing the process of communication in order to shape the opinions, attitudes, and behavior of a people, is capable of producing in the audience effects ranging from persuasion to coercion. Though it is not possible to specify precisely when the process ceases to be persuasive and becomes coercive, from the techniques and tactics employed and other instruments of strategy used—diplomatic, economic, and military—it is possible to identify the general character of a particular use as persuasive or coercive. The degree to which coercive effects can be produced on the audience is related to a great extent to the degree to which the strategists are able to control the processes of communication, information, and education. By using the instrument to influence external audiences, coercive effects may be brought to bear on an external elite, confronting it with the alternatives of adopting the policies desired by the strategists or facing the disloyalty of its rank and file, as well as adverse opinion among other audiences. The effect of communication may also be persuasion of the external elite.

One outcome of the use of the instrument is enlightenment of the audience in some degree or other. The other outcomes are deprivations, particularly of power, respect and well-being, of the external elite against which strategy is directed. Sometimes the strategy may have a boomerang effect, compelling the strategists to do what the audience, in the mood of an excited crowd, demands. The effects of the use of the instrument on world community values are threats to the maintenance of minimum order—that is, peace and security in the community—and interferences with the value processes of power, respect, well-being, and, to a lesser degree, other values.

The expectations, on the part of the elite and the decision-makers, of the outcome of the use of the instrument—affecting the attitudes and behavior of the audience and restricting the choice of alternatives of the elite against whom the strategy is directed—are dependent upon a number of factors. The more significant of these are: the character of the participants in the communication process, the audience, the objectives sought by the strategists as inferred from the context, the characteristics of the situation—geographical, temporal-duration, institutionalized, and crisis—the base values at the disposal of the strategists and those against whom the strategy is directed, and the various strategies employed. Such being the case, claims for authoritative decision have centered around: the relevancy of the character of the participants in the communication process and of the audience addressed; the permissibility of the objective sought; the relevancy of the characteristics of the situation, of the relative capabilities of the strategists and the target elite, and of the various strategies employed; and the outcome and effects.

The organized arena of decision-making in the world community being presently weak and imperfectly developed, the expectation of violence being very high, and the capabilities of the most important units of the community, the states, being extremely unequal, the decisions in relation to claims are marked by the following general features. The major preoccupation of national decision-makers is security from violence. Inclusive regulation of the use of the instrument is resisted in order that full control over the process of enlightenment within one's own state may be retained, and there may be full freedom to maintain among the internal audience attitudes necessary to meet external threats. The elites of states less menaced by coercions from outside, especially from the ideological instrument, oppose inclusive regulation, stating that it would affect the process of maximization of enlightenment. And those who fear that an unrestricted flow of information would jeopardize their power position, or subject them to coercive effects, oppose inclusive programs of promotion of freedom of information which tend to reduce the possibility of coercive use on the audience, stating that there should be full freedom to protect their home communities against abuses of the communication process. But all are seriously concerned about the outcome of the use of the instrument by their opponents.

To one who takes the position of an observer of the whole process of use of the ideological instrument and of decision, and who is interested in promoting human dignity and in optimal shaping and sharing of human values in the world community, three basic policies suggest themselves: (1) promotion of shaping and sharing of enlightenment, (2) minimization of coercion within and across state boundaries, and (3) promotion of human rights and optimum production and distribution of all human values. These goals are complementary and may be collectively referred to as optimum public order. The policy of minimization of coercion entails regulation of all coercion, with the exception of low level coercion which ought to be expected and tolerated as a normal incident of community interaction. And the process of regulation must necessarily vary with the degree of coercion involved in the context, the objective with which it is applied, the likely outcome, and the effect expected on community values. To the extent possible, the strategy of regulation should comprise not suppression of communication, but enlightenment of the audiences involved. In applying sanctions, persuasion should be preferred to coercion, and when coercion is employed, the principle of economy in such measures should be maintained, so that the sanctioning coercion is proportionate to the objective sought in applying it.

Regarding the goal of enlightenment, generally promotion of freedom of information is accepted by all. But due partly to the varied conceptions of freedom that currently obtain, partly to the demand of some that legal regulation of the freedom should help to balance others' higher capabilities in regard to the use of the instrument, and partly to the position taken by some that detailed definition of the freedom in semantic terms, specifying permissible grounds, would jeopardize that freedom, translation of the basic policy into treaty prescriptions has not made much progress. The necessity to develop the media of information and skills required to operate them, especially in the underdeveloped countries, and the magnitude of the task involved, are recognized. Indeed the liberal democratic doctrine that truth will be best ascertained in a free forum will be meaningful only if there is opportunity to present diverse versions and interpretations of events. Some effort has been devoted to the development of the media. To accomplish the goal we have posited, a liberal concept of freedom of information should prevail around the globe, and there should be less unequal distribution of resources and skills necessary to disseminate information and impart education. These conditions can be attained only by means of long-term programs.

On a short- and middle-term basis, two approaches suggest themselves. The first is to accept, by means of a treaty or convention, a compromise regime of freedom of information in the global community which explicitly requires or authorizes the elites to impose certain specified restraints. This may not appear desirable for two reasons. The essential task is to make inroads into the exclusive territorial power which the elites now claim, and are able to maintain by means of the force at their disposal, in an arena in which there is very little centralization of instruments of coercion. It is not to give express authorization for the elites to impose certain restraints which they now do in the exercise of their territorial power. Secondly, any restriction that may be specified, in the nature of things, is likely to be a reasonable one under certain circumstances but an unreasonable one under others, and community approval of such restriction without reference to the context described in detail is likely to be harmful to a policy of freedom of information. And in a treaty a detailed description of a number of contexts is not practical. Further, when a power is expressly conferred on the elite, it may be difficult later to secure a surrender of it in the interest of inclusive regulation.

The second approach, the one we suggest, is to evolve—through the time necessary for securing wider acceptance of liberal concepts and for accomplishing wider distribution of skills and resources—progressively higher standards of freedom of information, and to persuade, influence, and apply pressure on the elites to maintain such standards in their respective domains. These standards are to admit only such restrictions on the freedom as are reasonable, having regard to the objective sought in imposing restrictions and the proportionality of the restrictions to the objective. Even with respect to the use of the ideological strategy to neutralize the opponent's strategy, we suggest the maintenance of the principles of reasonableness and proportionality in regard to such measures as interfering with communications, jamming radio broadcasts, counter-propaganda, etc. In the arena of inclusive decision, all the nonviolent instruments of strategy may be employed to secure the maintenance of these standards, but in strict accord with the principle of economy in sanctioning coercion.

Coming to the regulation of coercion, the trend of decisions has been not to shape policy directly by reference to the effectiveness of the manifest communicators in influencing the audience, but to their status as officials or non-officials. This classification has no doubt some relevance to the estimation of effectiveness, but the dichotomy has no comprehensive reference. International civil servants are, by virtue of the conditions of their service, restrained from participating in the coercive strategies employed by national elites. This policy is useful from the point of view of maintaining the effectiveness of the organizations in the diplomatic arena, but it may be departed from with justification when the organizations are operating highly coercive strategies.

In regard to the claim that the responsibility of the state should extend to preventing dissemination from its territory of certain types of utterances, even if the communicator is a non-official, the trend, in spite of the fact that some treaties explicitly provide for such responsibility, cannot be said to be in favor of a general acceptance of that claim. On the other hand, the trend is against the position that private persons' activity is beyond the reach of international decision-makers.

It may be observed that the essential question here is what pattern of regulation the government of a state should apply, in the discharge of its obligation of due diligence, to prevent private persons from operating from its territory a strategy of coercion directed against a foreign government. In the nineteenth century, responsibility was variegated, with definite responsibility to prevent attacks of violence from its territory, at one end, and no responsibility in general to suppress utterances, at the other. At present, definition of responsibility by reference to utterances, referred to by such shorthand expressions as "war propaganda" or "subversive propaganda," as suggested by some scholars and governments, is fraught with jeopardy to enlightenment without a corresponding effective check on the use of coercion across state boundaries. In order to safeguard enlightenment and regulate coercion, responsibility of the state should be related to the coercive strategy involved in the context and not merely the utterance. A state's responsibility to prevent initiation from its territory of major coercion, impermissible under the U.N. Charter, cannot be denied. In the case of negligible coercion, indeed, there can be no responsibility at all. In respect of minor coercion by the ideological instrument, the responsibility becomes in theory determinable by reference to the expected degree of coercion on the one hand, and the legitimacy of the coercion under the circumstances and the internationally accepted standards of regulation of freedom of information which the states are required to maintain on the other. These standards are indeed not specific, and have to be inferred from the general trend of decisions relating to freedom of information. In practice, however, it may be expected that coercive use of the instrument by private persons in a state against the elite of another will encounter retaliation by the private media in the other, and if there are no private ones, by the state-owned agencies.

It seems more accurate to say, having full regard to the traditional doctrines, prescriptions of the Charter, and currently held expectations, that the responsibility of a state for the use of the ideological strategy by private persons in its territory varies with the expected degree of coercion and its legitimacy under the circumstances, and it is not determinable by reference to utterances alone. We are opposed to an alteration of the traditional doctrine, which does not in general permit attribution of utterances of private persons to the state, because such an alteration would necessitate strict governmental control over individual freedom of expression.

There is also the issue regarding the attributability of publications by the media in totalitarian states. Our suggestion is that attributability should depend upon the extent of formal authority and/or effective control exercised by the government over the disseminators, or by the latter over those who constitute the government.

Traditional law allowed greater latitude to the elites with respect to internal audiences than external audiences. But the underlying assumption of traditional law was that some communication would always be present across state boundaries as an incident of community life. The trend indicates that intensive use internally, if it jeopardizes the security of other states, is liable to be objected to as impermissible.

The use of the instrument for persuasion is quite permissible. The Covenant of the League of Nations, the Briand-Kellogg Pact, the Nuremberg and Tokyo trials, and the U.N. Charter indicate that the use of the instrument to promote a strategy of impermissible major coercion, or aggression, is impermissible. On the other hand, there is no objection if for self-defense. An impermissible minor coercion may be responded to by coercion under the rubrics of reprisals, permissible intervention, and self-defense or self-protection. Coercive use of the instrument with the objective of securing conformance to community prescriptions is permissible. Where coercive use is employed to promote an objective approved by the community, such as self-determination, protection of minorities, promotion of human rights, a straight answer regarding its legitimacy cannot be given. These objectives are related to the policy of promoting human rights and securing optimum access to human values.

At present, the expression "ideological aggression" is loosely employed by some to cover a wide range of activities that involve low level coercion. In our view it should be limited to impermissible major coercion.

In applying the polar and complementary doctrines stated above, the decision-makers will have to refer to a number of variables. In relation to major coercion, the question that has to be considered is who first resorted to major coercion without justification, and this will have to be done by reference to the participants in the process of mutual application of coercion, their objectives, relative capabilities, the various strategies employed, the expected outcome, the response of the participants to the directives of the community decision-makers, and the effect of the decision on the goal values of the community, including promotion of human dignity. In order to decide whether a particular minor coercion is impermissible, a similar contextual inquiry is necessary. A decision as to whether a particular use of coercion is legitimate, because the objective of applying it is to promote a policy approved by the community, has to be reached by balancing the overall objective of maintaining minimum order against that particular policy.

The trend is to recognize the geographical situation of the parties and the temporal-duration of the use of the instrument as relevant to decision-making. The institutionalized character of certain practices, such as slants given to publications in the press in favor of friendly states and against opponents, indoctrination of the rising generation to a certain degree in all communities, may be expected to receive due attention by the decision-makers as it affects the expectations of the outcome. The degree of crisis involved in the situation, too, may be expected to influence decisions as there will then be greater expectations of disturbance of the minimum order. When violence is being mutually employed, the trend has been to adapt the policies pursued in relation to the use of military instrument to the ideological as well.

The relative capabilities of the participants involved are regarded as relevant, and also the various instruments of strategy used by the participants in the context. Systematic analysis of the techniques and tactics of the ideological strategy employed does not appear to have been attempted in practice. Such analysis would indicate to a certain extent the degree of probability and imminence of overt response on the part of the audience, or severe inhibition of rational response which is generally called panic, and might supply guidance to the choice of policy.

In relation to the claims pertaining to the deprivation of power of the external elite against which the strategy is directed, suggestions have been made to prohibit certain types of propaganda, characterized as "subversive propaganda," "civil warmongering," etc. Our suggestion is that the choice of policy should be based upon the expected outcome, appraised in terms of major impermissible coercion, minor impermissible coercion, or coercion justified by virtue of the fact that the objective is promotion of a policy approved by the community, such as self-determination, respect for and observance of human rights, or protection of minorities.

According to traditional doctrine, states should afford redress to aliens subjected to loss of respect in their territory. Some states give special protection to heads of foreign states, some to heads of foreign governments in addition, while others give no special protection. In general, prosecution of persons for libels on heads of foreign states or governments has been somewhat rare. Group libels and libels on foreign states are not widely recognized as giving rise to the responsibility of the state to afford redress. In our view, a differentiation should be made between attacks on respect, which are not part of a strategy of major coercion, and attacks which are part of such a strategy. Where the expected outcome is confined mostly to loss of respect, suitable measures of rehabilitation of the deprived value should be adopted, but keeping the freedom to comment on affairs of public concern unimpaired. We believe that, in general, respect should not come under attack, in order that the value may be promoted and also that the scope for operation of the diplomatic strategy, which is a means of persuasion, may remain unaffected. But this policy must be balanced against the need to secure conformance to community prescriptions, to promote policies approved by the community, and to protect freedom of information.

Attempts to bring about treaty prescriptions which obligate suppression of incitement to terrorist acts directed against foreign elites, which affect well-being and possibly wealth, have not been successful, though incitement to assassination is generally regarded as impermissible even between belligerent states. While we favor suppression of incitements to assassination or terrorist acts, we suggest that in formulating policy, attention be given to instances of brutal suppression of human dignity which may have occasioned the incitement.

With a view to preventing outbreaks of violence, proposals have been made that treaty obligations should be accepted to prohibit "war propaganda" and certain other types of utterances. These proposals have met with opposition on the ground that treaty prescriptions of that kind will affect freedom of expression. The general trend, as can be observed for the most part in the resolutions of the U.N. General Assembly, has been to condemn "war propaganda," and simultaneously to affirm the necessity to promote freedom of information. We suggest that a distinction has to be made between elements of dissemination which are incidental to the present-day processes of collection and dissemination of information, bad practices on the part of those engaged in operating public information agencies, and the practice of indoctrination of youth in varying degrees in all states, on the one hand, and the use of the instrument as part of a strategy of major impermissible coercion, or use which creates an expectation that its proximate outcome will be a major impermissible coercion, on the other. The remedy for the former is to provide a free forum in which errors and misconceptions may be rectified. The latter merits prohibition on policy grounds and their prohibition can be implied from contemporary prescriptions.

Competence for inclusive decision in relation to the use of the instrument in the organized arena of international organizations—the United Nations and regional organizations—is clearly established, especially in situations when the employment of the instrument threatens peace or affects human rights. We are of the view that, so long as the procedures of these organizations are functioning, individual states should not be regarded as competent to make inclusive decisions and apply coercive sanctions. These international organizations are competent to employ, in accordance with their respective prescriptions and procedures, any, or any combination, of the instruments of strategy, diplomatic, economic, ideological, and military, in pursuit of the sanctioning objectives of *prevention, deterrence, restoration, rehabilitation,* and *reconstruction.* In the pursuit of restoration, the trend in the United Nations has been to bestow attention mostly on preventing the outbreak of violence, or stopping mutual application of it. In the OAS some attention is given to the propaganda employed by the parties as well. It is only under rare circumstances, as when an aggressor is completely defeated militarily, or an internal group overthrows those responsible for aggression and is prepared to surrender them for punishment, that it seems possible to adopt the strategy of subjecting individuals to criminal penalties.

Governments of states subjected to a coercive strategy are competent to take decisions for self-defense or self-protection or to resort to reprisals, but these exclusive decisions are open to challenge by other decision-makers in the arena. Diplomatic, ideological, economic, and military strategies can be employed by way of sanction, but the coercion so applied should be limited to the degree permitted by community prescriptions. Application of the strategy of subjecting individuals to criminal penalties is also possible to some extent.

The ultimate goal we recommend is the establishment of a process of inclusive decision in the organized arena to an optimal degree to regulate all coercive processes, and reduction to the minimal degree of the scope for exclusive decision. But as an interim policy, we recommend inclusive decisions to maintain minimum public order, enforced by employing all or any of the instruments of policy, and regulation of minor coercions with the help of nonviolent instruments of policy. Complementary to the process of inclusive decision, it is necessary to admit a competence for exclusive decision, and for applying sanctioning coercion, but in accordance with the basic principle of economy—that is, subject to the principles of necessity and proportionality to secure a cessation of the impermissible coercion involved.

Finally, we wish to emphasize that the problem of regulation of the use of the ideological instrument cannot be approached as one that can be solved by prohibiting a few types of disseminations. Meaningful choices of policy are possible only by a contextual approach along the lines suggested here. The problem is inextricably tied up with the promotion of an optimum public order in the world community. A policy designed to secure that order will help to attenuate the conditioning factors which have been mentioned as currently affecting decision-making, and will pave the way for regulation of the instrument in a manner compatible with the goal of a comprehensive world public order.

Index